DECISION
MAKING
for PATIENT
CARE

DECISION MAKING
for PATIENT CARE
Applying the
Nursing Process

Mary Jo Aspinall, R.N., M.N., C.S.
Surgical Clinical Nurse Specialist
Veterans Administration Medical Center
Long Beach, California

Christine A. Tanner, R.N., Ph.D.
Associate Professor of Medical-Surgical Nursing
University of Oregon Health Sciences Center
School of Nursing
Portland, Oregon

9 8 4 9

Appleton-Century-Crofts / New York

81 82 83 84 85 / 10 9 8 7 6 5 4 3 2 1

Prentice-Hall International, Inc., London
Prentice-Hall of Australia, Pty. Ltd., Sydney
Prentice-Hall of India Private Limited, New Delhi
Prentice-Hall of Japan, Inc., Tokyo
Prentice-Hall of Southeast Asia (Pte.) Ltd., Singapore
Whitehall Books Ltd., Wellington, New Zealand

Library of Congress Cataloging in Publication Data

Aspinall, Mary Jo.
  Decision making for patient care.

  Includes index.
    1. Nursing—Problems, exercises, etc.
2. Nursing—Case studies.   3. Nursing—Decision
making.   I. Tanner, Christine A.
II. Title.   [DNLM: 1. Decision making.
2. Nursing care. WY 100 A841d]
RT55.A84   610.73   81-861
ISBN 0-8385-1555-X   AACR2
Text design: Meryl Sussman Levavi
Cover design: Gloria Moyer

Contents

Preface

Virtually all scientifically-based health practitioners, including nurses, use a systematic clinical problem-solving process to determine (1) if a client has a problem requiring professional intervention; (2) what kind of intervention is needed; and (3) if the intervention has been effective. This process is initiated with data collection and analysis from which the initial diagnosis is derived, progresses through planning and implementation of appropriate nursing interventions, and culminates in the evaluation of the client's response to those actions. The process appears simple, straightforward, and logical. Yet the implicit requirement to apply theoretical nursing knowledge in the clinical situation is one of the more difficult skills for both nursing students and practicing nurses to learn.

This book is about the intricate and complex thinking processes that comprise the application of nursing knowledge in clinical problem solving. One of the critical elements in the process, described in detail in Chapter 1, is learning to consider multiple alternatives in each step. Indeed, one characteristic which seems to distinguish expert clinicians from novices is the number of plausible alternatives they may consider in their problem solving—in diagnoses, in intervention methods, and in explaining outcomes of interventions. Because such expertise appears to be, in part, a function of experience, we have attempted to provide you with some of that experience in the form of clinical simulations. These are written case studies, followed by a series of questions that require you to go through the problem-solving process, much as you would in clinical practice, while considering multiple alternatives every step of the way.

Another major element in clinical problem solving is the storage and retrieval of information held in memory. In order to consider multiple alternatives in the process of problem solving, one must possess a vast amount of information related to the meaning of clinical cues (e.g., signs and symptoms, laboratory data, and so forth). The way this knowledge is organized in your memory has a great deal of influence on whether or not you will be able to recall it at the appropriate time. For example, you may have studied problems in fluid and electrolyte balance extensively, learning the many signs and symptoms of fluid volume deficit. In the clinical setting, then, when a patient exhibits dry skin and complains of thirst, you may well recall fluid volume deficit as a potential problem. It may be more difficult for you, however, to think of other alternatives, organized under another category in your memory, such as side effect of atropine administration.

In order to assist you in organizing your knowledge so that it is more readily retrieved in clinical situations, we have organized the book around major cues indicative of health problems. We have selected nine major categories of cues (one for each chapter) that are frequently observed in patients experiencing medical or surgical conditions and which may signal you that there is a change in health status. For each category of cues, the relevant physiology and pathophysiology are reviewed, followed by a detailed description of assessment parameters and their meaning, and general approaches to intervention. This information should assist you in analyzing the case studies at the end of each chapter, identifying possible altered states of health, understanding the physiological basis for the altered state, relating cues to their causes and recognizing the rationale for therapy.

It is important for you to complete the skillbuilder exercises *before* you turn to the feedback section. It may help you in developing your problem-solving skills to discuss the hypotheses with a colleague or classmate, developing a rationale for your responses as you go along. In some skillbuilders, we suggest that you use one of the decision trees located in the appendix.

These tools were developed to help you overcome some of the difficulties that all clinicians experience in their diagnoses. When we are attempting to determine which of our diagnostic possibilities are most likely, we seek additional information which helps in confirming or ruling out each alternative. (For example, if you believe that one possible explanation for a patient's episodes of dizziness is postural hypotension, you would ask the patient if the episodes were related to assuming a standing position and you would, no doubt, check the lying and standing blood pressures to help you confirm or rule out postural hypotension as a plausible explanation.) Among the pitfalls in the diagnostic process are (1) not considering the important alternatives; (2) not collecting *all* the relevant information needed to confirm or disconfirm the diagnosis. Once you have identified a broad category of diagnostic alternatives, the decision tree will help you systematically collect the appropriate data and determine the most likely problems. Practice and further instructions for use of decision trees are included in the skillbuilders in Chapter 2.

In the feedback section following each of the skillbuilders, we have attempted to tell you about our thinking strategies in going through the problem-solving process. We explain what our diagnostic alternatives were, why we considered them, why we ruled out others—in terms of the underlying physiological and psychosocial principles, as well as the data provided. We describe what additional data we might obtain, if necessary, to confirm our diagnosis. Then based on the inferences we've made about the altered state, we detail the interventions and the criteria for evaluation.

It is our hope that the tools provided in this book will help you become superb clinicians in the care of patients with medical and surgical conditions. We wish you great success in your endeavors.

We are appreciative of the assistance of a number of persons, both within and without the field of nursing in the preparation of this book. We are especially indebted to David Michael Rose, M.D., Director, Surgical Intensive Care Unit, Veterans Administration Medical Center, Long Beach, and Assistant Professor of Anesthesiology, University of California at Irvine for his assistance in delineation of the critical indicators on the decision trees and review of the case studies. We are also indebted to Dennis G. Fryback, Ph.D., Associate Professor, University of Wisconsin for writing the introduction to the decision trees and collaborating on the development of the form for the trees.

CHAPTER 1

Clinical Decision Making and the Nursing Process

Process is defined by Webster as a particular method of doing something, with all the steps involved. It is an action of moving forward, progressing from one point to another on the way to a goal; it is a continuing development involving many changes.[1] The application of this definition to the process of nursing would suggest that it is a dynamic, continuously evolving, and deliberate sequence of steps directed toward the goal of the restoration, maintenance, or promotion of optimal levels of health for individuals, groups, and communities.

Such a definition of nursing process would suggest that it is central to most nursing activities and, indeed, it is. The sequence of steps depicted in the nursing process reflects the systematic use of problem-solving methods in clinical practice for the purpose of resolving, reducing or preventing health problems, and/or promoting the client's adaptation to those problems.

It is not surprising that when the term "nursing process" first found its way into the literature in the mid sixties, a frequent response by nurses was, "We've been doing it all the time."[2] Indeed, the activities embodied in the nursing process are not unlike the problem-solving processes used in everyday life. And, the steps of data collection, planning, intervention, and evaluation seem to be those naturally employed by problem solvers. However, a more elaborate and detailed explanation of these steps should provide improved clinical problem solving.[3]

Any process, by definition, is continuously evolving and interactive; therefore, any division into steps is both arbitrary and artificial. In practice, for example, the nurse may need to test the effectiveness of several interventions in order to confirm one diagnosis, simultaneously using the assessment, intervention, and evaluation components. However, as we shall see in our later discussion, there are many pitfalls in the intellectual strategies used in clinical problem solving. Recognition of the strategies being used by clearly identifying the components of the nursing process will assist the clinician in avoiding those pitfalls.

Although many readers already utilize the nursing process in clinical practice, this chapter will review the general components or subprocesses of clinical problem solving in order to assure a common frame of reference. A discussion of the intellectual activities or the thinking strategies involved in the nursing process, with a focus on assessment and diagnosis is included and will provide a framework for the remainder of the book.

ASSESSMENT: DATA COLLECTION PHASE

Assessment refers to the collection of data about a patient's health status for the purpose of determining health problems and identifying the patient's strengths and coping mechanisms. Data collection falls into two broad categories: (1) a complete and thorough assessment in which the data that are to be collected have been determined in advance or (2) a more focused assessment that is based on subjective reports by the patient and/or signs recognized by the patient or nurse.

The more complete assessment often follows a prescribed format. For example, the "data base" prescribed for the problem-oriented record usually includes the patient's chief complaint, the patient profile and related social data, history of the present illness, past history, review of systems, physical examination, base-line laboratory data, and nursing history. The nursing history in many hospital settings is compiled by using a printed interview schedule and/or a checklist related to the patient's health-related habits and lifestyle.

The focused assessment also involves the collection of data from the patient and a variety of other sources. It requires that the nurse form initial impressions about the meaning of the cues (signs, symptoms, and other data), then seek additional data to confirm or disconfirm these initial impressions. While the data collection process saves time compared to comprehensive assessment, the risk is that pertinent data will be missed. This process of determining initial hypotheses and testing them will be the focus of discussion later in this chapter.

In addition to these initial impressions, a number of factors influence the nurse's approach to data collection. The nurse's own philosophy and beliefs about basic human rights have a subtle, yet profound influence on both the kind of information she seeks and the way in which she communicates with the patient in obtaining it. The nurse's theoretical orientation will also influence the kinds of data collected as well as the way in which they are interpreted.

For example, the nurse using Byrne and Thompson's conceptualization of basic human needs will gather data related to seven basic needs: oxygenation, food and fluid, sex, preservation of physical integrity, activity-rest, elimination, and affiliative needs.[4] Consistent with this model, the nurse will interpret the data in light of actual or potential need deficits; if a need deficit in one area is discovered, the nurse will look for its effects in other need areas consistent with the interactive components of the model.

Similarly, the nurse subscribing to Roy's adaptation model will gather data related to the individual's behaviors (first level assessment) in each of four adaptive modes: physiologic, self-concept, interdependence, and role function.[5] Data pertaining to related stimuli (factors which influence the behavior) will also be collected. The nurse then evaluates the behaviors as adaptive or maladaptive and identifies problems relative to the patient's adaptation in each of the modes.

The advantages of using these frameworks are considerable. They assist the nurse in avoiding focusing too early in the assessment. They also provide a framework for interpretation of cues, different from the medical diagnosis, yet representing some very real, unmet health needs. In addition, nursing models also provide a framework for collection of data pertaining to strengths and coping mechanisms.

Another factor which greatly influences the data collection process, particularly in hospital settings, is the nurse's knowledge of the medical diagnosis. A study conducted by Kraus[6] examined the effect of providing information to nurses about a patient's condition before their initial encounter with that patient. The data the nurses subsequently gathered were limited in both amount and kind, and pertinent observations were frequently missed. While data related to the medical diagnosis are certainly important, focusing on that as the only basis for assessment may result in failure to identify other equally important nursing care needs.

A fourth factor which should increasingly influence the data collection process is the nurse's knowledge of the research literature. With the rapid growth of nursing knowledge predicted for the next decade, there will be greater understanding of behaviors associated with responses to illness, greater predictability of risk factors, and better understanding of factors influencing the development of healthy lifestyles. The result, when applied to clinical practice, will afford more refined assessment parameters that the nurse may use in selected situations.

An example may help clarify this point. There is now a tremendous body of literature about risk factors in coronary artery disease. We know that individuals with Type A personalities, with hypertension, diabetes, and a family history of vascular disease, obese individuals, and smokers are more prone to the development of coronary atherosclerosis. It is not now uncommon for nurses to assess the patient for the presence of these risk factors. The growing body of literature in areas such as pain experience, variables associated with sensory deprivation, sleep patterns, and exercise tolerance should assist nurses in their assessment of patients.

ASSESSMENT: PROBLEM IDENTIFICATION PHASE

The second component of the assessment process is that of identifying problems. Although problem identification, or diagnosis, has been termed the product of assessment, the *process* of diagnosis begins with data collection. As we shall see in a later discussion, the experienced clinician begins to formulate impressions or diagnostic hypotheses very early in the encounter with the client. This is true regardless of the approach to data collection, either comprehensive assessment or focused data collection. It seems to be a natural human tendency to give meaning to the phenomena we observe, and the diagnostic process is no exception.

The problem identification phase involves complex thinking and utilizes data obtained from the patient as well as information retrieved from memory about altered health states. There are two broad kinds of inferences which nurses must make about the state of patient: (1) those health problems ". . . which nurses, by virtue of their education and experience, are licensed and able to treat,"[7] nursing diagnoses, and (2) those health problems, which must be diagnosed and treated by other members of the health team, but which require continued nursing observation assessment, and implementation of the therapeutic regimen.

Generally, nurses have been reluctant to refer to their problem identification activities as diagnostic. Part of this reluctance may stem from lack of a clear operational definition of nursing diagnosis, a definitive distinction between medical and nursing diagnoses, or a standardized nomenclature for the labeling of health problems which fall into the domain of nursing practice.

A widely accepted definition of nursing diagnosis has been advanced by Marjory Gordon. She states that the diagnostic statement is ". . . a concise term representing a cluster of signs and symptoms and describing an actual or potential health problem. . . . In general, these problems encompass . . . disturbances in life processes, patterns, functions or development, including those secondary to disease."[8] A defining characteristic which appears frequently in the literature is that nursing diagnoses describe problems which the nurse can treat independently.

Efforts toward the development of a diagnostic nomenclature were initiated in 1973 with the formation of the National Conference Group on Classification of Nursing Diagnoses. The components of the nursing diagnostic categories developed by Gordon and used by this group include (1) problem, (2) etiology, and (3) signs and symptoms.[9] The problem is a term, or terms, describing the meaning assigned to the cluster of cues. For example, a patient who has been instructed to take diuretics and maintain a low sodium diet is admitted in decompensated congestive heart failure. A possible nursing diagnosis (which would require further data collection for confirmation) might be noncompliance.

The second component, the etiology, is a term or terms which will describe the cause(s) of the health problem. It is the etiologic statement which individualizes the diagnosis, makes it clinically useful, and suggests independent nursing action. In the example given, the noncompliance may be due to knowledge deficit, denial, powerlessness, and so on.

The third component used by the National Conference Group is the defining characteristics. These are the signs, symptoms, and other cues which characterize the particular diagnosis and distinguish it from other diagnoses.

To date, there are more than 100 categories that have been accepted by the National Conference Group.[10] Massive efforts are still required to validate and refine the nomenclature. In this text we have attempted to use a problem-etiology format for diagnoses that fall in the domain of independent nursing practice.

In addition to making inferences leading to nursing diagnoses, nurses must also make inferences about health problems that lie in the domain of physicians and other health professionals. While the nurse is not expected to make medical diagnoses, she must at least recognize the possible presence of a general category of conditions. The reason this recognition is important is that *it will guide the nurses' subsequent data gathering.* For example, the nurse, who recognizes that an elderly patient recovering from major abdominal surgery is particularly prone to atelectasis (medical diagnosis) will assess the patient for signs of its presence (e.g., auscultating the lung fields for fine rales). The nurse who does not recognize this as a potential problem may not gather the appropriate data and, therefore, miss making important modifications in the plan of care (e.g., increasing the frequency of postoperative respiratory hygiene activities).

Both kinds of inferences are included in this text, and for the sake of convenience and brevity are referred to as nursing diagnoses. The problem identification phase is probably the most complex, and, at the same time, the most critical component of the entire nursing process. The planning and subsequent interventions will be successful only to the extent that the data base and nursing diagnoses are accurate and complete.

PLANNING AND INTERVENTION

As soon as the patient's health problems have been identified, the nurse must set priorities, determining which are more urgent and which are less immediate. Short- and long-range goals that are acceptable to both the nurse and the client are mutually defined. These goals may be translated into more specific, measurable objectives which provide the direction for nursing care activities and which serve as outcome criteria for evaluation. Hence, for the patient with fluid volume deficit, for example, the overall goal may be "to meet fluid needs" or "to restore hydration." The specific objective stated in observable behavioral terms might be, "The patient will return to his normal hydration status as evidenced by: (1) normal skin turgor, (2) hematocrit within the range of 40 to 45 percent, (3) absence of thirst, (4) urine specific gravity between 1.010 and 1.020, and so on.

The planning phase represents individualization of care so that the goals, when possible, are mutually established, define what is probably attainable for the individual patient, and describe, in the outcome criteria, the evidence that this patient will demonstrate. For example, the outcome criterion of normal skin turgor may not apply to the elderly patient who is experiencing loss of subcutaneous tissue. A goal of "return to normal breathing patterns" may not apply to the patient with advanced chronic obstructive lung disease; instead, identification of the individual's optimal level of respiratory function will provide critical information in the establishment of realistic, attainable goals.

Once goals are established, appropriate interventions are determined. Like the problems identified, interventions can be broadly classified into dependent (e.g., implementation of physician's orders), interdependent (e.g., implementation of mutually agreed upon interventions which do not require a physician's order but may be based on the medical diagnosis), and independent (i.e., implementation of interventions which fall solely within the domain of nursing judgment, such as patient teaching and counseling, among many others).

During planning of interventions, it is important for the nurse to consider alternative interventions so if one is not effective in achieving the desired goals others will be available. As we shall see in our later discussion, generating multiple intervention alternatives will allow the nurse to predict which is (are) most likely to achieve the desired outcome and select one on that basis. Such "pausing" to consider alternatives prevents the nurse from automatically following the tried-and-sometimes-not-so-true intervention. A prime example of this is intervening with the patient experiencing pain. The nurse may decide to administer a pharmacologic agent for pain relief when other measures such as cutaneous stimulation, application of heat, and/or distraction may be more effective. Obviously, the effectiveness of the intervention chosen is related highly with the accuracy of the diagnosis; but frequently, for the same diagnosis, nurses may choose from a wide range of interventions.

Increasingly, as the body of nursing knowledge grows, the nurse will have to rely heavily on the nursing literature, which, when coupled with her own experience, will assist her in predicting outcomes of selected interventions. For example, as we learn more about patient education, we may find that certain kinds of teaching approaches are more effective for certain groups of patients than others.

EVALUATION

Evaluation, while often considered the final step of the nursing process, is actually an on-going cyclical activity, occurring during each step of the process. Hence, after identifying the patient's health problems, the nurse must ask the following evaluative questions:

1. Does the diagnostic statement explain all the data? Sometimes there will be cues which are simply inexplicable; however, at other times in the zeal to establish the diagnosis, some cues may be overlooked. Stopping to evaluate the diagnosis will help avoid this problem.

2. Is the diagnostic statement specific enough to intervene? Some diagnostic categories simply do not contain enough information to derive interventions. This is true of both nursing diagnoses and those considered within the domain of medicine. For example, the diagnosis of fluid volume deficit without an etiologic statement does little to assist the nurse in knowing what interventions are appropriate, and if, in fact, dependent or independent activities are indicated. Fluid volume deficit due to active gastrointestinal hemorrhage will require much different interventions than that caused by lack of knowledge regarding normal fluid needs.

Evaluation methods are also employed to determine if the intervention has been effective in achieving the desired outcome. If the goals are not achieved the nurse must ask the following series of questions:

1. Have all the intervention alternatives been exhausted? It may be that another approach will be more useful.

2. Are the goals realistic? If the intervention alternatives have been exhausted and the desired response is not achieved, it may well be that the goal was not realistic and attainable.

3. If it is deemed that the broad goals were realistic and attainable, then the nurse must reevaluate the accuracy of the initial diagnosis, in essence, beginning the process over again.

THE THINKING PROCESSES OF CLINICAL PROBLEM SOLVING

The model of the nursing process just described is depicted in Figure 1. It includes the major components of assessment (data collection) and diagnosis, planning, and intervention with evaluation occurring throughout the process. These components are indicated along the left-hand column of the model.

The thinking processes or intellectual activities that comprise each component of the nursing process are arrayed in the flow diagram to the right. The process activities requiring recall of knowledge from memory to interpret the meaning of cues are identified by the rectangular figures. The diamond shaped areas represent decision points in the process.

In our previous discussion, we have referred frequently to the intellectual strategies used in clinical problem solving. In general, the process consists of generating multiple alternatives and systematically testing those against additional information obtained from the patient and other sources. Note, for example, in the process of diagnosis that after attending to initially available data, the clinician generates diagnostic hypotheses (possible explanations for the cues). These hypotheses then are informally rank-ordered (e.g., from most likely to least likely, or from most urgent to least urgent) and additional data are obtained to assist in ruling in (confirming) or ruling out (disconfirming) the hypotheses. When sufficient data are obtained that strongly confirm one hypothesis, while disconfirming other possibilities, then a diagnosis is reached.

This is not the process that is always used. Nurses may take a variety of approaches to diagnosis. Let's take a look at a sample case study and examine how four different nurses might approach it.

Mrs. L is a 63-year-old diabetic woman who has been in coronary care for five days with the diagnosis of acute M.I. complicated with recurrent premature ventricular contractions. She has been receiving lidocaine IV drip at 2–4 mg/minute, currently at 2 mg/minute. She has an abrasion over the left eye, sustained in a fall prior to admission. Her history indicates one prior hospitalization for cataract removal. When the afternoon nurse comes on duty,

8

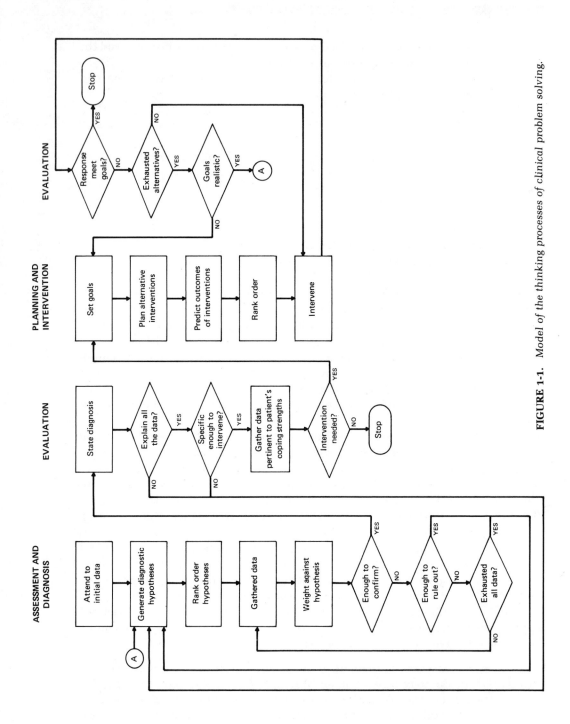

FIGURE 1-1. Model of the thinking processes of clinical problem solving.

Mrs. L is disoriented as to time and place. She is out of bed, brushing her teeth, and is quite agitated about the monitor wires restricting her freedom. When told that she's in the hospital, she comments that she's given enough time to the "equipment check" referring to "all the people coming in the room to check the monitor." There is no record of her having been confused before.

One approach that any of our four nurses might use would be the trial-and-error method: do a complete physical exam, gather all data from the chart related to Mrs. L.'s history, pull all the data together, and try to come up with all the possible explanations for her disorientation. Or they may try a variety of interventions and see if one of them works. Needless to say, the list of either possible diagnoses or possible interventions could go on forever. Unless we narrow down the list of possibilities, or in some other way reduce the complexity of the clinical problem, considerable time could be lost. Moreover, though our brains have huge storing capacity for information, they have a limited work space for processing current information. When trying to analyze the reams of information together with the endless list of possibilities, important details are likely to be forgotten. The trial-and-error approach to problem solving is just not very effective when attempted with complex problems.

Problem solvers tend to rely on what is known as heuristics to derive solutions. A heuristic is a quicker way to process information which allows us to use our limited work space in a more efficient manner. The unfortunate thing about these short-cut methods is that they are not 100 percent accurate; although, some are more accurate than others. The type of heuristic used and its effectiveness is probably dependent on the problem-solving task, the experience and knowledge of the problem solver, as well as other individual differences. Let's look at how our nurses each approach the problem.

Nurse A obtains the following information:

Assessment: Skin warm and dry
Pulse 72 and full
Blood Pressure Stable at 128/60
Last insulin was 8 hours ago, N.P.H. 40 units
N.P.H. peaks in *8-12* hours
Last S and A was at 11:30 A.M., 2 +/Neg.
7:00 A.M. FBS 138 mg/100 ml

Action: Nurse A gives Mrs. L 120 cc orange juice and draws blood for blood glucose

Assessment: She then checks:
IV patent with lidocaine at 30 cc/hour
She examines for evidence of tremors
She notes normal sinus rhythm with no dysrrythmias

Action: She decides to slow down the lidocaine to 1 mg/minute if Mrs. L. fails to respond to the orange juice

Assessment: She then checks:
Urinary output stable (800 cc) past 8 hours
Peripheral circulation good

HR stable at 72/minute
Decides the skin color is good
No evidence of low cardiac output which might result in disorientation.

Action: None indicated.

Assessment: She then checks:
Pupils—equal, react to light
Denies headache
Early admission data indicate no evidence of substantial head trauma sustained in fall prior to admission

Action: Decides to monitor neuro signs

Assessment: She then checks:
Degree of problems with vision
Presence of "meaningful" stimuli (books, clock, radio, calendar) in room
Frequency of visitors
The delusional quality of Mrs. L's disorientation

Action: Decides Mrs. L. needs to get her glasses from home, to relax the visiting restrictions, and to obtain some diversionary activities for her

Nurse B obtains the following information:

Assessment: *Rhythm Strip:* Normal sinus rhythm, no arrhythmias
Vital Signs: Pulse 72
Blood Pressure 128/60
Respiration 18 and unlabored
Temp 98.4 (0)
Urine Output: 800 cc's since 7:00 A.M.
IV: Patent at 30 cc/hour (lidocaine)
Chest PA: Lungs clear

Action: Noting nothing else abnormal in her routine assessment, Nurse A re-orients Mrs. L and charts her findings

Nurse C obtains the following information:

Assessment: Routine beginning of the shift assessment including V.S., rhythm strip, chest PA, urinary output
Package insert for lidocaine
Remembers caring for patient with lidocaine toxicity last week

Action: Reduce lidocaine drip to 1 mg/minute. Monitor PVC's over next hour; if less than 6, discontinue it

Nurse D obtains the following information:

Assessment: Skin warm and dry
Patient states she ate lunch well

Pulse 72 and full
Blood pressure stable at 128/60
Last S and A was 2 + and neg

Action: Reorient, record findings, and observe closely

Four different nurses, and four very different approaches to the problem. We will analyze each approach.

Nurse A is thorough and systematic. Notice that all of the data gathered in the initial assessment are related to a complication of insulin administration, i.e., hypoglycemia. The nurse is systematically testing this hypothesis by gathering data which will confirm or disconfirm the hypothesis.

The data do not clearly support hypoglycemia as an explanation of the patient's confusion. To be on the safe side, the nurse administers glucose since there still is a remote possibility that the patient is experiencing an atypical insulin reaction.

The nurse proceeds examining other diagnostic hypotheses. She evaluates the possibility that the confusion may be due to lidocaine toxicity. This, like insulin reaction, cannot be totally ruled out, so the nurse has an alternative intervention if the administration of orange juice fails to bring about the desired effects. Other diagnostic hypotheses the nurse considers are reduced cerebral perfusion due to low cardiac output, reaction to head trauma (i.e., increased intracranial pressure), and, finally, sensory deprivation.

It is quite likely that Nurse A initially considered all hypotheses. Because insulin reaction, based on the initial data, was the most probable hypothesis and, indeed, the most urgent, Nurse A began her hypothesis testing with this possibility. In other words, she went through a process of informally rank-ordering the likelihood of each hypothesis before seeking additional data.

Nurse B has gone through the nursing process in a quite different fashion. It appears that she has gathered data in a preprescribed manner, i.e., the type of information typically collected from every patient in the coronary care unit at the beginning of each shift. It also appears that the patient's disorientation did not trigger any hypotheses for this nurse. This example emphasizes how early hypotheses guide data gathering and subsequent nursing action.

Nurse C takes a different approach. She uses a heuristic, often employed by clinicians, to assist in the rapid generation and/or narrowing down of hypotheses. This heuristic depends on "availability of instances" for either retrieving hypotheses from memory or assigning the probability of the hypothesis being the diagnoses. If the nurse had recently cared for several patients with increased intracranial pressure, she may have overestimated the probability of that being the diagnosis, just because it seemed to be a common occurrence. Likewise, Nurse C may have used this heuristic in identifying lidocaine toxicity as a hypothesis.

The problem with using this heuristic is that the accurate diagnosis may not be even considered, or if it is, its probability relative to the favored hypothesis may be so low that further confirming/disconfirming data are not sought. The other risk inherent in using this strategy is that the favored hypothesis (in this case, lidocaine toxicity) may be accepted as the diagnosis without gathering sufficient confirming information and/or ignoring disconfirming information.

Nurse D demonstrates evidence of another problem occasionally encountered in diagnosis, that is, rejecting a hypothesis before enough information has been gathered to do so. Nurse D was evidently considering hypoglycemia as a hypothesis; to test this hypothesis, she used several possibly unreliable indicators of low blood sugar, such as a urine test 4 hours prior to her observations and the patient statements that she ate lunch well (which may be totally inaccurate given patient's confused state). The best indicators would be those used by Nurse A, that is, the patient's response to 120 cc of orange juice and blood glucose level.

To summarize then, we have discussed several potential problem areas in the diagnostic process: (1) failure to associate initially available data with plausible diagnostic hypotheses; (2) failure to include the accurate diagnosis in the initial set of hypotheses considered; (3) overestimating the probability of one hypothesis because of greater ease of recall, recent experience, etc.; (4) failure to use disconfirming data; and (5) overestimating the reliability of data or the information value in either confirming or disconfirming hypotheses.

Use of the systematic process depicted in Figure 1 will assist the problem solver in avoiding these pitfalls frequently encountered in diagnosis. The initial steps of attending to relevant cues and generating diagnostic hypotheses, are crucial to the remainder of the nursing process. Hypotheses guide subsequent data collection and, as we have seen in our examples, relevant data are likely to be missed if the related diagnostic hypothesis was not considered. If the clinician will pause to think of as many hypotheses as possible which explain the initial data, recognizing a natural tendency to reduce the possibilities as quickly as possible by using a variety of heuristics, s/he is more likely to be thorough in the subsequent data collection and accurate in the final diagnosis.

If the nurse uses similar caution in data collection, systematically testing each hypothesis and recognizing which cues may be unreliable, s/he is more likely to derive an accurate diagnosis. Profound influence on the diagnostic process can occur by the tendencies to favor, by "availability of instances," one hypothesis and to overestimate the value of confirmatory data. Carefully evaluating each hypothesis in the light of the evidence will help the nurse avoid these biases. It should be noted that these intellectual processes normally occur with such rapidity (fractions of a second) that one must consciously pause and evaluate his/her thinking process to assure relevant alternatives have been considered and biases have been minimized.

Once the diagnosis has been established, realistic goals are mutually defined by the patient and the nurse. As in diagnosis, pausing to consider the patient's own strengths and coping mechanisms as well as the optimal level of wellness is critical to the determination of attainable goals.

The identification of alternative interventions also requires the use of a complex thinking process subject to the same biases as the diagnostic process. The nurse must carefully predict outcomes of the interventions selecting the one which is most likely to attain the desired outcome. Very often, if the diagnosis is correct, the most desirable intervention is readily apparent.

It is hoped that the awareness of the intellectual activities comprising the nursing process, as well as an understanding of the potential pitfalls, will assist you in learning to become a superb clinical problem solver. Consciously thinking of alternatives throughout the entire process is critical in eliminating the biases naturally introduced by the human problem solver. In the chapters that follow, review information will be presented that is organized in such a way to help you think of these alternatives when needed in the clinical situation. You will then be provided with practice in applying this information to generate diagnostic hypotheses, evaluate the hypotheses in light of the data provided, confirm a diagnosis, determine an appropriate plan of care, and set criteria for evaluation of the effectiveness of the plan.

FOOTNOTES

 1. Webster's Third New International Dictionary. Springfield, Mass., Merriam-Webster, 1967.
 2. Yura H, Walsh MB: The Nursing Process. New York, Appleton, 1973, p 19.
 3. Ibid, p 19.
 4. Byrne ML, Thompson LF: Key Concepts for the Study and Practice of Nursing. St. Louis, Mosby, 1972.
 5. Roy C: The Roy Adaptation Model. In Riehl JP, Roy C: Conceptual Models For Nursing Practice. New York, Appleton, 1980, pp 179–188.
 6. Kraus VL: Pre-information—Its Effects on Nurses' Descriptions of a Patient, J Nurs Educ 15:15, pp 18–26, 1976.
 7. Gordon M: Nursing Diagnosis and the Diagnostic Process. Am J Nurs, 76:1298, 1976.
 8. Ibid., p 1298.
 9. Gordon M: The concept of nursing diagnosis. Nurs Clin North Am 14:3, 487–496, 1979.
10. Classification of nursing diagnoses: Proceedings of the Third and Fourth National Conferences. St. Louis, Clearinghouse, National Group for Classification of Nursing Diagnosis, in press.

CHAPTER 2

Blood Pressure Alterations

The blood pressure is the force exerted by the blood against the walls of the blood vessels. Measurements of the blood pressure are taken at specific hemodynamic periods. The systolic pressure is a measurement of the pressure when the ventricles contract and force the blood into the aorta. The diastolic pressure is a measurement of the pressure in the blood vessels during the filling of the heart when the aortic valve is closed. The difference between the systolic and diastolic pressures is termed the pulse pressure. The blood pressure is the product of the cardiac output and the peripheral resistance. The blood volume, elasticity of arterial walls, autonomic reflex mechanisms, hormonal activity, and nephrogenic factors are the major variables that affect the cardiac output and peripheral resistance. A short discussion of each of these factors should help in anticipation of changes in the blood pressure and recognition of the most likely cause for the change.

Cardiac output is the amount of blood ejected from the left ventricle every minute. It is the product of the stroke volume times the heart rate. Normal cardiac output at rest for the average adult is 5 liters/minute. The cardiac index is a more accurate gauge which takes body size into account. (An expression of the cardiac output per square meter of body surface.) Normal range is 2.5 to 4 liters/sq. meter. With strenuous exercise, the adult with a good "pump" responds with an increase both in heart rate and stroke volume, with the cardiac index increasing 4 to 5 times to 12 to 15 liters. Normally the systolic blood pressure increases with an increase in the cardiac output, but to a lesser extent; the maximum increase usually being 30 to 40 percent.

Peripheral vascular resistance is the resistance to the flow of blood that is made by the vessels in the peripheral vascular bed. The major determinant of resistance is the caliber of the arterioles and small arteries (lumen size), which primarily depends upon vasomotor tone. Vasoconstriction increases resistance to blood flow and increases blood pressure, while vasodilation decreases resistance and lowers blood pressure. Since resistance varies inversely with the fourth power of the radius of the lumen, it is apparent that small changes in caliber produce great changes in the resistance and in the blood pressure. For example,

15

a reduction of 16 percent in the radii of all vessels could double the blood pressure. Increases in the peripheral resistance increase both diastolic and systolic pressure; frequently the greatest effect is on the diastolic pressure.

The viscosity of the blood also affects the peripheral resistance, but to a lesser extent than the caliber of the vessels. Polycythemia is associated with increased blood pressure while persons with anemia usually have a low blood pressure. However, compensatory mechanisms for anemia that result in a higher cardiac output and a high degree of vasoconstriction may result in only moderately low, normal, or even, in a few instances, elevated blood pressure.

VARIABLES THAT AFFECT THE BLOOD PRESSURE

Blood volume in the circulatory system of an average adult is 6 liters. Increases in the volume are associated with elevations of the blood pressure while hypovolemia is usually evidenced by a decrease in the blood pressure. Compensatory mechanisms of increased cardiac output and vasoconstriction may effectively maintain the blood pressure within normal range in spite of hypovolemia. Although the end result of hypovolemia is a decrease in cardiac output, it is helpful to think of it separately since treatment needs to restore volume instead of primarily improving the cardiac pump.

Elasticity of arterial walls allow them to yield during systole with a rebound retraction during diastole. When the distensibility of the large arteries is limited by arteriosclerosis, the systolic blood pressure is increased and the diastolic decreased. The fall in diastolic pressure is due to loss of the elastic retractive support that maintains the pressure during diastole.

The autonomic nervous system is responsible for the operation of buffer systems that maintain arterial pressure. Stretch receptors in the aortic arch and the carotid sinuses send messages regarding pressure changes in the vascular system to the cardiovascular regulatory centers in the medulla. Elevations of arterial pressure increase the rate of discharge of impulses from the stretch receptors which increases the vagal discharge and inhibits the sympathetic discharge. As a result the heart is slowed and the peripheral vasoconstriction is decreased. Decreases in arterial pressure diminish the rate of discharge of impulses from the stretch receptors which in turn inhibits the parasympathetic (vagal) activity and activates the sympathetic nervous system with release of the catecholamines norepinephrine and epinephrine. The net effect is to return the blood pressure toward normal by increasing the heart rate, myocardial contractility, and peripheral vasoconstriction. Overproduction and/or release of excess catecholamine results in elevation of the blood pressure. Such overproduction may be due to a physiologic state such as pheochromocytoma or to an emotional state. Impulses arising in the brain as a result of anxiety, anger, fear, or moderate pain stimulate the vasomotor center in the hypothalamus and cause vasoconstriction and elevation of blood pressure. This is frequently referred to as the fight-or-flight mechanism. Severe emotional shock or intense physical pain may result in inhibition of the vasomotor center which can cause a vasodilation and fall in blood pressure so severe as to result in unconsciousness and even death.

Hormonal activity of the pituitary gland also acts to maintain blood pressure within normal range. A decrease in blood pressure normally causes an increase in the output of antidiuretic hormone (ADH) and adrenocorticotropic hormone (ACTH) with increased outputs of aldosterone. The effect is increased conservation of fluid and sodium which tends to return the blood pressure toward normal. The reverse happens when the arterial pressure is raised abruptly. Other hormonal and chemical influences on blood pressure include the thyroid hormone, adrenal hormones (both medullary and cortical), sodium, histamine, and serotonin.

Nephrogenic factors affecting the blood pressure are humoral vasoconstrictor substances that are released in response to renal ischemia or reduced renal blood flow with lower perfusion pressure at the renal arterioles. The enzyme, renin, acts upon a plasma substrate to produce angiotensin which has a bifold action of vasoconstriction and volume retention, with a resultant rise in blood pressure. Plasma renin substrate levels are elevated in pregnancy, as a result of oral contraceptive pills, with an excess of glucocorticoid or aldosterone hormone, and in many persons for whom no identifiable cause can be demonstrated. People with high plasma renin levels of unknown etiology comprise the largest single group of blood pressure elevation. The presence of other humoral agents produced by the renal tissue that cause vasodilation and natriuresis (sodium excretion) is fairly well substantiated, but there is a lack of consensus on the exact nature of the substances. Many authorities credit at least a portion of the activity to the prostaglandin designated PGA.

ASSESSMENT

Measurement of the Blood Pressure

Measurement commonly utilizes a pneumatic cuff and a manometer which in most instances provides a slight underestimation of the true arterial pressure. Errors in technique can give incorrect readings so diligence should be employed to minimize errors.

1. *Position.* The patient should be in a relaxed position and at least 30 minutes should have elapsed since eating or strenuous exercise. The position can be upright or supine, with the arm bared to the shoulder and the whole forearm supported at the level of the heart. Supine patients should be lying on their backs, since side position measurements have been found to be unreliable. Record arm and position used. Some clinicians recommend initial measurement of pressure in both arms to identify arterial disease and comparison of arm and leg pressures to recognize coarctation of the aorta. Additionally, measurement of both supine and standing pressures are recommended to determine if the nervous system's response to orthostasis is deficient or excessive. Changes in the mean arterial pressure of 10 mm Hg more or less are considered abnormal. Orthostatic (postural) hypotension is found more frequently than orthostatic hypertension.

2. *Cuff technique.* The width of the cuff should be 20 percent wider than the diameter of the extremity. Standard width is 13 cm for the adult arm, and 6–7 cm for the child. The cuff for a thigh or an obese arm is usually 20 cm wide. It is also essential that the rubber bladder in the cuff is long enough to reach around the extremity. Fit the cuff closely and evenly around the arm with the center of the rubber bladder over the brachial artery.

3. *Palpation and auscultation.* While palpating the radial pulse, place the diaphragm of the stethoscope over the brachial artery below the pulse and inflate the cuff fairly quickly until the radial pulse disappears. Then inflate the cuff an additional 30 mm Hg (overdistension of the cuff can cause arterial spasm and elevation of the blood pressure). Release the valve in the hand bulb so the pressure falls at a rate of 2–3 mm Hg per second. The systolic pressure is that at which the first sounds are heard and/or palpated. Most clinicians believe the systolic pressure by palpation is more accurate than by auscultation, but the usual practice is to record the highest, which is most often the ausculatory pressure. The inexperienced practitioner may have difficulty performing palpation and auscultation at the same time. If such is the case, palpation should be done before auscultation. Continue to let the pressure fall until the sounds become muffled and then disappear. The point of complete cessation of muffled sounds is recorded as the diastolic pressure. If there is a considerable gap between the time the sounds become muffled and when they disappear, both rates may be recorded as diastolic pressure, i.e., 140/85–70. When there is no cessation of sounds, record the pressure at which the sounds became muffled as the diastolic pressure. In a few patients, the sounds neither become distinctly muffled or disappear. This is usually indicated by a question mark in the diastolic recording place. With atrial fibrillation, the blood pressure measurement can only be an approximation. Record the pressure at which the majority of the sounds are heard and also when they become muffled.

Central arterial pressure. This measurement is taken by a cannula in a major artery that is connected to a pressure transducer. It is frequently used when alterations in the normal mechanisms of peripheral vascular resistance make cuff pressures less reliable. These central pressures can overestimate the systolic pressure when the highest point on the pressure waveform is recorded as the systolic pressure. For greater accuracy use the return to flow method to occlude the arterial flow by inflating a cuff on the extremity (arterial waveform will disappear). Release the cuff slowly and record the pressure at which the arterial wave form is again identifiable.

Identification of Variations in the Blood Pressure

Variations may be normal, pathognomonic, or idiopathic. Normal variations occur with age; neonates have lower pressures than adults. Although the blood pressure of many adults continues to rise after maturity, it is not desirable. Blood pressure has diurnal variation, being lowest in the morning. Other factors that affect the pressure are exercise, eating, weight, changes in posture, and emotionally stressful states.

Pathognomonic variations in addition to the previously mentioned higher pressure in the arms than in the legs characteristic of coarctation of the aorta are paradoxical pulse and pulsus alternans. Paradoxical pulse is an inaccurate descriptive term for the condition in which there is an exaggerated decrease in systolic blood pressure with inspiration. Normally the systolic pressure is 5−10 mm Hg less during inspiration than expiration. Persons with chronic obstructive pulmonary disease (COPD), extreme chest wall deformity, and those who breathe deeply frequently have a greater decrease in systolic blood pressure with inspiration. When not previously present, a decrease in the systolic pressure of more than 15 mm Hg during inspiration may indicate pericardial tamponade or constrictive pericarditis. Pulsus alternans is an irregularity manifested as a sudden doubling of the number of beats heard as the cuff is deflated to the pressure of the beats of smaller amplitude. It is associated with serious myocardial damage. Postural hypotension is said to be present when the difference in systolic pressure when supine and standing is greater than 10 mm Hg. Postural hypotension results from (1) a fluid volume deficit, (2) loss of compensating effect of sympathetic vasoconstriction to counterbalance the effect of gravity on the circulation, (3) intake of drugs that block the sympathetic nervous system, and (4) diminished responses to baroreceptor stimulation.

Variations in the blood pressure that are lower or higher than the normal range have been termed hypotension and hypertension, respectively. The defining characteristics, etiology, and intervention for each will be briefly discussed.

HYPOTENSION

Hypotension is frequently said to be present when the blood pressure (BP) is less than 90/60. Some people normally have low pressure with no untoward symptoms. Others with elevated pressures may have hypotensive symptoms with a blood pressure over 90. Thus a more accurate guideline of dangerously low blood pressure would be a sudden decrease in systolic pressure to three-quarters of previous pressure, or less than 85 mm Hg. Persons with hypotension are said to be in peripheral circulatory failure (shock) if they have inadequate perfusion of the brain, skeletal muscle, and vital organs. If shock is prolonged, it leads to generalized impairment of cellular function.

The major causes of arterial hypotension leading to shock are listed in Table 2-1. Shock from a decrease in cardiac output is referred to as cardiogenic shock, while that due to a fluid volume deficit is referred to as hypovolemic shock. Shock with decreased peripheral resistance due to vagal stimulation (resulting in vasodilation) or loss of vasoconstrictive mechanisms is termed neurogenic shock. When the decreased peripheral resistance results from dilation of arterioles and capillaries and increased capillary permeability with loss of intravascular volume, it is termed vasogenic shock.

TABLE 2-1.   Major Causes of Arterial Hypotension

Abnormal Initiating Mechanism	Pathophysiology	Clinical State
I. Reduction in cardiac output	Cardiogenic shock due to a decrease in the amount of blood pumped by the heart each minute. Causes include:	
	A. Decrease in the effectiveness of the heart as a pump (pump failure)	Myocardial infarction, severe congestive heart failure, myxedema crisis, severe hypoxia, severe metabolic acidosis
	B. Alteration of rate and rhythm of the heart	Severe paroxysmal tachycardia, ventricular fibrillation, severe bradycardia, heart block, digitalis toxicity, hyperkalemia, hypokalemia
	C. Interference with blood flow	Cardiac tamponade, pulmonary embolus, tension pneumothorax, valvular disease

II. Fluid volume deficit	Hypovolemic shock due to a decrease in the volume of blood in the intravascular space. Deficit may be due to:
	A. External fluid losses
	    Blood loss
	    Gastrointestinal loss of fluid and electrolytes
	
	    Renal loss of fluid and electrolytes
	
	    Cutaneous loss of fluid and/or plasma
		
		Hemorrhage
		Vomiting, diarrhea, fistula
		
		Uncontrolled diabetes mellitus, hyperosmolar nonketonic state, diabetes insipidus, excessive use of diuretics, Addison's disease, Thorne syndrome (salt-losing nephritis)
		Burns, extensive exudative dermatitis, unreplaced diaphoresis and insensible water loss

	B. Internal sequestration or translocation of fluid and plasma	Fractures, ascites, pancreatitis, perforated viscus, intestinal obstruction or ileus, second and third degree burns
III. Decreased peripheral resistance	A. Neurogenic shock due to loss or inhibition of sympathetic vasoconstrictive mechanisms Pharmacologic	 Anesthesia, sympatholytic antihypertensive drugs, sedative overdose (barbiturates, phenothiazines)

(continued)

TABLE 2-1.   Continued

Abnormal Initiating Mechanism	Pathophysiology	Clinical State
III. Decreased peripheral resistance (*continued*)	Interference with neural pathway	Transection of the spinal cord, neuropathies (multiple sclerosis, lateral sclerosis, tabes dorsalis, etc.), extensive lumbodorsal sympathectomy, idiopathic orthostatic hypotension
B.	Neurogenic shock due to vagal stimulation resulting in vasodilation	Syncope from severe emotional shock or pain
C.	Vasogenic shock due to presence of vasoactive substances that cause loss of vasomotor tone, increased capillary permeability, and loss of intravascular volume	
	Antibody reactions	Hemolytic transfusion reaction, allergic anaphylaxis
	Endotoxins	Septicemia

ASSESSMENT

Homeostatic compensatory mechanisms.   These are responsible for many of
the altered signs and symptoms seen with shock. Initially when the problem
occurs, the neural and hormonal defense mechanisms previously described are
activated to compensate for the assault and return the blood pressure toward
normal. In the case of shock from fluid volume deficit or reduction of cardiac
output, the presence of such compensatory mechanisms is manifested by
tachycardia, diaphoresis, and peripheral vasoconstriction with mottling or
pallor and coolness of the extremities. Early identification of shock increases the
success rate of effective management. Early hypovolemic shock may be manifested by a decrease in the pulse pressure before the systolic pressure falls. If the
compensatory reactions begin to fail and the blood pressure remains low despite
efforts to correct the underlying cause, the severe vasoconstriction may reduce
tissue perfusion even further, with widespread cellular injury from anoxia and
resultant lactic acidosis from anaerobic metabolism. Lactic acidosis interferes
with the energy-requiring active transport systems of the cell membranes. The
high-energy phosphate reserves are depleted and the integrity of the cells and
capillary membranes is compromised, and fluid and cellular contents of the
blood seep into the extravascular tissue space. The pooling of blood in the
extravascular space further reduces the available volume for circulation and
cellular starvation results.

   Although all forms of shock result in reduced tissue perfusion, shock from
loss of vasomotor tone presents a different chain of events. In these cases, functional or pathologic loss of sympathetic vasomotor activity results in a reduction
of the peripheral resistance with pooling of blood in the venous bed and di-

minished venous return. Without the vasoconstrictive response, the skin is warm and dry. The compensatory mechanism of tachycardia endeavors to maintain an adequate cardiac output in spite of the reduced circulating blood volume. In septic shock, the severe destruction of the microcirculation by the toxin causes a rapid loss of vasomotor tone. The specific parameters that are indicative of the presence of these adaptive mechanisms and the adequacy of tissue perfusion can be summarized as follows:

- *ECG monitoring of heart rate and rhythm*—Tachycardia is a compensatory mechanism with all types of shock except neurogenic shock due to vagal stimulation. Bradycardia is present with shock from vagal stimulation. Dysrhythmias may be the cause of a drop in blood pressure in some patients.

- *Arterial blood gas determinations* give information on the presence of acidosis and hypoxemia. The Po_2 of mixed venous blood drawn from the Swan–Ganz catheter is being increasingly relied on as an indicator of cellular perfusion. The venous Po_2 should be 30–40 torr. Values below 30 (and especially 25) are ominous signs of cellular ischemia and death which may be irreversible if uncorrected.

- *Level of cognitive functioning* and presence of lethargy, weakness, easy fatigability, and dizziness gives an indication of adequacy of brain perfusion.

- *Hourly urine output*—When the kidneys are not being adequately perfused, urine output ceases or is drastically reduced. Adequate perfusion is usually indicated by urine output greater than 30 ml/hour.

- *Pulmonary artery pressure* (PAP) is monitored using a Swan–Ganz balloon-tipped catheter in the pulmonary artery with hourly measurement of pulmonary artery wedge pressure (PAWP). The wedge pressure is measured by inflating the balloon with air. This wedges the catheter in the pulmonary capillary and cuts off the effect of proximal pressure, which results in a measurement of the pressure of the left side of the heart. A low PAWP of less than 10 mm Hg in an adult indicates that there is an inadequate volume of fluid within the intravascular space. A high PAWP of more than 25 mm Hg is indicative of an overload of fluid and/or failure of the left heart to pump out the volume of blood returned to it; this causes back up of fluid in the lungs (left heart failure or pulmonary edema).

- *Central venous pressure* (CVP) monitoring may be used when equipment for Swan–Ganz monitoring is not available. It is measured with a catheter in the superior vena cava or right atrium of the heart connected to a water manometer or transducer. It reflects the pressure on the right side of the heart. Since rather severe pulmonary edema can be present before the fluid backs up and pressure rises in the right side of the heart, it is not as reliable a measurement as PAWP.

INTERVENTION

The major goals of intervention for shock are maintenance of adequate circulation and oxygen to vital organs, reduction of anxiety, treatment of any underlying cause, and prevention of dysfunctional effects from ischemic injuries to the vital organs and tissues. Administration of oxygen is usually indicated for all forms of shock. Other intervention will be briefly discussed that is specific for each of the three major categories of shock.

Cardiogenic shock.   Management is directed toward restoration of cardiac function and increase of cardiac output. Positive inotropic agents that increase the force of the cardiac contraction such as digitalis, isoproterenol (Isuprel), or dopamine (Intropin) are the mainstay of therapy. A rapid-acting form of digitalis such as lanatoside C (Cedilanid) may be given initially, followed by a slower acting form such as digoxin (Lanoxin). More complete information on these drugs is included in the chapter on pulse alterations. If fluid retention is present, diuretics are given. If dysrhythmias are present which could contribute to the low cardiac output, they are corrected. When cardiogenic shock is refractive to other forms of treatment, circulatory assist devices such as external counterpulsation and diastolic augmentation by the intra-aortic balloon may be utilized.

Hypovolemic shock.   Management is directed toward restoration of the blood volume by rapid infusion of volume-expanding fluids. When large volumes of fluid are administered rapidly, they should be warmed to approximately 35 C before or during infusion. Blood is given for blood loss; while plasma, plasma protein fraction, dextran, or albumin plus isotonic electrolyte solutions are given for fluid deficit. Fluid cannot be adequately replaced by electrolyte solutions alone, because without colloid, fluid will not be retained in the intravascular space.

Decreased peripheral resistance.   Decreased resistance due to neurogenic or vasogenic causes also requires fluid replacement. The vasodilation with pooling of fluid in the venous bed results in a decreased venous return and a fall in cardiac output. Fluid replacement is similar to that of hypovolemic shock with the addition, for some patients, of vasoconstrictor drugs such as norepinephrine (Levophed) or metaraminol (Aramine). If the underlying cause is sepsis, prompt initiation of antibiotic drugs and drainage of a focus of infection is essential. Large doses of adrenal glucocorticoids may be given for septic shock. It is believed that their use decreases damage to the microcirculation.

HYPERTENSION

Hypertension is the term used for an abnormal elevation of arterial pressure. When the elevation is of the systolic pressure only, it is referred to as systolic hypertension. If both the systolic and diastolic pressures are elevated, it is termed diastolic hypertension.

Systolic hypertension is caused by a decrease in the distensibility of the major arteries from arteriosclerosis and/or an increase in the stroke output of the left ventricle. Systolic hypertension is less likely to result in organ damage than diastolic hypertension, although systolic pressures over 160 in persons under the age of 40 seems to increase the risk of coronary artery disease.

Diastolic hypertension, sometimes termed true systemic hypertension, is generally recognized as persistent elevation of the systolic pressure above 140 and the diastolic pressure above 90. Most of the major known causes of diastolic hypertension are related to a disease process in the renal, endocrine, vascular, or central nervous system. When there is an identifiable known cause, hypertension may be termed secondary. A specific cause for the elevated pressure cannot be identified for approximately 85 to 90 percent of the cases of diastolic hypertension; this is termed essential or primary hypertension. Regardless of the initial cause, the mechanism responsible for the rise in pressure in most instances is an increase in the peripheral arterial resistance as a result of generalized vasoconstriction or narrowing of the arterioles. The types and causes of hypertension are presented in Table 2-2.

Essential hypertension is correlated with the factors of heredity, stress, high dietary intake of sodium, overweight, pregnancy, and race; American Blacks have a higher incidence than the rest of the population. It is believed to be a multifactorial state related to abnormalities of the regulatory homeostatic mechanisms that normally control arterial pressure. The finding of high levels of the renal vasopressor substance, renin, in patients with essential hypertension has given credence to the renin-angiotensin theory previously discussed as the responsible mechanism in many cases. When the diastolic pressure is sustained over 130 mm Hg with rapidly progressing changes in the brain, eyes, and kidneys, the patient is said to have malignant hypertension. Approximately 5 percent of the patients with essential hypertension develop a malignant course.

Hypertensive emergency (or crisis) refers to a state in which the diastolic pressure is acutely elevated above 150 mm Hg (with or without symptoms) or above 130 mm Hg with any of the following: encephalopathy, acute pulmonary edema, cerebral hemorrhage, papilledema, (or multiple, fresh retinal hemorrhages), and/or decreasing renal function. It requires prompt hospital treatment with antihypertensive preparations to prevent further functional damage to the vital organs. Dissecting aneurysm is another emergency situation that requires rapid lowering of blood pressure.

ASSESSMENT

The usual diagnostic work up for patients with persistent diastolic hypertension attempts to identify any possible cause and to assess the damage the hypertension has caused to the heart, nervous system, and the kidneys.

History.   Items of significance include a family history of hypertension, urinary tract infections and symptoms, disturbances of the central nervous system, cardiac symptoms, and dietary intake of licorice and sodium. A history of menstrual irregularity, hypertensive episode with pregnancy, and the use of oral or conjugated estrogens are of significance with women. Because essential hypertension is affected by stress and dietary factors, questions should attempt to delineate the

TABLE 2-2. Major Causes of Arterial Hypertension

Abnormal Initiating Mechanism	Pathophysiology	Clinical State
SYSTOLIC HYPERTENSION		
I. Increase in cardiac output	Systolic blood pressure is increased as a result of an increased metabolic rate from excess thyroid hormone or temperature elevation	Thyrotoxicosis, sustained high fever
	Increased cardiac output resulting from increased venous return from circulation abnormalities or need for oxygen	Arteriovenous fistula, aortic insufficiency, patent ductus arteriosus, beriberi, severe anemia
	Sympathetic stimulation with vasoconstriction	Psychogenic hypertension
II. Loss of elasticity of major arteries	The distensibility of the aorta and large arteries is limited so they do not expand as the blood is received making the systolic pressure high. The associated lack of rebound retraction results in a rapid fall in pressure in diastole	Arteriosclerosis, coarctation of aorta
DIASTOLIC HYPERTENSION		
I. Renal ischemia		
A. Parenchymal disease	Hypertension results from renal parenchymal disease from loss of normally occurring vasodilator factor, excess of renin production, and hypervolemia with sodium and water retention	Acute and chronic glomerulonephritis, chronic pyelonephritis, polycystic kidney disease, renal tumor, diabetic nephropathy, renal involvement secondary to collagen disease, multiple myeloma, amyloidosis, etc.
B. Vascular occlusion	An obstructive lesion reduces the renal blood flow, decreases the renal arterial pressure, and stimulates the release of renin which acts to raise the blood pressure, increase aldosterone secretion, and increase sodium retention in an effort to increase the arterial blood volume and restore the renal arterial pressure	Fibromuscular hyperplasia of renal artery, thrombotic or embolic obstruction, arteriolar nephrosclerosis, periarteritis nodosa
II. Altered hormone level	By a poorly understood mechanism, probably associated with altered hormonal levels and preexisting diastolic hypertension, the renin-agiotensin-aldosterone pressor system is activated	Toxemia of pregnancy, intake of conjugated estrogens
	Excess secretion of adrenal hormones results in retention of sodium and water and sensitization of vascular smooth muscle to vasoconstrictive agents such as catecholamines	

(continued)

TABLE 2-2. Continued

Abnormal Initiating Mechanism	Pathophysiology	Clinical State

II. Altered hormone level (*continued*)	A. Adrenocortical excess
	   1. Aldosterone excess (mineralocortocoid excess)
	   2. Cortisol excess (glucocorticoid excess
	   3. Androgen excess
		Primary hyperaldosteronism (Conn's syndrome)
		Cushing's syndrome
		
		Andrenogenital syndrome

	B. Adrenal medulla secretion of excess catecholamines causing vasoconstriction	Pheochromocytoma
III. Fluid volume excess	An increase in intravascular fluid volume increase the pressure A. Red blood cell excess B. Sodium and fluid excess	Polycythemia, excessive transfusion Licorice ingestion, high sodium intake
IV. Excessive circulating catecholamine	Intake of drugs or certain foods with monoamine oxidase (MAO) inhibitors stimulates release of catecholamines causing vasoconstriction.	Addition of ephedrine, amphetamine, or tyramine to MAO inhibitors Ingestion of foods containing tyramine (some foreign wines and beers, unpasteurized cheeses, pickled herring, etc.) when taking MAO inhibitors
V. Excess stimulation of vasomotor center	Stimulation of the vasomotor center in the hypothalamus is followed by a sympathetic nervous system response with general vasoconstriction A. Psychogenic stimulation	Prolonged stressful states (conflicts), acute anxiety (transient elevation)
V. Excess stimulation of vasomotor center (*continued*)	B. Decreased oxygen supply to vasomotor center from increased intracranial pressure and brainstem compression.	Trauma (head injury, transection of cord), brain tumor, subdural hematoma, hemorrhage, inflammation, infections (encephalitis, bulbar poliomyelitis, etc.)
	C. Interference with neural pathways by lesions of vagus and glossopharyngeal nerves.	Polyneuritis, tabes dorsalis, acute porphyria
	D. Reflex sympathetic stimulation distension of hollow viscus (bladder or rectum)	Spinal cord lesions with paroxysmal hypertension
VI. Unknown	Pathophysiology is unknown, and initiating mechanism may vary, but incidence appears related to heredity, stress, sensitivity to activation of the ischemia−renin−angiotensin−vasoconstriction system, excess aldosterone production and sodium intake	Essential hypertension

individual's lifestyle. One effective method of questioning is to ask the person to describe a typical day, including diet and activity.

Symptoms.   There usually are no symptoms present in the early period of blood pressure elevation. Symptoms which appear as time progresses are occipital headaches (most often in the morning), vertigo, lightheadedness, tinnitus, fatigue, nervousness, vision disturbances, and sensation of flushing of the face. If hypertension is not controlled, signs and symptoms of damage to the vital organs from the sustained high pressures appear.

Physical examination.   Findings associated with etiology are disparities of the peripheral pulse (associated with atherosclerosis and aortic coarctation) and bruits (associated with renal arterial stenosis and/or arteriovenous fistula). The major cardiac, neurologic, and renal effects will be briefly discussed.

● *Cardiac abnormalities,* which occur in 75 percent of hypertensives, include left ventricular hypertrophy with a prominent fourth heart sound and angina. Ultimately left heart failure develops with exertional dyspnea, orthopnea, and paroxysmal nocturnal dyspnea. Right heart failure, which is a later development, is characterized by edema, venous distension, and enlargement of the liver. The incidence of myocardial infarction is increased in patients with hypertension.

● *Neurologic effects* of long standing hypertension can be found in the retina and central nervous system. Retinopathy progresses from narrowing of arterioles with exaggeration of light reflex to retinal hemorrhages and/or exudate to edema of the optic disc (papilledema). Central nervous system signs are the result of vascular occlusion or hemorrhage, with destruction of the brain tissue. Small lesions may result only in deterioration of mental functioning, but larger lesions produce major strokes and are responsible for 10−15 percent of the deaths secondary to hypertension.

● *Renal effects* result from arteriosclerotic lesions that decrease renal blood flow and tubular function. Patients have proteinuria and microscopic hematuria with progressive renal insufficiency. Approximately 10 percent of the deaths secondary to hypertension result from renal failure.

Essential laboratory tests.   For the diagnosis of the cause of hypertension lab tests include: (1) Serum BUN or creatinine for evaluation of kidney excretory function; (2) urinalysis for identification of renal parenchymal disease; (3) serum potassium, with low levels associated with aldosterone excess; (4) blood count for identification of polycythemia, and (5) chest x-ray and ECG to determine cardiac involvement.

Other diagnostic tests may be required for patients with certain positive history, physical examination, or initial laboratory screening tests. An intravenous pyelogram and renal arteriography provide data on obstructive uropathies; urinary catecholamines confirm or deny pheochromocytoma; and renin-sodium profiling identifies renovascular causes and provides information as to whether a beta-blocking drug is indicated to control inappropriate renin secretion.

INTERVENTION

Early detection and prompt effective treatment is of paramount importance in hypertension. A few patients have underlying diseases that can be surgically corrected or medically managed. For the large majority of patients, hypertension can only be controlled by long-term therapy. Education about the disease is crucial.

The most important goal of *nursing intervention* is for the patient to understand hypertension and the role he can play in its control. A review of the factors in his lifestyle (obtained from the history) which contribute to his hypertension should be discussed. Assisting him in identifying specific areas that can be changed is crucial. For example, the nurse should plan with the patient ways in which he may begin to reduce his weight, to restrict dietary intake of sodium and lipids, and to develop an exercise program. In addition, examining stressful situations in his life and learning to manage stress more effectively are important aspects of patient education. Smoking habits should also be examined and encouragement provided for curtailing smoking. Compliance with these regimes is variable and even for some compliant patients (if the diastolic pressure remains greater than 95–105 mm Hg) drug therapy is required.

Medical management utilizes diuretics to reduce the intravascular volume and agents to lower the systemic vascular resistance. Three major types of drugs are used to decrease peripheral resistance: (1) direct vasodilators such as hydralazine (Apresoline), sodium nitroprusside (Nipride), diazoxide (Hyperstat) and prazosin (Minipress); (2) renin lowering antivasoconstrictors such as propranolol (Inderal), clonidine (Catapres), etc.; (3) sympathetic inhibitors (also called adrenergic blockers or sympatholytics) such as reserpine (Serpasil), methyldopa (Aldomet), guanethidine (Ismelin), etc. Patients with more severe hypertension may be treated with a combination of drugs. Side effects can occur with all the drugs, and specific drugs and the dosage must be determined for each individual. A few patients who develop a malignant course that is not altered by drugs may be treated with sympathectomy.

EXPERIENTIAL INVOLVEMENT

Theoretical knowledge about blood pressure alterations will not guarantee success in the clinical situation. For example, when a patient has a sudden drop in blood pressure, will you be able to think of all the possible causes (generate the hypotheses) and collect the essential data needed to make the differential diagnosis? Handling the data alone is in itself a tremendous job. The reported symptoms gathered from the health history, significant signs found by the physical examination, clinical laboratory reports, medical diagnoses and treatment factors, psychosocial state, cultural background, and environmental factors all have to be *juggled*. From this myriad collection of data, the necessary information has to be selected, correctly interpreted, and synthesized into a diagnostic statement. The appropriate nursing intervention for the altered state has to be planned based on theoretical nursing concepts, taking into account the patient's physical, cognitive, emotional, cultural, social, and environmental state. Then you are ready to *DO* something for the patient; but doing alone is not enough, the patient's response to the treatment must be evaluated. If the patient does not exhibit the expected response, the intervention may need to be changed; there is also the possibility that the wrong diagnosis was made and you will have to start over.

Grappling with the whole process at once can be mind boggling. Taken step by step, using the problem solving process and some of the information-seeking strategies provided in the book, it can become more manageable. Learning any new skill is always difficult at first. None of us can remember learning to walk, but if we think about learning to drive a car (or skiing, swimming, playing the piano, playing tennis, etc.,) we can remember how difficult it was at first. We had to think of each action consciously, weigh the probable effects, make a decision, do it, and then see what happened. With practice, we found that we were doing many things without conscious effort, and the decision process was much easier because we had a wealth of concepts to draw from. These concepts, the product of theoretical knowledge and past experience, enabled us to internalize the learning process so we could draw on it when needed. To become proficient in the nursing process also requires theoretical knowledge and practice, which is what this book is all about.

In order to gain skill in problem solving, we will start out with a fairly simple case.

Case 2A. Mr. Brown, a 54-year-old male, was admitted to the hospital from the emergency room. He stated that he had awakened around 4:00 A.M. with severe abdominal pain, nausea, and vomiting. Just prior to coming to the emergency room at 7:00 A.M., he had emesis of a large amount of dark red material. His past history revealed that he had insulin dependent diabetes mellitus. He had been fairly well prior to admission, although he had an intermittent, gnawing, and burning pain in his epigastrium over the past three weeks. Pain had usually been relieved by Rolaids. He also had an ulcer on his right shin about 1½ inches in diameter, present for five weeks. The ulcer had developed after injury. He had not seen his physician for six months. He reported he had not taken his NPH insulin on the morning of admission because he was not eating. His vital signs were BP 110/60 (supine), 95/55 (standing), P 110, R 22 T 37 C (98.6 F). His Hct was 36 ml/dl. The patient was placed on nothing by mouth, and had blood drawn for type and crossmatch, CBC, and sequential metabolic analysis (SMA) 6. An intravenous of normal saline was started at 100 ml/hour.

A half-hour after his admission he became extremely restless and when he was questioned about the way he felt, his response was slow and somewhat inappropriate. His vital signs at this time were BP 85/50 (supine), 70/? (standing), P 116, R 26, and T 36.7 C (98 F). The results of his admission blood work were not yet available.

Skillbuilders:

1. On the practicum record 2A-1, enter the two most likely hypotheses for his hypotension.

2. Enter the data you have that support the hypothesis and additional data you will need to confirm or disconfirm.

3. Then enter the nursing intervention that would be appropriate if the diagnosis was confirmed.

4. In the evaluation column, enter the criteria by which the process will be measured.

5. On the practicum record 2A-2, enter the two nursing diagnoses which must be differentially considered as expressions of his problems in adjustment to diabetes.

6. Then briefly outline a plan that could be used for validation.

To acquaint you with the process, we'll start our thinking and recording together. We can get some help in generating the hypotheses from the list of causes of hypotension. As we scan the list for states that might have recently occurred or previous states that deteriorated, we realize that there is always an outside chance that some interference with the cardiac output such as myocardial infarction or dysrhythmia could cause the drop in blood pressure, but this does not seem likely. None of the neurogenic causes seems appropriate. We might wonder if he could have a septicemia from his leg ulcer. Theoretical knowledge of diabetic ulcers, however, indicates that there is a very poor blood supply and infections usually remain localized. Fluid volume deficit from hemorrhage is a distinct possibility, however. (He has had symptoms that sound like a peptic ulcer with earlier hematemesis.) Also since the patient is a diabetic who skipped his insulin, there is a possibility his diabetes is out of control and he is in ketoacidosis. (The stress of hemorrhage and vomiting activates the sympathoadrenal response which speeds up the conversion of glycogen in the liver to glucose, and results in elevated blood glucose, osmotic diuresis, and development of ketoacidosis.) Thus, it looks like the best bets for hypotheses are hypotension due to gastrointestinal hemorrhage or diabetic ketoacidosis. These have been entered on the practicum record. We need to keep in mind that some unusual cause not on the list could also be responsible.

Next we need to fill in the supporting data and additional data needed. For hemorrhage, the history of previous bleeding and possible ulcer can be entered as supporting data. To cue us on other data that can give us the most diagnostic information, we can use the decision trees in the Appendix. There will not be a tree for every diagnosis, and the wording may be different. It is not too difficult to deduce that fluid volume deficit would include hemorrhage. As we look at the

PRACTICUM RECORD 2A-1

Hypothesis/Possible Diagnosis	Supportive Data Available	Additional Data Needed to Confirm or Disconfirm	Nursing Intervention if Diagnosis Confirmed	Evaluation Criteria

Hypotension due to:
1. Fluid volume deficit from gastrointestinal hemorrhage
	History of previous bleeding and possible ulcer
	Postural hypotension BP 85/50–70/?
	in cognitive functioning
		Skin turgor
		Neck veins
		Creatinine and/or BUN
		Hct.
		Emesis (or N/G drainage of blood)
		Blood in stool
			Under direction of physician:
			Control the bleeding
			  Iced saline irrigation
			  Gastric drip of vasopressors
			  Gastric intubation and suction
			  Keep N/G tube patent
			Blood and IV fluid infusion
			  Control of rate
			  Accurate record of fluid balance
			Slight elevation of legs with flexion at hip
			Nurse-directed activities:
			  Relieve apprehension
			  Remain with patient
			  Give concise explanations
			  Keep requests at minimum
			  Medicate prn
			  Convey concern
			After critical period, education about disease, diet, and ordered medications
				Extent of hemorrhage
				Estimated blood loss
				Blood replaced
				Return to normalcy of BP, physical signs of fluid volume deficit, serum creatinine, Hct.
				Stools negative for blood
				
				Patient's report of feelings
				
				Verbalization of knowledge about disease, diet, and medications

2. Diabetic ketoacidosis				

PRACTICUM RECORD 2A-2

Hypothesis/Possible Diagnosis	Plan for validation of hypothesis:
Maladjustment to diabetes manifested by:	
1.	
2.	

column of observations on the tree for fluid volume deficit, we check to see if postural hypotension is present. There is a 15 mm Hg difference in his systolic pressure supine and standing, so that is recorded. We should note, however, that the patient also had a postural drop in BP on admission. We do not have any information about skin turgor, so this observation is written in the third column on the practicum record. There is a decrease in cognitive functioning which is entered in the second column, but we do not have information about the rest of the observations. (The Hct on admission was drawn before the drop in BP.) Since the patient does not have a Swan−Ganz catheter and we have no weight baseline, these data are not recorded in the third column. When additional information is available, the presence of flat neck veins, elevated BUN, and a decrease in the hematocrit (drawn after BP drop) in conjunction with the postural hypotension and the decrease in cognitive functioning would lend support to the hypothesis that hypotension is due to gastrointestinal hemorrhage. Other supporting data not listed in the tree are emesis (or N/G drainage) of blood or blood in stool.

Bear in mind that decision trees have their limitations. They can cue you to look at critical indicators, but you must use your background of theoretical knowledge in interpreting the findings. Thus it appears that Mr. Brown probably has a fluid volume deficit, but whether the deficit is due to GI hemorrhage or to loss of fluid from vomiting (and perhaps osmotic diuresis) cannot be determined without more data. When another hematocrit is available, it may also be inconclusive because we know that when a patient bleeds, he loses all elements of the blood such as water, plasma, red cells, electrolytes, etc. Immediately after a loss of blood, the hematocrit does not drop significantly because the concentration of red cells is the same, just the total volume in the intravascular compartment is decreased. After a period of time, homeostatic mechanisms attempt to restore the intravascular volume with the movement of water into the intravascular space; it is at this time (after dilution) that the hematocrit shows a decrease.

Even if there is sufficient information to support the hypothesis, we would still need to confirm or deny the likelihood of the second hypothesis being true since an alteration in the state of the patient can be caused by a combination of several factors. So we need to complete the nursing intervention and evaluation columns with activities that would be appropriate if the hypothesis of hemorrhage is supported, and then go through the same process for diabetic ketoacidosis.

Nursing intervention for this patient if he were hemorrhaging would include measures to control the bleeding, restoration of normal fluid and red cell volume, supportive measures during the period of blood loss, relief of apprehension, and education. Activities to control the bleeding would be ordered by the physician and could include iced saline irrigation for active bleeding, and, for some patients, gastric drip of an agent like levarterenol (Levophed) or vasopressin (Pitressin) that causes contraction of the smooth musculature of the stomach, capillaries, and small arterioles. If esophagoscopy and gastroscopy are to be done to identify the bleeding site, the nurse should explain what will happen and provide assistance to facilitate quick completion of the procedure with minimal discomfort. Activities to restore the fluid and red cell volume would include intravenous replacement of fluid and blood, with careful attention to infusion rate and accurate recording of fluid balance. Supportive measures would include gastric intubation and suction (if ordered by the physician) with maintenance of patency of tube, and slight elevation of legs with flexion at the hips.

If fluid and blood administration cannot keep up with the fluid lost by hemorrhage, the blood pressure may have to be maintained by cardiotonic drugs. Respiratory support such as administration of oxygen and, in extreme cases, use of a mechanical ventilator might be indicated. Morbidity increases as the number of units of transfused blood exceeds three times the body volume and the period of hypotension becomes prolonged. If bleeding does not respond to control effects, surgery may be undertaken. Specific measures for relief of apprehension might include spending time with the patient, giving clear, concise explanations of happenings, making only demands that are absolutely necessary on the patient, giving prescribed medication in response to patient's state, and conveying your concern for the patient. If the patient is found to have a peptic ulcer, education after the critical period has passed would include knowledge about the disease, diet, and prescribed drugs. Although we are talking about assessment and then intervention, we want to make it clear that assessment does not stop when intervention starts. It is a continuous ongoing process. Thus, BP, fluid volume, and cognitive level would be continuously monitored during intervention and may become the criteria for evaluation.

Evaluation criteria should include: (1) the extent of the hemorrhage, i.e., estimated blood loss and blood replaced; (2) return to normalcy of altered signs (BP, physical signs of fluid volume deficit, serum creatinine, Hct, and stools negative for blood); (3) patient's report of his feeling during the time and the degree of support he received from the health team; and (4) verbalization of knowledge about disease, diet, and medications.

Throughout this discussion the term "we" has been used as though the nurse had the total responsibility for the situation. Of course, this is not the case; but there are many differences among practice settings and the perceived responsibilities of the various members of the health care team. There are a few functions that are clearly in the realm of nursing and a few that undeniably belong to the physician, but the majority fall in the area of shared responsibility. The courts maintain that a nurse is accountable for her own actions, even when she is following a physician's order; therefore, it behooves us to be knowledgeable about all our actions, both the caring activities and the delegated medical activities directed toward cure.

Now for the next hypothesis, hypotension due to ketoacidosis. When ketoacidosis is present, hypotension results from a combination of fluid volume deficit (from osmotic diuresis) and a decrease in cardiac output from acidosis. The best decision tree to use is the one for metabolic acidosis. You've caught on to the system by now, so we'll let you fill out the rest of the practicum record. We do discuss each of the cases, but you can learn much more if you try it on your own and then compare your entries with our feedback. You may think of some essential point we've overlooked.

Feedback. Available data to support the hypothesis due to ketoacidosis would include (1) the history of diabetes, vomiting, and omission of insulin, (2) rapid pulse of 116, (3) deep and rapid respirations of 26, (4) decrease in systolic BP to 85, and (5) decrease in cognitive functioning. Additional data needed are arterial blood gases, blood sugar, serum acetone, and urine sugar and acetone. The presence of an anion gap greater than 12 mEq/liter would support the hypothesis, but, if sugar and acetone are elevated in this uncomplicated case, no more data are really needed to confirm the hypothesis. Nursing intervention should include carrying out the physician's orders for insulin, intravenous fluid, and, if acidosis is severe, giving sodium bicarbonate. (The average insulin requirement for the first 24 hours is 200 Units and 4−8 liters is the usual amount of intravenous fluid.) Fluid volume requirements are determined by monitoring of the pulmonary artery wedge pressure (PAWP) with a Swan−Ganz catheter. Other parameters that guide fluid replacement are urine output and physical signs of hydration. Insulin is ordered based on blood glucose which is usually determined every 2−4 hours during the critical period. The patient's safety must be safeguarded during the period of decreased responsiveness. If emesis continues, nasogastric intubation with suction or positioning semi-prone to prevent aspiration is important. Good oral hygiene decreases the discomfort of dry mucous membranes. Reassurance that the condition will respond to treatment should reduce anxiety. Evaluation would need to be done concurrently with intervention for this critical patient to assess the effectiveness of the treatment and direct additional therapy. Criteria could be blood pressure within normal range, return to previous cognitive level, chemistries returning to normal range, minimal glycosuria with ketonuria controlled within 48 hours, toleration of diet, absence of injuries (physical or aspiration), and only minimal anxiety.

In the next section on nursing diagnosis, did you record maladjustment to diabetes manifested by lack of knowledge about diabetes versus nonconformity to the diabetic regimen? After the critical period is passed, Mr. Brown will need to be interviewed to determine his knowledge about the disease and his usual routine regarding testing of urine, taking of insulin, and adhering to diet. A common misconception of many diabetic persons is that they only need to take their insulin when they are eating. We know he did not see his physician when he developed the ulcer and the reason for this needs to be explored with him. If it is found that Mr. Brown has knowledge but does not comply, the rationale for his behavior needs to be identified, if possible. Denial of the seriousness of his condition, extremely low self-concept, economic limitations, or philosophy of living only for the present are some of the factors that affect compliance.

Now that we have outlined the nursing process for Mr. Brown, we'll move on to another case study. On this case study, it will be all up to you.

Case 2B. Mr. McDonald is a 47-year-old married white male with a history of hypertension for 10 years, treated with hydrochlorthiazide (Hydrodiuril) and

PRACTICUM RECORD 2B

Hypothesis/Possible Diagnosis	Supportive Data Available	Additional Data Needed to Confirm or Disconfirm	Nursing Intervention in Order of Priority	Evaluation Criteria
Hypotension due to:				
1.				
2.				
3.				

propranolol (Inderal). He was admitted to the hospital for episodic dizziness, constant tinnitus, light headedness, occasional nausea and vomiting that increases with movement, and unsteadiness. He stated that every third day he felt like he was seasick. He had been impotent 1−2 years. Physical examination revealed nystagmus on extreme lateral gaze bilaterally and absent acoustic reflexes on the right. His laboratory reports were within normal limits except for fasting glucose 127 mg/dl. Skull films showed sellar enlargement with laminar demineralization. He was taken to surgery for resection of a chromophobe adenoma of the pituitary. Part of the pituitary was left after the tumor was resected. He did well postoperatively.

On the fourth postoperative day he was on a fluid restricted regular diet, ambulatory, with P70, R18, and BP 140/90 (supine), and 130/90 (standing). His 24 hour intake was 1490 ml with 24 hour output 1890 ml. Serum osmolality was 303 mOsm/liter and urine osmolality 260 mOsm/liter. Serum chemistries were within normal limits except for serum sodium elevated to 147 mEq/liter. His medications at this time were methyldopa (Aldomet) 250 mg 3 × day, hydrochlorthiazide (Hydrodiuril) 50 mg/day, and dexamethasone (Decadron) 4 mg every 6 hours. His dexamethasone was reduced over the next four days and was discontinued on his ninth postoperative day.

On the afternoon of his ninth postoperative day, Mr. McDonald was found slumped in a chair at his bedside. He had been incontinent of urine. His pulse was 56 (thready), respirations 16, and his blood pressure 88/60 (sitting). His pupils were equal and reacted to light. He was lethargic, but could be aroused with stimulation and was able to state his name and where he was. His only neurologic abnormality found by a brief examination was diminished deep tendon reflexes. His skin was cold and clammy, he was diaphoretic, and had cyanosis of his nail beds.

Skillbuilders:

1. On the practicum record (2-B) enter, in the order of their likelihood of occurrence, three most likely hypotheses for Mr. McDonald's syncopal hypotensive episode.

2. Then enter the data from the history that support the hypothesis and the additional data needed to confirm or disconfirm.

3. In the nursing intervention section, list, in order of priority, the actions for the next 15−30 minutes that would be the most beneficial for Mr. McDonald. The physician has said he will be at the hospital in 15 minutes and has ordered an intravenous of 5 percent D/W at 60 ml/hour.

4. In the evaluation column, list the anticipated outcomes of the intervention.

Feedback. Patients with pituitary resection are prime candidates for development of diabetes insipidus due to deficiency of antidiuretic hormone (ADH) which is normally released by the posterior lobe of the pituitary. The condition is characterized by excretion of excessive quantities of very dilute urine, and the urine osmolality is less than the plasma osmolality. (Normally urine osmolality is 100 mOsm/liter more than the plasma osmolality.) The post-operative course is usually triphasic, with polyuria for 2−5 days followed by a period of antidiuresis for 2−6 days. After the period of antidiuresis, polyuria may again recur. Thus, the most likely hypothesis is hypotension due to fluid volume deficit from ADH deficiency. Mr. McDonald had been receiving dexamethasone to reduce the cerebral edema associated with the neurosurgical procedure. The possibility of a drug-induced secondary adrenocortical insufficiency (Addisonian crisis) from the discontinuance of the cortisol drug is a good bet for the second hypothesis. The third hypothesis is a long shot but the iatrogenic effect of drugs should never be overlooked. The dosage of methyldopa may have been too high, or the additive effect of the hydrochlorthiazide to ADH deficiency could have caused excessive diuresis. By looking at the decision tree for fluid volume deficit, we are cued to the data that support the hypothesis of hypotension due to ADH deficiency. The only data which support the hypothesis are the history of pituitary resection, and the occurrence of high output (with low urine osmolality) and the central nervous system sign of lethargy. He had a high serum sodium and postural hypotension five days previously, and this has probably continued, although we would need new data to know for sure. Other data needed to confirm include skin turgor, state of the neck veins, and (not included on the fluid volume deficit tree but of diagnostic significance for ADH deficiency) urine specific gravity and/or urine osmolality.

For the second hypothesis, hypotension due to Addisonian crisis, the supporting datum is the history of cortisol administration with its suppression of adrenocortical function. Although laboratory tests such as response to ACTH stimulation testing combined with low serum sodium, high serum potassium, and low fasting blood sugar help to identify drug induced secondary adrenocorticol insufficiency, in crisis situations the physician usually administers an intravenous bolus of cortisol. A positive response from the patient substantiates the hypothesis. There are not many supporting data for the third hypothesis except the history of ingestion of methyldopa and hydrochlorthiazide. Again the major datum to support the hypothesis would come from observation of the blood pressure after discontinuance of the drugs. This hypothesis probably would not be tested unless both of the other hypotheses had been rejected. There may be some disagreement about the most effective ordering of nursing actions for Mr. McDonald, but of high priority is proper positioning, flat with legs slightly elevated, and starting an intravenous infusion. It is important to secure an intravenous line before the condition worsens since it is more difficult after vascular collapse. The intravenous line is essential in case of cardiopulmonary arrest (always a danger with shock) as well as for treatment of the present condition. While starting the intravenous, the patient should be watched closely for signs of deterioration such as further drop in blood pressure and loss of consciousness. Aqueous Pitressin and intravenous dexamethasone need to be ready at the bedside for the physician's use.

Mr. McDonald needs to be reassured that his condition is not unexpected after his type of surgery and that it can be corrected with no serious consequences. His incontinence needs to be handled matter of factly, conveying the nurse's recognition that the patient was not to blame for the incident. Although it is unlikely the patient will be able to void again so quickly, any urine should be saved for osmolality. Protection from injury is important in any period of lowered level of consciousness. The expected outcomes would be (1) stabilization of the BP above 100 systolic, (2) normal cognitive functioning, (3) absence of undue anxiety, and (4) absence of bodily harm.

The next case study is concerned with hypertension.

Case 2C. Mrs. Johnson is a 48-year-old Caucasian who has a history of recurrent urinary tract infections. Four years ago she was diagnosed as having chronic pyelonephritis. At this time she was also found to have a blood pressure of 160/110. Her weight was within normal range and she did not smoke. She was told to limit foods high in sodium and was started on a medication regimen. Her last checkup was six months ago. At that time her BP was 150/90. Her urinalysis showed specific gravity 1.014, pH 5, glucose and ketones negative, protein trace, and sediment containing a few white cells and casts. Her SMA 6 was within normal limits except for chloride 110 mEq/liter, total CO_2 20 mEq/liter, and BUN of 24 mg/dl. Her prescribed medications at this time included methenamine mandelate (Mandelamine) 1 g 4×/day, ascorbic acid 500 mg 4×/day, furosemide (Lasix) 40 mg 2×/day, potassium chloride 20 mEq 2×/day, and propranolol 40 mg 4×/day.

Three months before her admission to the hospital her husband had died suddenly of a myocardial infarction. He had not seen a physician although he had complained to her that he had chest pain with physical exercise. She was so preoccupied with her own problems associated with the menopausal syndrome and trying to help her 20-year-old pregnant daughter who had been deserted by her husband that she paid little attention to her husband's symptoms. The only income of the family was from a small garage her husband had operated. Since his death she had been attempting to hold the business together while she was searching for a general manager. Her menopausal symptoms of hot flashes, depression, insomnia, and joint pains worsened, and six weeks previous to her admission her gynecologist had prescribed conjugated estrogen 1.25 mg/day. Three days prior to admission she started having severe headaches in the back of her head which were not relieved by aspirin. The day of admission she not only woke up with a severe headache but her sight was blurred, and she could not see anything on the side with her right eye. When she tried to phone her daughter, she couldn't remember her daughter's number. A neighbor called her physician who told her to go to the hospital. On admission to the hospital her vital signs were BP 190/145, P 96, R 22, T 98.8. Examination of her eyes showed exudative retinopathy with papilledema. She had blood drawn for an SMA 6 and 12 and a urine specimen was obtained for urinalysis and electrolyte levels. She was started on intravenous sodium nitroprusside (Nipride) 165 mcg/minute.

Skillbuilders.

1. On the practicum record (2-C) enter the three most likely causes for Mrs. Johnson's hypertensive crisis (hypertensive encephelopathy).

PRACTICUM RECORD 2C

Hypothesis/Possible Diagnosis	Supportive Data Available	Additional Data Needed to Confirm or Disconfirm	Nursing Responsibilities During Nitroprusside Administration	Evaluation Criteria
Hypertension due to:				
1.				
2.				
3.				

2. Then enter the data from the history that support the hypothesis and additional data you would need to confirm or disconfirm.

3. Complete the information about administration and nursing observations and responsibilities during nitroprusside therapy.

4. List criteria for evaluation of nitroprusside therapy.

Feedback. Since we know that onset of acute renal insufficiency is one of the major causes of hypertensive crisis, this is a decided possibility for this woman with known chronic pyelonephritis for four years. Other possible hypotheses would be hypertensive crisis due to the additive effect of conjugated estrogen in a known hypertensive or crisis due to overwhelming stress in a known hypertensive. We can refer to the decision tree to confirm renal insufficiency. Supportive data include history of chronic pyelonephritis and hypertension. Six months ago, however, her renal function seemed to be adequate as shown by urine specific gravity 1.014 (indication that kidney had not lost its concentrating ability) and only a trace of protein. Her urea nitrogen was elevated to 24 mg/dl showing impaired, but adequate, ability of the kidneys to clear nitrogenous waste. The serum creatinine is a more reliable indicator of renal function than urea nitrogen, because the latter is elevated by blood in the gut, tetracyclines, high protein diet, and other factors. In clinical practice, urea nitrogen is usually screened first, and if the level is higher than anticipated, creatinine is also measured.

Not included on the decision tree for acute renal insufficiency, but of significance for a patient with chronic renal disease with loss of functioning nephrons, is the hyperchloremic acidosis manifested by the high chloride and low serum total CO_2. If you are unacquainted with serum CO_2, you may have difficulty interpreting the acid–base state from it. Since CO_2 is acid, you might equate acidosis with an elevated CO_2. The test, however, measures the CO_2 in bicarbonate as well as carbonic acid and dissolved CO_2. Clinicians generally equate total CO_2 with bicarbonate since carbonic acid and dissolved CO_2 account for such a small fraction of the total. Although it is necessary to know the pH to determine the acid-base state for certain, in many patients with normal respiratory function, a low total serum CO_2 is a fairly reliable indicator of metabolic acidosis. Thus six months ago she had a moderate hyperchloremic acidosis from impaired renal excretion of acid and reabsorption of bicarbonate. It is an indicator of diminished renal function with chronic disease. Since her urine was bacteria free, it appears that the prolonged bacteriostatic action of methenamine mandelate had suppressed the infection. To determine if her renal disease had progressed to acute renal insufficiency, additional data on admission will be needed. Supporting data would be urine output less than 30 ml/hour with a specific gravity less than 1.014, low urine osmolality and creatinine, and elevated urine sodium and serum creatinine. These laboratory reports indicate the impaired ability of the kidneys to concentrate the urine and the inability of the sick kidney to conserve sodium and excrete nitrogenous waste, with such wastes (urea nitrogen and creatinine) building up in the serum. The most effective diagnostic strategy for Mrs. Johnson would be to first confirm or disconfirm the presence of renal insufficiency. If disconfirmed, then the other two hypotheses should be investigated.

The only datum available on hypertension due to conjugated estrogen is the history of onset of severe hypertension shortly after start of therapy. The hypothesis would probably be supported by discontinuance of the estrogen and monitoring to see if the blood pressure returned to previous levels within $2-3$ weeks. Many clinicians believe that existing hypertension is a contraindication for estrogen therapy. You probably also questioned if the menopause was actually responsible for all her symptoms which brings us to the other hypothesis, hypertensive crisis due to overwhelming stress.

Stress contributes to hypertension because it stimulates the sympathetic nervous system (resulting in vasoconstriction) and stimulates production of adrenocorticoid hormones that cause increased sodium (and thus fluid) retention. There are indications that Mrs. Johnson has unresolved grief, probably contributed to by feelings of guilt, as well as limited economic and family support to help sustain her through the crisis. Anxiety over business, perhaps coupled with feelings of anger at her husband for leaving her in such a difficult situation, also contributes to stress. These possibilities would need to be explored with her in order to identify the presence and nature of the stressors and the extent of her resources and coping mechanisms to reduce or modify the stress.

To complete the practicum record about nitroprusside, we need to remember that the drug is a potent vasodilator that is unstable when exposed to light. The nitroprusside molecule contain five cyanide groups, and cyanide toxicity has been reported with large doses. With toxicity there is a decrease in the ability to utilize oxygen, so major signs are metabolic acidosis (from anerobic metabolism) and high mixed venous Po_2. Since myocardial infarction or stroke can occur during rapid lowering of the blood pressure, the nurse needs to be alert to these possibilities. The nurse is responsible for:

1. Accurate calculation of the dosage to insure that the volume infusing never exceeds the maximum limit of 10 mcg/kg/minute

2. Gradual tapering of the dose instead of abrupt discontinuance

3. Preparation of the drug in small amounts (usually 50 mg of nitroprusside is added to 150 ml of fluid) and remixed every $4-8$ hours

4. Wrapping the container in foil to protect from light

5. Using an electronic volume infusor with continuous monitoring of the arterial blood pressure.

Evaluation criteria would be reduction of the blood pressure, absence of metabolic acidosis or other complications, and improvement in cognitive level and eye pathology.

ADDITIONAL READING

Dunstan HP: Evaluation and therapy of hypertension 1976, Mod Concepts Cardiovasc Dis 45(5):97−103, May 1976.

Foster S, Kousch D: Promoting patient adherence, AJN 78(5):829−832, May 1978.

Jahre J. et al.: Medical approach to the hypotensive patient and the patient in shock. Heart Lung 4(4):577−587, August 1975.

Molyneux-Luick M, Knecht J: Hypovolemic shock. Nursing 77 7(11):33−37, November 1977.

Paine R, Sherman W: Arterial hypertension. In MacBryde C, Blacknow R (eds.): Signs and Symptoms, 5th ed. Philadelphia, Lippincott, 1970, pp 272−301.

Ward GW, Bandy P, Fink JW: Treating and counseling the hypertensive patient. AJN 78(5):824−828, May 1978.

CHAPTER 3

Pulse Alterations

The significance of the pulse as an indicator of the state of the patient was recognized in very early times. As early as 1500 B.C., the Egyptians were aware that the pulsations of the arteries coincided with the beats of the heart. In the second century A.D., Rufus of Ephesus described most of the characteristics of the pulse that are known today. Palpation of the pulse today is supplemented by other procedures for more definitive diagnosis of the cause of the alteration, but it remains a critical sign of a possible major health disturbance which can involve one or more body systems.

The arterial pulse is the result of pressure changes within the left ventricle of the heart that are transmitted as pressure waves to the root of the aorta during ventricular systole. When blood is ejected during systole, the ascending aorta is momentarily distended to accommodate the ejected volume. The pressures caused by the distension and relaxation of the ascending aorta are transmitted through the entire aorta and its branches, which results in a rhythmic expansion and relaxation of the peripheral arteries that is termed the pulse. Pressure waves are transmitted rapidly. Normally the impulse can be felt or seen in the dorsalis pedis artery 0.2 to 0.3 seconds after ventricular systole. The forward movement of blood follows the pressure wave, but blood moves more slowly, requiring 2.5 seconds to travel from the heart to the foot. Although arteries expand and relax along their entire length, palpable and visible arterial pulses are found at areas where the artery is over a bone and close to the skin. The accessible pulse points are the radial, brachial, carotid, temporal, femoral, popliteal, posterior tibial, and dorsalis pedis.

The pressure pulses from the arteries are not transmitted through the capillaries into the systemic veins. However, sometimes right atrial pulsations are transmitted backward and cause venous pressure pulses of a different character. Normally the venous pressure pulses are only present in the jugular veins of the neck and in the supraclavicular fossa. When the right atrial pressure is high, however, the pulsations may also be transmitted backward into the peripheral veins.

Since the pulses arise from dynamic forces within the heart, they are affected by disturbances in autorhythmicity and conductivity of the heart muscle, by structural abnormalities within the heart, and lesions or factors that alter the normal flow of blood through the vascular system. Each of these will be briefly discussed.

CAUSES OF ALTERATIONS

Autorhythmicity and Conductivity of the Heart Muscle

Cardiac muscle is characterized by an inherent automaticity; this means that it initiates its own rhythmic impulses which result in muscular contraction. The impulse activating normal atrial and ventricular contraction originates in the sinoatrial (SA) node and is termed a sinus rhythm. The SA node is a specialized tissue mass located in the wall of the right atrium near the entry of the superior vena cava. The impulse generated by the SA node spreads throughout the atria, resulting in atrial systole. The impulse then activates other specialized tissue lying between the atria and ventricles, the atrioventricular (AV) node and the bundle of His. The fibers in the AV node and bundle of His are termed the AV junction. The impulse, after crossing the AV junction continues through the right and left bundle branches and the Purkinje fibers. Because of the Purkinje system, the impulse is quickly transmitted to nearly all of the ventricular muscle, initiating an almost simultaneous contraction of ventricular muscle fibers and a sharp, rapid rise in intraventricular pressure.

An alteration in the normal pulse rate is termed a dysrhythmia. The major disturbances that result in dysrhythmias are related to changes in the autorhythmicity of the sinoatrial node, development of an ectopic focus, and alterations in the transmission of electrical impulse throughout the heart. The autorhythmicity of the sinoatrial node is influenced by chemical and neural control mechanisms. The exact mechanism of chemical control is unknown, but it is believed to be due to the changing electrical potential of the cell membrane that is produced by movement of electrolytes across the cell membrane. Normal levels of potassium, sodium, and calcium are required for adequate cardiac contraction. High concentrations of potassium and sodium are associated with slowing of the heart rate and force of contraction, while low levels of these electrolytes enhance both automaticity and excitability of the myocardial cells. Calcium has the opposite effect; an elevation of calcium levels is associated with excitation and increased systolic contraction. Hormones produced by the adrenal, thyroid, and parathyroid glands also influence the rate and force of the heart's contraction.

The autonomic nervous system modifies the rate and force of the heart's contraction through the vagus (which carries parasympathetic fibers) and the sympathetic nerves. Vagal innervation which is the dominant factor in the control of the normal heart rate is primarily, and perhaps exclusively, to the SA and AV nodes and to the atria. Sympathetic innervation includes the ventricles in addition to the atria. The vagus nerve exerts a restraining force on the heart rate while the sympathetic nerves increase the overall activity of the heart. This dual control of the heart allows the heart rate to be varied by four mechanisms. Heart rate is accelerated by inhibition of the vagus or stimulation of the sympathetic. Conversely, heart rate is slowed by stimulation of the vagus nerve or inhibition of the sympathetic nerves. When the heart rate is greater than 100, it is termed tachycardia; when it is less than 60, it is called bradycardia.

The slowing and accelerating effects on the heart are integrated in the cardioregulatory center in the medulla. Among the afferent impulses to the center that result in an increase in the heart rate are impulses from the cerebral cortex associated with emotions of anxiety, excitement, and anticipation, mild hypoxia and/or hypercapnia, elevated temperature, drop in arterial blood pressure, and somatic pain from the skin. Among the impulses that result in a slowing of the heart rate are an increase in intracranial pressure, severe hypoxia and/or hypercapnia, a rise in arterial blood pressure, and reflex effects of stimulation of the nerve endings in the carotid sinus, respiratory tract, viscera, eyeball, and skeletal muscles.

The development of an ectopic focus is another disturbance that results in dysrhythmias. The term, ectopic focus, refers to any impulse that arises from a site other than the SA node. When it is an occasional impulse that interrupts the normal rhythm of the SA node, it is called an ectopic beat. In other instances, an area of the heart with enhanced automaticity develops a rhythmic discharge rate that is faster than that of the SA node and takes over the pacemaker function. This ectopic pacemaker can be located elsewhere in the atria, in the AV junctional tissue, in the Purkinje fibers, or in the ventricular muscle.

There are a number of disturbances within the conduction system for transmission of electrical impulses which result in dysrhythmias. Perhaps the most frequent is a block at the AV junction, which can vary in severity. It is called first degree block when all the impulses are conducted but the conduction time is prolonged. Second degree block describes the state of prolonged conduction as well as the failure of some impulses to be conducted. When no impulses are able to reach the ventricles, third degree (or complete) AV block is said to exist. In this disordered state, the atria and ventricles maintain separate and independent rhythms. Another common block in conduction occurs in the bundle branches, with either the left or right bundle branch or both involved. The left bundle branch has two divisions or fascicles. A block in conduction through one of the divisions of the left bundle branch block is termed fascicular block (formerly called hemiblock). Fascicular block in a patient with preexisting right bundle branch block is a serious event, since it can herald the development of complete intraventricular block. The Wolff—Parkinson—White syndrome is a conduction disturbance in which an anomalous conduction pathway bypasses the AV node. The mechanisms of reentry, concealed conduction, and supernormal conduction are some of the other causes of dysrhythmias.

Structural Abnormalities within the Heart

Congenital abnormalities or damage from disease alter the ability of the heart to serve as an efficient pump. The ejection of a normal volume of blood requires satisfactory performance of both cardiac muscle and heart valves. Valves should offer no obstruction to forward flow when they are open (absence of stenosis). They should close completely so there is no retrograde flow when they are closed (absence of regurgitation). When either stenosis or regurgitation are present, the heart muscle has to work harder and becomes hypertrophied. Abnormalities of valvular function and stroke volume alter the character of the arterial pulse. These mechanical disturbances in the pumping activity of the heart also frequently result in characteristic abnormalities of initiation or conduction of the electrical impulse within the heart.

Alteration of Flow of Blood through the Vascular System

In addition to the effect of electrical and mechanical forces, the pulse is also affected by factors that alter the flow of blood through the vascular system. The major factors are the compliance of the arterial tree, presence of obstructive disease of the arterial system, and alterations in the venous return to the heart. The compliance of the arterial tree has been discussed in the chapter on blood pressure alterations. The major cause for loss of compliance (and therefore distensibility) of the arterial walls is old age when elastic and muscular tissue in the arterial walls is replaced with fibrous tissue and calcified plaques that are unable to accommodate the volume of blood pumped out by the heart. Obstructions to the flow of arterial blood by a blood clot or particulate matter or by arterial spasm are accompanied by loss of the pulse beyond the area of obstruction. Venous return flow to the heart is impeded by the presence of an obstructive lesion, hypovolemia, vascular pooling of blood, and a decrease in the venous gradient. For blood to be returned to the heart, the venous pressure in the extremities must be higher than that within the right atrium of the heart.

Table 3-1 lists the major alterations in the pulse and the associated abnormal mechanisms. The seriousness of the abnormality in the pulse is related to the character and magnitude of the dysfunctional effects on the cardiac output. The cardiac output is the product of the heart rate and the stroke volume (amount of blood pumped out of the left ventricle with each contraction of the heart). Normal cardiac output in someone at rest is 5 liters a minute. With exercise or other accelerated metabolic state, a healthy person is able to supply the increased metabolic needs by increasing both the heart rate and the stroke volume. The requirements of cardiac output during strenuous exercise can be as high as 30 liters/minute. An older patient or one with impaired myocardial or valvular function is frequently unable to maintain sufficient output to meet the increased needs and exhibits signs of low cardiac output. The effect of bradycardia on cardiac output in a patient unable to increase his stroke volume is readily apparent. Moderate tachycardia may be accompanied by normal or slightly increased cardiac output. More severe tachycardia, however, results in decreased cardiac output since there is a severe reduction in stroke volume because of the decrease in filling time associated with fast heart rates. Low cardiac output can also occur with irregular rhythms and ectopic pacemakers.

Patients with impaired compensatory mechanisms to maintain cardiac output have a reduction in cardiac output whenever the normal sequence between

TABLE 3-1. Major Pulse Alterations

Abnormal Initiating Mechanism	Pathophysiology	Underlying Clinical State	Manifestation
I. Increased auto-rhythmicity of SA node	Direct acceleration of pacemaker activity by: Sympathoadrenal response to stress	Anxiety state, neurocirculatory asthenia, somatic pain from skin	Sinus tachycardia, with rate over 100 (but usually less than 160) and regular or slightly irregular rhythm
	Stimulation from need to deliver more O_2 with high cardiac output states	Febrile illness, post strenuous exercise, thyrotoxicosis, severe anemia, pregnancy, beriberi, pulmonary emphysema, Paget's disease (widespread), arteriovenous fistula	
	High levels of epinephrine or intake of sympathomimetic or vagal blocking agents	Pheochromocytoma secreting epinephrine Administration of: Atropine, Sympathomimetic agents: isoproterenol, epinephrine, phenylephrine, norepinephrine, metaraminol	
	Reflex mechanism with inhibition of the vagus resulting in cardioacceleration. Reflex is in response to: Stimulation of the baroreceptors in aortic arch and carotid sinus by a fall in pulse pressure with increased sympathetic stimulation and reduced vagal stimulation	Hypotension, hemorrhage, extracellular fluid volume deficit	
	Stimulation of chemoreceptors in carotid body	Hypoxemia, mild or moderate, hypercarbia	
	Chemical alteration in ionic structure results in increased excitability of the membrane of the heart muscle cell	Hypokalemia, hypercalcemia, hyperparathyroidism	

(continued)

TABLE 3-1. Continued

Abnormal Initiating Mechanism	Pathophysiology	Underlying Clinical State	Manifestation
II. Decreased autorhythmicity of SA node	Increase in parasympathetic (vagal) stimulation with release of acetylcholine at the vagal endings and resultant decrease in the rate of the SA node and excitability of the AV junctional fibers. Causes include: Direct irritation Pressure on a hypersensitive carotid sinus	Increased intracranial pressure Carotid sinus syncope	Sinus bradycardia, with a rate less than 60 and regular rhythm
	Vagal stimulation by high level of enzymes and other substances resulting from ischemia and necrosis	Myocardial infarction/ischemia	
	Reflex stimulation of nerve endings in eyeballs, posterior pharynx, skeletal muscles, or viscera	Pressure on eyeballs or posterior pharynx, skeletal muscle or visceral pain, overdistended bladder, acute gastric distension	
	Reflex stimulation of chemoreceptors in carotid body	Severe hypoxemia, severe hypercapnia	
	Reflex stimulation of baroreceptors by a rise in pulse pressure	Acute nephritis, hypertension	
	Suppression of sympathetic activity, with resultant increase in vagal forces and slowing of the heart	Administration of: inhalation anesthesia, β-blocking agents, excess sedation	
	Failure of sinus node discharge results in absence of atrial depolarization and periods of ventricular asystole	Digitalis toxicity, excessive vagal tone, myocardial infarction involving SA node	Sinoatrial arrest, with absence of ECG activity unless escape beat or rhythm takes over

	Mechanism	Causes	ECG/Clinical findings
III. Abnormal ectopic pacemaker			
A. Atrial	Intermittent discharge of abnormal pacemaker in the atria	Emotional stress; intake of alcohol, coffee, tobacco, digitalis; myocardial ischemia, extracellular fluid volume excess	Ectopic atrial beats (premature atrial contractions-PAC's) which are preceded by an abnormally shaped P wave and followed by an incomplete pause
	Rapid ectopic foci in the atria takes over the pacemaker function	Excitement or fatigue; intake of alcohol/tobacco; secondary to underlying thyrotoxicosis or coronary artery disease	Paroxysmal atrial tachycardia (PAT) with a rate of 150-250/minute and a regular rhythm; abrupt onset and termination
	Rapid ectopic foci in the atria serving as pacemaker, with block of every 2nd or 3rd beat	Digitalis toxicity, cor pulmonale, coronary artery disease	PAT with block. Atrial rate may be as high as 220/minute with variable ventricular rate. Initially, ventricular rate is usually half of atrial rate
	By a mechanism not fully understood, the atria are bombarded by rapid and irregular impulses without effective atrial contraction. Impulses are conducted to the ventricles at an irregular rate	Digitalis toxicity. Underlying heart disease due to: mitral stenosis, thyrotoxicosis, cardiomyopathy, hypertensive heart disease, pericarditis, coronary artery disease, myocardial infarction	Atrial fibrillation with ECG showing irregular baseline undulations of 350-600/minute with a ventricular response between 60-160/minute. Pulse deficit between apical and radial pulse may be present
	Rapid ectopic foci in the atria serving as pacemaker, with ventricular response to every 2nd or 4th atrial stimulus	Severe low cardiac output states (Congestive heart failure)	Atrial flutter with atrial rate of 250-300/minute with a ventricular rate of 125-150/minute; ECG shows regular sawtooth-shaped undulations
B. Junctional	Intermittent or frequent ectopic foci in AV junction fires early, with impulse spreading both anterograde (to ventricle) and retrograde (to atria)	Stress, intake of stimulants, myocardial ischemia	Ectopic junctional beats, with inverted P waves (leads II, III, aVF) sometimes visible just before or after the QRS

(continued)

TABLE 3-1. Continued

Abnormal Initiating Mechanism	Pathophysiology	Underlying Clinical State	Manifestation
B. Junctional (continued)	Acceleration of the inherent junctional rhythm which takes over the pacing function when its rate exceeds the rate of the SA node	Digitalis toxicity, posterior myocardial infarction, acute rheumatic fever	Nonparoxysmal AV junctional tachycardia (idiojunctional tachycardia) with a rate of 70–130/minute
	When the sinus impulse fails to arrive at the AV junction, the junction takes over the pacing function at its inherent rhythm	SA arrest or block, digitalis toxicity	Junctional escape at a rate of 40–60/minute and a regular rhythm
C. Ventricular	Intermittent or frequent impulse originating from an ectopic focus in the Purkinje network of the ventricles that occurs earlier than the sinus impulse	Myocardial ischemia; Myocardial infarction; Myocardial irritability (hypokalemia, digitalis toxicity); hypoxia; intake of epinephrine, caffein, or amphetamines	Ectopic ventricular beats (premature ventricular contractions, PVC's) not preceded by a P wave, with a widened and distorted QRS complex and the T wave directed in the opposite direction from the QRS complex; they are usually followed by a compensatory pause Patterns include: ventricular bigeminy, ventricular trigeminy, multifocal PVC's, R^- on T pattern, fusion beats, ventricular parasystole
	Ectopic focus in the Purkinje network of the ventricle with a reentrant mechanism takes over the pacing of the ventricles, with the atria continuing to be paced from the SA node	Ischemic heart disease caused by same disorders as PVC's	Ventricular tachycardia, with rate of 140–200/minute and essentially regular rhythm; P waves, if present, are independent of ventricular rate. QRS complex is widened and distorted. First heart sound varies in intensity

Ventricles take over the pacing function when the rate of supraventricular pacemakers is less than the inherent ventricular rate or when impulses are blocked. When supraventricular pacing or conduction is variable, these will be intermittent escape beats	SA or AV block, slow SA or junctional pacemaker	Ventricular escape rhythm at a rate of 20–40/minute with widened QRS complex
Rapid, irregular, uncoordinated impulse arising within the ventricle that is not accompanied by an effective contraction or any cardiac output	Myocardial ischemia; Digitalis, quinidine, or procainamide toxicity; electrical shock, PVC's occurring on the T wave, advanced A-V block	Ventricular fibrillation with ECG showing a wavering baseline and bizzare waveforms; it may be preceded by ventricular flutter with a rate of 150–300 per minute and wide ventricular waves
IV. Alteration in cardiac conduction		
A. Atrial — Blockage of SA impulse so atria is not depolarized	Excessive vagal stimulation Acute infections: diphtheria, rheumatic carditis Drug intake: quinidine, procainamide, digitalis, potassium Myocardial infarction, atrial fibrosis	Sinoatrial block with absence of P waves and QRS complex for one or more expected beats
B. Junctional — Impulse from the atria is delayed or blocked at the AV node and His bundle. It may be permanent or transient, anatomical or functional. The extent of the block is classified by degrees. When block is complete, the ventricle has to have an independent pacemaker distal to the His bundle, and the atria and ventricles are thus dissociated	Drug toxicity: digitalis, procainamide, quinidine' Fibrosis of the conduction system, coronary artery disease, myocardial infarction, myocarditis, cardiomyopathy, valvular calcium deposits, surgical trauma to AV node	Heart block First degree, manifested by prolonged P-R interval (>0.20 second) with all P waves followed by QRS complexes Second degree, manifested by P waves that intermittently or frequently are not followed by a QRS complex; termed Mobitz Type I or Type II on the basis of

(continued)

TABLE 3-1. Continued

Abnormal Initiating Mechanism	Pathophysiology	Underlying Clinical State	Manifestation
B. Junctional (continued)			P-R interval, which may be normal, varying, or prolonged Third degree, or complete, manifested by an idioventricular rhythm at a rate of 30–40/minute with widened QRS complexes and P waves which are usually regular but have no relationship to the QRS; 2nd or 3rd degree may be accompanied by Stokes-Adams-Morgagni attack
C. Ventricular	Impulse from SA node is conducted normally until it is delayed in one of the bundle branches, resulting in one ventricle being depolarized and contracting before the other	Myocardial ischemia, congestive heart failure, rheumatic disease, congenital abnormalities, fibrotic or sclerotic disorders affecting the heart Transient, secondary to: tachycardia, infection, anemia, metabolic abnormalities Right bundle branch block (RBBB) may be associated with: pulmonary hypertension, pulmonary embolus Left bundle branch block (LBBB) may indicate acute MI: fibrosis, inflammation; aortic valvular disease	Bundle branch block, with P wave preceding a widened QRS. RBBB manifested by negative QRS deflection in leads I and V_6 and positive in leads III and V_1 LBBB has opposite directional deflections; the acute changes of a MI may be masked by this abnormality Bifascicular block is a RBBB combined with a block of either the anterior or posterior fascicles of the LBB Trifascicular block involves the right bundle and both branches of the left bundle, making a complete block

The atrial impulse prematurely activates a portion of the ventricular muscle by an anomalous conduction pathway which bypasses the AV node	Congenital or acquired disorder with a pronounced tendency for development of atrial tachydysrhythmias	Wolff–Parkinson–White (preexcitation) syndrome manifested by a short P-R interval and a widened QRS with a slurring of the initial part of the QRS (termed a delta wave)
V. Alteration in transmission of impulse throughout body		
Small pulse results from a low stroke volume of left ventricle, narrow pulse pressure, and/or increased peripheral vascular resistance	MI, hypovolemia, cardiomyopathy, cardiac tamponade, constrictive pericarditis, valvular stenosis	Hypokinetic pulse (pulsus parvus) that is small, weak, with a small pulse pressure
	Aortic stenosis, severe	Pulsus parvus et tardus, manifested by a small pulse with a delayed systolic peak
Large pulse results from a high stroke volume, wide pulse pressure, and/or decreased peripheral resistance	Increased metabolic states, stress, complete heart block with bradycardia, hypertension	Hyperkinetic pulse that is bounding, large, and strong
	Aortic regurgitation, severe	Extreme hyperkinetic pulse, termed water hammer or collapsing, because of its extremely rapid ascent and descent
Regular alternation in pulse size due to an alternation in the force of ventricular contraction due to severe left ventricular decompensation	Low cardiac output heart failure	Pulsus alternans manifested by alternating weak and strong impulse. It is usually associated with an abnormal ventricular gallop (S_3)
Irregular alternation in pulse size due to the occurrence of a small premature ventricular ectopic contraction after a larger normally conducted impulse, with inadequate cardiac filling time for the PVC	Ventricular bigeminy due to any of the causes listed above	Bigeminal pulse with a weak pulse and then a pause, with repetition of the pattern

(continued)

TABLE 3-1. Continued

Abnormal Initiating Mechanism	Pathophysiology	Underlying Clinical State	Manifestation
V. Alteration in transmission of impulse from heart throughout body (continued)	An abnormal decrease in the return of the blood to the left side of the heart with inspiration results in a subsequent decrease in left ventricular output with a decrease in the size of the arterial pulse and a drop in systolic blood pressure during the inspiratory period	Pericardial tamponade, airway obstruction, superior vena cava obstruction, severe CHF, constrictive pericarditis, extreme chest wall deformity	Pulsus paradoxus, manifested by a decrease in size or disappearance of the peripheral pulse with inspiration. It is best identified by difference greater than 10 mm Hg in systolic blood pressure during inspiration
	Narrowing or constriction of the lumen of the aorta results in diminution of the size and a delay in conduction of the pulse in the lower extremities	Coarctation of the aorta	Inequality of radial and femoral arterial pulses, with femoral weaker and delayed
		Dissection of ascending aorta	Inequality of radial and femoral arterial pulses of right or left side previously known to be equal
		Acute arterial occlusion, compartment syndrome, arteriosclerotic spasm, arteriosclerotic occlusive disease, Takayasu's disease, giant cell arteritis, Buerger's disease, Thoracic outlet syndrome	Absence or marked diminution in one or more extremities

atrial and ventricular systole is disturbed. Normally the atrial contraction preceding ventricular contraction acts as a booster pump that augments ventricular filling; loss of the atrial force can result in a lowering of the cardiac output by as much as 40 percent. The normal sequence is disturbed in all degrees of AV block, AV junctional rhythms, rhythms originating in the ventricles, and in some instances of atrial tachycardia, fibrillation, and flutter.

Oxygen requirements of the myocardium are related to the physiologic effort made during contraction. The amount of coronary blood flow also affects myocardial oxygen supply. Since coronary blood flow occurs predominately during diastole, a reduction in diastolic time with tachycardia may reduce the coronary blood flow, particularly in patients with narrowing of the coronary arteries. Thus, tachycardia can result in both greater oxygen consumption and decreased coronary blood flow. Myocardial ischemia and angina are signs of inadequate oxygen supply and/or coronary blood flow.

Another major alteration in cardiac output associated with dysrhythmias is altered ventricular contraction. When the sinus beat is normally conducted throughout the ventricle, contraction is synchronous, simultaneous, and maximally effective. Less effective contraction occurs when the rhythm originates in an ectopic focus in the ventricle, is conducted abnormally, or when there is an akinetic area that decreases the intraventricular pressure for forward propulsion of blood. This can result in a reduction in cardiac output, especially in the patient with cardiac disease.

ASSESSMENT

Assessment activities are aimed at detecting the nature of the pulse alteration. A history is taken which may indicate the cause for the alteration. Any deviations in other parameters are carefully assessed. The existence of any dysfunctional effects on the rest of the body as a result of the alteration in pulse is also examined.

History

History items of special importance for patients with an alteration in the pulse are the presence of symptoms of cardiovascular disease, the presence of any systemic illnesses that can have cardiac manifestations, past history of diseases that affect the heart, intake of drugs and alcohol, use of tobacco, recent stressful events, and family history of cardiovascular disease. Specific inquiries should be made concerning all the following symptoms of cardiovascular disease:

● *Palpitation,* which is the awareness by the patient of forceful, rapid, or irregular heartbeats. It may be described by the patient as pounding, fluttering, flopping, or skipping. Its occurrence can be indicative of a physical disorder or a psychic disturbance.

- *Dyspnea,* which is an abnormally uncomfortable awareness of breathing. The patient may describe it as inability to get enough air, a smothering feeling, or a choking sensation. If dyspnea is present, further questioning is needed to determine its relationship to exercise and body posture. When the term dyspnea is recorded, it should be quantified by the amount of physical exercise required to produce the sensation, and/or its occurrence when supine (orthopnea). Both respiratory and cardiac disorders can cause exertional dyspnea and orthopnea. Paroxysmal nocturnal dyspnea, in which the patient awakens from a sound sleep with extreme shortness of breath, however, is a sign of ventricular failure caused by edematous fluid returning to the vascular space which increases the circulating blood volume above the pumping ability of the heart.

- *Edema* of the extremities or dependent areas, which is most noticeable toward evening. The multiple causes of edema will be discussed in greater detail in a later chapter. It is present in congestive heart failure because of the emptying of the chambers of the heart that results in pressure backup in the venous circulation.

- *Abdominal pain.* An aching pain in the right upper abdomen may result from hepatic congestion and stretching of the liver capsule.

- *Angina pectoris,* which is frequently described as a substernal tightness, heaviness, or squeezing that occurs with physical exertion or emotional stress. It is caused by transient inadequacy of blood supply to the heart muscle (myocardial ischemia).

- *Fatigue,* which is a common symptom of cardiac failure, may develop so gradually that the patient is unaware of its presence. Questioning about the daily habits and activities may be necessary to discern changes in the activity level that may be due to a decreased tolerance for exertion. Fatigue occurs because the patient's heart is unable to increase its cardiac output in proportion to the metabolic demands.

- *Syncope,* which is due to a reduction in the cerebral blood flow, is manifested by a generalized weakness of the muscles with an inability to stand upright, and a momentary loss of consciousness. There are three major types of syncope: (1) Vasodepressor (vasovagal) syncope is the common faint that results from an initial marked fall in arterial pressure followed by a marked vagal slowing of the heart rate which further lowers the arterial pressure and reduces cerebral perfusion. It most frequently results from emotional stress, pain, poor physical state, organic heart disease, or stimulation of a sensitive carotid sinus. (2) Postural syncope may be due to an instability of vasomotor reflexes or primary autonomic insufficiency with degenerative changes in the autonomic neurons. Syncope occurs because the loss of reflex vasoconstriction of the systemic arterioles allows pooling of blood in the abdomen and legs and inadequate cerebral perfusion. (3) Cardiac syncope results from a sudden reduction in cardiac output. It most commonly results from a cardiac dysrhythmia; complete atrioventricular block is a frequent cause. This form of syncope was recognized and independently described by Stokes, Adams, and Morgagni. Their names have been given to the syncope, but the order of the names is frequently changed, and, in some literature, Morgagni's name is omitted. This book will refer to the syncope as Stokes–Adams–Morgagni syndrome. In addition to syncope with complete heart block, other types of cardiac syncope include pacemaker failure, onset or termination of tachydysrhythmias, shift of pacemaker to ectopic focus, and sinoatrial bradycardia. In all these disorders, the syncope results from the sharp reduction in cardiac output before the reflex vasoconstriction restores arterial pressure and aids ventricular filling.

Physical Examination

Palpation of the arterial pulses.   The radial pulse on the examiner's side is felt while the patient is lying with his palm upward. The examiner, with gentle pressure, places three fingers on the radial artery with the index finger nearest the heart. For many patients only the radial pulse needs to be evaluated. If there is any abnormality of the pulse or impairment of cardiovascular function is suspected, the pulse should be palpated bilaterally at the other pulse sites (carotid, apical, temporal, brachial, femoral, popliteal, posterior tibial, and dorsalis pedis). Both carotid pulses should not be palpated at the same time since diminished blood supply to the brain could result. Visual identification of the point of the maximal impulse (PMI) usually precedes palpation of the ventricular apical pulse with which it is considered synonymous. Normally the apical pulse is located just medially to the left midclavicular line in the fourth or fifth intercostal space. With normal functioning the impulse is localized to an area of 2 to 3 cm in diameter. Enlargement of the left ventricle as well other pathology can affect the position of the heart and displace the PMI. Palpable pulsations in sites other than the apex may indicate the presence of an aneurysm, pulmonary hypertension, or other disease abnormalities.

The pulses in the legs are reduced or absent when obstructive vascular disease is present. Other significant signs and symptoms, however, such as color, temperature, and skin condition must also be assessed to determine the extent of the circulatory insufficiency. These peripheral pulses should be examined not only when vascular disease is suspected but also so that baseline data may be established prior to diagnostic studies or treatment that entail the risk of circulatory impairment. Simultaneous palpation of the radial and femoral pulse may reveal a delay in the conduction of the pulse wave to the femoral artery when coarctation of the aorta is present. Assessment of the pulse should include a description of the following characteristics:

- *Rate*.   The normal range of pulse rate for a healthy nonexercising adult is considered to be 60–100/minute. With tachydysrhythmias, the atrial rate provides diagnostic information. The rate in sinus tachycardia can be due to any disorder that increases the metabolic rate, anemia, sympathetic stimulation, and myocardial disease. Paroxysmal atrial tachycardia usually has a rate of 140–240/minute. It may result from intake of stimulants or organic heart disease. With atrial flutter, the atrial rate is 250–350/minute; while with atrial fibrillation, the atrial rate is greater than 350/minute. With atrial flutter and atrial fibrillation, there is a difference in the atrial and ventricular rates so that an ECG is needed for accurate diagnosis. When the pacemaker function is assumed by the AV junction or the ventricles, the rate is slower. The normal rate of impulse formation in the AV junction is 40–70/minute and in the ventricles 30–50/minute. Nonparoxysmal junctional tachycardia which is characterized by a rate of 70–130/minute may indicate drug toxicity or underlying heart disease. Ventricular tachycardia, which may have a rate of 100–220/minute, is an ominous finding indicative of significant underlying cardiac disease. When untreated, it may progress to ventricular fibrillation and death. *Bradycardia* of approximately 50 beats per minute may be normal for some athletes. In nonathletes, especially in persons with heart disease, rates below 50 may be accompanied by a significant and dangerous reduction in cardiac output. Sinus bradycardia is usually the result of excessive vagal tone, and in some patients may predispose to the occurrence of premature ectopic beats. When the pulse rate is lower than the apical heart rate determined by auscultation, it is termed a pulse deficit. This phenomenon occurs because some of the ventricular contractions are too weak to be transmitted to the radial pulse site. A pulse deficit commonly accompanies atrial fibrillation and may occur with premature contractions.

● *Size of pulse.* The size of the pulse is the second assessment characteristic. It is dependent on the degree of filling of the artery during systole and of emptying during diastole. The size of the pulse reflects the pulse pressure (difference between systolic and diastolic blood pressure). A small pulse is characteristic of a small left ventricular stroke volume. The small stroke volume may be due to a number of factors such as hypovolemia, increased vascular resistance, left ventricular failure, restrictive pericardial disease, or mitral stenosis. In contrast, a large pulse is usually associated with an increased left ventricular stroke volume and a decreased peripheral resistance. *Size of beat.* In addition to the determination that the pulse is small or large, there may be alterations in the size of the beat. Pulsus alternans is a regular alteration in the size of the beats, with a small pulse following a large pulse. It is due to an alternating left ventricular contractile force, and usually is a grave sign denoting severe left ventricular decompensation. In a few instances, the weak beat is so small that it cannot be palpated at the periphery. Pulsus paradoxus also has an alteration in size, with a decrease in size, or momentary disappearance during inspiration. It is found with constrictive pericarditis, pericardial tamponade or effusion, airway obstruction, or superior vena obstruction. It may be due to the decrease in venous return to the left side of the heart due to pulmonary vascular pooling during inspiration or to impediment to venous return to the right side of the heart from high intrapericardial pressure.

● *Type of wave* is another assessment characteristic. The pulse varies in the steepness of its rise and fall. Although the type of wave can be determined by palpation, more accurate identification can be made by study of the pulse pressure tracing made from a transducer attached to an arterial line. The type of pulse wave is frequently related to its size, and both alterations are discussed for the following disturbances. In aortic insufficiency, the large volume of blood ejected at a rapid rate from the left ventricle causes a rapid rise to a high peak, which is sometimes termed the water hammer pulse. The rapid ascent is followed by an extremely rapid downstroke, which is sometimes termed a collapsing pulse. A few patients with aortic insufficiency also have a bisferiens pulse. This pulse is interrupted on its downstroke by a momentary increase in pressure that results in a second apex wave. In addition to aortic insufficiency, a large bounding pulse accompanies hyperkinetic states that occur with severe emotional stress, increased metabolic rates, and cardiac defects that have a high stroke volume.

In aortic stenosis the pulse is the antithesis of that found in aortic insufficiency in that it is both small and rises and falls slowly. Severe aortic stenosis may also be accompanied by a small wave on the ascending limb (the anacrotic pulse), but it is of little diagnostic significance.

- *Rhythm* is an important characteristic to assess. Normal rhythm is regular, although the rate may decrease slightly with inspiration. When the rhythm is irregular, it should be determined whether it is regularly irregular or irregular with no recognizable pattern. When every normal systole is followed by a premature contraction (bigeminy), the irregular rhythm has a regular pattern. Such a regular pattern may also be seen when every third beat is premature (trigeminy) or when second degree block of the AV junction blocks every second, third, or fourth beat. In contrast, atrial fibrillation, occasional and/or multifocal premature contractions, and varying block of the AV junction have a completely irregular rhythm. Palpation is an important assessment parameter for recognition of abnormal rhythms, but an ECG is necessary for definitive diagnosis.

- *Tension* is a characteristic of little diagnostic significance today. It is tested by obliterating the distal radial artery by firm pressure with the index finger of one hand while the index and second finger of the other hand are placed over a more proximal segment of the radial artery. Pressure is then exerted on the proximal radial artery by the index finger while the pulse is felt with the second finger. A soft compressible pulse is obliterated with slight pressure while a hard pulse requires strong pressure. A hard pulse may be an indication of a high diastolic blood pressure, but actual determination of the blood pressure with a sphygmomanometer is necessary.

Examination of the jugular venous pulse. Since there are no valves between the right atrium and the superior vena cava or between the superior vena cava and the internal jugular veins, the jugular venous pulse reflects the phasic pressure changes in the right atrium. Hemodynamic disturbances in the right side of the heart and malfunction of the tricuspid valve are reflected in abnormal venous pressures and waveforms. Although venous pressure may be measured by a transducer or water column attached to a central venous line, the noninvasive technique of measuring the distance from the right atrium to the top of the oscillating venous column in the neck (with the trunk elevated 30°−45°) provides a fairly accurate estimate of central venous pressure. The hepatojugular reflux may be tested by the application of firm pressure in the right upper quadrant of the abdomen for 30−60 seconds. The level of venous pulsation (venous pressure) usually increases with impaired right heart function. The increase probably occurs because increased abdominal pressure enhances venous return and the failing right heart cannot increase its output.

The nurse generally is not responsible for assessment of the waveform of the jugular pulse. The normal venous pulse consists of three positive waves (a, c, and v) and two negative troughs (x and y). In order to examine the pulsations, the patient must be properly positioned. The right internal jugular, which is most frequently used, is observed below the sternomastoid muscle and lateral to the clavicular insertion of the sternomastoid. The patient should be positioned with his trunk elevated 30 to 45 degrees with his head turned slightly to the left and his neck muscles relaxed. Shining a light tangentially across the skin overlying the vein may make the pulsations more visible. Simultaneous palpation of the left carotid artery helps to distinguish between venous and arterial pulsations. The major disorders that are associated with abnormalities of the jugular venous pulse are absence of the a wave in atrial fibrillation, accentuation of the a wave in pulmonary stenosis, pulmonary hypertension, and tricuspid stenosis, and accentuation of the v wave in tricuspid insufficiency, heart failure, and constrictive pericarditis.

Auscultation of the heart. The use of auscultation to improve identification of abnormalities of the pulse has been mentioned. Of perhaps greater value than identification of disorders of rate and rhythm of the heart beat, is its use in determining the blood flow through the heart chambers and functioning of the valves. Physical assessment books contain detailed descriptions of the normal first and second heart sounds in adults and the extra heart sounds that are indicative of a heart disorder. These abnormal sounds include a third heart sound (called a ventricular gallop), a fourth heart sound (atrial gallop), ejection and midsystolic clicks, murmurs, and pericardial friction rubs. Abnormal heart sounds may be indicative of an underlying cardiac disorder that is also manifested by an alteration in the pulse, but the nurse is generally only responsible for auscultation of the heart rate and rhythm. Accuracy in auscultation of the heart requires extensive supervised experience; therefore, more detailed discussion will not be undertaken.

Electrocardiographic examination. The ECG is a graphic tracing that depicts the timing, magnitude, and direction of the heart's electrical activity. It is required for accurate diagnosis of the nature and site of origin of any dysrhythmia, whether it is due to increased or decreased automaticity of the normal pacemaker, an ectopic pacemaker, premature ectopic contractions, or disturbances of electrical conduction within the heart. By calculation of the electrical axis from the ECG, ventricular hypertrophy and more precise information on any conduction abnormality or area of the heart affected by an infarct can be identified. Analysis of an ECG tracing should begin with the recognition that the various waveforms of the ECG represent specific electrical events occurring in the myocardium. Absence of a characteristic waveform, abnormality of any time interval, and alteration in the normal configuration of a wave are clues that point to the nature of the underlying disturbance. Perhaps the most frequent assessment error is equating electrical activity with mechanical activity. Although electrical activity is essential for mechanical function, adequate electrical activity does not guarantee adequate mechanical function and adequate cardiac output. Like auscultation, ECG interpretation is complex and requires extensive theoretical knowledge and practice. A complete presentation is not within the scope of this book.

Radiologic examination of the chest. The posterior-anterior (PA) and lateral chest X-rays provide information about heart size and shape, enlargement of the aorta, pulmonary artery, or left atrium, intracardiac calcification, and pressure and flow in the pulmonary arteries. A barium swallow can confirm left atrial enlargement and fluoroscopic examination helps differentiate between a pulsatile mass as an aneurysm and a solid tumor.

Laboratory and Other Tests

Electrolyte level determination. As has been previously stated, normal levels of potassium, sodium, and calcium are required for propagation of the electrical impulse and adequate cardiac contraction. For patients on digitalis, low serum potassium can potentiate digitalis toxicity in addition to causing hypokalemic dysrhythmias. Abnormal levels of potassium and calcium may sometimes be assessed by characteristic changes in the ECG as well as by serum levels. In addition to the levels of potassium, sodium, and calcium, the bicarbonate concentration is important for assessment. Acute metabolic acidosis can decrease the cardiac output and lead to vascular collapse and shock. A low serum bicarbonate is indicative of metabolic acidosis, but arterial blood gas and pH studies are required for precise determination of the extent of the deficit. A pH below 7.35 with a bicarbonate less than 22 mEq/liter and a normal or low Pco_2 (less than 45 torr) is indicative of metabolic acidosis. Evaluation of the anion gap will help determine the underlying cause for the metabolic alteration.

Serum enzyme studies. Since injured cells and overactive cells release specific enzymes which are picked up by the circulating blood, the levels of the various enzymes can be utilized to detect the site and extent of cellular damage. Physical overactivity or muscle trauma must be excluded as possible causes of the elevation. The enzymes of greatest diagnostic importance for cardiac injury are creatine phosphokinase (CPK), lactic dehydrogenase (LDH), and serum glutamic oxaloacetic transaminase (SGOT). The fractionation of CPK into its isoenzymes gives more specific information about the muscle involved. CPK-MB is highly specific for myocardial infarction. The elevations of these enzymes that are indicative of cardiac injury varies with the method used by the laboratory and the time between the injury and the drawing of the specimen. The CPK is the fastest rising enzyme but the elevation is only sustained for 24 to 48 hours. The extent of a myocardial infarction has a fairly high correlation with the height and duration of the enzyme elevation.

Other diagnostic procedures. There are a number of other diagnostic procedures which the physician utilizes to evaluate the nature, cause, and extent of an alteration in the pulse wave accompanied by other abnormal physical assessment findings of abnormalities in the ECG, chest X-ray, and serum enzymes. Many new noninvasive techniques are being developed to reduce the morbidity associated with the invasive procedures. Since these techniques are the responsibility of the physician, they will only be mentioned in this book. Noninvasive techniques such as reflected ultrasound (echocardiography) and radioisotopes with subsequent scanning are of the greatest value. In addition to blood pool scans, new techniques for radioisotope myocardial imaging that allow the detection of areas of myocardial necrosis look extremely promising. Other noninvasive methods include phonocardiography, apexcardiography, and indirect carotid artery pulse wave recording. The invasive procedure of cardiac catheterization and angiocardiography probably provides the most accurate anatomic and functional diagnosis of complex cardiac lesions.

Assessment of Dysfunctional Effects

It has already been said that the seriousness of the abnormality of the pulse is related to the character and magnitude of its dysfunctional effects on the cardiac output. Therefore, assessment should include the volume of the cardiac output as well as the nature and cause of the alteration in the pulse. Cardiac output can be measured by a specially constructed Swan–Ganz catheter. Normal cardiac output at rest is 5 liters/minute and output is inadequate when it is less than 3.5 liters/minute. Greater accuracy is obtained with the use of the cardiac index, which is based on body size. Inadequate cardiac output is indicated by a cardiac index less than 2.5 liters/minute per square meter of body surface. When the cardiac output is not being monitored, it is necessary to use other output indicators. These parameters will be briefly discussed:

• *Blood pressure* falls when cardiac output is decreased. The systolic blood pressure is mainly affected. Blood pressure should be compared to the patient's previous pressure rather than an absolute norm.

• *Pulmonary artery wedge pressure* (PAWP) rises above 25 mm Hg with a failing heart. The PAWP can also be elevated with fluid volume excess; but, when it is elevated in a patient with a low systolic pressure, it is a sign of low cardiac output.

• *Central venous pressure* (CVP) may be monitored when the patient does not have a Swan–Ganz catheter for PAWP monitoring. An elevation of CVP above 20 cm H_2O in a patient with a drop in blood pressure is indicative of low cardiac output. In some facilities CVP is measured by a transducer rather than by a water manometer. It is important to remember that pressure readings from a transducer are in millimeters of mercury (Hg) rather than centimeters of water. Centimeters of H_2O can be converted to mm Hg by dividing by a factor of 1.36. Thus a CVP reading from a water manometer of 20 cm is equivalent to a transducer reading of 14.7 mm Hg. When a central venous line is not available for direct measurement of CVP, the pressure can be estimated by observing the height of distension of the neck veins above the level of the right atrium with the head elevated 30°.

• *Tissue perfusion* is another indicator of cardiac output. When renal perfusion is adequate, urine output exceeds 30 ml/hour. Normal cognitive functioning is a sign of adequate cerebral perfusion. Adequacy of the peripheral circulation can be determined by assessment of the temperature, color, and fullness of the veins of the extremities and the presence and strength of the peripheral pulses. Cardiac output less than 3 liters/minute is correlated with absent or questionable peripheral pulses and coolness and cyanosis of extremities.

• *Oxygenation* of blood is frequently low when cardiac output is decreased. Arterial P_{O_2} less than 70 torr or mixed venous P_{O_2} less than 30 torr are signs of inadequate supply of oxygen to the tissues.

• *Other physical signs* of low cardiac output can include tachycardia, diaphoresis, rales at the lung bases, and dependent pitting edema. Symptoms which may be reported by the patient include dyspnea, chest pain, and faintness.

• *Effectiveness of psychologic adaptive mechanisms* (coping responses, defense mechanisms, mental mechanisms) can provide clues regarding the extent the mechanisms are bolstering the patient's ego defenses and psychologic adaptation. Adaptive behaviors are mechanisms that attempt to avoid some aspect of reality. The hospitalized patient may perceive the alteration in pulse as a threat that will change his self-concept and self-esteem. He may grieve over the separation from family and friends and the need to relinquish cherished plans or goals. He may respond to this threat by denial, repression, rationalization, or other mechanisms that allow him time to bolster his psychologic resources and make the necessary adjustments. In some instances, though, the use of denial or other mechanisms may compromise the treatment and be detrimental to the patient's recovery. The patient may manifest his difficulty by disturbed behavior. Thus an attempt to exert control over his environment and to regain a measure of autonomy may be evidenced by complaining and demanding behavior. The man whose self-concept as a virile male is threatened may attempt to bolster his self-esteem by sexually provocative behavior toward female attendants.

INTERVENTION

The nature and major responsibility for intervention in a patient with an alteration in pulse depends on the cause. When a dysrhythmia is a sign of underlying cardiac pathology, it will probably require medical intervention to terminate the dysrhythmia, to reduce its dysfunctional effects, and/or to treat the underlying disorders. Dysrhythmias due to a noncardiac disorder or those that are physiologic responses to stressors may require both medical and independent nursing intervention. The type of intervention would depend upon the nature of the disorder, and naturally priority is given to treatment of life-threatening states. Some of the major goals and the activities which might be indicated for goal attainment follow.

Correction of Dysrhythmia

Activities will be discussed for the major disturbances.

• *Sinus bradycardia* accompanied by a decreased cardiac output is generally treated by the administration of atropine to block the vagal slowing of the heart. An intravenous bolus of 0.5–1.0 mg is usually given with additional doses as needed every 5 minutes up to 2 mg. Atropine may be contraindicated for patients with glaucoma, or those with extreme hypothermia, and its use can also cause urinary retention. Isoproterenol may be given when atropine is contraindicated or ineffective. Its use will be discussed in more detail under improvement of cardiac contractility.

• *Sinus tachycardia* is generally due to excessive sympathetic stimulation from fear, anxiety, exercise, fever, or the administration of chronotropic or vagolytic drugs. It usually responds to treatment of the underlying cause.

• *Supraventricular tachycardia* is a general category for a number of fast dysrhythmias which may arise in the atria or in the AV junctional tissue. Since many of the rapid supraventricular rhythms may be due to digitalis toxicity, this possibility needs to be assessed carefully. Paroxysmal atrial tachycardia with block and nonparoxysmal AV junctional tachycardia are usually caused by digitalis toxicity and atrial fibrillation is sometimes caused by digitalis. Dysrhythmias from digitalis toxicity are treated by discontinuance of the drug and administration of potassium (unless potassium is high). Diphenylhydantoin and, occasionally, propranolol may be indicated for selected patients.

Paradoxically, supraventricular tachycardias in patients not on digitalis are frequently treated by the administration of digitalis. In patients who do not have cerebrovascular disease, the rapid dysrhythmia will frequently be treated initially by carotid sinus massage. Stimulation of the pressoreceptors in the carotid sinus may inhibit the vasomotor center and the sympathetic nervous system, producing a relative increase in vagal tone. The application of unilateral pressure on the carotid sinus for 5 or 6 seconds is generally the responsibility of the physician. Other physical measures that slow the heart rate include the performance of a Valsalva maneuver (expiring against a closed glottis) and inducement of coughing, gagging, and/or vomiting.

If these physical maneuvers are ineffective, digitalization or electrical cardioversion may be initiated. The choice of the treatment modality depends on the need for rapid control and various other patient factors. For example, cardioversion is used with reluctance for patients with recent myocardial infarction or heart surgery. Digitalization may be accomplished by the intravenous administration of 1–1.5 mg of digoxin in divided doses. Quinidine may be used in place of digitalis for patients with atrial fibrillation; but patients with atrial flutter should be digitalized before quinidine is given to prevent an increase in the ventricular rate from increased AV conduction. One of the factors that favors the use of cardioversion before digitalization is that cardioversion increases the sensitivity of the heart to digitalis. If the patient has been digitalized, the drug is usually withheld for 24 hours before cardioversion. This delay in control of the dysrhythmia may be detrimental to the patient.

Cardioversion is accomplished with a DC defibrillator in the synchronous mode, so the electrical impulse is timed to occur 0.4–0.8 seconds after systole (ventricular depolarization). This timing reduces the danger of the shock being delivered during the vulnerable period of ventricular repolarization when it could trigger ventricular tachycardia or ventricular fibrillation. The treatment is naturally frightening to the patient, so adequate explanation is important. Sedation is usually accomplished by means of rapid-acting intravenous agents such as diazepam or sodium methohexital. Low energy levels of 25–50 watt-seconds are utilized, with gradual increases when cardioversion is ineffective.

Rapid atrial pacing may be used for serious rapid atrial dysrhythmias that fail to respond to other methods of treatment or where other treatment modes are contraindicated. The pacemaker is passed into the right atrium; the pacemaker rate is set higher than the patient's rate for a few seconds in an effort to overdrive the atrium and convert the dysrhythmia. Since it is vital that the pacing electrode is properly positioned in the atrium, the procedure is usually done under fluoroscopy. If the electrode passes into the ventricle, dangerous ventricular tachycardia could occur.

• *Ventricular tachycardia* is a life-threatening dysrhythmia that requires prompt intervention. In the conscious patient, it is usually treated by an intravenous bolus of lidocaine (1 mg/kg to 100 mg) followed by infusion at a rate of 1–4 mg/minute. In an unconscious patient, immediate cardioversion is the treatment of choice. The method is similar to that used for atrial tachycardias, but the energy levels may need to be increased. Ventricular tachycardia may quickly deteriorate into ventricular fibrillation. If this occurs, the synchronizer switch needs to be turned off and defibrillation promptly attempted, using a setting of 400 watt-seconds for the average sized adult.

Administration of an electrical shock demands careful attention to the prevention of unnecessary harm to the patient from burns or bridging. A conductive substance as electrode paste, saline soaked pads, or commercially prepared defibrillator pads should be used to reduce the skin resistance to the transmission of the electrical current. Bridging is prevented by the proper placement of the paddles so there is no contact between the paddles or the conductive material under them. Firm pressure of 20–25 pounds on each paddle should be applied when the electrical charge is delivered. For reasons of safety the intention of defibrillating should be announced and no one should be in contact with the bed or the patient.

● *Ectopic beats* are treated if they impair hemodynamics or if they have a possibility of triggering more dangerous dysrhythmias. Atrial ectopic beats are rarely of hemodynamic significance. Quinidine may be given to revert the rhythm to normal. Ventricular ectopic beats, also referred to as premature ventricular contractions (PVC's), may be caused by ischemia, hypoxia, heart failure, digitalis excess, or intake of epinephrine, coffee, or amphetamines. Therapy is directed toward treatment of the underlying cause and suppression of the ectopic foci. Factors associated with increased danger from PVC's are high frequency of occurrence, involvement of several ectopic foci (multifocal), occurrence during the vulnerable period of ventricular repolarization (prior to, or at peak of T wave), and rapid heart rate. The usual treatment is administration of lidocaine as outlined for ventricular tachycardia. In a few patients resistant to lidocaine, procainamide, bretylium tosylate, quinidine, or diphenylhydantoin may be used. Oral forms of some of the drugs are available when needed for long-term therapy. There are contraindications and untoward reactions with all these drugs. A complete discussion of drug therapy is not within the scope of this book, but it is essential for the nurse administering the drugs to be aware of their harmful effects.

● *Conduction disturbances* are of concern because they may reduce the cardiac output, predispose to ectopic ventricular dysrhythmias, or progress to complete heart block. Treatment directed at the underlying cause includes withholding of digitalis or quinidine if drug toxicity is present and correcting the heart failure or hypotension that is contributing to the ischemia. Atropine or isoproterenol may be administered to accelerate the heart rate or increase the conduction in the AV junction. Isoproterenol is rarely given to myocardial infarction patients because it tends to increase the myocardial oxygen demand more than it increases the coronary blood flow; thus, the area of myocardial ischemia might become enlarged.

Electric cardiac pacing is indicated for patients with complete heart block (both with and without Stokes–Adams–Morgagni attacks), or bifascicular block. It may also be indicated for lesser degrees of heart block associated with other potentially dangerous clinical states. A temporary transvenous pacemaker catheter attached to an external pacemaker generator is utilized initially. In emergency situations with inadequate time for the transvenous placement under fluoroscopy, percutaneous transmyocardial catheters may be inserted through the chest wall into the ventricle. If the conduction block persists, the patient may be treated with a permanent implanted pacemaker.

The majority of pacemakers used are of the demand type, with the catheter lodged in the right ventricle. This means that when the patient initiates and conducts his own electrical impulse the output of the pacemaker is suppressed. Although a complete discussion of pacemakers is not within the scope of this book, a few essential points will be briefly discussed. External generators can pose an electrical hazard from contact with the electrical terminals during attachment or removal of the generator from the pacing catheter. The generator should be turned off and rubber gloves should be worn during these procedures. Other hazards of temporary pacing are cardiac perforation, dislocation of the catheter with loss of capture, stimulation of ventricular ectopic beats, and development of infection from loss of barrier of intact skin.

With both temporary and permanent pacemakers, the nurse needs to be aware of the possibility of competition that can develop when the pacemaker fails to sense the patient's own beat. Electrical stimulation, especially when it occurs during the vulnerable period of ventricular repolarization, can trigger ventricular tachycardia or fibrillation. The sensitivity can be regulated on all external generators and on some implated models. Failure to capture must also be recognized. This is evident when a pacer blip is visible on the ECG but no QRS complex follows. Failure to capture can be caused by high myocardial threshold which is usually due to development of edema around the electrode, displacement of the electrode, broken electrode wire, or battery failure. Increasing the amplitude of the electrical impulse may improve capture for high myocardial threshold. Any patient with an implanted pacemaker needs to be educated in its use. The signs of malfunction (syncope, blackout spells, chest pain, dizziness, or pulse rate below a certain figure) that need to be reported to the physician should be clearly discussed. Newer pacemaker models have improved shielding against electrical devices, but patients should be instructed to avoid close contact with microwave ovens.

- *Cardiac arrest* requires prompt intervention to maintain circulation of blood to the tissues during the period the heart is not pumping. Respiratory arrest may precede or quickly follow cessation of heart activity. The American Heart Association has published standards for management of cardiopulmonary resuscitation which are universally used. All rescuers should be trained in basic cardiopulmonary resuscitation (CPR). If the arrest is witnessed, and the cause of the arrest is believed to be a rhythm disturbance such as a heart block, it may be treated by a precordial thump. If the arrest is not witnessed or hypoxia is present, the patient should receive CPR. Artificial ventilation is supplied by mouth-to-mouth breathing or by use of a bag-valve-mask device after the airway has been cleared of any obstruction and the patient placed in the sniffing position. Proper technique for establishment of an open airway is discussed more completely in the chapter on respiratory alterations. Artificial circulation is done by external cardiac compression or, in a few instances, open chest massage. Further treatment includes the use of defibrillation, drugs, and adjunctive equipment as required. CPR must continue until the patient needs no further assistance or until it is discontinued by a physician.

Improvement of Cardiac Contractility

It has already been stated that cardiac electrical activity needs to be accompanied by adequate mechanical activity for maintenance of an adequate cardiac output. Factors directly associated with the heart that decrease cardiac contractility are

(1) presence of a ventricular aneurysm, (2) area of myocardial ischemia or necrosis, (3) accumulation of pericardial fluid or blood with resultant compression of the heart and limitation of diastolic filling, (4) depression of the myocardium which may be related to depletion of the stores of norepinephrine, and (5) impedance to left ventricular ejection from a high aortic root pressure. High aortic root pressure is frequently referred to as high ventricular afterload. The responsibility for improvement of cardiac contractility rests primarily with the physician, so these activities will only be briefly discussed. Some of the activities are directed toward treatment of the underlying cause such as resection of a ventricular aneurysm, revascularization of an area of ischemic myocardium, and pericardiocentesis for fluid.

Depressed myocardial states are treated by the administration of digitalis to increase cardiac contractility and by drugs that stimulate the sympathetic nervous system. The terminology associated with these drugs is frequently confusing to the nurse since many terms are used interchangeably. Sympathetic stimulation normally releases the hormones norepinephrine and epinephrine which are called sympathetic amines or catecholamines. Drugs that mimic the action of these amines are called sympathomimetic drugs. Since they act on the postganglionic adrenergic nerves, they are also called adrenergic drugs. Not all adrenergic drugs have the same action, however. There are two types of adrenergic receptors in the vascular system which are identified as alpha (α) and beta (β). Drugs that stimulate the alpha receptors, producing peripheral vasoconstriction, are termed alpha adrenergic. Those that stimulate the beta receptors, producing vasodilation and increased cardiac contractility, are called beta adrenergic. Some drugs have both alpha and beta action, but one action usually predominates. Sympathomimetic drugs that increase the rate and force of the heart's contraction may also be termed cardiotonic. This terminology is further complicated by the use of the terms positive inotropic effect for agents that increase the strength of the contraction and chronotropic effect for agents that increase the heart rate. Sympathomimetic agents most frequently employed include dopamine, isoproterenol, and, in emergency states, epinephrine. It is important to remember that these drugs, in turn, can induce ectopic and/or rapid dysrhythmias. Thiamine is indicated when the underlying cause is alcoholic cardiomopathy or beriberi heart disease.

Ventricular afterload is reduced by administration of agents that decrease peripheral resistance by vasodilation. The rationale for reducing afterload is that the heart can pump out a larger volume of blood when the pressure in the aorta it is pumping against is lower. Agents most frequently used to reduce the afterload are phentolamine, nitroprusside, trimethaphen, and nitroglycerin. Since vasodilation can cause a marked drop in the blood pressure, these agents are most helpful for patients with a normal or elevated pressure but cold and clammy skin. When given to patients with low blood pressure, cardiotonic drugs such as dopamine or isoproterenol must be given simultaneously. An additional advantage of vasodilation is reduction of the preload as well as the afterload. Preload is reduced since vasodilation increases venous capacitance and venous pooling and this decreases venous return.

Management of Factors that Increase Cardiac Work

Anything that increases the heart rate, the metabolic rate, or the volume of blood returned to the heart increases the work of the heart. Patients with impaired myocardial reserve may develop myocardial ischemia or congestive heart failure with such increases. Rapid heart rates may be part of a metabolic response to an underlying state and respond to treatment of the responsible disorder. If the cause is unknown or treatment cannot be immediately initiated, medication to slow the heart may be used when the rapid rate is contributing to myocardial ischemia. Propranolol, a beta-adrenergic blocker may be used when the blood pressure is adequate. It is usually given in increments to reduce the rate to between 60 and 70. Such slowing of the rate along with the reduced myocardial contractility can result in dangerous reduction of cardiac output, so careful monitoring is indicated.

The volume of blood returned to the heart is termed the preload or left end diastolic pressure since it determines the hemodynamic load on the left ventricle just prior to contraction. Vasodilation has already been discussed as a method of preload reduction since it decreases the venous return to the heart. The major method of reducing preload is by the administration of diuretics. Intravenous administration is indicated in acute states, with oral administration for maintenance. Diuretic drugs act by varied mechanisms and on different portions of the nephron to prevent sodium reabsorption. Some patients may be on more than one type of diuretic to increase diuresis. In emergency situations phlebotomy or rotating tourniquets may be required.

The metabolic rate can be increased by activity, physiologic disorders, and psychologic factors. Fever always increases the metabolic rate, and the rate is generally elevated with pheochromocytoma, thyrotoxicosis, and pregnancy. With anemia and low hemoglobin states, there is a decreased ability to carry oxygen, since oxygen must be combined with hemoglobin for transport. When oxyhemoglobin is decreased, the heart rate increases to supply adequate oxygen to the tissues. With hearts unable to compensate, there may be both myocardial ischemia and hypoxia. The major responsibility for control of many of these states that increase the metabolic demand and the work of the heart lies with the physician. Activities which might be indicated for which the nurse generally has the major responsibility include the following.

- *Reduction of effort expenditure.* Activities can include use of bed and/or chair rest, meals of small quantity, prevention of constipation and straining at stool, and assistance with activities of daily living. Elevation of the head decreases venous return and enhances preload reduction. Other activities may include limitation of number of visitors as well as the length of the visits, and prompt recognition and management of any other disorder that increases work such as airway obstruction. Since bed rest increases the hazard of phlebothrombosis and pulmonary embolism, leg exercises and elastic stockings are indicated. Some patients may be on prophylactic anticoagulation.

- *Control of anxiety and other stress* which activate the sympathoadrenal response with increased production of adrenocorticosteroid hormones, antidiuretic hormone, and catecholamines should be attempted. Activities are directed toward reducing the stressors and/or strengthening the patient's ability to cope with the stress. Some new therapeutic modalities that strengthen a person's ability to resist stress are based on the concept of hemisphere dominance. It is believed that at any one period of time, an individual is operating with either left or right brain dominance. The left brain is dominant when a person is thinking or talking, while the right brain is dominant during emotional experiential activities. The person can only experience stress when the left brain is dominant, as the right brain refuses to be stressed. Therefore shifting to right brain activities such as absorption in music or other art form can reduce the level of stress. Some persons find it easier to focus attention on breathing patterns or word repetition since it is easier than becoming involved in music. Encouraging the anxious patient to verbalize his feeling is a well-known intervention which can be effective in reducing stress. Talking is a left brain activity, however, and it is important to assess the level of stress before encouraging conversation. When stress is rather high, it may be more helpful to shift to a right brain activity. At a later time when the stress is at a tolerable level, conversation may reveal the underlying concerns of the patient. Sedatives are sometimes ordered to decrease stress. Since drugs do not affect all persons in the same way, the patient's response to any sedative or tranquilizer must be carefully evaluated.

- *Control of pain* and discomfort which can also activate the sympathoadrenal response must be attended to. Intervention is discussed more fully in the chapter on pain.

- *Weight reduction* for patients who are overweight helps to reduce the workload on the heart.

- *Maintenance of normothermia* by the use of aspirin or acetaminophen, cooling sponges, or hypothermia blanket is indicated for a patient with fever and impaired cardiac function.

- *Correction of hypoxemia.*   Inadequate oxygenation can be both the cause and the result of pulse alterations. If the P_{O_2} cannot be maintained above 70 torr with oxygen supplement, the patient may require intubation and ventilation on a mechanical respirator. Intervention for hypoxemia is discussed more fully in the chapter on respiratory alterations.

- *Management of systemic factors that decrease tissue perfusion.*   Major factors are hypovolemia, electrolyte abnormalities, and metabolic acidosis. Intravenous fluid, plasma, plasma expanders, or blood is given as indicated to restore the fluid volume. Abnormal levels of sodium, potassium, and calcium require correction. Sodium bicarbonate is given for severe metabolic acidosis.

- *Surgical correction of abnormalities.*   Surgical procedures include replacement of damaged valves, repair of ruptured chordae tendineae, bypass grafting to revascularize an ischemic myocardium or an extremity with impaired blood supply, resection of an aneurysm, and repair of congenital defects. Endarterectomy, embolectomy, and/or sympathectomy may be indicated for peripheral vascular disease. Amputation may be required for arterial occlusion when circulation cannot be restored.

- *Provision of mechanical assistance to the circulation.* When the patient is unable to maintain adequate cardiac output after correction of systemic factors and administration of cardiotonic drugs and drugs to reduce the preload and afterload, mechanical counterpulsation may be initiated. The goal of counterpulsation devices is to improve ventricular emptying and decrease the work of the heart by reducing the afterload. The devices function by altering the volume (and thus the pressure) in the aorta in the various stages of the cardiac cycle. They are synchronized to the electrocardiogram so that the aortic volume is reduced at the onset of left ventricular systole (preceding the QRS complex). This facilitates left ventricular ejection since it is easier for the heart to pump into the aorta when the aortic pressure is low. During ventricular diastole (T wave on the ECG), the volume in the aorta is increased, which improves myocardial and systemic perfusion. Myocardial perfusion benefits since coronary blood flow occurs during diastole, and the higher aortic pressure increases the flow into the coronary arteries.

Several models of noninvasive devices that provide external counterpulsations have been developed. All methods employ the application of pressure cuffs that are deflated just before systole to decompress the vessels of the extremity, which results in lower aortic pressure. The cuffs are inflated during diastole, compressing the extremities, which results in higher aortic pressure during diastole. Some models employ cuffs on the lower extremities only, while other models use cuffs on the upper extremities as well. The advantages of external devices is that their use can be rapidly initiated without the complications associated with an invasive method. The disadvantages are that they cannot be used over a period of time because of leg muscle pain and they are probably not as physiologically effective as the intra-aortic balloon.

The intra-aortic pressure balloon (IAPB) is the most frequently used method of counterpulsation. It consists of a sausage-shaped polyurethane cylinder on the end of a catheter. It is inserted into the femoral artery and passed up the abdominal and thoracic aorta until the tip lies at the level of the origin of the left subclavian artery. The ECG is usually used for timing the inflation and deflation of the arterial balloon. The correctness of the timing and the effectiveness of the diastolic augmentation and presystolic lowering of aortic root pressure is evaluated by study of the arterial pulse waveform. Setting the machine on 1:2 ratio for a short period aids evaluation. Diastolic augmentation is usually most effective when its onset coincides with the dicrotic notch and when peak diastolic pressure equals or exceeds systolic pressure. Proper timing of deflation should result in a lower left ventricular end diastolic pressure with counterpulsation.

The nurse's responsibilities for the patient on IAPB therapy include monitoring for desired pressure alterations and prevention of complications during therapy. Anticoagulants are usually administered to prevent clot formation. As with all patients with alteration of clotting factors, close observation for bleeding is indicated. In spite of anticoagulation, some patients develop systemic emboli which need to be recognized. Probably the most common problem is circulatory insufficiency of the leg distal to the site of balloon insertion. Problems can be minimized by protective care of the extremity similar to that given with vascular insufficiency. This includes prevention of damage from pressure of bed covers, protective wrapping to keep the extremity warm and prevent accidental trauma, and prevention of hip flexion greater than 30 degrees.

Other mechanical devices for circulatory assistance which are in the developmental stage or have received only limited clinical use are the partial cardiac bypass oxygenators and counterpulsation utilizing a permanently implanted aortic patch in the lateral wall of the descending thoracic aorta.

● *Eradication of infections.* Bacterial endocarditis, acute or subacute, is a most serious infection. It requires prompt initiation of appropriate antibiotic therapy. Myocarditis and pericarditis may result from an inflammatory reaction or a viral infection. Viral infections are usually treated with aspirin or, in some cases, antiinflammatory doses of indomethacin or corticosteroids.

● *Identification and alleviation of untoward effects* of the altered state or its therapy. Untoward effects of the disorder include systemic emboli from the clot that frequently develops in the atrium with atrial fibrillation, renal failure from inadequate kidney perfusion, and venous stasis from impaired circulation. Untoward effects of the treatment regimen are primarily related to the drugs administered. Diuretics alter the electrolyte levels, frequently leading to potassium depletion. All of the cardiac drugs can cause untoward effects. The occurrence of premature ectopic beats and fast rhythms with sympathomimetic drugs has already been mentioned. The frequent use of digitalis and the small margin between a therapeutic and a toxic dose for the patient with a damaged myocardium make it vital for the nurse to recognize early signs of digitalis toxicity. Dysrhythmias which may be a sign of digitalis toxicity in a patient receiving digitalis have already been mentioned. The nurse routinely counts the pulse before giving a dose of digitalis and withholds the drug and notifies the physician when the pulse is less than 60/minute. This action usually affords recognition of the development of block of the AV junction. It does not, however, lead to recognition of digitalis toxicity that may be manifested by ventricular ectopic beats or the rapid rhythms of paroxysmal atrial tachycardia or nonparoxysmal junctional tachycardia. The alert patient may report gastrointestinal and/or neuro-ophthalmologic symptoms of digitalis toxicity. Gastrointestinal symptoms may include anorexia, nausea, vomiting, and diarrhea. Neuro-opthalmologic symptoms may include headache, visual disturbances (such as colored vision or photophobia), and changes in mood, irritability, and cognition. These symptoms either may not be reported by a very ill patient or they may be masked. Thus, the nurse must be suspicious of any change in pulse in a patient receiving digitalis. It is important to remember that hypokalemia potentiates digitalis toxicity. Patients on long-term diuretic therapy frequently have a low potassium level. The extent of the body deficiency with a low serum potassium needs to be recognized. In an average sized adult, a serum potassium of 3 is indicative of a deficit of 200-300 mEq of potassium.

● *Development of effective psychologic adaptation.*   Some patients have adequate psychologic resources to cope with illness and are able to make the necessary adaptations in their life style. When the alteration in pulse is a sign of a life-threatening or potentially disruptive disorder, the patient may require help in making an effective psychologic adaptation. Collation of history information of past illnesses, assessment of the effectiveness of the patient's present psychologic adaptation mechanisms, and the nature of the limitations imposed by the present illness helps to identify the patients who need assistance. The patient's ability to adapt to his illness may be strengthened by giving him some forewarning about what he is likely to experience. Explanations geared to his level about his condition which realistically enhance feeling of security and hope should be given. The treatment plan can be modified to reduce the stressors and the environment (temperature, noise, sensory stimuli, etc.) can be controlled. Early initiation of a graduated program of physical conditioning seems to promote a positive psychologic outlook.

When the adaptive responses the patient is utilizing are impeding his recovery, he may need assistance in substituting more therapeutic coping mechanisms for maladaptive behaviors. The establishment of a therapeutic relationship in which the patient feels accepted and free to express his feelings is basic to assisting him to change his behavior. The authors have found that assumption of the attitude that the patient will be able to recognize the changes he needs to make and able to make realistic plans to handle the situation increases the patient's confidence in his own ability and supplies motivation for change. The family frequently needs assistance with their own psychologic problems and can be taught how to exert a positive influence on the patient's psychologic adaptation. When behavioral or emotional disturbances are more severe, administration of tranquilizer drugs and/or psychiatric consultation may be indicated.

● *Education about prescribed treatment and modification of risk factors* can decrease the incidence of recurrence of the same or related disorders. Patients should be instructed as to the action and dosage of the medications they will be taking after discharge, dietary restrictions, activity levels and reportable symptoms. Providing a list of activities graded in terms of MET's will help in determining activity. (One MET is the amount of oxygen required to maintain basal resting state.) Patients should also be aware of factors that increase the risk of cardiovascular disease such as untreated hypertension, elevation of cholesterol and/or triglyceride level, obesity, and smoking. The educational program must be tailored to each individual's goals, intellectual and physical abilities, and emotional acceptance of his disorder. Frequently referral to community agencies for follow-up will be beneficial.

EXPERIENTIAL INVOLVEMENT

Case 3-A.   Mr. Black is a 68-year-old man who had been in good health prior to the development of difficulty with urination. He had a transurethral resection of the prostate (TURP) under enflurane anesthesia. The operation went well except for a period of hypotension that responded to rapid infusion of a volume of fluid. His vital signs on admission to the recovery room were BP 105/80, P 70, R 16. He was receiving 5 percent dextrose in Ringer's lactate at a rate of 100 ml/hour and his Foley catheter drainage was bright red with clots. An hour later his pulse rate suddenly dropped to 46; the pulse was weak and thready and BP was 86/60, R 28. He had received no drugs in the recovery room.

Skillbuilders:
1. On the practicum record 3-A, enter the four most likely hypotheses for the decrease in Mr. Black's pulse rate.
2. Then enter the data that support the hypotheses and additional data you would need to confirm or disconfirm.
3. In the intervention column enter the immediate actions that would be indicated if the diagnosis was confirmed.
4. In the last column list the evaluation criteria for the short-term management of Mr. Black.

Feedback: Before proceeding to find out the cause for the slow pulse, his normal preoperative pulse rate and blood pressure should be checked. This important information should be part of the recovery room admission assessment. We were not given these data on Mr. Black and they are necessary to make accurate inferences and judgments. Obviously a pulse rate of 46 is more serious when the preoperative rate was 110 than if it was 60. Since Mr. Black has had a general anesthetic, the first cause for the drop in pulse that comes to mind is the continued depressive effect of the anesthesia, which could compromise normal compensatory mechanisms. This may cause a number of problems with bradycardia and hypotension among the more frequent. Bradycardia probably occurs first, and the drop in BP is a direct effect of this in patients with altered compensatory mechanisms. It is easy to understand how this may happen if you remember that blood pressure is the product of the cardiac output and the total peripheral resistance, and cardiac output is the product of the stroke volume and heart rate. Under normal conditions, a lowering of peripheral resistance, stroke volume, or heart rate stimulates the sympathetic nervous system to restore the disordered factor toward normal or to cause compensatory action by the other two factors to maintain homeostasis. Without this compensatory mechanism, a decrease in the heart rate will result in a decrease in the blood pressure. The other possible hypotheses for the decrease in pulse rate are hypoxia, myocardial infarction during surgery, and acute urinary bladder distension. It is possible that more than one of these is responsible. Two other possibilities that may be immediately determined are postoperative hemorrhage and pain. Hemorrhage

PRACTICUM RECORD 3-A

Hypothesis/Possible Diagnosis	Supportive Data Available	Additional Data Needed to Confirm or Disconfirm	Nursing Intervention if Diagnosis Confirmed	Evaluation Criteria
Decrease in pulse rate due to:				
1.				
2.				
3.				
4.				

usually causes a decrease in stroke volume which provides the stimulus for a compensatory increase in heart rate and peripheral resistance. Thus, with hemorrhage, hypotension would probably occur with an elevated (or at least unchanged) pulse. Although Mr. Black may have lost his compensatory ability to increase his heart rate in response to a drop in fluid volume, it would be unusual for his pulse to fall.

While pain can stimulate the vagus nerve and slow the heart, it is unlikely that the patient would have severe pain one hour after a TURP with general anesthesia. To complete the practicum record for the hypothesis of decrease in pulse rate due to continued depressive effect of anesthesia with loss of compensatory mechanisms, the history of enflurane anesthesia is the main supporting datum. We don't have a decision tree to serve as a guide here, but the diagnosis of this can be made by excluding other causes. If the diagnosis was confirmed, intervention would consist of activities that would hasten return of consciousness and muscle tone; intravenous atropine could also be administered to block the prolonged vagal effect of the anesthesia. Atropine is usually given in increments of 0.5 mg to a total of 2 mg under close observation. Continuous monitoring of the ECG is essential for careful therapy. In a few instances, infusion of Isuprel may be used. Criteria for evaluation are return of the pulse rate toward the preoperative level and the absence of any dysfunctional effects from the period of reduced perfusion. Such effects could include a decrease in cognitive level, metabolic acidosis, or kidney damage from reduced renal blood flow. If any of these were present, their extensiveness would need to be assessed before instituting treatment. The decision tree on respiratory insufficiency can serve as a guide in conducting the search for clues to support the hypothesis of hypoxia. Tissue oxygenation cannot be measured, but low arterial oxygenation (hypoxemia) is indicative of hypoxia. Since there are no supporting data, except that the respiratory rate has increased from 16 to 28, theoretical knowledge indicates that this may be connected to the anesthesia since respiratory depression causes hypoventilation. Other effects may be increased right to left shunting, airway closure, decreased compliance, and airway obstruction. Inspired air cannot get to the lungs when there is obstruction from the tongue in an obtunded patient or from edema or bronchospasm following intubation. Additionally, shivering, which frequently occurs postanesthetically, raises the oxygen requirements. These factors are discussed more fully in the chapter on respiratory alterations. All of the observations in the two columns of the decision tree would be helpful in providing additional data to confirm the diagnosis of hypoxia. However a blood gas finding of Po_2 less than 70 torr on room air is most conclusive. Intervention when hypoxia is suspected should not wait for blood gas reports and determinations of other parameters. Usually oxygen therapy is indicated immediately. Masks are most frequently utilized in the recovery room in patients without obstructive pulmonary disease with the flow between 4−6 liters/minute. Turning, encouragement to cough, and deep breathing are the cornerstones of intervention. Hyperextension of the head and lifting the mandible upward and, in some instances, use of an oral airway helps to relieve oropharyngeal airway obstruction. Warm humidified oxygen and bronchodilators are helpful for bronchial edema and bronchospasm respectively. Application of warm blankets is indicated to control shivering. Although in a few cases, drugs such as chlorpromazine might be given to control shivering, it would be contraindicated in a patient with hypotension and probable central nervous system depression.

Evaluation criteria would be the same as with loss of compensatory mechanisms from anesthesia as well as the addition of Po_2 maintained above 70 torr. To determine whether a myocardial infarction (MI) during surgery is responsible for the slow pulse, it may be helpful to look at the decision tree for myocardial ischemia. It is readily apparent that our present knowledge does not supply us with any supporting data, although we know that an MI can occur during surgery and the only apparent signs may be a drop in blood pressure and ST segment displacement on the ECG. Since the anesthetic can mask symptoms and impair a patient's ability to report, the data most essential for confirmation would be the ST segment displacement, T wave changes, and presence of a Q wave on a 12 lead ECG. Of course, not all these changes are immediately apparent, and they can be masked by previous abnormalities. Other data include serum enzyme changes, ventricular S3 gallop rhythm on auscultation, leucocytosis, and, possibly, vascular congestion seen on chest X-ray. An alteration in these parameters would need to be evaluated carefully to ascertain that an MI had occurred, since alterations can also be due to other disorders. Intervention in the immediate period is mainly supportive. The use of atropine to increase the pulse rate, oxygen to improve myocardial oxygenation, lidocaine to suppress ventricular ectopic beats, and cardiotonic drugs such as dopamine or Isuprel to increase the cardiac output and maintain adequate tissue perfusion would be indicated. It would also be important to decrease the work of the heart by provision of rest and activities to allay any anxiety the patient might be experiencing. Evaluation would essentially be the same as with loss of compensatory mechanism from continued anesthesia effects. The extent of any permanent damage to the heart will not be known for several weeks.

The last of the hypotheses, i.e., that acute urinary bladder distension is the cause of the problem will now be discussed. The main supporting data for this hypothesis are found in that his urine contained blood and clots and an understanding of physiology. Although the vagus does not innervate the bladder, overdistension initiates a reflex stimulus to the vagus, which causes a slowing of the heart rate. This stimulus seems to be triggered only when the bladder is stretched to a critical limit. Although Mr. Black has a Foley catheter, it can become obstructed by clots. Since fluid administration was vigorous during the surgical procedure, his urine output could be high in the early postoperative period. Thus, obstruction of the catheter for a relatively short period could result in overdistension of the bladder. The bladder should be palpated to determine if there is distension. The intervention would be to irrigate the Foley catheter and to judge the effectiveness by a return of the pulse and blood pressure to normal.

Case 3-B. Mr. Lopez is a 62-year-old hospitalized man weighing 104 pounds with a history of a myocardial infarction 8 years prior to admission (PTA). He has had increasing dyspnea and weakness over the last three years. He stopped working at his job as a house painter six months ago because he could no longer do the work. He had the flu one month PTA and has not felt well since. He has had no appetite, and felt nauseated at intervals, but no emesis. He still has some residual cough, and dyspnea has worsened. During the three nights PTA he awakened around 3:00 A.M. with coughing and a feeling that he was going to suffocate because he couldn't get enough air. Sitting up helped a little, but he felt exhausted from coughing and working to breathe. He was admitted to the hospital with a diagnosis of congestive heart failure (CHF). His physical findings included rales in the posterior lung bases, S_3 gallop rhythm, edema of the ankles, distension of the neck veins when head is elevated, enlarged liver, and a positive hepatojugular reflux. His chest X-ray showed an enlarged heart. His ECG was indicative of left ventricular hypertrophy with nonspecific ST segment and T wave changes, left axis deviation (−30 degrees), and abnormal R wave in lead V_5 and V_6.

His blood chemistry and hematology reports were as follows:

	Patient	Normal
Metabolic I		
Chloride	90	95−105 mEq/L
Carbon dioxide, total	22	24−32 mEq/L
Potassium	4.2	3.5−5 mEq/L
Sodium	128	135−145 mEq/L
Urea Nitrogen	26	10−20 mg/dl
Glucose	96	58−100 mg/dl
Metabolic II		
Protein	6.5	6−8.5 g/dl
Albumin	3	3.5−5 g/dl
Calcium	9	8.5−10.5 mg/dl
Phosphorus	3	2.5−4.5 mg/dl
Cholesterol, total	290	150−250 mg/dl
Uric Acid	6	2−8 mg/dl
Creatinine	1.7	0.7−1.4 mg/dl
Bilirubin total	1.0	0.2−1.2 mg/dl
Phosphatase, alkaline	65	30−85 mU/ml
Hematology Profile		
Leukocyte count (WBC)	9,000	5−10 thousand/cu mm
Erythrocyte count (RBC)	5.2	4.5−6 million/cu mm
Hemoglobin (Hgb)	14.5	14−18 g/dl
Hematocrit (Hct)	43	40−54 ml/dl
Lactic dehydrogenase (LDH)	160	100−225 mU/ml

(continued)

	Patient	Normal
Glutamic pyruvic transaminase (GPT)	40	8−40 mU/ml
Glutamic oxalacetic transaminase (GOT)	42	7.5−40 mU/ml

He received digitalizing doses of digoxin followed by 0.25 mg daily. Other treatment included intravenous furosemide and then oral hydrochlorthiazide (Hydrodiuril) 50 mg twice a day, a sodium restricted low cholesterol diet, and bed rest with bathroom privileges. He had no more episodes of paroxysmal nocturnal dyspnea and lost 3 kilograms (6.6 pounds) weight in 4 days. He was anticipating discharge, but his physician, when visiting him on the morning of his fifth hospital day, told him he wanted him to remain for more diagnostic tests with a possibility of heart surgery. He refused his lunch tray saying he felt nauseated and didn't feel like eating. He asked for a wheel chair to go to the bathroom stating that his legs felt so weak they just wouldn't hold him. He was very restless and somewhat diaphoretic. In response to questioning, he reported that he had such a feeling of tightness in his chest that he could hardly get his breath. His vital signs at this time were BP 140/90 P 110 (regular) R 28 T 98.4 F. His SMA reports received a short time ago from the laboratory are as follows:

	Patient	Normal
Chloride	92	95−105 mEq/L
Carbon dioxide	28	24−32 mEq/L
Potassium	3.2	3.5−5 mEq/L
Sodium	132	135−145 mEq/L
Urea, nitrogen	29	10−20 mg/dl
Protein, total	6.4	6−8.5 g/dl
Albumin	3.1	3.5−5 g/dl
Calcium	9.2	8.5−10.5 mg/dl
Phosphorus	3.2	2.5−4.5 mg/dl
Cholesterol, total	270	150−250 mg/dl
Glucose	152	58−100 mg/dl
Uric acid	9.5	2−8 mg/dl
Creatinine	1.9	0.7−1.4 mg/dl
Bilirubin, total	1	0.2−1.2 mg/dl
Phosphatase, alkaline	65	30−85 mU/ml

Skillbuilders:

1. On the practicum record 3-B, enter the three most likely hypotheses for Mr. Lopez's increase in pulse rate and associated behavior.

2. Enter the data from the history that support each hypothesis and additional data needed to confirm or disconfirm.

PRACTICUM RECORD 3-B

Hypothesis/Possible Diagnosis	Supportive Data Available	Additional Data Needed to Confirm or Disconfirm	Nursing Intervention if Hypothesis Confirmed (next 24–48 hours)	Evaluation Criteria
Alteration in the pulse rate is due to: 1.				
2.				
3.				

3. List the nursing activities both independent and delegated by the physician that would be indicated for the next 24–48 hours if the hypothesis was confirmed.

4. List appropriate evaluation criteria.

Feedback: When a patient is receiving digitalis and a thiazide diuretic, the diagnosis that alteration in pulse is due to digitalis toxicity is certainly likely. Since the problem developed shortly after the physician informed him of the possibility that heart surgery would be required, a second hypothesis could be that the alteration is due to an acute anxiety state. A third hypothesis is myocardial infarction.

How did you do? Of course there are other possibilities that you may have listed. Another possibility that came to mind was that his CHF had worsened and he might now have acute pulmonary edema. We rejected this as unlikely, since he had been receiving treatment and shown improvement. One or more of the hypotheses on our list could precipitate acute decompensation, but if that were the case, it is preferable to work from the precipitating cause rather than its dysfunctional effect.

The supporting data for the hypothesis that the alteration in pulse is due to digitalis toxicity are the history of digitalis intake, the patient's report of anorexia and nausea, and a low serum potassium of 3.2. An awareness that digitalis can cause a number of dysrhythmias and that toxicity can be potentiated by hypokalemia adds additional support to the hypothesis. The faster heart rate could reduce the cardiac output and cause myocardial ischemia, which can be manifested by a feeling of tightness in the chest. Also, since hindsight is better than foresight, it can be noted that both the BUN and the serum creatinine are in the slightly elevated range on admission. Although these levels are not indicative of renal insufficiency, they are indicative of impaired renal function for this patient. With Mr. Lopez's weight of 104 pounds and reduced physical activity, he has small muscle mass and probably is incapable of producing as much creatinine as the averaged-sized muscular person. Thus a creatinine level that would be normal for most people is elevated for him. Additionally, he had edema, a sign of fluid volume excess, which dilutes all solutes. His blood chemistries on the fifth hospital day with the slight increase in BUN and creatinine as well as a number of other solutes reflect the hemodilution present on admission. This reevaluation of his admission laboratory values leads us to the conclusion that Mr. Lopez probably had impaired renal clearance and therefore the daily dosage of 0.25 mg of digoxin may have been an overdose for the patient. Additional data needed would include presence or absence of neuroopthalmologic symptoms, serum digoxin level, and an ECG.

To evaluate the importance of these data, we recognize that the gastrointestinal symptoms of nausea and vomiting only weakly support the hypothesis of digitalis intoxication since these symptoms were present on admission before he received any digitalis. Patients with CHF quite frequently report anorexia and nausea. Some of the probable causes are congestive hepatomegaly, abdominal fullness, and impaired intestinal absorption due to congestion of the intestinal veins. Thus it is important to question Mr. Lopez about other signs of digitalis toxicity such as headache and visual disturbances (colored vision and photophobia). Since cardiovascular signs are the first manifestation of digitalis toxicity in about half the patients, the absence of both gastrointestinal and neuroopthalmologic symptoms does not rule out the hypothesis. To continue with the other supporting data, one isolated digoxin level does not actually provide a great deal of information. The therapeutic range of digoxin is generally considered to be 0.8–2.1 ng/dl. There is a great deal of difference, however, in the level tolerated by an individual before signs of toxicity occur. Generally, patients with poor myocardiums develop toxicity at a lower level. Thus the change in level for an individual is more useful than an isolated reading. The most helpful data for confirmation of the hypothesis are those provided by the ECG. Since his pulse rate was 110 and regular, paroxysmal atrial tachycardia with 2:1 block might be suspected. An ECG pattern showing regular small P waves with every other P waved followed by a QRS would confirm the dysrhythmia. An occasional premature ventricular extrasystole lends support to the hypothesis that the cause of the PAT with block is digitalis toxicity. The physician might seek other support for the hypothesis by massaging the carotid sinus while observing the ECG. Supportive datum would be dramatic accentuation of the AV block, with the 2:1 ratio (every other beat blocked) changed to a 3:1 or 4:1 block. Intervention is generally initiated if digitalis toxicity is suspected since it cannot be definitely confirmed and the potential harm to the patient is high. There should have been no trouble with intervention here. The digitalis is stopped and potassium chloride is given. Diphenylhydantoin might be used for some patients to suppress the dysrhythmia associated with digitalis. Electrical countershock should be avoided because of the danger of precipitating ventricular tachycardia or ventricular fibrillation. Depending on the patient's response, the diuretic might be changed to an agent that spares potassium such as triamterene or spironolactone. There are some other indicators that Mr. Lopez is having side effects from the thiazide diuretic. His glucose level has gone from normal to 152 mg/dl, and his uric acid is also elevated. The probable reason for these elevations is that thiazides inhibit the release of insulin and cause increased tubular reabsorption of uric acid. In many patients, the concurrent administration of potassium supplement to maintain normokalemia minimizes these effects. In other patients, the therapeutic plan has to be altered.

Evaluation needs to be done continuously with this patient since a worsening state could be life threatening. Restoration of normal sinus rhythm on the ECG and disappearance of the abnormal physical signs and symptoms is the desired state. Now let's consider the hypothesis that the alteration in pulse rate is due to an acute anxiety state. The supporting data again come primarily from the history, physical findings, and knowledge of physiology. Mr. Lopez has already experienced a number of alterations in his life style. He may have unresolved grief over the losses, failure to integrate the changes into his self-concept, and/or reduced psychologic reserves to make new adaptations. The emotional component that most people associate with the heart increases the vulnerability when its function is threatened. These factors combined with the natural anxiety associated with any major surgery could be overwhelming. Physical findings that support the hypothesis in addition to the rapid pulse are restlessness, diaphoresis, nausea, and increase in respiratory rate. The physiologic mechanism of acceleration of the heart rate from sympathetic activation in response to anxiety and stress also lends support to the hypothesis. Additional supporting data would be obtained by analysis of the ECG and observation and communication with the patient. A sinus tachycardia is the regular rhythm that is most frequently associated with anxiety. Additional signs of anxiety which could be observed for confirmation of the hypothesis include presence of muscle tension, narrowing of perceptual field, inability to focus attention, decrease in cognitive functioning, trembling, and, perhaps, bizarre behavior. Exploration with the patient of his feelings and concerns might provide data to confirm the hypothesis but such activity might be contraindicated at this time if it could intensify the anxiety. At some time during his hospitalization, data should be obtained about the extent of his unresolved grief or conflicts, and the meaning he ascribes to the possibility of surgery.

Intervention for the next 24 to 48 hours would primarily be directed toward establishing a therapeutic relationship with the patient. Attitudes and behaviors on the part of the nurse that facilitate such a relationship are demonstration of concern and acceptance of the patient, a respect for the patient's privacy, empathetic understanding of the meaning the patient ascribes to experiences, an attitude of hopefullness, and demonstration of trustworthiness. Trustworthiness encompasses a number of concepts. It includes knowledge and ability to provide safe care, honesty, willingness to serve as the patient's advocate, and the ability to keep promises. Establishment or strengthening of the therapeutic relationship at this time is essential for success in assisting the patient to deal with this and future anxiety. For some patients, tranquilizing drugs might be given to depress their awareness of the disturbing situation. Evaluation of this diagnosis is difficult within a short time frame. A decrease in the pulse rate and a lessening of the signs of anxiety would be the desired effect. If drugs were given, close observation for untoward effects of the drug is essential, since many patients have idiosyncratic reactions.

Now let us look at the last hypothesis that ascribes the pulse alteration to a myocardial infarction. It is important to remember that the patient may have more than one cause for an altered state. Thus, even though anxiety may be confirmed as a diagnosis, other possibilities are not rejected until they have been disconfirmed. The decision tree for myocardial ischemia will assist us in the diagnostic process. Supporting data for myocardial infarction are the physical findings of the altered pulse, restlessness, and diaphoresis, plus the patient's report of anorexia and nausea, weakness, difficult breathing, and tightness in his chest. Although we usually associate a myocardial infarction with severe chest pain, some patients have no pain at all while others describe states of discomfort without using the word pain. Additional data needed to confirm the hypothesis would include a more complete description of the sensations he was feeling, ausculatory findings, ECG tracing, and laboratory reports. Exploration with the patient to determine the character of his discomfort should include ascertaining if he had ever experienced this type of tightness in his chest before, and if it was worse when he took a deep breath. Information should also be sought about the presence or absence of discomfort in his shoulder, throat, jaw, teeth, or left arm. Additionally, his anorexia and nausea should be compared with his preadmission experience. Data on presence of an S3 ventricular gallop rhythm, if not present a day or two before, would indicate that some incident had triggered left ventricular failure, with myocardial infarction the highly probable precipitating incident. The ECG, serum enzyme, and white blood count reports provide the most conclusive evidence, but the period of delay before these abnormalities become manifested has already been discussed. The physician frequently orders a trial dose of nitroglycerin for the patient. Pain or discomfort not relieved by nitrates is more apt to be caused by a myocardial infarction. As discussed in the previous case study, intervention in the first 24–48 hours for a myocardial infarction is mainly supportive. The overall goal is to decrease the metabolic demand on the heart and maintain an adequate cardiac output in order to prevent death and to limit permanent damage to the heart and dysfunctional effects on other body organs. Intervention to decrease the metabolic demand on the heart includes reduction of effort expended, control of pain, anxiety, and stress, and control of physiologic alterations such as hypoxemia, metabolic acidosis, and electrolyte abnormalities. To maintain an adequate cardiac output requires attention to both electrical and mechanical factors. The list of specific activities should be compared with those discussed in the intervention section.

The effectiveness of intervention would be evaluated by the extent of normalization of the altered symptoms, signs, laboratory reports, and special diagnostic studies. Since the course of a myocardial infarction is frequently accompanied by the development of new dysrhythmias and other complications, evaluation would include the effectiveness of monitoring and treatment activities in the prevention or early detection of these occurrences. The major complications in the early period after infarction are:

1. Life-threatening electrical abnormalities of ventricular tachycardia, ventricular fibrillation, and complete heart block.

2. Pump failure (cardiogenic shock).

3. Mitral regurgitation (or insufficiency) from dysfunction of the papillary muscle or tear of the chordae tendineae.

4. Dislodgment of mural thrombus and other thromboembolic states.

5. Development of pericarditis and pericardial tamponade (more likely to occur on the third to fifth day).

6. Extension of the myocardial infarction.

ADDITIONAL READING

Gazzaniga: The split brain in man. Sci Am 217(2), 1971.
Guyton A: Textbook of Medical Physiology, 5th ed. Philadelphia, Saunders, 1976 (Rhythmic excitation of the heart, pp 163–171; The systemic circulation, pp 218–228).

Hurst JW, Schlant R: Examination of the arteries and their pulsation. In Hurst JW
    (ed): The Heart. New York, McGraw-Hill, 1978, pp 183–192.
Imboden J, Urbaitis J: Practical Psychiatry in Medicine. New York, Appleton 1978
    (Coping behavior, pp 9–22; Psychologic reactions during hospitalization, pp
    40–59).
Major R: Physical Diagnosis, 8th ed. Philadelphia, Saunders, 1975, pp 358–516.
Massie E: Palpitation and tachycardia. In MacBryde E, Blacklow R (eds.): Signs and
    Symptoms, 5th ed. Philadelphia, Lippincott, 1970, pp 304–322.
Patient Assessment: Abnormalities of the heartbeat, programmed instruction. AJN
    77(4):1–26, 1977.
Patient Assessment: Pulses, programmed instruction. AJN 79(1):115–132, 1979.
Sobel B, Braunwald E: Cardiac dysrhythmias. In Harrison T (ed.): Principles of
    Internal Medicine, 8th ed. New York, McGraw-Hill, 1977, pp 1187–1206.
Sparks C: Peripheral pulses. AJN 75(7):1132–1133, 1975.

CHAPTER 4

Respiratory Alterations

Respiration is the term for a series of processes that supply oxygen and eliminate carbon dioxide; these functions are essential for cellular metabolism and energy production. Oxygen is required for the oxidation of simple sugars (reduced substrate) to high energy adenosine triphosphate (ATP). Carbon dioxide is a waste product of the oxidative process and must be removed from the cell and body. Respiration involves not only gas exchange but also all the physiologic reactions involved in its utilization at the cellular level in the body tissues. Although the lungs are the primary organs for respiration, the circulatory system is essential for the exchange and transport of the gases, and the central nervous system regulates many of the respiratory functions. With such a complex function it is easier to consider each of the components individually. There are many terms used to describe the different processes. Some authors divide respiration into external and internal; external referring to the process at the alveoli of the lung, and internal to the gas exchange at the cellular level. Here we will consider all the respiratory functions under the four main processes: (1) *ventilation*, or the movement of air in and out of the lungs; (2) *distribution* of the inspired air throughout the lung fields; (3) *diffusion* of gases across the alveolar membrane in the lung and across the capillary wall in the tissues; and (4) *perfusion* of the blood through the pulmonary capillaries and the body.

RESPIRATORY PROCESSES

Ventilation

Ventilation is a cyclic process initiated by the contraction of the diaphragm and intercostal muscles that transfers a volume of air from the atmosphere to the alveoli of the lungs (inspiration), and moves a volume of air from the lungs to outside the body (expiration). The key factor is volume. The basic measurement is minute ventilation, which is the product of the respiratory rate and the tidal volume (the amount of air moved in and out of the lung with each breath during regular breathing). Normal tidal volume in a middle-aged adult can be roughly considered to be three times the weight in pounds, with older adults having a lower volume. Thus a 150-pound 40-year-old with a respiratory rate of 16 would be expected to have a minute volume of 7.2 liters. (Tidal volume is $150 \times 3 = 450$ ml; minute volume is 450 ml $\times$ 16 = 7200 ml or 7.2 liters.) Inadequate volume is termed hypoventilation. Greater volume than normal is termed hyperventilation. Ventilatory failure is manifested by carbon dioxide retention, or hypercarbia. In hyperventilation, there is increased expiration, or "blowing-off" of carbon dioxide, manifested by hypocarbia. There are a number of pulmonary function tests that measure the volume or capacity of the lungs at various phases of the inspiratory-expiratory cycle. These are helpful in identification of the causal factors for hypoventilation that are due to altered states within the lung or in the muscles involved in the respiratory process. Essentially they demonstrate whether the problem lies in a restrictive disorder that reduces the vital capacity (VC) of the lung (maximum breathing ability) or in an obstructive disorder that decreases the expiratory flow rate. An appreciation of the effect of the various alterations in lung volumes and flow rates is helpful to the nurse, but precise interpretation of the tests is the responsibility of the pulmonary specialist. The nurse, however, must understand the mechanisms and regulators involved in ventilation so that any alterations in the ventilatory pattern of the patient can be accurately assessed.

The effect of dead space volume on ventilatory volume is an important concept to understand. Lung volumes reflect the amount of air inspired and expired at the nose or mouth. Gas exchange takes place at the alveolar membrane. With each breath, a portion of the air inspired goes to fill the respiratory passages in the tracheobronchial tree and does not reach the alveolar membrane. This volume of air that remains in the conducting airways is termed the *anatomic dead space volume*. In a normal adult, dead space volume equals approximately the weight in pounds, i.e., for a man weighing 150 pounds, the dead space volume would be 150 ml. Since no gas exchange takes place in the dead space the most significant volume measurement is minute alveolar ventilation, or the volume of air reaching the alveoli each minute. This is calculated by subtracting the dead space volume from the tidal volume and multiplying by the respiratory rate. For the 40-year-old patient weighing 150 pounds with a respiratory rate of 16, the expected minute alveolar volume would be 4.8 liters (450 ml − 150 ml = 300 ml; 300 ml $\times$ 16 = 4800 ml, or 4.8 liters). In healthy states, changes in the minute ventilation have a fairly constant relationship with changes in minute alveolar ventilation. In altered states, minute volume can remain normal while large deficits can occur in minute alveolar volume. Although anatomic dead space remains relatively constant, additional dead space may develop from pathologic dead space that results when alveoli are ventilated and there is no capillary blood flow. A major cause of increased alveolar dead space is pulmonary embolus; however, it may be present in severe emphysema and other disorders.

Compliance is another essential concept that should be understood. Compliance refers to the volume of air that is able to move into the lung for each unit of pressure change. A noncompliant lung offers greater resistance to the flow of air and requires greater pressures, so resistance (or elastance as it is commonly called) is the reciprocal of compliance. With different disorders, the source of increased resistance may be in the airways, within the lung, or in the distensibility of the chest wall. When compliance is reduced, the work of ventilation is increased.

The central neural control of ventilation is in the respiratory center located in the medulla and pons. The respiratory center determines the rate and depth of respiration in response to various chemical stimuli, reflex stimuli, and sepsis. Sepsis is an extremely powerful stimulus to the respiratory center, due to the elaboration of endotoxin. Reflex stimulation to ventilation comes from the stretch receptors in the lung and the higher centers in the cortex and thalamus. The stretch receptors stimulate deeper inspiration such as the sighing mechanism that hyperinflates the lung periodically. Ventilation can be increased by cortical control, and thalamic impulses alter the respiratory rate in response to emotions. Arterial and venous baroreceptors in the aorta and carotid bodies also stimulate the respiratory center in response to a significant drop in blood pressure. The greatest effect on the respiratory center comes from the chemical stimulation of hypercarbia, hypoxemia, and acidosis.

Carbon dioxide (CO_2) in the blood diffuses freely into the cerebrospinal fluid (CSF). With increased CO_2, the pH of the CSF decreases, providing a powerful stimulus to the respiratory center which increases ventilation. Both rate and volume of ventilation is increased in normal individuals, but when the ability to increase volume has been lost, there will be an attempt to maintain minute ventilation by a greater increase in respiratory rate. The sensitivity of the respiratory center to hypercarbia (especially to levels greater than 70 torr) decreases over a period of time. Thus patients with chronic severe hypercarbia may have very little respiratory center stimulation from elevated CO_2.

Hypoxemia stimulates the respiratory center by specific chemoreceptors in the carotid bodies located at the bifurcation of the carotid arteries and the aortic arch. The chemoreceptors respond to a decrease in oxygen tension (or pressure) in the blood, but hypoxemia is a weaker stimulus to ventilation than hypercarbia. Consequently a drop in the arterial oxygen tension below 60 torr is required to stimulate ventilation. Unlike the response to hypercarbia, however, the response to hypoxemia persists until death.

Acidosis even when not accompanied by hypercarbia, increases both the respiratory rate and the tidal volume. However hydrogen ions and bicarbonate ions diffuse more slowly across the blood-brain barrier than carbon dioxide, so the effect is not as rapid as with hypercarbia.

Distribution

Distribution of the inspired air throughout the lung fields follows ventilation. Distribution is primarily affected by the distending pressure within the lung, ventilatory volume, closure of airways, and level of surfactant. In normal states, air is distributed fairly uniformly. With abnormal states, unequal distribution of the air can compromise adequacy of respiration. The distending pressure (sometimes termed transpulmonary pressure) is the pressure throughout the lungs after the airway resistance has been overcome. It is affected by gravity, with the pressures in the apex of the lungs higher than in the dependent portions. Thus, at low lung volumes, air is poorly distributed to the dependent areas of the lung. This maldistribution results in underventilation of some areas.

Small airways in the dependent portions of the lung tend to close early in expiration. They also open later during inspiration; so with low lung volumes, the volume of air within the alveoli is inadequate to maintain alveolar integrity. Airways also close because of obstructions such as a foreign body, inflammatory process, tumor, mucous plug, or external pressure. The alveoli beyond the site of the blockage collapse because the air in them is absorbed and a new supply is blocked from entering. This collapse of alveoli in the small airways beyond obstructions is termed atelectasis.

Surfactant is essential for adequate respiration because it is needed to reduce the alveolar surface tension which otherwise predisposes to alveolar collapse. Inhalation of high oxygen concentrations over a period of time, overdistension of the alveoli, and presence of vasoactive substances following shock are some of the major causes of decreased surfactant.

Diffusion

Diffusion of oxygen from the inspired air across the alveolar membrane into the red blood cells of the pulmonary capillaries is the next respiratory process we shall discuss. Carbon dioxide diffuses in the opposite direction, i.e., from the capillaries into the alveoli. Air diffuses across the membrane from an area of higher concentration to an area of lower concentration. Thus diffusion of oxygen can occur when the concentration of oxygen in the alveoli is higher than in the capillary bed. Oxygen also diffuses from the peripheral capillaries into the tissues when the arterial oxygen concentration is higher than that in the tissues. Carbon dioxide diffuses quite readily, so hypercarbia due to impaired diffusion is unlikely.

Hypoxemia due to impaired diffusion across the alveolar membrane may occur, although it is rarely the sole respiratory abnormality. Increased interstitial fluid, which increases the distance between the red cell membrane in the pulmonary capillary and the alveolus, is the most frequent cause of impaired diffusion.

Perfusion

The perfusion of the blood through the pulmonary capillaries and the body is an essential part of the respiratory process. The primary determinant is the cardiac output, with other influencing factors being the blood volume, pressures within the pulmonary and systemic circuits, and the pulmonary vascular resistance. The permeability of the pulmonary capillary also affects perfusion and other respiratory processes. When either capillary permeability or hydrostatic pressure is increased, fluid moves from the vascular space into the interstitial fluid spaces and alveoli and results in decreased perfusion; this is referred to as pulmonary edema.

The distribution of the blood flow within the lungs is largely determined by gravity with greater perfusion in the dependent areas of the lungs. Thus, with decreased cardiac output and hypotension, the apices of the lung are frequently underperfused. It has already been said that air is unevenly distributed within the lung, and greater ventilatory volume goes to the apices in an erect person. Since perfusion is greater to the dependent portions of the lung, an imbalance between ventilation and perfusion can exist. The relationship of ventilation to perfusion is expressed as the alveolar ventilation–perfusion ratio ($\dot{V}/\dot{Q}$). Normally the average alveolar ventilation is 4 liters minute and the perfusion is 5 liters/minute, giving a $\dot{V}/\dot{Q}$ of 0.8. When the ratio of dead space (combined anatomic and alveolar) to tidal volume (V_D/V_T) increases, the $\dot{V}/\dot{Q}$ is greater than 0.8—indicating ventilation without adequate perfusion. The ventilation–perfusion ratio is less than 0.8 when the lungs are perfused but there is inadequate ventilation. This $\dot{V}/\dot{Q}$ imbalance is referred to as right to left physiologic shunting or venous–arterial admixture because a portion of the blood circulating through the lungs returns to the left side of the heart without picking up oxygen. Anatomic shunts from congenital or posttraumatic lesions also cause $\dot{V}/\dot{Q}$ imbalance, but their effect is constant rather than a changed state.

Disturbances in any of these respiratory processes require compensatory mechanisms which increase the work of breathing and thereby oxygen consumption. If the problem becomes more severe, or the extent of the compensation decreases, the carbon dioxide in the arterial blood increases and the oxygen decreases with resulting respiratory insufficiency or failure. Table 4-1 lists some of the major clinical states, both acute and chronic, associated with altered respiratory functioning.

Discussion of all these disorders is not within the scope of this book, but because of its complexity and high mortality, the acute respiratory failure termed adult respiratory distress syndrome (ARDS) will be briefly discussed. Many conditions in which respiratory insufficiency is secondary to an acute insult to the lung are now commonly considered under the heading of ARDS. Some of the pathologic states responsible for the syndrome are referred to as shock lung, traumatic wet lung, pump lung, and septic lung. The pulmonary changes in these disorders are probably caused by blood-borne vasoactive substances (catecholamines, serotonin, histamine, bradykinin, etc.) and/or lysosomal enzymes released from damaged, necrotic, or infected tissues. These substances alter the function and structure of pulmonary arterioles, veins, and capillaries. Other major causes of ARDS are fat emboli, particulate emboli from multiple transfusions, disseminated intravascular coagulapathy (DIC), aspiration, pulmonary infections, toxins, fluid overload, oxygen toxicity, immunologic reactions, and cerebral hypoxia with resultant pulmonary constriction. In many cases, two or more of these are present.

In spite of the diverse etiology, the respiratory pathophysiologic derangement and clinical characteristics follow essentially the same pattern. The major sequential changes that occur are damage to the pulmonary capillary membrane with fluid moving from the capillaries into the interstitial spaces; this increases interstitial edema which in turn decreases lung compliance and oxygen diffusion. As the pulmonary capillaries become further damaged, red blood cells may

TABLE 4-1. Major Respiratory Alterations

Abnormal Initiating Mechanism	Pathophysiology	Clinical State
I. Difficulty in maintaining adequate volume of inspired air	Interference with volume of air inspired during normal respiratory effort. Many cases will have hypercapnia (high P_{CO_2}) and respiratory acidosis. If able to increase respiratory effort and increase minute alveolar ventilation, may have normal (or even low) P_{CO_2}.	
A. Upper airway obstruction or constriction	Obstruction to flow of air in epiglottis, larynx, or trachea. Effects are same as lower airway obstruction.	Foreign body, acute epiglottis, laryngospasm/edema
B. Lower airway obstruction or constriction	Obstruction to flow of air in the bronchi, bronchioles, and/or alveoli resulting in increased work of breathing. If body tires or is unable to increase the respiratory effort, will have low tidal volume with inadequate air to dependent areas of the lung, or to the area beyond the obstructive process.	Asthma, emphysema, bronchitis, pulmonary tuberculosis, bronchospasm
C. Loss of mechanical integrity	Limited ability to increase the size of the thorax with inspiration, with resultant inadequate tidal volume due to: Anatomic defects Injury to nerves or muscles	Kyphoscoliosis, spinal arthritis Post abdominal and thoracic surgery
	Presence of air or blood within the pleural cavity.	Pneumothorax, hemothorax, pleural effusion
	Upward displacement of the diaphragm by the pressure of abdominal contents.	Gastric dilation, ascites, obesity
D. Alteration in sensitivity of the respiratory center	Depression of the respiratory center with inadequate tidal volume to eliminate the carbon dioxide produced by the body processes.	Myxedema coma; drug depression by: anesthetics, sedatives, narcotics, curare
	Excessive deposition of fat with obesity increases work of breathing, resulting in fatigue, somnolence, and sleep apnea.	Primary alveolar hypoventilation (when occurring with obesity, referred to as Pickwickian syndrome)
	With chronic hypercapnia, respiratory center becomes less sensitive to the stimulus of an increase in P_{CO_2}, and oxygen lack is only stimulus. Administration of oxygen raises P_{O_2} to normal levels, suppressing the mechanism of low oxygen that stimulates respiration.	Iatrogenic administration of excessive oxygen to patient with chronic hypercapnia
	Ventilatory compensation for metabolic alkalosis is manifested by a decrease in the respiratory rate and depth in order to conserve CO_2	Metabolic alkalosis

(continued)

TABLE 4-1.   Continued

Abnormal Initiating Mechanism	Pathophysiology	Clinical State
E. Neurologic and neuromuscular dysfunction		
1. Central nervous system disorders	Damage or disease of the respiratory integrating neurons in the medulla causes an irregularity in the respiratory rate and rhythm which can progress to apnea	Head injury, cranial lesion, cranial infection
2. Peripheral disorders	Skeletal muscles of the diaphragm, chest wall, abdomen, and neck become weakened or paralyzed by neurologic disorders that affect the neuromuscular system or by diseases of the striated muscles. The result is hypoventilation due to inadequate muscular contraction. Affected sites are:	
	Disorders of the anterior horn cell and peripheral nerves.	Poliomyelitis, Guillain-Barré syndrome, aminoglycoside antibiotic intake, amyotrophic lateral sclerosis
	Disorders of the myoneural junction	Myasthenia gravis, botulism, tetanus, polymyositis, muscular dystrophies, myotonia
	Lesions of the spinal conduction pathways.	High cervical trauma, acute myelitis
II. Inadequate oxygenation in the lungs	Some areas of the lung are perfused but there is no ventilation, so have right-to-left shunting and hypoxemia, since the blood that leaves the lung from the pulmonary veins is not oxygenated. If able to compensate by hyperventilation, the initial manifestation may be respiratory alkalosis. Respiratory acidosis is an indication that the condition is severe or inability to compensate.	
A. Interference with gas exchange in the alveoli	Causes of impaired alveolar functioning are the following:	
	Invasion of interstitial spaces or alveolar spaces by edema, acid gastric contents, lipid substances, inhaled chemically active or immunogenic particles, vasoactive substances, proteolytic enzymes, fibrous tissue, granuloma, or tumor cells. The foreign substances stimulate inflammatory processes with release of substances damaging to the membranes and resulting in an infiltrative response.	Pulmonary edema, massive fibrosis, granulomatosis, lymphangitic metastasis, pulmonary aspiration of gastric contents, sarcoidosis, hypersensitivity pneumonitis, acute pancreatitis

(continued)

TABLE 4-1. Continued

Abnormal Initiating Mechanism	Pathophysiology	Clinical State
	Retention of secretions in the alveoli and bronchioles. When secretions completely obstruct an airway, the air beyond the obstruction is gradually absorbed into the blood stream and the alveoli collapse.	Atelectasis secondary to pulmonary infiltrative disorders listed above and states that decrease efficiency of secretion removal. Contributing factors are decreased surfactant and inhalation of high concentrations of oxygen, with loss of nitrogen skeleton.
	Disruption of exchange of gas in the alveoli by exudate from infectious process.	Pneumonia
	Damage to bronchial epithelium by inhalation of hot gases, resulting in edema and sometimes bronchospasm.	Thermal injury
	Severe damage to alveolar capillary membrane (from any of above or as a result of other system disorders), with leakage of fluid and cellular components into the interstitial spaces and eventually the alveoli.	Adult respiratory distress syndrome
B. Anatomic shunt	Diversion of the flow of blood within the cardiac and pulmonary circulation so a portion of the cardiac output bypasses the lungs and is not oxygenated.	Arteriovenous fistula, atrial and ventricular septal defects, transposition of aorta and pulmonary artery
III. Disorders of perfusion	Impaired blood flow to the lung (or portion thereof) due to arterial obstruction or pathological changes in the arteries that interfere with the flow of blood.	Pulmonary embolus, fat embolism, primary pulmonary hypertension, scleroderma
	Inadequate cardiac output due to mechanical or electrical conduction disorders results in reduction of blood flow through both pulmonary and tissue capillaries, with inadequate supply of oxygen on the tissues.	Left ventricular failure, Shock: hypovolemic, cardiogenic, septic; cardiac tamponade, heart block, dysrhythmias
IV. Alteration in transport of oxygen to tissues	Reduction in oxygen-carrying capacity of the blood due to:	
	Deficiency of hemoglobin	Severe anemia
	Alteration of hemoglobin by toxic agents	Methemoglobinemia, carbon monoxide inhalation
	Reduction in dissociation of oxygen from hemoglobin at the tissue level.	Metabolic alkalosis, hypothermia, deficiency of 2,3-DPG: multiple transfusions of stored blood; sepsis
V. Reduction in availability of oxygen	Deficient oxygenation of the arterial blood due to:	
	Interruption of flow of gas to lungs	Asphyxiation
	Insufficient O_2 in inspired air	High altitude sickness

(continued)

TABLE 4-1. Continued

Abnormal Initiating Mechanism	Pathophysiology	Clinical State
VI. Hyperpnea without hypoxemia		
A. Primary	Hyperventilation blows off CO_2, resulting in a respiratory alkalosis with a P_{CO_2} less than 35 torr and a pH greater than 7.45. Causes include:	
	Direct stimulation of respiratory center from:	
	Central neurogenic hyperventilation	Lesion of upper pontine or low midbrain structure, secondary brainstem compression, brainstem hemorrhage
	Stimulus to respiratory center and inhibition of enzymatic processes from endotoxin release.	Sepsis
	Intake of salicylate	Salicylate poisoning
	Impaired cerebral metabolism due to:	
	Deficiency of the substrate, glucose	Severe hypoglycemia
	Ammonia and other toxic nitrogenous substances.	Hepatic insufficiency
	Psychogenic stimulation of the autonomic nervous system increases respiratory rate.	Anxiety state, anxiety neurosis, hyperventilation syndrome
B. Compensatory	State of metabolic acidosis initiates compensatory mechanisms to return the acid-base state toward normal by blowing off CO_2.	Diabetic ketoacidosis, uremia
	Hyperventilation in response to increased metabolic oxygen requirement.	Fever, strenuous exercise, status epilepticus

migrate into the interstitial spaces and fluid moves from the interstitial spaces into the alveoli, which inactivates the surfactant and causes progressive atelectasis. Infection frequently develops due to ease of bacterial growth in alveolar fluid with atelectasis.

Clinical changes are usually absent initially, with tachypnea and hypoxemia the first signs. As hyperventilation increases, hypocapnia as well as hypoxemia is present, and perfusion without ventilation in areas of collapsed or fluid-filled alveoli results in physiologic shunting. The functional residual capacity is markedly decreased. If treatment is not initiated before the development of frank respiratory failure, the damage to the lungs is so severe that recovery is doubtful. Details on the methods of assessment of these changes are included in the next section.

ASSESSMENT

Since so many disorders can result in respiratory impairment, the assessment process can be lengthy. This book will focus primarily on the parameters for which the nurse has some responsibility as well as those that are most helpful in determining the cause and extent of an acute disorder.

History

Items of special importance include occupational, personal, genetic, and previous health disorders. Occupational history is directed toward documentation of exposure to coal, silica, asbestos, oxides of iron, titanium, iron, etc. Location of previous residence can implicate coccidiomycosis or histoplasmosis. Personal habits of tobacco consumption and family history of genetic disorders or tuberculosis are helpful.

Information should be obtained on the presence of symptoms of cough, dyspnea, or chest pain. If cough has been present, a detailed description may assist in the diagnosis. It must be remembered that dyspnea is a subjective symptom of difficulty in breathing. It may be described by the patient as shortness of breath, uncomfortable breathing, or the sensation of difficult or labored breathing. Not every patient who appears to have labored breathing, however, has dyspnea. A patient with chronic obstructive pulmonary disease (COPD) may appear to be having difficulty breathing, but when asked to validate if it was hard to breathe, a negative response might be received. If dyspnea is confirmed, it helps to identify the disorder as functional (occurring with rest) or secondary to cardiac or pulmonary disease (occurring with exercise). Chest pain can be caused by inflammation of the pleura, in which case it is usually localized to one side of the chest and related to movements of the thorax and respiration. Pleuritic pain needs to be differentiated from pain arising from disorders of the heart, aorta, or esophagus, and from referred pain from nerve or muscle disorders.

Physical Examination

Observation, palpation, percussion, and auscultation are included. Observation provides the most helpful information about the presence and extent of respiratory alterations. Some alterations may be compensatory. Alterations that can be observed include:

Change in respiratory rate. This is one of the earliest indicators of a developing problem. Tachypnea is usually a homeostatic response to hypoxemia or hypercarbia. The increased respiratory rate, by increasing minute ventilation, may, at least initially, compensate for the disorder so no other abnormality may be present. The cause for tachypnea, therefore, should always be investigated. When increased respiratory rate is accompanied by an increased depth of respiration (hyperpnea), the underlying cause may be metabolic acidosis (due to diabetic coma, uremia, or ingested organic acids) or hyperventilation from central neurogenic causes or from acute anoxia, hepatic coma, or sepsis. Bradypnea may result from administration of narcotics or sedatives, central nervous system disorders, metabolic alkalosis, or from the administration of high oxygen concentrations to patients with COPD. Since the respiratory center in these persons has lost its sensitivity to hypercarbia, hypoxemia is their only respiratory stimulus. When oxygen is supplied in amounts to eradicate the hypoxemia, respirations may become extremely slow or cease altogether.

Decrease in cognitive functioning.   Euphoria, irritability, restlessness, anxiety, and/or delirium usually accompanies the acute development of hypoxemia. Mental cloudiness and apathy are signs of increasing hypercapnia.

Respiratory effort.   The effort needed for respiration is an important assessment parameter. Signs of increased effort are flaring of nares and opening of mouth with inspiration, visible retraction of the intercostal and supraclavicular structures, use of accessory muscles such as the sternocleidomastoid and abdominal, inability to talk except during expiration (staccato speech), pursing of lips during expiration, presence of wheeze during either inspiration or expiration, and absence of bilateral chest expansion.

Respiratory pattern alterations.   These are usually a reflection of neurologic damage. Progressive rostral (head) to caudal impairment of brain-stem function is accompanied by sequential respiratory abnormalities changing from periodic respiration to ataxic breathing. Any deviations from the regular, rhythmic movements of respiration should be noted and carefully described. A decrease in the ratio of inspiration to expiration should also be noted. Ideally, inspiration is twice as long as expiration, when the process becomes equal or reversed, airway obstruction is probably present.

Volume measurements.   Measurement is essential when any respiratory disorder exists. Pulmonary studies are necessary for accurate diagnosis of many disorders, especially chronic obstructive respiratory states. Acute volume changes which can be measured at the bedside by the nurse are the tidal volume and the vital capacity. A respiratory spirometer is required. To measure the tidal volume, the patient is asked to hold the mouth piece between his lips and breathe normally through his mouth. A nose clip may sometimes be used to assure mouth breathing. The usual procedure is to activate the "on" switch after the patient has taken five or six breaths, since it is difficult to breathe normally when you are thinking about it. Greater accuracy is achieved when the volume of 10 breaths is measured without interruption, with the registered total volume divided by 10 to obtain the volume of one breath. Normally tidal volume is 7 ml/kg; less than 5 ml/kg is a cause for concern. Low volume may be adequate if the patient has been able to increase his respiratory rate to maintain adequate minute alveolar ventilation. Because the dead space volume is increased with higher respiratory rates, actual ventilation for the patient will need to be computed.

The vital capacity is the volume of air that can be exhaled after a maximal inspiration. Usually the patient is asked to do the activity three times, with the highest volume being the one recorded. There is a wide range between normal values (2–6 liters in adults depending on age) and dangerous levels, but a vital capacity less than 1 liter is serious.

Cyanosis.   This is not a reliable indicator of early hypoxemia. Presence of cyanosis is difficult to detect in the black patient, and its development varies with amount of hemoglobin and capillary circulatory factors as well as with the oxygen saturation. With normal hemoglobin levels and capillary circulation, cyanosis develops when the arterial oxygen saturation drops to 80 percent. With normal acid–base level and temperature, this level of oxygen saturation is indicative of severe hypoxemia with a partial tension of oxygen in the arterial blood of 50 torr. Thus, cyanosis is not a reliable early assessment parameter.

Palpation.   Confirmation of differences between excursions of the two sides of the chest that were noted by observation can be palpated. Detection of mediastinal shift and evaluation of tactile fremitus, which are not usually the responsibility of the nurse, are covered in all physical assessment books.

Percussion.   This helps to detect the presence of pleural fluid, free pleural air (as in pneumothorax), and consolidation of the lung parenchyma, as with pneumonia or atelectasis. When percussion cannot be accomplished in the upright position, the patient should be turned from side to side to compensate for the position. Although hyperresonant sounds indicate air and dull or flat sounds indicate consolidation or fluid-filled tissue, a great deal of practice is required to become proficient in exact identification of the responsible disorder.

Auscultation.   Information about abnormal breath sounds, rales, and rhonchi is obtained by auscultation. Normally breath sounds are heard over the entire lung field, with little sound during expiration, termed vesicular sounds. When tissue is consolidated, the sounds transmitted to the periphery are of the bronchial type, which are harsher and higher pitched, and are heard during both inspiration and expiration, with a short silent gap. The finding of rales (usually heard only during inspiration) is indicative of fluid or mucous in either the small or large airways. Clearance with coughing may be indicative of minimal atelectasis. Rales due to congestion do not generally clear with coughing. Rhonchi which have a rumbling sound occur with a narrowing of the airways. They may clear with coughing and are more frequent during expiration, although they may be present throughout the respiratory cycle. Some inaudible wheezes can be heard with auscultation. Wheezes are caused by a high velocity flow of air through restricted air passages of the lower airways. With bronchospasm, wheezing may be present during inspiration as well as expiration. Wheezing in a patient with COPD is only heard at end expiration. Obstruction of the upper airway is characterized by inspiratory stridor. In adults, inspiratory stridor does not usually develop until the laryngeal or tracheal lumen is at least 70 percent obstructed, so it is an indication that immediate action is required. Breath sounds are decreased or absent with pneumothorax and severe atelectasis.

Palpation, percussion, and auscultation are used infrequently for detailed assessment of respiratory status in hospital settings since X-ray and blood gas analysis are so readily accessible. Obviously, greater reliance is placed on these assessments out of the hospital.

Tests

Chest x-ray. Roentgenographic examination of the chest is the most definitive tool to establish the existence of moderate or severe atelectasis, pneumonia, pneumothorax, pulmonary aspiration, and mediastinal shifts. The presence of interstitial fluid, mild atelectasis, and early ARDS, however, may not be detectable. Standing films are superior to portable ones. When portable X-ray is necessary, the patient should be positioned as upright as possible. Although interpretation of roentgenographic films has not been the responsibility of the nurse, many nurses in intensive care areas have contributed to the care of their patients by detection of improper positioning of the endotracheal tube, presence of a pneumothorax, or an increase in density indicative of atelectasis or consolidation in lung areas that appeared normal on previous films.

Sputum. Gram stain, culture, and sensitivity should be obtained whenever pulmonary infection is suspected. Sputum induction and transtracheal aspiration may be indicated for some patients.

Arterial blood gas and pH. These studies are essential for determination of the presence, nature, and extent of respiratory insufficiency and the appropriate management. Respiratory insufficiency is the term used here for combined respiratory acidosis (ventilatory insufficiency with impaired elimination of carbon dioxide) and hypoxemia (impaired oxygen supply to the tissues). Although the term respiratory insufficiency in some literature may be used when only one of the conditions exists, it is more helpful to identify the specific impairment since different management is indicated (i.e., respiratory acidosis or hypoxemia). Interpretation of blood gas and pH values is rather complex. Some values that are outside the normal range may actually be the result of normal compensatory processes. When COPD results in a chronic elevation of carbon dioxide in the blood, interpretation is difficult without serial studies. The interpretation of blood gas values should also take into account the variables that decrease the availability of oxygen to the tissues, since oxygen availability is not synonymous with partial tension of oxygen in the arterial blood. These factors will be briefly discussed, with the focus of the discussion primarily on acute or abrupt changes in the blood gas values. As with most altered body states, a systematic ordered approach as outlined below (and used in the decision tree for respiratory insufficiency) will help to reduce errors. The beginning nurse would not be expected to be proficient in assessment of complex disorders, but some advanced concepts are presented for the nurse desiring to increase her basic skills.

The pH should be examined first. It is a measure of the hydrogen ion activity. Different values can be found for the normal range, with 7.35−7.45 probably the most commonly accepted range. When the pH is less than 7.35, the patient is said to have acidemia; when it is greater than 7.45, he has alkalemia. Since the acid-base state can be altered by both metabolic and respiratory disorders, the next step is to look at the P_{CO_2} to ascertain the nature of the disorder.

The P_{CO_2} is a measure of the partial pressure of carbon dioxide in the blood. In respiratory texts, it is usually written Pa_{CO_2} to show that it is the partial pressure of CO_2 in arterial blood. Since arterial blood is commonly used in hospitals, the symbol is usually shortened to P_{CO_2}. The normal range is generally considered to be 35−45 torr. The unit of measurement in some tests may be millimeters of mercury (mmHg) rather than torr. For accuracy in interpretation, however, the pressure should be corrected for altitude, and torr is a unit of pressure equal to 1/760 of an atmosphere. The P_{CO_2} is an indicator of alveolar ventilation. With hyperventilation, CO_2 is blown off, and the P_{CO_2} is less than 35 torr. With hypoventilation, CO_2 is retained and, P_{CO_2} rises above 45 torr. P_{CO_2} needs to be looked at in relation to the acid-base state previously determined. In the patient with acidemia, the acidemia is respiratory when the P_{CO_2} is elevated above 45 torr; the acidemia is metabolic when the P_{CO_2} is less than 45 torr (termed metabolic acidosis). In the patient with alkalemia, the alkalemia is respiratory when the P_{CO_2} is less than 35 torr (respiratory alkalosis); the alkalemia is metabolic when the P_{CO_2} is greater than 35 torr (metabolic alkalosis). Respiratory alkalosis occurs with hyperventilation and is frequently due to early sepsis, anxiety, early pulmonary embolus, or overventilation on a mechanical respirator. Respiratory acidosis is caused by hypoventilation from numerous disorders; the most frequent causes are neurologic disease or depression, respiratory muscle disease, and acute disorders imposed on a patient with COPD. When the P_{CO_2} is greater than 50 torr in a patient with previous normal values, the patient is said to be in ventilatory failure. A patient can have a metabolic acidosis superimposed on an existing respiratory acidosis. This is manifested by elevation of the P_{CO_2} above 45 torr but with a decrease of the pH to less than 7.3 and a low bicarbonate. It is important to note that although respiratory acidosis is present in the later stages of many alveolar, interstitial, or vascular lesions of the lungs and in terminal ARDS, metabolic acidosis with a normal or even low P_{CO_2} is frequently present in the earlier stages as a result of compensatory hyperventilation. When someone with metabolic acidosis develops an elevated P_{CO_2}, it is a sign of severe pulmonary insufficiency. It is also important to realize the effect of metabolic alkalosis on respiration. The body's compensatory response to alkalemia is conservation of acid. Thus patients with metabolic alkalosis hypoventilate. The presence of elevation of the three parameters (pH, P_{CO_2}, and HCO_3^-) indicates that the acid−base state requires prompt intervention to prevent further respiratory depression. In ARDS, elevation of the P_{CO_2} above 45 torr is a grave sign, indi-

cating that there are so few perfused functioning capillaries in the lung parenchyma that CO_2 cannot be eliminated even by hyperventilation.

Bicarbonate (HCO_3^-) and/or base excess (B.E.). These values in a patient
with abnormal Pco_2 values are helpful in determining if there is an underlying
metabolic acidosis or if the problem has existed long enough that compensation
by renal conservation or excretion of bicarbonate has taken place. Normal
HCO_3^- is $22-26$ mEq/liter. Some laboratories may use B.E. which is calculated
from the predicted bicarbonate. Normal B.E. is -2 to $+2$ mEq/liter. Base excess
of less than -2 correlates with a low bicarbonate and metabolic acidosis.

The PO_2 is a measure of the partial pressure of oxygen in the arterial blood.
It is an indication of the tissue oxygen state, but it does not always accurately
reflect tissue oxygenation. The inspired O_2 concentration ($F_{I_{O_2}}$) should always be
reported with the Po_2. The normal range varies with age and a number of other
lesser factors. Normal range for a person under 30 years of age who is breathing
room air ($F_{I_{O_2}}$ 0.21) is generally considered to be 85 to 100 torr. After 30 years of
age, the Po_2 falls 3 or 4 torr per decade, so a healthy person of 80 years would
have an expected arterial Po_2 between 65 and 75 torr. Many healthy persons,
however, have been found to consistently have Po_2 values less than predicted for
their age, so normal ranges cannot be rigidly applied in the assessment process.
Hypoxemia is generally considered to be present in a patient under 65 years with
a Po_2 less than 70 torr, and oxygenation failure with a Po_2 less than 55 to 60 torr.

Assessment of variables is necessary to determine the adequacy of tissue
oxygenation accurately in a patient with a low Po_2. Oxygen is more strongly
bound to hemoglobin and is less available to the tissues with alkalosis, hypothermia, and deficiency of 2,3-Diphosphoglycerate (2,3-DPG). Administration of
stored blood which is low in 2,3-DPG, and sepsis which decreases the concentration of 2,3-DPG result in less oxygen being released. Conversely acidosis and
heat, and an increase in 2,3-DPG makes the hemoglobin give up its oxygen more
readily. The combined effect of these three variables on dissociation of oxygen
from hemoglobin is referred to as the Bohr effect. All respiratory texts contain
a drawing of the oxyhemoglobin dissociation curve which is the basis of compu-
tation of oxygen saturation. The percent of oxygen saturation is a measure of
the amount of oxygen combined with hemoglobin. With a Po_2 of 60 torr previously given as an indicator of oxygenation failure, the corresponding oxygen
concentration with normal pH, temperature, and 2,3-DPG is 90%. Most laboratories no longer report oxygen concentration, but supply the raw values and
then a correction for temperature and pH.

In addition to the variables that affect the dissociation of oxygen from hemoglobin, the amount of oxygen available to the tissue is also affected by the
concentration of hemoglobin and the cardiac output. Since oxygen is primarily
carried combined with hemoglobin, a reduction of hemoglobin to 10 gm/100 ml
will reduce the oxygen content available to the tissues by a third. This factor
needs to be taken into account when analyzing blood gases since the values of Po_2
and oxygen saturation are not affected by concentration of hemoglobin and can
be well within normal levels.

Adequate cardiac output is necessary to transport the oxygen to the tissues. To a certain extent, when the heart is able to increase the cardiac output and the hemoglobin is normal, a borderline low Po_2 may be tolerated relatively well. A combination of low Po_2 and low hemoglobin, and low cardiac output, however, is associated with a high mortality.

Mixed venous Po_2.   This is drawn from a pulmonary artery catheter and is helpful in assessment. The Po_2 of mixed venous blood should be between 35 and 40 torr. When venous Po_2 drops below 30, the gradient is not high enough at the capillaries distant from the mitochondria in the tissue cells for the tissues to extract adequate oxygen. Mixed venous Po_2 below 30 torr is a grave prognostic sign.

Calculation of the physiologic shunting in the lung (Q_S/Q_T).   This provides the most sensitive information on the severity of ARDS. It is measured by comparing oxygen content of arterial blood and of mixed venous blood (drawn from a pulmonary artery catheter) with the maximum oxygen content that could be present with the FI_{O_2} used. Initially Q_S/Q_T was measured with 100 percent oxygen ($FI_{O_2} = 1.0$). Since the high FI_{O_2} can itself increase shunting, the measurement now is usually made on FI_{O_2} of 0.4 or 0.6. Normal Q_S/Q_T should be less than 5 percent at bedrest. Values greater than 15 percent are considered abnormal. A rough estimate of physiologic shunting can be made by estimating the expected Po_2 by multiplying the percentage of oxygen by 6. Thus a patient on 40 percent oxygen would be expected to have a Po_2 of 40×6 or 240 torr. If the patient's actual Po_2 was lower than 204 torr (15 percent less than 240), the patient has more shunting than normal. If more exact information about the extent of the shunting is needed, calculation of the Q_S/Q_T would be indicated.

Since the correlation between assessment findings and underlying pathophysiology is complex, the basic knowledge that is essential for the beginning nurse will be briefly summarized in the following paragraphs.

An increase in the respiratory rate may be a sign of a psychologic disorder or of compensation for a metabolic acidosis, but is more frequently an indication of a developing respiratory problem. The increased respiratory rate may be the only early measurable abnormality, but if the underlying cause is not corrected, other parameters will be altered.

Initially the respiratory problem may be due primarily to inadequate ventilation or inadequate oxygenation. If the Pco_2 with tachypnea has increased over previous levels, the problem is inadequate ventilation. Essentially, the tidal volume is not large enough to provide adequate air supply to the alveoli so the respiratory rate is increased in an effort to provide greater minute alveolar ventilation. With shallow breathing (low tidal volumes), dead space ventilation may consume most of the increase, with alveolar hypoventilation and carbon dioxide retention resulting. The underlying cause can be an obstructive disorder of the airways or interference with the ability to breathe deeply (surgical incision, depression of respiratory center, neuromuscular disease, etc.). When the Pco_2 becomes moderately or severely elevated, the Po_2 will be lowered; this can be easily restored to normal levels by oxygen administration. The elevated P_{CO_2} can only be corrected by measures that increase alveolar ventilation.

If the abnormal parameter is a reduction in P_{O_2} with a normal or low P_{CO_2}, the problem is inadequate oxygenation. The respiratory rate (and usually the depth) is increased in response to the need for oxygen and this hyperventilation results in a lowered P_{CO_2} and respiratory alkalosis. The underlying causes are disorders that interfere with diffusion and perfusion such as infiltrative diseases of the lung, pulmonary vascular disorders, and disorders of other body systems that result in pulmonary dysfunction. This deficiency requires measures to increase the oxygen supply to the tissues.

Depression of the respiratory rate may be due to a central nervous system disorder or as a compensatory mechanism to metabolic alkalosis. If not corrected, it can result in both hypercarbia and hypoxemia.

Although initially most respiratory disorders are characterized by either ventilatory or oxygenation inadequacy, in end stage disorders, both are present. The methods for correction of these abnormalities will be discussed in the next section.

INTERVENTION

Knowledge of the nature and extent of the respiratory disorder gained from assessment will guide the intervention. As with all disorders, underlying states such as sepsis, necrotic tissue, heart failure and DIC require treatment in addition to management of the respiratory problem. The ordering of the intervention also would depend on the nature of the disorder. Some of the major overall goals and activities for their accomplishment are briefly discussed. The goal statement would need to be made more specific for the individual patient, based on the exact nature of the problem.

Maintenance of an Open Airway

Occlusion of the airway. This is caused by the tongue in states of reduced consciousness; it may be corrected by turning the patient on his side with his face down. If this is contraindicated or ineffective, use the sniffing position and, if required, an oral airway. To place the patient in the sniffing position, a folded bath blanket 3 or 4 inches thick should be placed under the patient's head to flex the neck. Then the head is extended at the junction of the spine and skull by moving the chin up and back. This is the position instinctively assumed by a long distance runner and is described more fully in the book by Applebaum and Bruce.

Laryngeal or subglottic edema. This may be minimized by the administration of humidified oxygen, antihistamines, steroids, and nebulized epinephrine. Intubation may be necessary and the patient should be placed in the sniffing position for the procedure. The procedure should be explained to conscious patients and a topical anesthetic such as Cetacaine spray should be used.

Bronchospasm. This can be controlled by the use of a bronchodilator. It is important to remember that asthma (which can occur in a patient with normal lungs) can result in as severe a state of respiratory insufficiency as gross pulmonary pathology. In acute disorders, intravenous epinephrine, isoproterenol, or aminophylline is used. Corticosteroids may also be used. In chronic obstructive airway disorders, aerosolized isoetharine, metaproterenol, disodium cromoglycate, and oral terbutaline, aminophylline, or theophylline are utilized.

Foreign bodies. These should be removed by suctioning, use of forceps, bronchoscopy, sharp blow between the scapulae, or the Heimlich maneuver. When the foreign body cannot be removed, emergency tracheotomy may be performed.

Secretions. Clearing of secretions is probably the most frequently indicated and vital nursing intervention for airway obstruction. The method used depends on the patient's state. The following listing is arranged in order of decreasing patient participation.

• *Coughing* is the most effective method when the patient has a vital capacity of 15 ml/kg and the ability to contract his abdominal and diaphragmatic muscles. Coughing is productive when the volume of air is sufficient to penetrate the small airways, and the cough is forceful. A forceful cough results in an expiration that carries the secretions upward. The following steps will assist a patient to cough effectively:

1. Explain what will be done and the rationale.
2. Place the patient in an upright position.
3. If the patient has had abdominal or thoracic surgery, decrease discomfort by medication and the use of a pillow over the incision area.
4. If the mouth is dry, give fluids or mouth care.
5. Encourage the patient to take a maximal deep inspiration and hold it (count as patient inspires).
6. Instruct the patient to contract his abdominal muscles on the count of two. Application of sharp external abdominal pressure while "hugging" the patient from behind will often be helpful for this step.
7. On the count of three, instruct the patient to cough.
8. Offer container for mucus and encourage the patient to expectorate.

• *Postural drainage* with chest physiotherapy is indicated for the patient unable to cough. For localized collection of secretions, a number of positions to promote drainage of the various lung areas can be found in the literature. For postoperative and COPD patients, secretions tend to collect primarily at the base of the lungs and lowering of the head of the bed with the patient prone or on his side is usually the position of choice. Clapping (or percussion) may be done over the entire lung field, but is especially helpful at the lung bases. Vibration, which is difficult to do correctly without a great deal of practice, should be done only with expiration. After postural drainage, the patient should be assisted to cough to bring up secretions that have been loosened and moved to the larger airways by gravity.

● *Suctioning* may be required for the patient who cannot get rid of his secretions even with postural drainage. Effectiveness of suctioning also depends on use of proper technique.

1. Preferably, position the patient sitting upright or at a 45 degree angle with the head tilted backward and the chin extended.

2. Wearing sterile gloves, introduce a sterile lubricated catheter with thumb control for suction at a slight downward slant into nostril.

3. When the catheter is in the nasopharynx (approximately the distance from the tip of the nose to the ear), ask the patient to stick out his tongue and pant. If the patient is unable to cooperate, a second person may be required to grab the tongue with a gauze sponge and pull it forward. Panting (or coughing) causes the glottis to retract and allows passage of catheter into trachea.

4. Advance the catheter down the bronchus as far as it will go.

5. If secretions are dry, instill 3–5 ml of sterile saline into the catheter.

6. Apply suction as the catheter is slowly withdrawn to the main bronchus. Limit suction to 10 seconds.

7. Supply oxygen as indicated before successive suctioning activity.

● *Bronchoscopy* may be required for the removal of excessive secretions and matter not removed by suctioning.

● *Intubation* may be necessary for control of secretions in a few patients. Proper positioning of the endotracheal tube to prevent slipping into the right bronchus is important. Obstruction of the tube can be caused by biting, kinking, as well as clogging with mucus; these problems should be anticipated and prevented. Long-term management may include a tracheotomy.

Maintenance of an Adequate Volume of Inspired Gas

Periodic deep breathing. This helps reopen alveoli that have been partially closed by atelectasis. Somnolent patients may require both tactile and verbal stimulation to arouse them before cooperation is secured. The use of an inspiratory incentive spirometer provides feedback to the patient about his inspiratory volume. Adequate instruction and the opportunity for surgical patients to practice in the preoperative period usually increases the patient's cooperation. To be effective, the volume of air inspired has to be sufficient to fill the airways.

Patients with a vital capacity of less than 800 or 900 ml will benefit very little from the treatment. Vital capacity can be roughly measured by the markings on the incentive spirometer. In borderline cases, a respiratory spirometer should be used. Vital capacity can sometimes be increased by appropriate measures.

Lower abdominal and thoracic surgical patients have a 50 percent reduction in their vital capacity postoperatively; this reduction continues for 72 hours. Upper gastric surgery patients have up to 75 percent reduction during the same period. Appropriate use of multiple small doses of pain medication, splinting the wound with a pillow, and positioning may limit the reduction. Elevation of the head usually increases vital capacity since the abdominal viscera are not exerting pressure on the diaphragm.

Greater volumes of air may be inspired if the patient is encouraged to expel all his air before he inhales. Pursing of lips and audible sighing with expiration may be helpful. Only one deep breath should be taken at a time, with two or three regular respirations intervening before a second deep breath. When several deep breaths are taken in succession, the resulting hypocapnia causes cerebral vasoconstriction and possible cerebral anoxia. The patient should also be taught to pause at the end of inspiration to allow air to penetrate the airways before exhalation.

Prevention of abdominal distension.   Nasogastric suction to relieve distension eases breathing. The patency and proper functioning of a nasogastric tube needs frequent checking. Nonfunctioning tubes not only do not decrease the distension, but they can also be harmful since pharyngeal irritation may result in aspiration of vomited or regurgitated contents. Additionally, gastric contents can run along the side of the tube to the pharynx and larynx and be subsequently aspirated into the lungs.

Hyperinflation of lungs.   Use of a resuscitation bag to hyperinflate the lungs may be indicated for the patient who cannot inspire an adequate volume without assistance. If the patient is conscious, an explanation regarding the use of the bag is essential to avoid emotional trauma as well as to enlist the patient's cooperation. Asking the patient if he would be willing to have the treatment can increase his cooperation and effectiveness of the procedure. The patient can also be given more control over the situation by raising a finger as he exhales and is ready for the mask to be applied to his face. As with the incentive spirometer, the patient should only receive one lung hyperinflation at a time. The mask should be removed between deep breaths.

IPPB.   Intermittent positive pressure breathing is being used less frequently for alveolar hypoventilation. The major limitation is that application of pressure at the face level does not assure adequate inflation pressure at the site of the disease. It is probably effective for simple alveolar hypoventilation due to disorders or depression of the central and peripheral nervous system and respiratory muscles. Its effectiveness is decreased with respiratory pathophysiology since the decreased compliance requires greater pressures to deliver the same volume. Pressures of 40−50 cm/water may be required to deliver 800 ml. Most IPPB equipment does not generate pressures of this magnitude. Whenever IPPB is used, it should be evaluated by measurement of the actual volume delivered by a respiratory spirometer on the exhalation port. If the volume is less than 800 ml, the therapeutic effectiveness of the treatment is highly doubtful.

Mechanical ventilatory assistance.   This may be indicated for alveolar hypoventilation when it is accompanied by hypoxemia. It is discussed in a later section.

Slowing of respiratory rate.   Slowing will decrease the anatomic dead space to tidal volume ratio (V_D/V_Y). If increased depth results as a compensatory reaction, there will be a resulting increase in minute alveolar ventilation, with a decrease in the work of breathing (and the oxygen consumed for respiratory work). It is difficult to get the tachypneic patient to slow his respiratory rate voluntarily, since rapid breathing is a normal response to the body's perceived respiratory insufficiency. Behavior modification techniques and control of anxiety and apprehension may be successful with some patients.

Since morphine decreases the respiratory rate and has a minimal effect on the respiratory volume, it is sometimes used in small doses, with careful observation of its effect on the patient. It is important to remember that restlessness is a sign of hypoxia, and no depressant medication should be given for restlessness until the oxygenation state is determined.

Correction of Pleural Effusion.   To avoid limitation of lung expansion from pleural effusion, the effusion should be aspirated and, when possible, the underlying cause should be treated. Causes include inflammation, neoplasm, congestive heart failure and hypoalbuminemia.

Maintenance of Normal Distribution of Air

Normal distribution should be maintained throughout the lung fields. Any patient at risk for respiratory insufficiency who does not turn voluntarily should be turned every 2 or 3 hours around the clock. Severely ill patients may require even more frequent turning to prevent ventilation of the nondependent portions of the lung without perfusion, since the blood flow would be primarily to the dependent portions. Elevation of the head and chest produces the best overall ventilation−perfusion ratios throughout the lung.

Maintenance of Normal Diffusion

Diffusion across the alveolar membrane is important. Since interstitial fluid in the lung impairs diffusion, fluid restriction and diuretics are given to decrease the fluid gradually while maintaining an adequate intravascular volume for tissue perfusion. A slow progressive increase in the serum osmolarity to 320 mOsm/liter without hypotension or oliguria is an indication that fluid restriction is successful. Septic patients often require large amounts of fluid to maintain an adequate intravascular volume, and tolerate fluid restriction poorly.

Albumin and/or other colloids may be cautiously given for moderate to severe hypoproteinemia. With normal pulmonary capillary permeability, increasing the colloid osmotic pressure promotes movement of fluid from the interstitial space into the intravascular space. With damage to the capillary membrane, however, infused colloids are able to leave the intravascular space and enter the interstitial space, where they can exert an osmotic pull resulting in even greater volumes of fluid in the interstitial space. Thus the desirability of maintenance of colloid osmotic pressure is weighed against the severity of capillary membrane damage.

Corticosteroids in large doses may be effective in restoring the integrity of the cell membrane and slowing the inflammatory process. They are most effective with immume reactions, following thermal injuries, and after inhalation of irritating gases and/or chemicals.

Maintenance of Adequate Oxygenation.

Supplemental oxygen.   Oxygen may be required to maintain adequate tissue oxygenation. The goal for most patients is to maintain the Po_2 between 50 and 70 torr. Therapy is not directed toward restoration of the Po_2 to normal, since the oxyhemoglobin dissociation curve demonstrates that increasing Po_2 above 70 torr increases only minimally the hemoglobin saturation and total oxygen content of the arterial blood. Additionally, normal levels of Po_2 in the patient with chronic hypercapnia decreases the stimulus to respiration, as previously discussed. The two most common means of delivery of oxygen are nasal prongs and masks based on the Venturi principle.

Nasal prongs are generally better tolerated by the patient when a low flow rate of oxygen is needed. The disadvantages are that they are ineffective for mouth breathers and the F_{Io_2} the patient receives depends on the minute ventilation of the patient as well as liters per minute flow rate.

Venturi masks entrap air, which is mixed with the oxygen being delivered, to deliver accurate concentrations of oxygen up to F_{Io_2} 0.4. More precise concentrations of oxygen for both the mouth and nose breathers are supplied, but many patients cannot tolerate a mask over their nose and mouth. Any patient who requires oxygen by mask, but keeps removing the mask, should have nasal prongs in addition to the mask, since dangerous hypoxemia can develop within minutes of removal of oxygen adjunct. Inability to maintain adequate oxygenation may require ventilator therapy. This is discussed in a later section. If transfusions are necessary, the use of stored blood should be avoided since it lowers 2,3-DPG and makes it more difficult for hemoglobin to give up its oxygen at the tissue level. Severe anemia is corrected, with hemoglobin maintained at $10-12$ gm/100 ml.

Prevention of oxygen toxicity.   The use of high oxygen concentrations over a period of time injures the lungs; severe injury is generally irreversible. Although toxicity is affected by many variables, persons receiving an $F_{I_{O_2}}$ over 0.6 for 2 or more days are definitely at risk. Whenever possible, $F_{I_{O_2}}$ is kept at 0.4 or less. Of greater risk than inspired oxygen concentration, however, is the arterial P_{O_2}. When P_{O_2} exceeds 140 torr, oxygen toxicity can develop with concentrations less than 40 percent. There is some indication that high oxygen concentrations do not cause toxicity when the P_{O_2} is less than 70 torr. Thus, oxygen should not be withheld since hypoxia is a greater danger than oxygen toxicity. Reduced surfactant and the use of high inflation pressure increases the development of oxygen toxicity. Measures to prevent oxygen toxicity in ventilator patients who require high oxygen concentrations include intermittent lowering of the $F_{I_{O_2}}$, provision of adequate humidification by heated nebulization, administration of small quantities of an inert gas (as nitrogen) along with the oxygen, and reduction of pulmonary shunting. Shunting will be discussed in the next section.

Limitation or decrease in physiologic shunting.   Major overall activities are mechanical ventilatory assistance and improvement of tissue perfusion. When the physiologic shunt is 40 percent or more and other clinical or laboratory indicators of respiratory failure are present, mechanical ventilary assistance is indicated. Other laboratory indicators include an arterial P_{O_2} less than 60 torr (particularly if there is no improvement with O_2 adjunct by mask or prongs), and P_{CO_2} greater than 50 torr in patients with previously normal lung function and no metabolic alkalosis. Some clinical states may improve with early ventilatory assistance, even when ventilation and blood gases are relatively normal. Flail chest, generalized subdiaphragmatic peritonitis, massive smoke inhalation, and aspiration of gastric contents are instances in which early mechanical ventilation is beneficial. In addition to improving ventilation, a respirator can decrease oxygen requirements (by decreasing the work of the respiratory muscles) and also improve the distribution of the inspired gas. There is no agreement on the best protocol but a volume-cycled ventilator with intermittent mandatory ventilation (IMV) and positive end expiratory pressure (PEEP) has gained wide acceptance. The most frequently used management methods and the associated delegated and independent nursing activities will be briefly discussed.

●   *High tidal volumes* of 12−15 ml/kg are used for inflation of both small and large airways and distribution of gas to entire lung fields.

●   *Oxygen adjunct to maintain P_{O_2}* between 50 and 70 torr. Oxygen concentration is kept as low as possible to decrease O_2 toxicity and atelectasis. Since nitrogen is absorbed more slowly than oxygen, there is less alveolar collapse with air than with oxygen.

●   *Respiratory rate of 10−12/min initially* with the patient allowed to breathe on his own between ventilations through the IMV valve. This reduces the incidence of "fighting the respirator" while maintaining normal P_{CO_2}. Ventilatory rate is gradually decreased if tolerated to 6/minute or less. High ventilatory rates with large tidal volumes result in hypocapnia with respiratory alkalosis and cerebral vasoconstriction. When respirators without an IMV mode are used, a rapid respiratory rate may be reduced by administration of morphine or induction of respiratory paralysis with curare-like drugs. For these patients, the tidal volume is slightly lower (10–12 ml/kg) with intermittent sighs (deeper inspiratory volume) three or four times an hour.

- *Adequate humidification* of inspired gases is necessary to prevent drying of secretions and destruction of surfactant. Heating elements are used to supply the gas at the patient's body temperature, since water vapor per cubic meter of air is greater as the temperature is increased. The water reservoir requires refilling and the thermometer in the line to the patient needs to be checked to assure that gas is being delivered at body temperature.

- *Management of PEEP* to utilize the most effective pressure and prevent complications. PEEP increases the volume of air within the lungs at the end of respiration and thus prevents the transtracheal pressure from falling to zero during expiration. In the presence of alveolar instability (loss of surfactant and other abnormal states), alveoli that close completely at the end of expiration tend to become "stuck" and resist reopening with the next inspiration; this can lead to alveolar collapse and increased shunting. Management includes:

Blood pressure monitoring and/or determination of the cardiac output to assess the effect of PEEP on the cardiovascular system. Since the positive pressure exerted by the volume of air increases intrathoracic pressure, the resultant decrease in the venous gradient can cause the cardiac output to drop. (A difference in pressure between the venous and thoracic structures is required for normal return flow of blood to the heart.)

If cardiac output (and blood pressure) drop, the mechanical ventilator rate may be decreased to decrease the impairment of venous return and increase the filling pressure of the heart.

In some patients, continuous positive airway pressure (CPAP) with no augmentation of the ventilatory volume may be utilized. (There are many different terminologies used in respiratory therapy. Although CPAP sometimes refers to positive pressure without intubation, this discussion concerns its use with intubation.) Although this may be initially effective, as compliance of the lungs decreases, hyperinflation of the lungs for at least 6 respirations per minute will usually be required. A rough measurement of compliance can be obtained by dividing the administered tidal volume by the pressure exhibited on the pressure dial. When the quotient is less than 25, the lungs are becoming stiffer (less compliant).

To be most beneficial, PEEP must be continuous, not intermittent. Endotracheal tubes should be fitted with a special adaptor that permits suctioning without loss of PEEP.

The physician determines the amount of PEEP. Initial pressure is usually 5 cm H_2O, but pressures can be increased. Some patients may require 20–40 cm H_2O PEEP.

The nurse must continually check the patient's response. The pressure dial (an indicator of the pressure within the airways) should return to the ordered PEEP (rather than zero). Pressures required to inflate the lungs should be recorded. Any rather sudden increase in the pressure required to deliver the volume of ventilation (inflation pressure) should be investigated. The major causes of an increase in pressure are kinking in the conducting tubing, biting of the endotracheal tube, malpositioning of the tube with tube slipping down below the level of the carina (most frequently into right main bronchus), obstruction of the airway by a mucus plug, or pneumothorax.

An increased incidence of pneumomediastinum, subcutaneous emphysema, and pneumothorax accompanies the use of mechanical ventilators. The higher pressure within the airways is transmitted to lung cysts or blebs, and these, or a vulnerable alveolus, may rupture. Unless pneumothorax involves a minimal area of the lung, it is promptly treated by insertion of a chest tube (or tubes) and connected to waterseal drainage. Failure to drain a simple pneumothorax promptly and adequately can result in its conversion into a tension pneumothorax. A tension pneumothorax occurs when air leaking from the lung during inspiration cannot escape during expiration. The resulting pleural pressure on the involved side exceeds atmospheric pressure and pushes the flexible mediastinum toward the uninvolved lung.

Tracheal injury due to excessive pressure in the occluding cuffs of endotracheal or tracheal tubes must be prevented. The use of low-pressure cuffs and careful inflation will reduce the incidence of injury. The cuff should be inflated to "minimal leak" at the peak pressure of the ventilator.

Maintenance of Adequate Tissue Perfusion

Activities that decrease shunting by maintenance or restoration of adequate tissue perfusion include the use of (1) cardiotonic drugs to stimulate the heart; (2) vasodilating drugs to decrease the afterload (reduce the left end diastolic pressure); (3) diuretics to decrease fluid retention; (4) corticosteroids to reduce inflammation and stabilize capillary membranes; (5) antibiotics to reduce the damage to the reticuloendothelial system from sepsis; and (6) correction of any fluid volume deficit, including replacement of hemoglobin for severe anemia. Sodium bicarbonate may be given for severe concomitant metabolic acidosis, since the myocardium is depressed and cardiac dysrhythmias occur with severe acidosis. With pH values greater than 7.25, sodium bicarbonate is rarely given, since oxygen is released to the tissues more readily with acidosis. A positive response to mechanical ventilation and efforts to increase tissue perfusion is evidenced by a decrease in the Q_S/Q_T. Weaning from the respirator is a gradual process that requires close monitoring. When mechanical ventilation with PEEP and high oxygen concentrations does not result in improvement in altered parameters, a pump and a membrane oxygenator may be utilized.

Correction of metabolic alkalosis.
The major deleterious effects of metabolic alkalosis are a compensatory decrease in the rate and depth of respiration and a

decrease in dissociation of oxygen from hemoglobin at the tissue level. Hypochloremia and hypokalemia are almost always present in metabolic alkalosis; the restoration of these ions to normal levels combined with measures to reduce loss of hydrogen ions from the upper gastrointestinal tract is usually effective in restoration of normal acid-base balance. A few patients, however, have alkalosis due to other causes than chloride deficiency; they can be identified by a urine chloride greater than 20 mEq/liter. These persons will require treatment with intravenous hydrochloric acid. The iatrogenic contribution to metabolic alkalosis from overzealous administration of bicarbonate during cardiac arrest and the depletion of potassium caused by diuretic should be avoided.

Maintenance of normothermia.   The metabolic requirement for oxygen increases 13 percent for every 1 degree centigrade increase in temperature. Although hypothermia decreases the oxygen requirement, the associated decrease in dissociation of the oxygen from the hemoglobin at the tissue level as well as the discomfort experienced by the patient usually counteracts the benefits of hypothermia.

Control of pulmonary infection and/or sepsis.   If infection is suspected, all secretions (sputum, blood, urine, other drainage, IV sites, etc.) should be examined and cultured. Immediate gram stain provides earlier feedback than culture and sensitivity. Since infections caused by anaerobes are increasing, appropriate techniques for securing and culturing these specimens as well as aerobes must be used. Effectiveness of antibiotic therapy depends on the use of the right drug in the right amount. Toxic levels of the drug can occur without exceeding the usual dosage if renal and/or hepatic failure is also present or developing. Serum drug levels are frequently utilized to guide continuing therapy. Drainage and/or eradication of the foci of infection are important. This may necessitate the removal of all intravenous, arterial, and urinary catheters, removal of pulmonary secretions, and surgical drainage of abscesses.

Prevention of respiratory aspiration of gastric contents.   Aspiration can be the initiating mechanism of respiratory insufficiency, or it can be an added insult to an existing respiratory disorder. The severity of the damage increases when the pH of the aspirate is less than 2.5, the volume is large, it is poorly localized, and it is contaminated with bacteria, such as occurs with bowel obstruction. Aspiration can follow regurgitation as well as vomiting. Patients at risk are those with altered states of consciousness, diseases or states that affect normal swallowing or protective mechanisms (including tracheotomy), and those undergoing emergency anesthesia with a full stomach. Preventive activities include positioning the patient on his side or semiprone with elevation of the head, decompression of the stomach before surgery or, if not feasible, endotracheal intubation preceding induction of anesthesia, and use of oral antacids or oral or intravenous cimetidine to decrease gastric acidity. Treatment which is primarily the responsibility of the physician can include vigorous endotracheal suctioning with concomitant oxygen administration, bronchoscopy if large particle aspiration is suspected, and aggressive ventilatory support with maintenance of an adequate fluid volume.

Adjustment to physical and emotional dependency.   During the acute stage, the patient has to accept a dependent role. The loss of the ability to breathe on one's own is frightening. Patients who require mechanical respiratory assistance also lose the ability to talk. The patient will be more receptive to his dependency when he understands the functions of the respirator and when his feelings of powerlessness are reduced. Explanations should be simple and geared to the patient's level. Frequent repetition may be required since the stress reduces cognitive functioning. Providing feedback on the patient's progress is also helpful. A positive attitude toward recovery can be fostered by enumerating or demonstrating positive factors to the patient of which he may not be aware. Concrete examples are more effective than verbal reassurance. These include: (1) reporting that the pressure required to get the oxygen to his lungs has gone from 50 down to 40, showing that his lungs are not as stiff as they were; (2) showing him X-rays of his chest, past and present, with a reduction in the "white" areas in the present film indicative of improvement; and (3) reporting to him that the oxygen concentration has been reduced from 40 to 30 percent.

The feeling of powerlessness can be reduced by instituting a method of written communication (with adequate time to write), and giving the patient as much control in the situation as possible. Examples of methods to increase the patient's control are asking his permission before beginning certain procedures and offering him choices whenever possible as, "Would you like to have your back washed and your sheets changed now or just before your family comes this afternoon?" or "Would you like some medication for pain?" Reminding the patient that the present situation is a temporary one also helps. Explanation and assistance to the family is important. The family should be encouraged to touch the patient and talk to him in a normal manner.

INTERVENTION FOR CHRONIC RESPIRATORY DISORDERS

Goals

For a patient with a continuing or chronic respiratory disorder, additional goals could include the following.

Physical reconditioning and mastery of proper breathing technique.   A general reconditioning exercise program to improve muscular tone and posture will often increase general independent functioning. Minute alveolar ventilation in patients with COPD can be increased by abdominal diaphragmatic and pursed-lip breathing. Pursed-lip breathing prolongs expiration and increases exhalation of carbon dioxide. The work of breathing is also decreased when the useless uncoordinated patterns of respiratory muscle activity are replaced by abdominal diaphragmatic breathing. The ability to cope with dyspnea can be improved by relaxation exercises and assumption of upright positions. Energy conservation techniques and ways to coordinate breathing with activity provide greater independence even for patients with severe disorders.

Control of air pollution. Respiratory irritants can come from smoking, the home environment, as well as certain occupations. The three sources can interact so that the cumulative effect is more severe than just additive. Patients generally comply more readily with suggestions for changing environment and occupation than with those regarding smoking.

Maintenance of hydration. Hydration is essential for keeping the tracheo-bronchial secretions loose. Methods to improve hydration include increasing fluid intake, use of room humidifiers, and inhalation of moisture from a steam nebulizer. The use of aerosol brochodilators (previously mentioned) often precedes steam inhalation, with expulsive coughing and/or postural drainage following.

Control of obesity. Overweight patients have a reduced expiratory reserve volume owing to decreased diaphragmatic respiratory excursion. Limitation of caloric intake to promote gradual weight loss is beneficial.

Psychosocial rehabilitation. As with other illnesses that result in physiologic impairment, problems in psychosocial adaptation can be anticipated. Frequently occurring problems include role change, loss of employment, financial insecurity, reactive depression, change in self-concept, alteration in socialization, and altered sexual activity. Intervention is directed toward assisting the patient to make the necessary changes in his life style and limiting the reactions and changes which have an adverse effect.

Vocational rehabilitation may help a few patients regain employment. Compliance with the regimen for physiologic rehabilitation is often markedly decreased in the patient who does not make an adequate psychosocial adaptation. An essential ingredient for successful adaptation is the patient's positive attitude and confidence in his ability to make the necessary adaptations.

EXPERIENTIAL INVOLVEMENT

CASE 4-A. Mr. Raleigh is a 64-year-old man with no major illnesses except for duodenal ulcer disease for the past 10 years. With the exception of three or four exacerbations, he has managed fairly well until about 3 months prior to admission (PTA). At this time he experienced increased pain unrelieved by antacids and vomiting of undigested food. Since that time his appetite has been poor and he has continued to have periods of pain and vomiting. He has had a weight loss of 15 pounds over the past 3 months. An attack of severe upper abdominal pain and prostration prompted admission to the hospital. An abdominal film showed free air under the diaphragm, which, combined with other findings, led to the diagnosis of perforated duodenal ulcer. Past history was not remarkable. He had surgery for repair of an inguinal hernia 20 years previously.

Five hours after admission he was taken to surgery. In addition to the perforation, he was found to have nearly complete obstruction of the gastroduodenal junction as a result of scarring from cycles of inflammation and repair. He had a vagotomy with a gastrojejunostomy and was taken to the Recovery Room in fairly good condition. His vital signs were within expected limits postoperatively, but he had an ileus that required continuing nasogastric suction and nothing by mouth.

On his fourth postoperative day, he developed abdominal pain, rigidity, leukocytosis, and tachycardia. Investigation revealed he had leakage at the gastrojejunal anastomosis and a sump drainage tube was placed in the wound to limit peritoneal contamination from leakage of intestinal contents. He continued to have severe abdominal pain for which he received meperidine hydrochloride (Demerol). He called for his medicine every 3 hours and when the nurse attempted questioning about the extent of his pain, he replied, "The Doctor told me to ask for the shots whenever I need them and you have no right to say I shouldn't have them." Drainage from the sump tube was profuse, and was replaced with electrolyte solution. Nourishment was by parenteral hyperalimentation. No one had visited or called about him since his admission All attempts by the staff to engage in conversation were rebuffed. About 18 hours after sump drainage was started, his respiratory rate decreased from 18 to 10. He responded to questioning, but appeared lethargic.

Skillbuilders:

1. On the practicum record 4A-1, list the two most likely hypotheses for Mr. Raleigh's decrease in respiratory rate.

2. Then enter the data that supports each hypothesis and additional data you would need to confirm or disconfirm.

3. In the intervention column, enter the immediate actions that would be indicated if the diagnosis were confirmed.

4. In the last column, enter the evaluation criteria for the short-term management of Mr. Raleigh.

5. On practicum record 4A-2, list the three most likely nursing diagnoses present or potential based on the case study information.

6. Briefly outline the nursing intervention that would be indicated for these diagnoses and the criteria for evaluation of the effectiveness of the intervention.

Feedback: Since there are not too many disorders that cause a decrease in the respiratory rate, the selection of these hypotheses should not have been too

PRACTICUM RECORD 4A-1

Hypothesis/Possible Diagnosis	Supporting Data to Confirm or Disconfirm	Additional Data to Confirm or Disconfirm	Nursing Intervention if Confirmed	Evaluation Criteria
Decrease in respiratory rate due to:				
1.				
2.				

PRACTICUM RECORD 4A-2

Nursing Diagnoses (Present or Potential)	Nursing Intervention	Evaluation Criteria
1.		
2.		
3.		

difficult. The most likely causes are metabolic alkalosis and respiratory depression from meperidine hydrochloride. The supporting data for metabolic alkalosis is the history of prolonged loss of gastric secretions rich in hydrochloric acid, the decrease in the respiratory rate, and the lethargy. Metabolic alkalosis is probably the most common acid-base disturbance in surgical patients. It is discussed in greater detail under vomiting in the chapter on output deviations. Additional supporting data would be arterial blood gas analysis consistent with metabolic alkalosis and low urinary chloride. The anticipated arterial blood findings would be pH greater than 7.45 with a bicarbonate greater than 26 mEq/liter (or base excess greater than +2). If the decreased respiratory rate has resulted in retention of CO_2, the Pco_2 would be slightly elevated to 45−50 torr. This compensatory response is limited due to hypoxia. Thus if the Pco_2 was greater than 50, it would be suggestive of an underlying respiratory acidosis. The main goal of intervention would be to restore the metabolic acid-base balance. In most patients this can be done by the administration of fluid and replacement of chloride, potassium, and sodium. (Adequate volume repletion promotes excretion of HCO_3^- by the kidney.) A few patients will require hydrochloric acid replacement; this can be added to the intravenous infusion. Remember that hydrochloric acid must be added to a glass bottle of fluid and a metal needle is required for administration. (Note: Spilling the solution on your uniform can be hazardous!) Evaluation criteria would be normal acid-base state, electrolytes (Cl^-, Na^+, and K^+) within normal limits, and absence of damage from hypoxia. (Remember that oxygen is released to the tissues less readily with alkalosis, so a low Po_2 is more apt to result in hypoxia.)

Now let's discuss the next hypothesis that respiratory rate is decreased by depression from meperidine hydrochloride. Supporting data would be the every three-hour administration of meperidine and the knowledge that meperidene, like most opiates and sedatives, can cause respiratory depression. Additional supporting data would be the demonstration of absence of respiratory alkalosis and the return of the respiratory rate to normal when meperidene was withheld. Intervention in addition to withholding of meperidene would include stirring up activities, hyperinflation of the lungs with oxygen-enriched gas from a ventilation bag, and, in some instances, administration of a narcotic antagonist such as naloxone hydrochloride (Narcan). When a narcotic antagonist is used, continued surveillance is crucial because of the short duration of effect and the danger of resumption of respiratory depression. Evaluation criteria would be the return of the respiratory rate to normal and absence of dysfunctional effects from hypoxia.

And that takes us to the nursing diagnoses for Mr. Raleigh. With the profuse sump drainage of intestinal contents, perhaps the most immediate diagnosis is the potential loss of skin integrity from the irritative effects of the outpouring of gastric acid, bile, and pancreatic enzymes. Preventive intervention would include scrupulous cleansing followed by protective applications of an acrylic emulsion or karaya gum powder. A disposable ileostomy type of plastic bag can be placed over the tube with bottom opening taped closed around a catheter attached to suction to prevent collection of drainage in the bag. After a drainage tract has been established, the sump tube can be removed with the drainage which flows into the bag promptly removed by suction. The criteria for evaluation would be maintenance of good skin condition.

The second nursing diagnosis on our list is potential or existing inadequate nutrition with negative nitrogen balance. Accurate measurement of sump tube output as well as other fluid loss is necessary for adequate replacement. Electrolyte levels of drainage are sometimes measured to guide replacement. Mr. Raleigh was in a debilitated state upon admission and his continuing inability to take nourishment orally has undoubtedly resulted in electrolyte deficiency and a negative nitrogen balance. Parenteral hyperalimentation should be administered using strict aseptic technique; urine sugar and acetone should be checked regularly. Significant glycosuria is an indicator for insulin administration to promote metabolism and utilization of glucose. Amino acids, instead of being used for tissue repair, will be metabolized unless sufficient calories (in the form of glucose or fat) are supplied. When Mr. Raleigh's condition has stabilized and intestinal activity has returned, he will probably be fed by means of a long tube passed through the stomach and into the distal loop. Evaluation criteria would be weight gain, signs of tissue healing, and electrolytes within normal limits.

Perhaps the last nursing diagnosis is a toss up. We felt there was some difficulty in his ability to form interpersonal relationships as indicated by the absence of family or significant others. Thus, he will have an inadequate support system during the stressful lengthy illness. Our runner-up possibility could be excessive reliance on pain medication, unrelieved pain, and manipulation of staff. You may have even thought of other likely possibilities. Planning of intervention for an inadequate support system would be based on the more definitive problem identified by assessment. The basic approach would be consistently to demonstrate quiet friendliness and acceptance, allowing Mr. Raleigh to set the pace, and to show appreciation for his efforts. Evaluation criteria could be evidence of an enhanced perception of himself, initiation of contact with others, and trust in others.

Measures for pain are discussed more fully in the chapter on pain. If the patient continues to insist he needs "shots" for his pain and refuses any other comfort measures, the physician might order an injection of a placebo of distilled water. In administering a placebo, it is important to convey the belief that it will relieve the pain. If pain is not reduced or relieved, the diagnosis of excessive reliance on pain medication could be incorrect and the patient may truly have severe pain.

Intervention for manipulation of staff includes consistency among all staff members and setting limits on the patient's behavior. Personnel should not accept gifts, favors, or flattery. Positive reinforcement should be given when the patient attempts to use cooperation, compromise, or factual discussion rather than manipulative behaviors such as playing one against the other, intimidation, or derogation. Evaluation could be the number of manipulative actions of the patient.

CASE 4-B. Mrs. Seagram is a 29-year-old Caucasian admitted to the hospital three days ago for acute pancreatitis. Her past history showed no major illnesses or operations, but intermittent attacks of asthma over the past 15 years. She had been hospitalized twice for acute asthmatic attacks. Her medications prior to admission (PTA) were terbutaline (Brethine) 2.5 mg three times daily and birth control pills. Her pancreatitis was treated by prohibition of oral intake and maintenance of gastric suction to keep pancreatic secretory activity at a minimum, and intravenous therapy to maintain an adequate circulating blood volume and nutrition. Her progress was satisfactory, but the results of diagnostic testing showed a moderately severe pathologic process that would require treatment for a period of time. Thus she was started on parenteral hyperalimentation on her second day after admission via a percutaneously placed subclavian catheter. Shortly after initiation of parenteral hyperalimentation she complained of dyspnea. Her respiratory rate at this time had increased from 20 to 32, and she was extremely restless. Our problem with Mrs. Seagram is to determine the cause of her increased respiratory rate and dyspnea.

In order to help you organize your thinking and limit the possibilities to a manageable number, we are giving you two blood gas reports which could have been received from analysis of an arterial blood sample drawn at this time.

	Sample A	Sample B
pH	7.32	7.49
P_{CO_2}	51	31
P_{O_2}	69	69
B1 bicarb	26	23
Base excess	+1	−1
$F_{I_{O_2}}$	0.21	0.21

Skillbuilders: We are asking you to complete two practicum records for Mrs. Seagram, with one based on each of the two arterial blood reports. First you will need to analyze the blood gas reports to determine the nature of the disorder. You may need to refer to the decision trees on respiratory and metabolic acidosis and alkalosis for correct interpretation. After you have identified the specific blood gas alteration for sample A and sample B, look over the chart for the altered pathophysiology that could be responsible. Remember that the alteration occurred abruptly in a fairly healthy young woman so you need to think of the early changes that could occur instead of end stage alterations.

We are asking you to:

1. Record on practicum record 4-B (Sample A) the abnormality indicated by the blood gas analysis in sample A and the most likely hypotheses for Mrs. Seagram's increased respiratory rate with the blood gas values given in sample A.

2. Record on the practicum record 4-B (Sample B) the abnormality indicated by the blood gas analysis in sample B and the three most likely hypotheses

PRACTICUM RECORD CASE 4B (SAMPLE A)

Hypothesis/Possible Diagnosis	Supporting Data to Confirm	Additional Data Needed to Confirm or Disconfirm	Nursing Intervention if Diagnosis Confirmed	Evaluation Criteria
Increased respiratory rate and dyspnea with arterial blood analysis indicative of _____ due to: 1.				

PRACTICUM RECORD CASE 4B (SAMPLE B)

Hypothesis/Possible Diagnosis	Supporting Data to Confirm	Additional Data Needed to Confirm or Disconfirm	Nursing Intervention if Diagnosis Confirmed	Evaluation Criteria
Increased respiratory rate and dyspnea with arterial blood analysis indicative of _____ due to: 1.				
2.				
3.				

for Mrs. Seagram's increased respiratory rate, based on the blood gas analysis given in sample B.

3. For both sample A and B enter the data that support the hypothesis and additional data you would need to confirm or disconfirm.

4. In the intervention column of both sample A and B enter the intervention you would plan for the next 24 hours if the hypothesis were confirmed.

5. In the last column of both sample A and B list the appropriate evaluation criteria.

Feedback: This was a toughie. We found, however, that the only way we could make sense of blood gases was just to wade in and work through them. So here we go. In sample A, if you look at the pH first, you recognize that there is acidemia. To determine whether it is respiratory or metabolic, look at the Pco_2. If the Pco_2 is elevated, the problem is respiratory, with inadequate ventilatory volume to blow off the CO_2. Thus we decide that respiratory acidosis is present. We can refine our diagnosis a little if we look at the bicarbonate to determine if there is a concomitant metabolic acidosis. (Remember that respiratory processes do not alter bicarbonate, it only reflects metabolic state.) A low bicarbonate (or negative base excess greater than -2) would be indicative of a mixed metabolic and respiratory acidosis. Since the bicarbonate is normal, the problem is purely respiratory. To determine the adequacy of oxygenation, we next look at the Po_2. The low Po_2 is indicative of hypoxemia. Thus we have respiratory acidosis with hypoxemia, which is generally referred to as respiratory insufficiency. In this case the hypoxemia has probably resulted from an inadequate volume of air, an indication that the increased respiratory rate has not adequately increased minute alveolar ventilation.

Following the same process with sample B, we recognize that the pH is indicative of alkalemia. The low Pco_2 tells us that it is due to respiratory causes, in this case hyperventilation that resulted in blowing off of CO_2. We note again the bicarbonate is normal so there is no metabolic component. (Metabolic alkalosis would be manifested by an elevated bicarbonate and a base excess greater than $+2$.) The low Po_2 is indicative of hypoxemia. So we can say there is respiratory alkalosis and hypoxemia, with the alkalosis probably resulting from a compensatory effort to amend the oxygen deficit by increasing the ventilation. Now that we have identified the acid-base abnormality, we are ready to select our hypotheses. Thus we need to recall (or refer to the chart to find) the disorders that could be responsible for an increase in respiratory rate. Since both samples indicate hypoxemia and no metabolic component, we can probably rule out as possibilities those disorders on the chart associated with hyperpnea without hypoxemia or metabolic acid-base disorders. We can also probably rule out psychogenic stimulation since with psychogenic tachypnea there would be no hypoxemia.

Having narrowed down the field of possibilities a little, let's see if you found the most likely possibility for sample A. With respiratory acidosis associated with an inadequate minute alveolar ventilation, we need to look at the acute disorders that can decrease the volume of inspired air. Some of you may have listed acute asthmatic attack as the most likely hypothesis. Since asthma causes increased airway resistance from a narrowing of the tracheobronchial tree, it is reasonable to think that it could decrease the minute alveolar ventilation. It has been found, however, that persons with otherwise normal pulmonary function are able to compensate for the hypoxemia and usually initially have hypocapnia and respiratory alkalosis. Normal Pco_2 with hypoxemia is considered a sign of a severe attack, and elevated Pco_2 is associated with an emergency state that may be terminal.

You can go to the top of the class if you selected pneumothorax as the cause of the increased respiratory rate. The supporting data are the history items of asthma and placement of a subclavian catheter. Asthma can result in a pneumothorax due to rupture of bleb or cyst on the pleural surface of the lung. The most likely cause for Mrs. Seagram's pneumothorax, however, would be puncture of the lung during placement of the subclavian catheter. The decision tree for respiratory insufficiency can guide us in assessment, but we need to know the specific alterations with pneumothorax, since the parameters on the tree are general parameters that may be altered with respiratory insufficiency due to any cause. Supporting data would include the rapid respiratory rate, dyspnea, and respiratory acidosis. Additional data to confirm the hypothesis would be gained by physical examination of the lungs, chest X-ray, and questioning regarding the presence of chest pain. Pain is unilateral, frequently referred to the shoulder or arm on the involved side, and is made worse by movement or coughing. Physical examination findings in the involved area are decreased chest movement, hyper-resonance to percussion, and decreased (or absent) breath and voice sounds. The chest X-ray is important for exact diagnosis of the presence and extent of the pneumothorax. Both an inspiratory and expiratory film should be taken. If only an inspiratory film is taken, a small pneumothorax may be missed since it can be obscured by a nearly expanded lung. The chest X-ray reveals retraction of the lung from the parietal pleura.

Intervention is primarily directed by the physician. A symptomatic pneumothorax almost always requires insertion of a chest tube (or tubes) with connection to waterseal drainage. The nurse is responsible for insuring that all connections are tight so no air can be sucked into the lung. There should be bubbling in the watertrap for at least several hours, since air leaking from the lung with inspiration must be removed to prevent the development of a tension pneumothorax. It is important to alternate the patient's position from the back (with head elevated 30 degrees or more) to the involved side. The good lung should always be up to allow maximum expansion. There is also less incidence of mediastinal shift when the good lung is kept up. Other intervention would include measures to control pain and administration of oxygen to correct hypoxemia. Any narcotic pain medication needs to be administered cautiously to prevent respiratory depression. Non-narcotic analgesics and comfort measures are usually tried initially. Provision of support to the body and putting desired items within close reach will help to reduce movement and minimize pain. Most patients report that their pain subsides rather quickly after chest tube placement. Reporting the self-limiting nature of the pain to the patient may help her mobilize her resources and reduce its perceived severity. As the lung gradually reexpands, the dead space should return to normal with correction of the respiratory acidosis. The hypoxemia however, will probably require oxygen administration for a period of time.

Evaluation criteria would be:

1. Chest X-ray showing good lung reexpansion.
2. Absence of tension pneumothorax.
3. Po_2 between 80 and 100.
4. Normal pH and Pco_2.
5. Patient validation of effectiveness of pain control measures.

We are now ready to consider the hypotheses for sample B. We've already tipped you off that we have an acute asthmatic attack at the head of our list. Our other hypotheses are increased respiratory rate and dyspnea due to pulmonary embolus or pulmonary infiltration from pancreatitis. How did you do? If you missed one or more, we hope it will be clearer after we discuss it. We have discussed the possibility of an acute asthmatic attack to some extent already. Supporting data come primarily from the history of asthma, the presence of tachypnea, dyspnea, theoretical knowledge, and blood gas reports. Acute pancreatitis is a stressful disease and stress can cause reflex bronchoconstriction that may trigger an asthmatic attack. The blood gas picture is compatible with an acute attack in a person with otherwise normal lungs. Additional supporting data would be the presence of wheezes during both inspiration and expiration, signs of increased respiratory effort, coughing, pulsus paradoxus, negative chest X-ray findings, and altered pulmonary function studies. To elaborate on some of these findings, increased respiratory effort is manifested primarily by the use of accessory muscles and flaring of the nares. It is a helpful observation that can cue you to increasing severity of the airway obstruction. One of the causes of pulsus paradoxus is an obstructive airway disorder. A decrease in systolic arterial pressure greater than 10 torr with inspiration can be indicative of narrowing of the airway. Pulmonary function tests in patients with asthma show abnormalities in forced vital maneuvers. A reduction of forced expiratory volume to less than 750 ml in one second is a cause for concern, while a volume less than 500 ml in one second is indicative of impending respiratory failure.

Intervention would be primarily directed toward reversing the airway narrowing and provision of oxygen to remedy hypoxemia. Major aspects in addition to administration of oxygen include:

1. The use of bronchodilators to relieve bronchoconstriction.
2. Assistance in removal of mucus and secretions (coughing, chest physiotherapy, postural drainage, mucolytic agents, suctioning, etc.).
3. Early recognition of complications such as pneumothorax or cardiac dysrhythmias from bronchodilators and/or hypoxemia.
4. Correction of any hypovolemia.
5. Treatment of any underlying bronchopulmonary infection.
6. Provision of ventilatory assistance for respiratory fatigue or hypoxemia nonresponsive to oxygen administration.
7. Administration of corticosteroids if eosinophils are increased in the blood or present in the sputum.
8. Control of anxiety.

Most of these activities have been discussed in considerable detail in other parts of the book. We will only elaborate on a couple of points. It must be remembered that oxygen is more strongly bound to hemoglobin and less available to the tissues with alkalosis. Thus Mrs. Seagram must be closely monitored for the development of serious hypoxia. Her initial restlessness may have been a sign of hypoxia. An increase in restlessness or agitation and/or cognitive impairment could be a sign of worsening hypoxia that should be checked by blood gas analysis. It is a rare patient with an acute asthmatic attack that does not show moderate or severe anxiety. Since anxiety increases hyperventilation and respiratory alkalosis while decreasing the patient's feeling of security, it is important to control whenever possible. Sedation is contraindicated because of its depression of alveolar ventilation. Measures to control anxiety have been discussed in some detail elsewhere in the book. For Mrs. Seagram it would probably be helpful to remain with her, keep her informed of her progress, remind her that she recovered quickly from previous attacks, and promote confidence in those who are caring for her.

Evaluation criteria would be (1) Po_2 between 80 and 100 on oxygen adjunct; (2) absence of complications (pneumothorax, dysrhythmias, etc.); and (3) absence of signs of airway obstruction (wheezes, dyspnea, use of accessory muscles, pulsus paradoxus). Longer range criteria would be normal Po_2 without oxygen and normal forced expiratory volume, although it may take 1 to 2 weeks for Mrs. Seagram to progress to this stage.

Now let's consider the hypothesis that the increased respiratory rate and dyspnea is due to a pulmonary embolus (PE). The supporting data come primarily from her history of intake of birth control pills and the knowledge that the incidence is increased with the "pill" and decreased physical activity. Dyspnea, as with our other hypotheses, is the major presenting symptom. The other supporting datum is the blood gas analysis of respiratory alkalosis with hypoxemia. This alteration is characteristic of, but not specific for, pulmonary embolism. We do not try to remember all the characteristics of each disorder, our minds just can't hold all those details. But when we think of the involved pathophysiology, we can get a fairly good idea of what to expect. Since a pulmonary embolus occludes one or more vessels in the pulmonary arterial tree, the back pressure in the pulmonary vessels is high, and this high pressure is reflected back to the right side of the heart, which can cause right-sided heart failure.

Thus the additional physical findings that you would expect to find are related to right heart failure and turbulence of flow in vessels partially obstructed by emboli. They would include (1) tachycardia; (2) a systolic ejection type murmur over the pulmonic area and a continuous murmur accentuated by inspiration over the lung fields; (3) ausculatory findings consistent with right ventricular failure; (4) distended neck veins with a prominent A wave; and (5) hepatomegaly. You would also want to check for deep venous thrombosis in the legs. Some patients may have few or no abnormal physical signs. If embolism leads to infarction, pleuritic chest pain, hemoptysis, fever, and a pleural friction rub or evidence of pleural effusion may be present. Less than half of the patients with PE have signs of deep venous thrombosis. A rough indicator of thrombosis of the leg is a positive Homan's sign, i.e., forced dorsiflexion of the foot results in pain behind the knee. More definitive methods such as venography, Doppler ultrasonic, and radioactive fibrinogen studies are being developed for greater accuracy in diagnosis of deep venous thrombosis.

Laboratory techniques to diagnose pulmonary embolism rely primarily on scanning, with a perfusion scan frequently combined with a ventilation scan. (Remember that PE is a disorder of perfusion but normal ventilation.) Intervention would be directed toward prevention of further clot formation and assistance as needed in maintenance of life and breath during the period of compromised function. Anticoagulation therapy with heparin would probably be ordered. The nurse needs to measure the dosage accurately and give it on time to maintain uniform inhibition of the coagulation system. After the initial dose of heparin, maintenance doses are usually given every 4 to 6 hours to keep the clotting time or partial thromboplastin time at 1.5 to 2.5 times normal. Heparin is given either intravenously or subcutaneously. Attention to technique for subcutaneous injection is essential to prevent hematoma formation.

Mrs. Seagram should have antiembolic hose, gentle exercise of the legs (dorsiflexion of the foot and flattening of the knee to the mattress), positioning to prevent pressure on legs, ambulation to allowed maximum, and no massage of the calves of the legs. Measures for hypoxemia would be the same as discussed for the other disorders. For some patients, mechanical ventilation is indicated. Hypotension, if present, is treated with sympathomimetic drugs. When there is severe hemodynamic compromise unresponsive to supportive measures, pulmonary embolectomy with cardiopulmonary bypass may be indicated. Evaluation criteria would be (1) Po_2 between 80 and 100 on oxygen adjunct; (2) absence of bleeding from heparin administration; and (3) no further emboli.

Now we're ready for the last stretch with a discussion of the hypothesis that increase in respiratory rate and dyspnea is due to pulmonary infiltration and/or atelectasis secondary to acute pancreatitis. Supporting datum is primarily the knowledge that a number of patients with acute pancreatitis develop lung pathology which can range from moderate involvement to the adult respiratory distress syndrome (ARDS).

It is believed that the passage of vasoactive products across the diaphragm is the mechanism whereby damage develops. Other supporting data are the tachypnea and blood gas findings of hypoxemia and respiratory alkalosis. Additional data would include:

1. Ausculatory findings of rales, dullness to percussion, and diminished breath sounds, especially over the left lower lobe of the lungs.

2. Chest X-ray showing fluid, infiltrate, or atelectasis.

3. Measurement of physiologic shunting (Q_S/Q_T).

Shunting would probably be first estimated with the patient breathing 40 percent oxygen. The expected Po_2 would be 240 torr. If Mrs. Seagram's Po_2 were less than 204, it would be indicative of an abnormal state. If the Po_2 were less than 170 torr (showing roughly 30 percent shunt), more definitive testing would probably be done in order to detect ARDS in the early stages.

Intervention for pulmonary infiltration and/or atelectasis would include:

1. Administration of oxygen at lowest $F_{I_{O_2}}$ that would prevent hypoxia (to avoid washing out the nitrogen skeleton and decreasing surfactant, actions that lead to increasing atelectasis).

2. Use of chest physiotherapy, postural drainage, and coughing to clear secretions.

3. Prevention of an imbalance between ventilation and perfusion in which ventilation was primarily to the apices of the lungs. The bases of the lung are usually the involved areas, and, at least periodically, a large volume of air must be inhaled to inflate the alveoli at the base of the lung adequately. Turning should be combined with deep breathing maneuvers. If these methods are ineffective, intubation and placement on a volume respirator with PEEP may be necessary.

The criteria for evaluation would be maintenance of the P_{O_2} between 70 and 90 torr and clearing of atelectasis and/or infiltrate.

ADDITIONAL READING

Applebaum E, Bruce D: Tracheal Intubation. Philadelphia, Saunders, 1976, pp 40–51.

Aspinall M: Nursing the Open Heart Surgery Patient. New York, McGraw-Hill, 1973, pp 49–93.

del Bueno D: A quick review on using blood-gas determinations. RN 78:68–70, 1978.

Keyes J: Blood-gas analysis and the assessment of acid-base status. Heart Lung 5(2):247–255, 1976.

Kurihara M: Postural drainage, clapping, and vibrating. AJN 65(11):76–79, 1965.

Levy M, Stubbs J: Nursing implications in the care of patients treated with assisted mechanical ventilation modified with positive end-expiratory pressure. Heart Lung 7(2):299–305, 1978.

Major RH: Physical Diagnosis, 8th ed. Philadelphia, Saunders, 1974, pp 89–118.

Moser K: Management of acute respiratory failure. In Harrison T (ed): Principles of Internal Medicine, 9th ed. New York, McGraw-Hill, 1980, pp 1278–1282.

Tinker J: Understanding Chest X-rays. AJN 76(1):54–58, 1976.

West J: Disturbances of respiratory function. In Harrison T (ed.): Principles of Internal Medicine, 9th ed. New York, McGraw-Hill, 1980, pp 1191–1199.

Wilson R: Principles and Techniques of Critical Care. Kalamazoo, Mich., The Upjohn Co., 1976, Sections F–H.

CHAPTER 5

Temperature Alterations

The temperature of the human body must be maintained within a relatively narrow range for optimal functioning. Significant alterations from the normal range are associated with illness and death. The normal range of temperature of body tissues and organs (commonly called the "core" temperature) taken orally is 35.8–37.2 Celsius (C) or 96.5–99 Fahrenheit (F). Rectal temperature is 0.65 C (1.2 F) higher. With oral temperature below 32.8 C (91 F), the cognitive level, pulse, and respiratory rate are all decreased. As the temperature drops below 28.5 C (83.3 F), the electrocardiogram frequently shows slow atrial fibrillation, and/or a J wave occurring at the junction of the QRS complex and the S-T segment. Consciousness gradually decreases and is lost completely at levels below 26.7 C (80 F). Elevations of temperature are also accompanied by serious derangements of bodily function. Convulsions frequently occur when the temperature exceeds 40.5 C (105 F). Irreversible brain damage occurs with temperatures greater than 42.2 C (108 F). In the very young, the aged, and other susceptible persons, death may occur before the temperature reaches either of these extremes.

The temperatures of the skin, muscles, and subcutaneous tissues are generally cooler than the core temperature, and can fluctuate over a wider range without damage. Tissue injury does occur, however, when the temperature of local skin tissue is less than 18 C (64.4 F) or greater than 45 C (113 F).

Normal body temperature is dependent on homeostatic mechanisms that maintain the balance between heat production and heat loss. The main source of body heat is derived from the combustion of fats, carbohydrates, and proteins during normal metabolism. The thyroid gland, by its secretion of thyroxine, controls the metabolic rate. Metabolism can also be increased by muscular contraction and such substances as norepinephrine and epinephrine. Although the entire complex process whereby increases in the metabolic rate increase the production of heat is not known, it is believed that the basic process is a reduction of the phosphorus-oxygen ratio for the formation of adenosine triphosphate (ATP), resulting in greater utilization of oxygen for metabolism. The metabolic rate is lowest with sleep and increases with exercise and involuntary muscular tensing and relaxation. The muscular activity is usually not apparent, but when

131

there is a strong stimulus for heat production, the muscular contraction increases and shivering is observable. Small quantities of heat are also derived from external sources such as radiation from the sun, conduction from a local source of externally applied heat, and ingestion of hot foods and liquids.

An increase or decrease in heat production is normally compensated by a similar increase or decrease in heat loss. The principal means of regulation of heat loss is by varying the volume of blood flowing to the body surface. Vasodilation, which increases the flow of blood to the surface, is associated with greater heat loss. Vasoconstriction with decreased blood flow results in heat conservation. Heat is eliminated by the mechanisms of radiation, convection, conduction, and evaporation. Radiation, convection, and conduction are all forms of heat loss to the environment. The amount of heat lost by these means is determined to a great extent by the movement of air and the difference between the temperature of the body and the external environment. Evaporation accounts for less than 30 percent of the total loss in normal states, but is the major mechanism for heat loss when the ambient temperature is almost the same or greater than body temperature. Vaporization of the water from the surface of the body and the respiratory passages, of which one is unaware, is termed insensible perspiration. The process of conversion of a liquid to a vapor cools the body. For an average adult, the amount of fluid lost by insensible perspiration is 500 ml in 24 hours. Sweating greatly increases the loss of fluid and heat when the ambient temperature is elevated. Fluid loss in some patients can be as great as a liter an hour. Sweating is influenced by the humidity, with high humidity associated with a decrease in the ability to lose heat from sweating.

The control center for regulation and integration of the various physical and chemical processes for heat production and loss is located in the hypothalamus. Combined stimuli from peripheral and central thermodetectors are interpreted by the thermoregulatory center in the hypothalamus which in turn activates autonomic mechanisms to return the temperature toward the normal range. In normal states, when the core temperature rises, cells in the anterior section of the hypothalamus stimulate the parasympathetic division of the autonomic nervous system causing vasodilation and sweating to increase heat loss. When core temperature falls, cells in the posterior section of the hypothalamus stimulate the sympathetic division of the autonomic nervous system causing vasoconstriction and heat conservation. These mechanisms that maintain temperature within normal range are altered in febrile states and in disturbances of functioning of the regulatory centers in the hypothalamus. When fever develops, the normal thermoregulatory set-point of the hypothalamus is increased, and body temperature rises until it reaches the higher setting. Thermoreceptors sense the body temperature as low during the early period of rising temperature, so the initial response is shivering and vasoconstriction. Disturbances of function of the regulatory center in the hypothalamus can result in hypothermia (with involvement of the posterior section) or hyperthermia (with anterior hypothalamic involvement). Body temperature with a disorder of central neural control is said to be poikilothermic, i.e., it fluctuates markedly with changes in environmental temperature.

There are a number of regularly occurring variations in body temperature that are not considered pathologic. Most people have a diurnal variation of approximately 1 C (1.8 F), with the lowest temperature between 2:00 and 4:00 A.M. and the highest between 6:00 and 10:00 P.M. Strenuous exercise and high ambient temperatures are frequently accompanied by an elevation of temperature. Persons with altered thyroid functioning may exhibit temperatures outside the normal range, with elevated temperature corresponding to higher metabolic activity. Persons with congestive heart failure often have an elevated temperature. The impaired heat dissipation as a result of the decrease in cardiac output and the insulating effect of the edema are probably the major reasons for the elevation. When there is some impairment in the sweating mechanism, temperature may be elevated in a warm environment. Sweating is impaired by congenital absence of the sweat glands, skin disorders such as ichthyosis, and anticholinergic drugs such as atropine and propantheline.

Disturbances in heat regulation manifested by hypothermia and fever will be briefly discussed.

HYPOTHERMIA

Hypothermia with lowering of the body temperature below 32 C (89.6 F) is usually a medical emergency which requires prompt treatment. The injury can be generalized, local, or both. Exposure to low environmental temperature and underlying vascular or systemic diseases are the major causes. Disordered states that can result in hypothermia are listed in Table 5-1.

ASSESSMENT

Measurement of core temperature.   This is needed to find the extent of temperature depression. Since standard clinical thermometers do not register below 35 C (95 F), temperatures must be checked with a special thermometer with low range capability.

History.   To determine the incidence of exposure to cold, intake of alcohol and/or drugs, and the presence of cardiovascular or endocrine disease an accurate history is essential.

Physical examination.   To reveal alterations in other body functions a comprehensive physical must be done. Frequent alterations include:

● *Vital sign changes* – A decrease may be noted in the pulse and respiratory rates, in the depth of respiration, and in the blood pressure.

● *Skin* is cold and pale. If local tissue has been frozen (frostbite), the affected area will initially be white (a reflection of decreased blood flow) and hard (from

TABLE 5-1.   Major Causes of Hypothermia

Abnormal Initiating Mechanism	Pathophysiology	Clinical State
Metabolic disorder	Prolonged low blood sugar with deficiency in substrate essential for functioning of central neural control mechanism.	Hypoglycemia, most frequently caused by hyperinsulinism, acute pancreatitis, hepatic enzyme deficiency, hepatic disease (severe), anterior pituitary hypofunction, adrenocortical hypofunction, alcohol ingestion
	Deficient thyroid function with an abnormally low basal metabolic rate. Different types include:	
	Thyroid deficiency from birth	Cretinism
	Thyroid deficiency in adult	Myxedema
	Thyroid deficiency with goiter	Goitrous hypothyroidism
	Deficiency of insulin necessary for metabolism of carbohydrates	Diabetic ketoacidosis
Severe weight loss	Inadequate heat production due to unavailability of adequate protein, carbohydrate, and fat for combustion.	Starvation, malabsorption, malignant disease, colon disorder, anorexia nervosa
Advanced shock (Vasomotor collapse)	As shock progresses, the cardiac output is decreased and tissue perfusion is inadequate, with anaerobic metabolism due to inadequate oxygen for aerobic metabolism. The disturbed metabolism results in inadequate production of energy with inability to maintain normothermia.	Hypovolemic shock, cardiogenic shock, anaphylactic shock, hypodynamic septic shock
Damage to central nervous system	Destruction of the thermal regulatory mechanism in the posterior hypothalamus with loss of the sympathetic response of vasoconstriction and heat conservation	Hypothermia is not frequent, but may occur with: cerebral abscess, tumor, or hemorrhage; cerebral abscess or tumor
Side effects of drugs or alcohol	Temporary loss of power of heat regulation due to depression of central nervous system	High intake/or potentiating additive effect of: morphine, alcohol, barbiturates, other sedatives, anesthetic agents, phenothiazines
Exposure to cold	Exposure to extremely low environmental temperatures for a period of time with exhaustion and inability to increase heat production by shivering or exercise. Vasoconstriction limits heat loss from internal organs but results in hypoxia with damage to nerve and muscle tissue of extremities which can progress to freezing.	Accidental hypothermia, frostbite, nonfreezing (immersion-foot) injury

edema). Anesthesia may be present. With rewarming, the skin may be red and mottled.

- *Cognitive level* is decreased. Early signs are lethargy and confusion, with progression to unconsciousness.

- *Musculature* is stiff. With very low temperatures, the stiffness of the muscles resembles rigor mortis.

- *Pupils* are constricted.

- *Generalized edema* may be present.

Electrocardiographic examination.   Abnormalities frequently present include atrial fibrillation and/or alteration of the terminal portion of the QRS complex by a J wave. Distortion of the ECG by muscular tremors may make accurate interpretation difficult.

Laboratory tests.   To determine causal factors and extent of disturbances resulting from the hypothermic state lab tests must be done. The tests of greatest significance are serum glucose (for detection of hypoglycemia or severe uncontrolled diabetes mellitus), serum amylase (for detection of pancreatitis), and thyroid function tests (for detection of myxedema). Laboratory data useful in determining the extent of the alteration in bodily functions are the hematocrit and serum sodium (an index to the presence of hemoconcentration with a fluid volume deficit) and arterial pH and gas analysis. The pH is an indication of the presence and severity of acidosis, while the Pco_2 and Po_2 are an indication of the adequacy of respiratory function. The white count and differential can provide useful information about the presence of infection. If alcohol or drug ingestion is suspected, determination of the blood levels of these substances is indicated.

INTERVENTION

The major overall goals of treatment for hypothermia are gradual rewarming, prevention and/or prompt management of complications, and management of any underlying disorder. The physician has the major responsibility for direction of the treatment. Short-term goals and related activities for the treatment of hypothermia and prevention of complication include:

Passive rewarming.   This is accomplished by exposure of the lightly covered patient to normal room temperature. Body temperature is expected to increase 0.5–1.0 C (1.0–1.8 F) an hour. The use of external sources of heat is contraindicated, since with dilation of the constricted peripheral blood vessels, blood is diverted from the vital organs, with resultant cardiovascular collapse. After core temperature has been restored to near normal levels, a frostbitten extremity should be gradually rewarmed by immersion in water at 10 to 15 C (50 to 59 F) with gradual increases of 5 C (9 F) every five minutes to a maximum of 40 C

(104 F). With extremely low core temperatures, hemodialysis with dialysate at normal body temperature may be used to warm the blood externally and limit the length of the period of hypothermia.

Maintenance of normal fluid volume.   Intravenous administration of fluid and albumin will return the patient to a normal fluid level. Peripheral vasodilation and hyperemia during warming frequently require large volumes of fluid to maintain an adequate cardiac output. Monitoring of central venous or pulmonary artery wedge pressure may be done to guide volume replacement.

Prevention of intravascular aggregation.   This can result in infarction from increased blood viscosity in central hypothermia and circulatory damage to extremities in patients with frostbites. Low molecular weight dextran is given to reduce intravascular clumping and expand blood volume.

Maintenance of an open airway.   With severe respiratory depression, intubation and mechanical ventilatory assistance may be required.

Improvement of peripheral circulation.   With frostbite or other cold injuries of extremities, circulation is impaired. Methods to improve circulation include elevation of extremity and, in select cases, regional sympathectomy. The beneficial effect of regional sympathectomy is probably due to the decrease in vasospasm. Vasodilator drugs are sometimes given, but their value is uncertain.

Prevention of complications.   The complications that occur most often are development of dysrhythmias during rewarming, and infection and/or gangrene in tissue with inadequate perfusion. The ventricular myocardium shows increased irritability as rewarming results in core temperatures around 32 C (90 F). Lidocaine hydrochloride is given for ventricular premature beats or ventricular tachycardia. An electrical defibrillator should be available for ventricular fibrillation or ventricular tachycardia with moderate to severe hypotension. Severe cold injuries to extremities are treated with tetanus antitoxin, prophylactic antibiotics, protection from injury from bed covers, etc., early drainage of blebs and bullae with strict aseptic technique, and physiotherapy to minimize loss of function.

Education.   Information about ways to reduce adverse residual effects after frostbite must be presented. Measures include avoidance of exposure to cold, and use of gentle massage of extremity (rather than external heat) when exposure is unavoidable.

FEVER

Fever has long been recognized as a cardinal sign of disease. It can be defined as a disturbance of temperature regulation resulting from tissue injury. The products released into the bloodstream following injury which initiate a rise in core temperature are termed pyrogens. One form of bacterial pyrogen which is present within the cell or produced by gram-negative bacteria is called endotoxin. With bacterial invasion by the gram-negative bacteria, the endotoxin may directly stimulate the thermoregulatory center. The more commonly held belief, however, is that the endotoxin plays an intermediary role. As the endotoxin is removed from the bloodstream by the reticuloendothelial system, it activates phagocytes (polymorphonuclear and mononuclear neutrophils) and tissue macrophages to release fever-producing substances into the bloodstream. These agents, which have been called endogenous pyrogens, are believed to elevate the central thermoregulatory setting, activating the mechanisms for heat production and conservation, with resultant fever. It is believed that other infectious disorders in which endotoxin is not present, are also the result of release of endogenous pyrogens. In inflammatory states, mononuclear phagocytic leukocytes, tissue macrophages, or Kupffer cells probably activate the synthesis of endogenous pyrogens. The cause of fever in disorders other than infectious and inflammatory and the exact mechanism whereby endogenous pyrogens stimulate the hypothalamus to increase temperature setting is unknown.

Elevations of temperature due to disorders that directly damage the thermoregulatory center are not true fevers in the strictest sense, since they are not accompanied by tissue injury. Damage to the center can result from cerebral disorders such as tumors, infectious degenerative diseases, and vascular accidents. It can also occur when high environmental temperatures exceed the body's available homeostatic mechanisms for compensation. When these mechanisms fail, sweating ceases. Since sweating is the major mechanism for heat loss with elevated ambient temperature, the core temperature rises. The rising temperature becomes part of a vicious cycle: increased body temperature increases metabolism by accelerating chemical reactions and the increased heat thus produced, in turn, raises the temperature even more. Temperature frequently exceeds 41 C (105.8 F). This syndrome is termed heat stroke or heat hyperpyrexia.

Thus we see that in heat stroke and other disorders of the thermoregulatory center, the physiologic alteration is a failure to lose heat rather than the presence of an endogenous pyrogen that increases the thermoregulatory setpoint of the hypothalamus. Table 5-2 lists all the disorders that can result in an elevation of temperature. Regardless of the initiating mechanism, there are many commonalities in assessment and intervention. Thus, all elevations of temperature will be considered together, with identification of parameters of assessment and modalities of intervention that are specific for one disorder.

ASSESSMENT

When encountering a patient with a fever, it is the nurse's responsibility to determine:

1. The extent of the elevation
2. Whether the fever is expected in light of the medical diagnosis or due to another cause

TABLE 5-2. Major Causes of Fever

Abnormal Initiating Mechanism	Pathophysiology	Clinical State
Microbial Infection (Bacteria, viruses, chalmydias, mycoplasmas, rickettsias, spirochetes, fungi, protozoa)	Endogenous pyrogens produced in response to endotoxins from gram-negative bacteria and/or phagocytic activity to destroy microorganisms cause a change in the setting of the thermostat in the hypothalamus, resulting in fever	Gram negative sepsis, systemic staphylococcal infections, abscess, pneumonitis, meningitis, hepatitis, typhoid, tuberculosis, malaria, bacterial endocarditis, other infectious invasion
Malignant lesion	Liberation of products from the tissue destroyed by the neoplasm	Neoplasms most frequently accompanied by fever: lymphoma, hypernephroma, carcinoma of liver, pancreas, or lung, sarcoma
Nonmalignant alteration of tissue structure	Inflammatory reaction and tissue necrosis with/without alteration of phagocytes such as macrophages and Kupffer cells	Cirrhosis, regional enteritis, Whipple's disease, granulomatous hepatitis, sarcoidosis
Blood disorder	Alteration in normal hematopoietic cells in the bone marrow, infiltration of other organs by leukocytes, hemolysis and fragmentation of red blood cells, and impairment of normal inflammatory responses stimulate activation of endogenous pyrogens.	Acute agranulocytosis, acute leukemia, sickle cell crisis, thrombocytopenic purpura
Autoimmune disorders	Protein antigens combined with their antibodies activate the complement system, with a resultant inflammatory response and cell damage, with elevation of temperature	Acute rheumatic fever, systemic lupus erythematosus, rheumatoid arthritis, periarteritis nodosa, post-streptococcal glomerulonephritis, dermatomyositis, post-cardiac-injury syndrome
Tissue necrosis or trauma	Products of cellular breakdown and hematomas trigger the inflammatory reaction, with activation of endogenous pyrogens and resulting fever	Myocardial infarction, pulmonary embolism, gangrene of extremity, accumulation of blood in body cavities or intestinal tract, thrombosis, crushing injuries, fracture of large bones, surgical manipulation
Accelerated metabolic state	Increase in the metabolic rate from increased thyroid or norepinephrine secretion increases heat production	Thyrotoxocosis, pheochromocytoma
Allergic reaction	Antibodies formed in response to red blood cell incompatibility, animal serum, or antibiotics cause an immune reaction due to release of endogenous pyrogen	Blood transfusion reaction, serum sickness, antibiotic reaction

(continued)

TABLE 5-2. Continued

Abnormal Initiating Mechanism	Pathophysiology	Clinical State
Side effects of drugs	Alterations that may result in fever:	Drugs most frequently associated with fever:
	Inhibition of parasympathetic	Anticholinergic drugs (atropine, propantheline)
	Stimulation of sympathetic	Amphetamines, Methylphenidate, Imipramine
	Development of blood dyscrasia	Phenylbutazone, Sulfonamides
	Idiosyncratic reaction of excitement and increased metabolic rate	Barbiturates, Dilantin
	Hypersensitivity reaction	Antipyretics, Phenothiazines, Iodides, Thiouracils
Abnormality of sweat glands	Loss of mechanism of cooling by evaporation of water from the skin	Congenital absence Ichthyosis
Impaired heat dissipation	Decreased cardiac output and insulating effect of edema slow process of heat loss from body	Congestive heart failure
Disorder of heat regulatory mechanism	Injury or trauma to the central integrative mechanism in the posterior hypothalamus	Cranial lesion (CVA, tumor, hematoma, aneurysm), head injury, upper cervical cord injury, post brain surgery
	Failure of central regulating mechanism for cooling by sweating due to unknown cause, combined with high environmental temperature	Heat stroke (Heat hyperpyrexia)
	Suppression of central thermoregulatory reflexes for hyperthermia by anesthesia, with rapid temperature rise accompanied by intense muscular spasticity and rigidity, tachycardia, and dysrhythmias	Anesthetic hyperthermia
Disordered emotional state	Emotional stimulus of anxiety or excitement and some personality disorders stimulate the hypothalamic-pituitary-adrenocortical system with increased release of epinephrine and norepinephrine and resulting vasoconstriction leading to heat conservation	Psychogenic fever, stress reaction

3. Whether the patient has the adaptive mechanisms necessary to increase heat loss and prevent dangerously high core temperatures

4. Whether the fever with its accompanying increase in metabolic rate may have a deleterious effect on the patient suffering from another problem such as congestive heart failure, respiratory disease, neurologic disability, or dehydration.

The ordering of the assessment process would depend on the patient and the height of his fever, but the following parameters are generally included.

Measurement of core temperature.   This must be determined to find the extent of elevation. For accuracy in measurement, oral temperatures should not be taken until 15 minutes have elapsed after eating, drinking, or smoking. Either rectal or axillary temperatures should be taken when the patient is receiving oxygen or unable to close his mouth. Route of measurement needs to be indicated. Thermometers should be left in place for the full period of time recommended by the manufacturer. If there is a question about the accuracy of the temperature, it should be checked with another thermometer. When disposable heat-sensitive or electronic thermometers are used, checking should be by a different mode, since errors can result from improper storage of disposable thermometers or miscalibration of electronic thermometers. If it is suspected the patient has produced a purposeful elevation in temperature (factitious), the nurse should remain with the patient while the thermometer is in place. It should be remembered that aged and debilitated patients and persons receiving cortisone therapy may have an infection without a febrile response.

When fever has been present over a period of time, the pattern of the fever may be a clue to the cause. Most fevers are of the remittent type, i.e., they fall to normal (or near normal) each day. When the fever shows a persistent elevation, it is termed a sustained fever. This type of fever is present with damage to the thermoregulatory center in the hypothalamus or with untreated typhoid or typhus. When short periods of fever occur between 36 to 72 hours of normal temperature, it is termed a relapsing fever. Malaria is the most frequently seen condition, but parasitic relapsing fever, rat-bite fever, and, in some cases, Hodgkin's disease and localized pyogenic infections can be accompanied by periodic exacerbations of fever.

History.   Accurate history taking to elicit chronologic development of symptoms and clues to cause of fever should include:

1. Any exposure to high environmental temperatures.
2. Geographic or known human contact with infectious organisms.
3. Factors that predispose to infection by destruction of physical or chemical barriers or reduction of immune defense mechanisms.
4. Ingestion of drugs which precipitate hyperthermia.

Drugs which either stimulate the sympathetic nervous system (sympathomimetic) or block the parasympathetic (anticholinergic or parasympatholytic) can increase body temperature by increasing vasoconstriction or blocking the stimulus for vasodilation. Amphetamines are the sympathomimetic drugs most frequently responsible, while atropine or propantheline are the main anticholinergic drugs. Other drugs of importance are thyroid, antipyretics, antibiotics, and cortisone. Thyroid increases the metabolic rate, and antipyretic drugs such as aspirin and acetaminophen depress a fever or alter its pattern. A number of antibiotics can cause fever, which is probably due to hypersensitivity to the drug. Cortisone masks many of the warning signs of infection, including fever and elevation of the white count. In addition to drug intake history, questioning should determine the presence or absence of systemic symptoms which frequently accompany fever such as photophobia, headache, gastrointestinal disturbances, pain in the back, or generalized pain in the muscles or joints. Previous illness history may give clues to the cause, or supply information about the patient's ability to tolerate the fever.

Physical examination. To determine other altered functioning in response to the fever special attention must be paid to the following parameters.

• *Vital sign changes.* The pulse rate increases, respirations are rapid and shallow, and the blood pressure increases initially. In heat stroke with high elevation of the temperature, the blood pressure falls as shock develops.

• *Skin color and moisture* are determined by the stage of the illness and the underlying cause. With heat stroke, the skin is hot and dry. With the onset of fever due to an endogenous pyrogen, the skin is pale and cold. As the core temperature rises the skin begins to feel warmer. About two hours after the fever starts to rise, the skin appears flushed and feels warm. Mild perspiration to frank sweating occurs with fevers due to an endogenous pyrogen, with resultant lowering of temperature to some extent. The absence of skin moisture in a patient with an elevated temperature is a grave sign of failure of the central neural control center.

• *Chills* (or rigor) are present with fever due to some endogenous pathogens. They are most typical of pyogenic infections with bacteremia, but may also occur in noninfectious diseases such as lymphoma. The time of occurrence of chills corresponds with the period just before the fever starts to rise, when the patient is feeling cold. Duration is usually some 10−40 minutes.

• *Portal of entry* or signs of infection may be identified. Possible foci to be investigated include the teeth, oropharynx, tonsils, insect bites, skin lesions as boils, carbuncles, or furuncles, abdominal tenderness (indicative of abscess or peritonitis), wound from trauma or surgery, urinary indwelling catheter, swelling of lymph nodes, redness or rupture of ear drum, abnormality of drainage or output, or presence of signs of an inflammatory reaction. Occurrence of redness, heat, tenderness, and/or swelling in an area is indicative of an inflammatory response to an infectious process. The appearance and distribution of a rash, petechial hemorrhages, and other skin lesions are pathognomonic of certain infectious diseases.

• *Cognitive level* is impaired. Deficit can range from restlessness with inability to concentrate through lethargy and drowsiness to delirium, convulsions, loss of consciousness, and deep coma with decerebrate rigidity.

• *Herpes labialis* is frequently present. Fever seems to activate the herpes simplex virus with resultant lesions that are commonly called fever blisters.

• *Muscle twitching and/or flaccidity* with decreased tendon reflexes may be present with the extreme temperature elevation that accompanies heat stroke.

• *Abnormal chest ausculatory findings* may indicate cardiac or respiratory disorders. Heart murmurs not present previously may be due to rheumatic fever, bacterial endocarditis, or atrial myxoma. Friction rubs are an indication of an inflammatory process of the pleura or pericardium. Rales and rhonchi are an indication of lung congestion.

Laboratory tests. To determine the presence and identity of an infectious pathogen, the extent of the patient's defenses against an infection, or the presence of a noninfectious disorder responsible for the fever, testing must be done. Frequently utilized tests include:

• *White blood count and differential.* The homeostatic response to microbial infection is an increase in the white cell count, especially in the number of the cells with phagocytic action, or primarily the polymorphonuclear neutrophils (PMNs), which are sometimes called segmented neutrophils. In a patient with a previously normal white count, elevation greater than 12,000/cumm is suspicious, with levels above 15,000/cumm highly indicative of a microbial infectious process, particularly when PMNs comprise greater than 75 percent of the white cells. With severe septic states, the supply of PMNs may become exhausted. The presence of less mature forms of neutrophils as (in order of decreasing maturity) bands, metamyelocytes, myelocytes, promyelocytes, and myeloblasts are a sign of depletion of PMNs and mobilization of immature cells from the bone marrow in response to the infectious process. This can be an indication that the patient is beginning to exhaust his ability to mobilize an adequate number of phagocytic neutrophils to combat the infection.

• *Microscopic examination, culture, and sensitivity* of tissue, fluid, or body discharges from suspected foci of infection. The gram-stained smear provides the quickest information about whether the bacteria is gram negative or gram positive. Direct examination of unstained material may allow identification of ova, intestinal parasites, and some forms of fungus and yeast. Electron miscroscopy is required for visualization of viruses. Both aerobic and anaerobic techniques should be used for cultures from many areas. The incidence of anaerobic infections has been increasing, and it is important to recognize their presence early. Anaerobic cultures need to be obtained by careful methods to prevent exposure to oxygen during collection. When needle aspiration is used, any air in the syringe should be immediately expelled and the needle capped with a sterile solid rubber stopper. When tissue biopsy is taken, it should be promptly placed in a tube of prereduced anaerobically sterilized semisolid transport medium. Rubber stoppered tubes that have been gassed out with oxygen free carbon dioxide are also available for collection and transport. Cultures should be incubated for at least two weeks to permit recognition of the slow-growing organisms such as the Bacteroides group. Blood cultures need to be drawn at least three times over a period of 2 to 3 days. The optimal time for drawing a blood culture is when the temperature is rising, just before it reaches its peak. Cultures drawn after the temperature has reached its peak may not reveal the pathogen due to its alteration by the host's defenses. Cultures, whenever possible, should also be drawn before initiation of antibiotic therapy, since the drug can remain active in the specimen to interfere with the growth of a pathogen. The nurse obtaining specimens for analysis is responsible for insuring that: (1) the quantity is adequate for study; (2) the specimen is collected in a sterile manner; (3) the material comes from the source of the suspect area; (4) the specimen is packaged to prevent inadvertent contamination of those who handle it; and (5) the specimen is promptly delivered to the laboratory.

● *Immunologic examination* is being increasingly used to identify the responsible pathogen. Many of the techniques, such as counter-immunoelectrophoresis, provide information more rapidly than culture. Other tests utilize gas-liquid chromatography and mass spectroscopy to detect microbial byproducts. Measurements of the serum antibody titer are based on the premise that antibody production will increase during the source of an active infection. Baseline levels need to be obtained to compare with later samples. Tests to measure antibody content have a number of different names, depending on the nature of the reaction between the antibody and antigen. Most frequently ordered tests are febrile agglutinins, complement fixation, and fluorescent antibody (FA).

● *Blood smears* are examined for parasites, and lupus erythematosis (LE) cells, and abnormal morphology. Acute hemolytic crises are accompanied by marked fever, especially those due to sickle-cell disease.

● *Serum sodium and elevation of the blood urea nitrogen (BUN)* and serum osmolality gives an indication of the extent of the sodium and fluid volume deficit.

● *Serum enzyme* studies. Alkaline phosphatase is elevated in some malignancies; amylase is elevated with pancreatic disorders and cirrhosis, and transaminase is elevated with myocardial infarction and liver disease.

● *Bone marrow examination*—Material obtained from bone marrow biopsy is studied for tumor cells, LE cells, and abnormal red or white cells.

● *Arterial blood* is analyzed for pH and blood gases to determine acid-base state and adequacy of oxygenation.

● *Urine examination* frequently shows proteinuria, and may show bacteria.

Roentgenograms.   X-rays are necessary to locate evidence of an infectious or obstructive process. Plain films of suspected areas shows consolidation, pathologic changes characteristic of infection or tumors, and changes in size of organs. Dye contrast studies may be required to diagnose obstruction to flow of blood or other products, mass lesions, or other pathologic state.

Radioactive scans.   These can detect abscesses, osseous metastases, and liver pathology.

INTERVENTION

Ordering of intervention depends on the assessment of the state of the patient. When a high fever is life threatening, the first goal is to reduce the fever. When temperature is only moderately elevated and can be tolerated by the patient, the major focus of the intervention is to treat the underlying cause. Frequently occurring goals for the patient with an elevation of temperature and the main activities for their attainment will be briefly discussed.

Reduction of Temperature to Below 40 C (104 F)

If heat stroke is present, the patient has lost the mechanism of losing heat by evaporation, so the means of cooling is generally immersion in a cold water bath until the rectal temperature falls to 38.8 C (102 F). Temperature should not be allowed to fall below 38.3 C (101 F), because of the danger of severe potentiation of hypotension. Phenothiazine may be given to reduce shivering which decreases heat loss. Vigorous massage of the skin during cooling accelerates heat loss and stimulates the flow of the cooled peripheral blood to the brain and internal organs. After the temperature is lowered, the patient should be kept in bed lightly covered in a well ventilated cool room. Core temperature needs to be continually monitored since the patient may remain poikilothermic for several days.

When the high fever is due to an endogenous pyrogen, activities to lower the fever are directed toward bolstering the patient's own adaptive mechanisms. Only a light sheet should be used for covering and the room should be kept cool. The patient should be sponged with cool to tepid water without towel drying. The cooling effect comes from the evaporation of water from the skin, it is not necessary to use ice water or alcohol to lower the temperature. When the fever is expected to continue, a hypothermic blanket placed under the patient is frequently used. In rare instances the patient may require covering with a second hypothermic blanket to reduce a dangerously high fever. When a hypothermic blanket is used, care must be taken to keep the blanket temperature within a safe range, and the patient must be turned regularly to prevent injury from excessive skin cooling. When two blankets are used, the extremities should be wrapped with an insulating material to prevent frost bite. Antipyretics such as aspirin and acetaminophen may be given for comfort with moderate temperature elevation. They have an analgesic effect, and also act on the thermoregulatory center to lower the fever. Their use with temperatures greater than 40.5 C (105 F) in patients with hypotension, however, is contraindicated because of the danger of potentiation of the hypotension.

Maintenance of Normal Fluid Volume and Electrolyte State

Both sodium and water are lost with sweating; this is increased with higher metabolic rates. If the patient can take fluid orally, increasing the fluid intake may be adequate to replace losses. Parenteral intake may be required for those with a fluid volume deficit. Monitoring of electrolyte levels and fluid volume state is done to prevent overinfusion and the danger of left heart failure and pulmonary edema. Fluid volume state is assessed by urinary output and measurement of the central venous or pulmonary artery wedge pressure. Septic shock requires vigorous infusion of fluid because of the pooling of blood in the microvascular tissue beds with a resultant decrease in cardiac output and tissue anoxia.

Elimination of an Infectious Pathogen

Antibiotics are effective against many microbial infections. They have frequently been misused when they are prescribed indiscriminately rather than in relation to the infecting organism. Information regarding previous reaction to antibiotics should be obtained before any drugs are given. In most situations antibiotic therapy will be initiated before culture and sensitivity data are available. If anaerobic infection is suspected, Clinamycin may be given alone or combined with another antibiotic effective for gram-negative bacteria. When the report has been received from the lab, the regimen may be revised. Broad spectrum agents are frequently used without laboratory testing. It should be remembered that no agent is effective against all microbes. Not only must the right drug be given but it is crucial that the antibiotic level in the blood be adequate to kill the pathogen. The use of bolus doses of intravenous antibiotics is considered to be the most effective form of therapy for severe infections. The nurse is responsible for careful administration of the ordered dosage at the ordered time interval. Whenever antibiotics with known toxic effects are used, it is important to recognize early signs of toxicity. With developing renal failure, the administration of drugs excreted by the kidneys must be drastically reduced in dosage and frequency to avoid toxicity and further damage to the kidney. Audiology testing may be done every 2 to 3 days when ototoxic antibiotics are used. Potent diuretics are given with great care when the patient is on an antibiotic that is ototoxic. Although knowledge is incomplete on the mechanism by which diuretics increase the ototoxic potential of aminoglycoside antibiotics, it is believed to be related to the decrease in fluid in the inner ear. Serum drug level determinations are used to maintain therapeutic levels of the antibiotic and decrease the incidence of toxicity. When antibiotics that cause bone marrow depression and blood dyscrasias are used, baseline blood studies and follow-up studies every 2 to 3 days are indicated.

In addition to drug therapy, it is important to eradicate all necrotic tissue and provide adequate drainage for any present or potential focus of infection.

Wounds and burns are debrided of necrotic tissue. The use of wet to dry dressings is a commonly used means of debridement of small necrotic areas. Moist dressing are applied to the wound and allowed to dry. When they are removed after drying, the devitalized tissue adheres to the dressing. Drains are used in surgical wounds to prevent bacteria from growing in the blood and tissue exudates and forming an abscess. If an abscess does develop, the area is opened and drained. The nurse is responsible for maintaining patency of any catheter used for wound drainage. If suctioning is ordered, clots can form any time the catheter is clamped off, and when the catheter is not draining the blood properly, a hematoma may develop in the wound area. Hematomas later decompose and are a good media for growth of bacteria. Thus, portable devices that provide suction such as a Hemovac need to be used during transport.

Improvement of Adaptive Mechanisms

To fight present infection and resist development of new infections, adaptive mechanisms must be improved. Any patient with an infection at one site is at high risk for development of infection at another site. Care must be exercised to keep the skin intact to maintain its physical barrier to infection. Additionally, antibiotic therapy can alter normal body chemistry and cause a change in the normal flora of the gastrointestinal tract so that organisms not generally pathogenic such as yeast and enteric bacteria can flourish. Oral intake of yogurt and/or acidophilous milk has been found to decrease the overgrowth of some gastrointestinal organisms. Since milk products interfere with absorption of tetracycline, they must be given only between doses of this drug. Maintenance of an acid urine likewise decreases the incidence of *Pseudomonas*.

Adequate nutrition bolsters the body's defenses against infection. The accelerated metabolic state resulting from fever leads to nitrogen wasting and weight loss. A diet high in protein and calories is required to restore the positive nitrogen balance necessary for fighting an infectious process. The patient with a diminished appetite will need much encouragement to eat an adequate amount. If oral intake is not tolerated, total parenteral nutrition, sometimes termed hyperalimentation, may be utilized.

Increasing the patient's immune defenses by injection of antisera is indicated in a few instances. Examples are the local injection of rabies antiserum around the site of an animal bite and the use of immune globulin in individuals who are deficient. Passive immunization by the injection of antitoxin produced in lower animals is indicated for bacterial infections that are accompanied by the production of highly injurious or lethal toxins. The antitoxin neutralizes the toxin. The administration of antibiotics prevents further toxin production by inhibition of bacterial growth, but has no effect on toxin already produced. Disorders treated by antitoxin include diphtheria, tetanus, gas gangrene, cholera, and botulism. In a few patients with extremely low white counts (leukopenia), an infusion of polymorphonuclear neutrophils may be given. Reverse isolation is also used for these patients to decrease their exposure to pathogens.

Factors that limit a patient's ability to resist infection such as diabetes and renal problems must be carefully treated. Patients receiving drugs or other treatment that suppress the body's immune system may need to have some reduction in their therapy during the period of a severe infection.

Limitation of Discomfort

When systemic symptoms of photophobia, headache, backache, and aches in the muscles and joints are present, activities to lessen the discomfort are indicated. Drugs with antipyretic and analgesic actions are frequently given. Their use may be contraindicated, however, in the early stages of an illness because they mask the natural course of the fever. Other measures include elimination of glare, soothing back rubs, support of dependent body portions with pillows, and the use of a method of distraction chosen by the patients. Some persons enjoy soft music; others like to read; while there are some that prefer the company of others.

Discomfort caused by chills can be reduced by the intravenous administration of calcium gluconate. Oral hygiene should be done regularly for comfort as well the prevention of stomatitis and parotitis.

Control of Stress

Fever stimulates the hypothalamic-pituitary-adrenocortico system, with a resultant increase in heart and respiratory rate. When psychologic stress is superimposed on fever, the effect on the cardiovascular system and the patient's integrative ability may be greater than can be tolerated. Thus measures to limit the stress experienced by the patient are indicated. Effective measures with some patients include:

1. Providing knowledge about the patient's condition
2. Giving the patient more control in the situation.
3. Encouraging the patient to talk about his concerns.
4. Accepting the patient as he is.
5. Instituting measures to modify confusion and delirium.
6. Preventing undue fatigue by providing periods of uninterrupted rest.

Control of Deleterious Effects

Fever is accompanied by an increase in the metabolic rate and the inflammatory reaction to an infection results in chemical and mechanical injury of varying degrees. The metabolic rate (and thus oxygen consumption) is increased 12 percent for each degree increase in Celsius temperature and 7 percent for each degree increase in Fahrenheit temperature. Although most patients increase their cardiac output to meet this need, those with poor myocardial reserve will be unable to do so. Additionally, blood may not be adequately oxygenated in patients with respiratory disorders. When arterial blood gas studies show hypoxemia, supplementary oxygen is indicated. Mechanical ventilation may be required. Cardiotonic drugs that do not cause peripheral vasoconstriction are given to increase the cardiac output. Drugs commonly used are dopamine and isoproterenol.

With inflammatory reactions, local mechanical injury can result from the exudate and swelling. If the swelling puts pressure on the nerves and impedes circulation to other areas, severe damage can result. Prompt recognition and management is essential. Mild cases can be managed by elevation of the involved extremity. When the anterior compartment of the leg is the involved area, appropriate management is most often a fasciotomy to release the pressure on the nerves and circulation.

Chemical damage following an inflammatory reaction is due to the toxic products of disintegrating cells and microorganisms. These toxic substances can enter the blood stream and be carried to other organs, especially the lungs. A serious condition referred to as "shock lung" can result. Renal failure and disseminated intravascular coagulapathy are other possible serious complications. These will be discussed in more detail in later chapters.

Prevention of Spread of Infection

Since the mode of transmission varies with different pathogens, measures to prevent the spread depend on the pathogen involved. When spread is by direct contact with the patient, protective clothing needs to be worn. All items and equipment used by the patient should be removed from the room when they are no longer needed. The use of disposable dishes and supplies decreases the number of items that need to be disinfected or sterilized. Prophylactic immunization against some of the more serious contagious diseases is to be encouraged.

Knowledge About Future Activities

A patient with heat stroke needs to be cautioned about future exposure to high environmental temperatures. Many of the disorders responsible for fever are either recurrent or have no cure at the present time. The patient needs to be assisted to adjust his life to the disordered state and recognize the warning sign of fever as an indicator that the physician should be consulted.

EXPERIENTIAL INVOLVEMENT

CASE 5-A. Mrs. Sanford is a 68-year-old woman with progressively disabling osteoarthritis in her left hip. She entered the hospital for a left total hip prosthesis. Her surgery under general anesthesia was uneventful. She had to be catheterized twice (at 8-hour intervals) after surgery but was then able to void. She is tolerating a diet but has continuous intravenous (IV) for antibiotic infusion. She is still on bed rest with a thigh spreader to keep her hip in abduction. All her vital signs were normal until the afternoon of her second postoperative day at which time her findings were: BP 140/90, P 88, R 22, T(oral) 38.3 C (100.9 F).

Skillbuilders:

1. List on the practicum record (5-A), in order of likelihood of occurrence, the four most probable hypotheses for Mrs. Sanford's elevated temperature.

2. Then enter the data that supports the hypotheses and additional data you would need to confirm or disconfirm.

3. Record the major nursing activities if the hypothesis was confirmed.

4. In the last column list the criteria that would be used to evaluate the effectiveness of the process.

Feedback: All of our hypotheses for the cause of Mrs. Sanford's elevated temperature are related to infection. The ordering is based on the frequency of the cause of fever 48 hours postoperatively. We listed altered pulmonary function first, followed by urinary infection, wound infection, and phlebitis. Altered pulmonary function, which can be due to pneumonia or retained secretions with atelectasis, is the most frequent cause of early postoperative fever. It can cause fever within 24 hours after surgery. Urinary infections will be manifested by fever 24 hours after the initiating cause, but they occur less frequently than respiratory problems. Wound infections generally do not cause fever until 3 to 5 days post op, and phlebitis rarely develops before the fourth day of intravenous infusion. The supporting data for each hypothesis would be the temperature elevation of 38.3 C and the predisposing cause. All patients with surgery under a general anesthetic are at risk for development of pneumonia, particularly those with preexisting chronic obstructive pulmonary disease, the elderly, and those who cannot achieve mobility. Mrs. Sanford has two of these risk factors. Predisposing causes for the other hypotheses are obvious, i.e., bladder catheterization can result in urinary tract infection, a surgical wound can become infected, and phlebitis can occur with IV therapy.

Our search for additional data to confirm the hypothesis that fever is due to altered pulmonary function can be guided in part by the decision tree for respiratory insufficiency. A decrease in tidal volume can be both the cause for, and the effect of, altered pulmonary function. Low tidal volume breathing leads to progessive collapse of the alveoli and retained secretions. Accumulation of secretions results in obstruction of small bronchi, absorption of air, and collapse of the segment supplied by the occluded bronchus. The secretions are rich in sugar and protein and thus provide a good medium for the growth of bacteria. Other data to support the hypothesis would be observation of signs of labored respiration, decrease in cognitive functioning, presence of rales, and low arterial Po_2. Chest X-ray and collection of sputum for gram stain and culture would help confirm the hypothesis.

Nursing intervention if the hypothesis was confirmed has been outlined in considerable detail in the chapter on respiratory alterations. Major activities would include stimulating Mrs. Sanford to breathe deeply and cough productively. An incentive spirometer when accompanied by adequate instruction

PRACTICUM RECORD 5-A

Hypothesis/Possible Diagnosis	Supportive Data Available	Additional Data Needed to Confirm or Disconfirm	Nursing Intervention if Diagnosis Confirmed	Evaluation Criteria
Elevation in temperature due to:				
1.				
2.				
3.				
4.				

and supervision may result in deeper breathing. If she is not able to raise her secretions when assisted to cough, she may require postural drainage with chest percussion. These nursing interventions need to be evaluated simultaneously. Thus coughing is immediately evaluated for its effectiveness in raising secretions. If secretions are not raised, then postural drainage would be indicated. If the postural drainage was not effective, nasotracheal suctioning should be initiated. If none of these measures is successful, bronchoscopy might be indicated. The volume of air inspired with the maximal deep breath (vital capacity) should be measured to evaluate the effectiveness of the deep breathing. Intermittent positive pressure breathing (IPPB) might be used if volume was less than 800 ml after the airway was cleared of secretions. Again, IPPB needs to be evaluated. Since the machines are pressure-cycled, they cannot be set to deliver a certain volume. Spirometric measurements of exhaled volume must be made to determine if the machine is actually delivering the desired volume (800 ml is the minimum that would be considered adequate).

If the arterial blood gas reports showed a Po_2 less than 80 torr, oxygen would probably be indicated to prevent hypoxemia. The concentration of oxygen and the need to continue its use would be determined by repeat blood gases. The nurse would follow the physician's order for administration of antibiotics. Selection of the drug is generally based on the gram stain report but may await the culture and sensitivity report. Most of the evaluation criteria have been mentioned with the intervention. Additional criteria would be absence of fever, lungs clear to auscultation, normal chest X-ray, arterial Po_2 at preoperative level, and no growth on sputum culture.

The second hypothesis we will discuss is that the fever was due to a urinary tract infection. We have said the supporting data were the fever and history of catheterization. Additional data would include the finding of pus or bacteria in the urine sediment and identification of organisms on gram stain and culture. Some patients report frequency and urgency associated with urination and burning pain in the urethra afterward. Flank pain or tenderness is suggestive that the infection involves the kidney pelvis, a pyelonephritis. Denial of pain or discomfort, however, does not rule out urinary tract infection, because it can be present without any symptoms. Intervention if the diagnosis was confirmed would include forcing of fluids and encouragement of activity to facilitate complete emptying of the bladder. Antibiotic drugs ordered by the physician would be carefully administered. Since some drugs given for urinary tract infections are only effective if the urine is acid (with a pH below 5.5), supplemental ascorbic acid might be ordered. Evaluation if Mrs. Sanford were on this type of regimen would include testing of the urine pH. The major evaluation criterion would be urine free from bacteria.

This brings us to the third hypothesis, that the fever was due to a wound infection. Although symptoms of most wound infections do not begin to appear until the third day postoperatively, streptococcal and a few other organisms multiply rapidly and give signs of infection within 24 to 48 hours of contamination. Additional data to confirm the hypothesis of wound infection would be the presence of redness, swelling, and/or drainage from the wound site. If the infection had progressed beyond localized involvement of the superficial layers of the skin, systemic signs of infection would be present. The decision tree for sepsis will help guide our search for additional data to confirm the presence of systemic infection. The characteristic signs of chills, malaise, myalgia, photophobia, lymphadenopathy, and gastrointestinal upset may be present, but their absence does not rule out the possibility of infection. The most informative data would come from the wound culture and the white blood count differential.

Intervention if the hypothesis of wound infection was confirmed would be directed by the physician. Streptococcal infections are generally nonnecrotizing and can usually be adequately treated with specific systemic antibiotics. This would probably be the treatment for Mrs. Sanford since her early fever is indicative of a nonnecrotizing process. If the responsible pathogen were necrotizing with a collection of pus, the wound would be opened widely so it could drain and heal by granulation. Wet to dry compresses are frequently utilized to promote healing. As the compresses are removed, they debride the wound of devitalized tissue and debris. Although antibiotics are not given for every wound infection, they would probably be ordered for Mrs. Sanford because of the seriousness of an infection that could progress to involve the prosthesis. Since the prosthesis has no blood supply, infections that involve prostheses usually do not respond to antibiotics and may require removal of the prosthesis. Evaluation criterion would be wound healing with no infection.

This brings us to the hypothesis that phlebitis is responsible for the fever. Although it is the least likely cause for fever on the second post op day, the IV site should be checked promptly, since phlebitis can be readily identified in superficial sites and early recognition and treatment may prevent further complications. Additional data to support the hypothesis would be the presence of local pain, induration (hardness) along the course of the vein, swelling, and erythema. It is more difficult to recognize early phlebitis in the deep venous channels such as the subclavian. Distension of the venous tributaries distal to the IV site is indicative of extensive involvement with venous obstruction. Culture of the catheter tip after removal will help to identify whether the phlebitis is accompanied by an infection in the vein. Many cases of phlebitis are due to chemical irritation. Intervention for phlebitis consists of removal of the IV needle or catheter and application of heat to the inflamed area. Evaluation would be based on the absence of signs of phlebitis. Evaluation would need to be continued, however, for two weeks after removal of an indwelling intravenous catheter used for more than 5 days. The reason for the long surveillance is that septic phlebitis may be clinically hidden for two weeks after long-term intravenous catheter use. Additionally, since septic thrombus can be located at a considerable distance from the insertion site, the vein must be carefully observed at one or more points proximal to the insertion site to rule out intravascular sepsis.

EXPERIENTIAL INVOLVEMENT

CASE 5-B.   A woman was brought to the emergency department of a big city hospital at 11:00 P.M. She had been found in a semicomatose state on a bench in a small park in a residential section. She could be roused by stimulation, but

only groaned in response to questions and quickly drifted back to unresponsiveness. Her clothing was of good quality, but she was wearing only a light-
weight coat, although it was close to freezing. She carried no identification.
She was described as a clean, severely emaciated female with no scars, lacerations, or needle marks. Her breath had no detectable odor of alcohol, acetone, or
fruitiness. She had no icterus or edema, and her pupils were reactive with no
conjugate deviation. Her age was estimated between 60 and 80. Her vital signs
were T (rectal) 32.2 C (90 F), BP 90/70, P 60 (regular), R 14.

Skillbuilders:

1. On the practicum record (5-B), enter the three most likely hypotheses
for an abnormal initiating mechanism that could have contributed to the
hypothermia in this woman exposed to the cold.

2. Then enter the data from the history that support each hypothesis and
additional data you would need to confirm or disconfirm.

3. Since the specific nursing intervention for the associated disorders is
either obvious or discussed rather fully in other case studies, we are asking you
this time to outline only the nursing intervention for the hypothermic state, and

4. The criteria for evaluation of the intervention.

Feedback:
When you are unable to obtain a history from a patient, it is
difficult to narrow down the list of possibilities to the three most likely hypotheses. A few possibilities, however, have almost been ruled out by the description.
Absence of needle marks makes hypoglycemia due to insulin administration or
use of morphine unlikely. Absence of breath odor of alcohol, acetone, or fruitiness makes alcoholic intake or diabetic ketoacidosis unlikely. Myxedema usually
is manifested by puffiness of the eyes and abdominal fullness, while this woman
had no edema and was emaciated. The absence of icterus and edema makes
hepatic disease less likely, since one or both of these signs are usually present.
Central nervous system damage frequently causes alterations in the reaction of
the pupils to light or in the conjugate gaze. Thus having ruled out some possibilities, the three most likely hypotheses are severe weight loss (probably due to
anorexia nervosa), advanced shock (most likely due to sepsis), and intake of
barbiturates.

The supporting data for the hypothesis that hypothermia is associated with
severe weight loss is her emaciated appearance. Since she has no scars suggestive
of surgery for malignancy or colon disease, the most likely cause for severe
weight loss in a patient able to afford good clothes is a psychologic disturbance
resulting in anorexia nervosa. Support for a psychologic disturbance is her action of going outdoors with only a light wrap in the freezing weather. This action
seems to point to extreme disorganization that caused her to interpret the environment inaccurately or embark on self-destructive behavior. Additional data to
confirm the hypothesis would be negative findings for systemic disorders that
could be responsible for the weight loss or potentiate the hypothermia. When
she recovers sufficiently, psychologic assessment would be needed to confirm or
disconfirm the hypothesis.

The second hypothesis was that the hypothermia was associated with shock,

Hypothesis/Possible Diagnosis	Supportive Data Available	Additional Data Needed to Confirm or Disconfirm	Nursing Intervention for Hypothermia	Evaluation Criteria
Hypothermia following cold exposure associated with: 1.				
2.				
3.				

with septic shock the most likely cause. The low blood pressure of 90/70 gives a little support to this hypothesis, but blood pressure is nearly always low with hypothermia. Without knowing her previous blood pressure, the extent of the depression is difficult to evaluate. Thus, the supporting data come mainly from theory. In a debilitated patient with no signs of hemorrhage, the most likely cause of shock is sepsis. In an older person, sepsis can occur with an unrecognized primary infection, or accompanying an infection that was not considered serious enough for physician consultation. Thus endotoxin can be released into the circulation with a bacterial infection in the lungs or genitourinary tract. Supporting data would be positive blood culture, location of infection focus, and the leukocytosis with the increase in percentage of neutrophils and bands and presence of immature forms of white cells as depicted by the decision tree for sepsis. Since the patient is unable to answer questions, you would not be able to collect the history data listed on the decision tree. Her hypothermia clouds some of the other symptoms such as tachycardia, hyperpnea, and temperature of extremities. One parameter that would be meaningful, however, is pulmonary artery wedge pressure (PAWP) less than 10 torr (mm Hg). Since this measurement reflects intravascular volume and left ventricular function, it is low in shock associated with low cardiac output but normal heart function. It is elevated in cardiogenic shock with left ventricular failure. Although hypodynamic sepsis is the most likely cause for shock, failure to find a focus of infection should prompt a search to rule out the other types of shock. The decision tree for fluid volume deficit could guide the search for cues of hypovolemic shock. Since we are unable to secure history information and the central nervous system signs could be due to the hypothermia, we can get the most information from determination of the presence or absence of postural hypotension and flat neck veins when supine. Laboratory data on hematocrit, hemoglobin, total protein, and serum sodium should help confirm or disconfirm the diagnosis. The major problem we have is that in sepsis the blood is pooled in the capillary bed and plasma leaks into the interstitial spaces, with resultant deficit of circulating fluid volume. Therefore, the diagnosis of fluid volume deficit doesn't rule out sepsis.

The decision tree on low cardiac output heart failure can guide our search for data to support cardiogenic shock. The parameters that would be meaningful for this patient without edema are rales at lung bases, liver enlargement, distended neck veins when head elevated above 45 degrees, presence of metabolic acidosis, and PAWP greater than 25 torr. Further studies would be indicated to determine if the underlying cause was a myocardial infarction or another disorder. The possibility of shock due to anaphylaxis is highly unlikely.

Without patient history of intake, we only have few data for the hypothesis that the hypothermia was associated with intake of barbiturates. The supporting data come from theory that supplies a plausible explanation and a clinical picture that is not contradictory. Ingestion of 3 to 5 times the usual dosage of barbiturates results in impaired judgement, mild disorientation, drowsiness or sleep state, but normal pupillary reflexes. Additional data to confirm would be the presence of barbiturate in the blood and/or residual barbiturate obtained from gastric lavage. This discussion has followed the usual nursing process of assessment and diagnosis preceding intervention. This patient, however, is an example of one of the situations in which the hypothermic state is life threatening and intervention to treat the state and limit any dysfunctional effects would have been initiated without definitive diagnosis.

Nursing intervention would include:

1. Passive rewarming by placement of the lightly covered patient in a room at 20 C (68 F) temperature.

2. Careful intravenous infusion of fluid and albumin as ordered.

3. Maintenance of an open airway and adequate ventilation.

4. Observation of extremities for development of redness and mottling with rewarming which can indicate frostbite.

5. Provision of safety while patient has reduced cognitive function and increased myocardial irritability.

Evaluation criteria for rewarming would be increase in body temperature of 0.5–1 C (1–1.8 F) an hour. Therapeutic infusion of intravenous fluid would be indicated by maintenance of PAWP between 12 and 20 mm Hg, urine output above 30 ml an hour, and absence of postural hypotension or pulmonary edema. Criteria for evaluation of ventilation would be normal blood gases and normal chest X-ray. It is important to remember that blood gases need to be corrected for temperature. Arterial P_{O_2} and P_{CO_2} can be spuriously high if uncorrected. Criteria for frostbite would be related to minimal residual damage or loss of function. Safety would be evaluated by the absence of injury or infection and prevention of ventricular fibrillation.

ADDITIONAL READING

Atkins E: Fever. In MacBryde C, Blacklow R (eds.): Signs and Symptoms, 5th ed. Philadelphia, Lippincott, 1970, pp 451–470.

Davis-Sharts J: Mechanisms and manifestations of fever. AJN 79(11): 1874–1877, 1979.

Guyton A: Textbook of Medical Physiology, 5th ed. Philadelphia, Saunders, 1976, pp 831–843.

Petersdorf R: Disturbances in heat regulation. In Harrison T (ed.): Principles of Internal Medicine, 9th ed. New York, McGraw-Hill, 1980, pp 53–68.

CHAPTER 6

Edema

Edema is a sign of expansion of the extracellular fluid in the interstitial spaces as a result of movement of fluid from the plasma in the intravascular space into the tissues. There are two major pathophysiologic mechanisms for the formation of edema. The process is initiated by changes in the vascular system or in the composition of its components that results in transudation of fluid from the plasma. As a consequence, mechanisms are initiated that cause the renal retention of water and electrolytes to prevent hypovolemic shock. The second mechanism is a result of renal hemodynamics or renal hormonal influences that cause retention of sodium and water by the kidneys, with the transudation of fluid a secondary occurrence.

The most frequent vascular cause of edema is an increase in capillary blood pressure which can result whenever the venous pressure is increased. This mechanism is seen in the nonpathologic occurrences of swelling in the ankles of persons who stand for long periods of time with little muscular activity to promote venous return. Sleeping while seated may also result in edema because venous obstruction that occurs in a sitting position is added to the reduced cardiac work while sleeping which causes the blood to back up in the venous system. It is seen in heart failure where inadequate cardiac output results in accumulation of blood in the heart and great vessels. Edema also results when there is an obstruction to the venous or lymph flow.

Other vascular factors that result in transudation of fluid into the tissue are damage to the capillary endothelium (which increases capillary permeability) and a decrease in the plasma oncotic pressure. When the plasma protein is low, there is a reduction in the colloid osmotic pressure that normally pulls fluid back into the vascular compartment.

Edema is a manifestation of abnormal renal retention of sodium and water when more sodium is ingested than the kidney can excrete or when there is a decrease in the renal excretion of sodium by the kidneys. There are two major hormones that stimulate the renal tubular readsorption of sodium. Aldosterone is secreted by the adrenal cortex probably in response to a decreased volume of plasma. It causes a decrease in the renal excretion of sodium and an increase in the excretion of potassium. The retention of sodium and the decreased effective

157

TABLE 6-1. Major Causes of Edema

Abnormal Initiating Mechanism	Pathophysiology	Clinical State	Identifying Characteristics
A. Increased intravascular pressure due to:			
1. Cardiac disease	Incomplete systolic emptying of the chambers of the heart leads to an accumulation of blood in the heart and venous circulation causing an increase in venous volume and pressure resulting in transudation of fluid. The increase in venous volume causes a corresponding decrease in arterial volume with initiation of the mechanisms of aldosterone and ADH secretion to increase retention of sodium and water.	Anatomic lesions, bacterial endocarditis, beriberi (wet), cardiomyopathy, constrictive pericarditis, cor pulmonale, dysrhythmias, heart failure (right), myocardial infarction	Pitting edema occurring primarily in the ankles and pretibial regions, ascites, distension of neck veins when head elevated 45 degrees, cardiac enlargement, diastolic murmurs, gallop rhythm, hepatomegaly
	Increased pulmonary capillary blood volume and pressure plus increased capillary permeability from poisons and inhalation of smoke or toxic gases	Pulmonary edema	Chronic-paroxysmal nocturnal dyspnea
			Acute: interstitial edema in early stages with first sign being tachypnea. With alveolar involvement, wet rales and rhonchi with diffuse haziness on chest X-ray, deterioration of blood gases, acidosis, and frothy sputum.
2. Hepatic disease	High venous pressure which develops from a combination of increased resistance to flow, sustained high splanchnic inflow, and inadequate collateral decompression causes hepatic capsular weeping. Hypoalbuminemia (due to decreased liver production of albumin) and impaired water and sodium excretion that accompanies hepatic disease are responsible for the dependent edema in the early stages and contribute to ascites in the later stages.	Cirrhosis, hepatic amyloidosis, carcinoma infiltration, portal vein thrombosis, schistosomiasis	Ascites, edema of lower extremities (dependent edema)

158

	Mechanism	Condition	Effect
3. Hypertension, acute, severe	Vasoconstriction is a response to hypertension, but arteries in eyeball and brain are unable to constrict to the same degree as peripheral so they become engorged with blood with the pressure causing transudation	Hypertensive encephalopathy	Edema of optic disc and brain
4. Obstruction of circulation			
a. Venous	Interference with venous return	Thrombophlebitis, phlebothrombosis, varicose veins	Localized edema of area drained by the affected veins
		Compression of superior vena cava	Edema with cyanosis of upper body
b. Lymphatic	Interference with lymphatic drainage from tissue spaces to vascular bed	Lymph nodes removed, lymphangitis, filariasis, Milroy's disease	Edema of involved area, with edema fluid rich in protein since lymphatics removed protein lost from capillaries. High tissue oncotic pressure makes it difficult to reduce edema.
	Obstruction or damage to the abdominal lymphatic system	Chylous ascites	Ascites, fluid appears milky and contains fat
5. Increased body sodium and fluid volume from:			
a. Excess fluid and/or sodium intake	When intake of salt and fluid exceeds kidney's excretory ability, have increased intravascular pressure resulting in transudation.	Hypervolemia, sodium overload	Generalized hypotonic edema
b. Renal retention of sodium and water	Mechanical retention of sodium and water due to inability of kidney to excrete them	Renal disease, end stage	Hypotonic edema, primarily of lower extremities
	Sodium retained due to high levels of estrogens and progesterone	Toxemia of pregnancy	Excessive weight gain with puffiness of the face, fingers, and ankles; sometimes cerebral edema with convulsions.
	Hormone produced with maturation of corpus luteum causes retention of sodium and water.	Premenstrual tension	Weight gain and ankle edema with occasional abdominal distension. Condition more severe in evening.

(continued)

TABLE 6-1. Continued

Abnormal Initiating Mechanism	Pathophysiology	Clinical State	Identifying Characteristics
	Pathologic changes in glomeruli resulting in renal retention of sodium and water	Glomerulonephritis, acute	Edema of periorbital area, lower extremities, and sacrum, hematuria, proteinuria
	Excess steroids act upon renal tubules to stimulate the reabsorption of salt from the glomerular filtrate	Hyperaldosteronism Adrenocortical hyperfunction	Gain in weight If severe, generalized edema may be evident; hypokalemia
	Diminished renal perfusion and decreased water excretion	Myxedema	Periorbital edema, facial edema, nonpitting edema of extremities, diminished thyroid function
B. Increased capillary permeability: 1. Increased glomerular permeability	High urinary loss of protein due to increased permeability of glomeruli, with a resultant decrease in colloid osmotic pressure	Nephrotic syndrome, diabetic nephropathy	Periorbital edema, pleural effusion, generalized edema progressing to anasarca, heavy proteinuria, hypoalbuminemia, hypercholesterolemia
2. Allergic disorders	Allergen triggers histamine secretion which increases capillary permeability	Angioneurotic edema, urticaria, serum sickness, insect bites and stings	Edema may affect eyelids, lips, face, and/or mucous membranes of mouth, larynx, and gastrointestinal tract. White raised wheals surrounded by erythomatous areas over body or on mucous membranes
	Increased capillary permeability plus constriction of airways increases respiratory efforts, increasing intrapleural pressure, with resultant increase in venous pressure and transudation of fluid	Bronchial asthma	Edema of bronchial mucosa

3. Trauma	Tissue injury liberates vasoactive substances (histamine, kinins, prostaglandins) that cause vasodilation and increased capillary permeability with transudation of fluid	Tissue injury, burn, fracture, sprain, tendon injury	Edema of area distal to the site of trauma
4. Toxic damage to capillaries	Venom causes increased permeability of capillaries	Snake bite	Local edema that spreads in all directions accompanied by bullae and ecchymosis over involved area
	Capillary damage from toxin produced by bacteria	Cellulitis	Edematous swelling of skin and subcutaneous tissues accompanied by local pain, redness, and heat
5. Peritoneal irritation	Inflammation causes damage to capillary endothelium with transudation of fluid	Peritonitis Rupture of a hollow viscus Chronic pancreatitis	Ascites Abdominal pain, ileus Pancreatitis has high amylase in ascites fluid
6. Vitamin deficiency	Deficiency of ascorbic acid interferes with collagen synthesis and integrity of blood vessels	Scurvy	Edema of joints and lower extremities
C. Decreased colloid osmotic pressure	Hypoproteinemia results in a decrease in osmolality of plasma, with loss of fluid into interstitial space	Starvation, malabsorption of amino acids	Generalized edema but most evident in the eyelids and face, being more pronounced in the morning after sleeping
D. Damage to autonomic nervous system	Loss of vasoconstrictive mechanism predisposes to arteriolar dilation, with pooling of fluid in involved area. Decreased lymphatic and venous circulation from inactivity heightens edema	Hemiplegia	Edema of affected side

arterial blood volume seem to trigger the release of the antidiuretic hormone (ADH) from the posterior lobe of the pituitary which increases the reabsorption of water in the distal renal tubules with resulting transudation of fluid into the interstitial compartment. It is important to remember that in many types of renal insufficiency such as chronic pyelonephritis, polycystic disease, and medullary cystic disease there is salt wasting and these patients have high urinary loss of sodium and no edema.

Edema fluid can be hypotonic, isotonic, or hypertonic. When it is isotonic, the function of the cell is not affected. However, if the edema fluid is hypotonic or hypertonic, the integrity of the cell membrane may be disturbed. The amount of sodium in the extracellular compartment determines its osmotic effect, so cells swell in the presence of low sodium hypotonic edema and shrink with high extracellular sodium concentrations. Thus, the effect of edema on cellular metabolism should be considered when the extracellular fluid has either abnormally high or low levels of sodium. The accompanying Table 6-1 lists the abnormal mechanism, pathophysiology, and clinical state (with identifying characteristics) that results in edema.

ASSESSMENT

History

Any previous disorders responsible for edema or predisposition to such disorders by ingestion (diet, drugs, ethanol, etc.) or trauma will help identify the cause for edema and direct the search for cues.

Physical Examination

Distribution of the edema.   This is an important guide to its cause. Generalized noninflammatory edema is usually associated with cardiac, hepatic, renal, or nutritional disorders. Localized edema is usually due to inflammation, hypersensitivity, localized loss of vasomotor tone, or obstruction in venous or lymphatic systems. These causes of localized edema can be further differentiated by the assessment of the color and sensitivity of the skin. Local tenderness and warmth is suggestive of inflammation while local cyanosis and coldness may signify venous obstruction. The ankles are the first site to show edema, although in a patient confined to bed, edema would be evident first in the sacral areas.

Extent.   Edema is termed "pitting" when there is persistence of an indentation of the skin following pressure. It is sometimes rated on a scale of 1+ to 4+. The meaning of scales varies, however, so it is important to know the scale used in your health facility. One scale uses 1+ to indicate edema of the feet, 2+ to indicate edema ascending to the calves, 3+ to indicate edema above the knees, and 4+ to represent involvement of the entire extremities. In other facilities, 1+ indicates that pitting is a depth of 1 mm, 2+ a depth of 2 mm, and so on. Pitting edema is characteristic of extracellular fluid excess, and is a hallmark of dilutional hyponatremia. (Low serum sodium, but excess of total body sodium due to excess fluid). Anasarca refers to gross, generalized edema, which is usually due to excess fluid in the intracellular as well as extracellular compartment.

Weight.   When the edema is generalized over a large portion of the body, an increase in weight is one of the earliest indicators of excess fluid. Before edema can be detected by physical examination, the body weight can increase by nearly 10 percent. This means the average-sized person of 60 to 70 Kg (132 to 154 pounds) can store 6 to 7 liters of fluid before the edema is clinically evident. (Each kilogram of weight gained is equivalent to a liter of fluid.)

Presence of ascites.   Ascites is an accumulation of fluid in the peritoneal cavity. It may be difficult to assess by physical examination. Bulging flanks may be present in the supine position, although massive ascites can be present without this sign. A fluid wave and shifting dullness may indicate ascites, but they can also be present with a distended viscus, fat, pelvic cyst, or a neoplasm. A fluid wave is elicited by sharply tapping one side of the abdomen with the right hand with the left hand placed on the opposite side of the abdomen to receive the transmitted wave. The impulse is felt after a perceptible time lag. To differentiate between a wave from fat in the mesentery, an assistant needs to place the ulnar surface of his hand along the midline of the abdomen to block a wave from fat. To test for shifting dullness, the abdomen is percussed with the patient supine, marking the areas over the flanks that are dull to percussion. Then, after a minute of lying on the side, the abdomen is percussed again. A considerable shift in the area of dullness with increased dullness on the side that is down indicates the probability of fluid.

Measurement of circumference of extremity.   If edema is localized in one extremity, the amount of fluid retained can be estimated by measuring the circumference of the extremity. A 1-in. increase in the circumference of one thigh (measured at the mid-thigh level) is indicative of transudation of some 1 to $1^{1}/_{2}$ liters of fluid.

Venous pressure.   The venous pressure is an aid in the evaluation of all fluid volume states. Elevation in a portion of the body indicates venous obstruction. Elevation of the central venous pressure is indicative of fluid overload. The cause may be congestive heart failure (with failure of the heart to pump out the blood) or acute renal insufficiency (with failure to excrete fluid).

Laboratory Tests

Those that are needed to provide helpful information are serum albumin, serum sodium, serum and urine osmolality, and urinalysis for protein and sodium. The laboratory determination of total serum protein and albumin differentiates the patients in whom decreased intravascular colloid pressure contributes to the edema. A low serum protein is referred to as hypoproteinemia, and albumin less that 2.5 g/dl is termed hypoalbuminemia. The presence of protein in the urine (proteinuria) points to renal and/or cardiac disease. Slight to moderate proteinuria is indicative of cardiac disease, with large urinary protein losses characteristic of the renal disease termed the nephrotic syndrome. Proteinuria also helps evaluate the sign of hepatomegaly, which can be present in either cardiac or hepatic disease. In the absence of proteinuria, hepatomegaly is more likely due to hepatic disease.

INTERVENTION

The specific treatment modality for any patient is aimed at correcting the abnormal state that produced the edema when it is possible and in reducing its dysfunctional effects. Therefore, accuracy in diagnosis of the underlying problem is crucial. Supportive measures and some treatment modes are common for all generalized edema regardless of the abnormal state that produced it.

Diuretics

Usually diuretics are given to rid the body of excess water. If the edema is a threat to life, diuretics are given by intravenous push. Occasionally if response to diuretics is slow, the patient will be treated with rotating tourniquets to pool the blood in the extremities and reduce the volume (and thus the venous pressure) of the circulating blood. *Fluid restriction,* at least during the acute period, is essential. Patients on diuretics need to be monitored for potassium since hypokalemia can result from loss of potassium with fluid. Diuretics are given with caution to patients with liver disease since their use may potentiate hepatic encephalopathy.

Sodium Restriction

Sodium intake is restricted. Even though the serum sodium may be low, the patient usually has an excess total body sodium.

Drainage

Some localized edema that exerts a deleterious pressure may be removed by drainage. Examples are ventriculostomy drainage for cerebral edema, pericardiocentesis for drainage of pericardial fluid, and, in a few instances, paracentesis for drainage of ascites fluid. It is important to remember that fluids must be restricted after paracentesis and the patient monitored for signs of hypovolemia, since protein and fluid tend to move from the vascular space into the abdominal cavity. If fluids are allowed ad lib, the osmolality of the serum is lowered, favoring increased movement of fluid out of the vascular compartment.

Promotion of Venous Return

Elevation of an edematous extremity. This may be indicated to promote return of fluid to the vascular system. However, if heart failure is an underlying problem, increasing the blood volume returning to the heart will increase the heart failure. When the pressure on tissues caused by edema is in danger of damaging the nerves of the extremities, fasciotomy is indicated.

Muscular exercise (or range of motion exercises). Exercise of the edematous extremities and the use of support stocking on the legs may be indicated to promote venous return.

Maintenance of Skin Integrity

Edema in tissues limits the blood flow to the tissues, interfering with their nutrition, and making them more vulnerable to injury. Bed patients with generalized edema who have to have their head elevated to breathe are particularly prone to decubiti on the buttocks. They need frequent shifts of position to prevent tissue breakdown from continuous pressure on edematous tissue. Cleanliness and prevention of moisture accumulation are also important for decubiti prevention.

EXPERIENTIAL INVOLVEMENT

Case 6-A. Mrs. Hill is a 68-year old-woman, 5 feet 2 inches in height, weighing 170 pounds. She was admitted to the hospital in a semicomatose state with an initial medical diagnosis of stroke. The absence of blood or elevation of pressure in the spinal fluid, neurologic manifestations, and angiography resulted in the definitive diagnosis of occlusion of the superior branch of the right middle cerebral artery. Her condition remained unchanged for 48 hours and then gradually improved. A week after admission, she had a left hemiparesis with some spasticity, urine and bowel incontinence, motor (ataxic) aphasia, and facial asymmetry. She was fed through a nasogastric tube. She seemed to recognize what was said and usually followed simple commands. When the head of the bed was elevated, she continually fell toward the left side. She did not follow movements of people or notice objects on her left. While bathing Mrs. Hill on her eighth day, it was noticed her left leg was considerably larger than the right. The skin was tightly stretched and the tissue felt hard when pressed.

Skillbuilders:
1. On the practicum record (6A-1) list the two most likely hypotheses for Mrs. Hill's left leg edema, listing the most critical state first.
2. Then enter the data that support each hypothesis and additional data you would need to confirm or disconfirm.

PRACTICUM RECORD 6-A1

Possible Hypothesis/ Diagnosis	Supportive Data Available	Additional Data Needed to Confirm or Disconfirm	Nursing Intervention if Diagnosis Confirmed	Evaluation Criteria
Left leg edema due to: 1.				
2.				

PRACTICUM RECORD 6-A2

Problems (Present or Anticipated)	Nursing Intervention	Evaluation Criteria
From neurological deficit:		
1.		
2.		
3.		
4.		
5.		
From adaptation:		
1.		
2.		
3.		
4.		

3. Enter the appropriate nursing intervention for each diagnosis (in the order of priority) and the criteria for evaluation.

4. On the practicum record (6A-2) enter the five major problems related to the neurologic deficit that are important to consider in planning care for Mrs. Hill. Then list four psychosocial problems that Mrs. Hill is likely to experience as a result of her stroke. Briefly outline the nursing intervention and the evaluation criteria for each identified problem. Use numerical estimates to express the goal of the percent of function to be regained whenever feasible.

Feedback: This was an easier one, wasn't it? But time consuming! We're sure you identified the most critical hypothesis as edema due to venous thrombosis because it can lead to pulmonary embolism. The second hypothesis would be edema secondary to hemiplegia, with arteriolar dilation and decreased venous circulation. The supporting datum for venous thrombosis is the history of venous stasis, a major element in the development of thrombi. Factors that contributed to venous stasis are venous dilation in the recumbent position, paralytic loss of the muscular pumping activity that massages the veins and promotes the return of blood to the heart, and the 50 percent decrease in blood flow that accompanies bed rest. Another factor predisposing to the development of venous thrombosis is obesity (weight 170 pounds). Additional physical observations to confirm are somewhat difficult with a limb which has reduced sensation and a patient who responds poorly. The presence of pain, tenderness, warmth, and a positive Homan's sign are data that support the hypothesis. Even with sensory impairment, most patients will grimace (or otherwise demonstrate pain) when the foot is forcibly dorsiflexed to elicit Homan's sign. The greatest difficulty in confirming the hypothesis comes from the theoretical knowledge that more than half of the patients with deep venous thrombosis (which poses the greatest threat for pulmonary embolism) may have no symptoms at all, or only one or two.

Diagnostic tests used by physicians include venography, radioactive fibrinogen, electrical impedance plethysmography (IPG), and ultrasound. The nursing activities would primarily be guided by the nature of the phlebitis and the physician's orders. Superficial phlebitis is usually treated by application of moist heat locally, elevation of the extremity above the heart level (with only slight bending at the knees), and use of elastic support hose. In addition to these measures, deep venous thrombosis is treated by anticoagulation with heparin. Careful monitoring of the patient for bleeding is, of course, in order for any patient on heparin. Of vital importance is observation for development of pulmonary embolism which may be accompanied by difficult tachypneic breathing, cough, hemoptysis, tachycardia, chest pain, rales, and accentuation of the pulmonary second sound.

Evaluation criteria are resolution of venous thrombosis, decrease in edema, absence of bleeding, and absence of pulmonary embolism. If the hypothesis of venous thrombosis was not supported, the hypothesis of edema secondary to hemiplegia would probably be accepted. The supporting datum available is the same as that of venous thrombosis, since venous stasis is primarily responsible for both. Additional data needed would include careful examination of the left arm and left side of the face to determine if edema is of entire left side. The main data would be the absence of venous thrombosis. Except for some long shots as unidentified trauma or snake bite, there is no other explanation for the edema.

The most important nursing intervention would include turning every 2 to 4 hours with passive range of motion to extremities (including dorsiflexion of foot to massage veins) with every position change. Other intervention would include elastic support hose, elevation of the foot of the bed, and care to prevent pressure on the calf of the leg. The evaluation criteria would be absence of edema of the left leg, absence of venous thrombosis, and absence of myoglobinuria. Perhaps you are not familiar with myoglobinuria, but it can result from muscle ischemia caused by prolonged compression of the muscle due to the weight of an immobile patient. Fasciotomy may be required in rare instances to prevent muscle necrosis. The myoglobin that is released into the circulation when muscle is impaired can cause renal failure.

There are several problems present or anticipated from her neurologic deficit. She has paralysis of both left arm and leg, but the early development of spasticity is a good sign that at least some function will return. Other obvious problems are urine and bowel incontinence and motor aphasia. Did you get the two more obscure (and less talked about problems) of spatial-perceptual deficit and one-sided neglect (hemianopsia)? Patients with left hemiplegia are apt to have spatial-perceptual difficulties as evidenced by Mrs. Hill's inability to keep from falling to one side when her head was elevated. Other problems are an inability to judge position, speed of movement, and distance to objects. One-sided neglect was evidenced by Mrs. Hill's inability to see objects on her left side. People with this problem do not turn their heads or attempt to see the other part of an object of which they only see a section. The extent of her neglect will need to be evaluated, as some patients neglect auditory input as well as visual. Perhaps if you missed these problems, you would like to go ahead and fill in the intervention and evaluation before you read more of the feedback. We realize you may have also listed problems that were common to patients with right-sided brain damage, but for which no information was given in the case study. This is great, but there is no way we could hope to discuss all the possible problems. More detailed assessment would be required in the clinical situation to insure that all such problems are identified.

Let's look at nursing intervention and evaluation of the neurologic deficiency first. Intervention for paralysis of the left arm and leg needs to be started early to prevent contractures and deformities and for most complete return of function. Nursing intervention would include:

1. Maintenance of body alignment with left arm supported on a pillow, a soft rubber ball in left hand, and the use of a footboard and a trochanter roll for the left leg.

2. Active and passive range of motion exercises to all extremities every 2 to 4 hours.

3. Encouragement of left hand finger stretching and movement of the left arm with her right hand and arm.

4. Assistance with transfer to chair (with bed in lowest position) by standing on right side, and supporting Mrs. Hill while instructing her to step on her right foot first; it's better not to call it the good foot because that implies the other foot is bad. It is helpful to tap the foot the patient is to move.

5. Assistance and instruction for walking in a walker and with a cane as needed.

We're sure you may have thought of others as there are many possible activities in this area. We didn't include supportive actions as skin care to prevent decubitis, which is of course important, but not a specific activity for this problem.

Evaluation criteria are absence of contractures and minimal muscle wasting. Muscle wasting should be stated in measurable terms, i.e., measurement of left extremities at mid-deltoid, mid-thigh, and calf at least 90 percent of measurement of right side. Other criteria would include left hand grasp at least 75 percent of right, able to raise left arm 120 degrees, able to transfer from bed to chair with minimal assistance, and able to walk length of hall with walker. It is difficult to tell at this time what the potential is for regaining the use of her left side. However it is important to develop the habit of stating the outcome behavior specifically in measurable terms whenever possible.

Let's now look at the intervention for the problem of urine and bowel incontinence. Most patients can regain control of bladder and bowels with retraining. Bowel training usually employs suppositories (and sometimes digital stimulation) every other day. Gradual weaning from dependence on suppositories can usually be accomplished. Bladder retraining is initiated by establishing a pattern for voiding. A bedside commode (or toilet if patient can walk) is used every 2 or 4 hours (based on patient's previous habits). Patient should be assisted to lean forward and contract the abdominal muscles to stimulate voiding. Catheterization for residual urine may be required for a brief period. Evaluation criteria would be urine continence and control of bowels (either with or without use of suppositories).

When we look at the next problem of motor aphasia, we realize that it is easier to manage than central aphasia from left side brain damage. Mrs. Hill's aphasia is manifested by difficulty in speaking but she has normal auditory reception (absence of receptive aphasia). The speech therapist will guide her therapy, but the following nursing actions will help:

1. Wait patiently when she struggles with a word. If she is becoming frustrated, either supply the word for her (and encourage her to repeat it after you) or, if you don't know what she is trying to say, reassure her that she'll be able to think of it later and can tell you then.

2. Keep practice periods brief, and give positive encouragement.

3. Keep noise and other distracting influences at a minimum to increase concentration.

4. Use any aids that are helpful such as pictures with names printed underneath, tape recordings of words and sounds needing practice.

Outcome criteria could be: ability to speak 5 new words each week (or whatever figure is realistic at the time). The figure should increase as time goes by.

Now we'll move on to discuss spatial-perceptual deficits. This is probably the least understood and recognized deficit. Since it will have a great influence on Mrs. Hill's learning self-care skills, it is important to assess the extent of her deficit accurately and plan intervention to help her compensate for the identified weaknesses. Intervention that we have found effective includes:

1. When seating patient in a chair, place the chair in front of a mirror or with the left side against the wall to provide a cue as to whether body is upright or leaning.

2. Ask patient to talk her way through a task before attempting it. For tasks that are hard to master, write out simple, brief instructions for the steps in the process.

3. Check patient on each activity before she is allowed to do it on her own. (This counteracts for overestimation of abilities which is characteristic of the left hemiplegic, in contrast with the cautiousness of the right hemiplegic.)

4. Provide appropriate verbal instructions and cues rather than demonstration for a task. Cues are frequently needed to guide patient in top and bottom, wrong side and right side, and movement toward right or left to avoid hitting doorframe, furniture, etc.

Evaluation criteria would be (1) able to perform self-care abilities of dressing, bathing, eating, and ambulating; and (2) recognizes activities she is incapable of doing without assistance.

The last problem for us to discuss is one-sided neglect. Since Mrs. Hill does not have auditory aphasia, her neglect is probably (although not necessarily) limited to visual. Intervention for visual neglect with Mrs. Hill would include:

1. Approach patient from the right side while problem severe.

2. Place bed so patient's right side is toward the major activities in her environment. (This is usually with the door of the room on the patient's right.)

3. When placing food in front of the patient, encourage her to name all items on her tray (to train her to see the whole tray, not just the right half).

4. When traveling outside the room, point out distinguishing features and colors of the left side of the corridor (to prevent her from seeing only the right side and not recognizing the corridor when she returns).

Evaluation criteria could be simply stated for this problem as absence of one-sided neglect. It would be helpful in evaluation, however, if you also included measurable specific behavior such as:

1. Will identify persons approaching from the left as well as the right.

2. Will respond to activities occurring on both left and right side.

3. Will eat food from both sides of her tray.

4. Will not become confused when transported outside her room.

That takes us to the psychosocial problems Mrs. Hill is likely to experience as a result of her stroke. It is unlikely that any two people would word the adaptation problems in the same way or would even include the same general areas. Obviously there are many responses here, and some of yours may be better than some of ours. We have identified the broad areas of (1) depression, or more descriptively labeled "despair" (also called grief reaction); (2) changes in self-concept or body image; (3) social isolation or loneliness; and (4) role conflict, especially in relation to family or significant others. Immobility is of course a problem, but we didn't include it because it has been discussed under neurologic deficit. The presence of all of these problems would, of course, need to be validated.

Nursing intervention for depression would include:

1. Provide stable emotional environment.

2. Give tasks that are within the patient's ability.

3. Call attention to progress patient is making, praising her for her accomplishments.

4. Accept labile emotional upsets matter of factly; utilize distraction for their termination.

Evaluation criteria would be improvement of depression, with specific behaviors of patient such as:

1. Less than three periods of frustration each day.

2. No refusal of patient to attempt tasks.

3. Less than two emotional upsets per day.

4. Demonstration of interest in environment and hope for future.

Intervention for change in self-concept or body image would include:

1. Listen to what patient is saying to determine the meaning of the change to the patient.

2. Convey your interest and concern for patient as a worthwhile human being. (Don't forget to use *touch!*).

3. Assist patient in maintaining an attractive appearance.

4. Consult the patient about her wishes, allowing her to make decisions whenever possible. Evaluation criteria would be absence of derogatory remarks about self, realistic appraisal of what she can or cannot do, and increased interest in appearance.

Intervention for social isolation would include:

1. Select social activities that she will enjoy which are within her capacity.

2. Encourage family or significant others to help patient in her rehabilitation program, discussing with them specific activities that would contribute to rehabilitation.

3. Seek other persons to provide companionship if no family is available.

4. Provide diversional activities that require skills or abilities she has.

Evaluation criteria would include:

1. Active participation in activity.

2. Development of a meaningful relationship with family, significant other, or new companion.

3. Presence of actively seeking company of others.

You may have used other terminology for role conflict such as denial of need to make changes in pattern of daily life or unwillingness to give over previously held authority, etc. Regardless of what you call it, intervention would include:

1. Validate with patient the changes she is planning to make to adjust to her illness.

2. Explore need for certain role changes within family.

3. Assist with planning daily schedule that allows for periods of rest.

Outcome criteria would be acceptance of changes in role and realistic plans for life with avoidance of fatigue.

In clinical practice you rarely get history, physical examination, and laboratory reports in a neat summarized paragraph. You usually have to scan the profiles and compile your own data base. Like most everything you do, it is difficult at first, but becomes fairly easy with practice. We are using profiles for some of the patient situations in this book to give you that practice. There are several styles used for recording the information. The physician's history, system review, and physical examination are frequently on separate forms. Nursing history and physical assessment data are usually on other forms, with much repetition of data. In an increasing number of settings, the responsibility for obtaining the medical history and physical examination rests with the nurse. Because of this, and because it facilitates getting a complete picture of the patient, we are using a combined medical and nursing form with information obtained in the physical examination placed opposite the history information for that system.

Case 6B. Study the history and physical data on Mr. Johnson. The medical impression has been recorded at the end. Record the nursing diagnosis that you would be entering on the nursing care plan on admission. Include potential problems where nursing activity plays a major role in prevention and/or early recognition.

PATIENT PROFILE

NAME: John Johnson SEX: Male ETHNIC EXTRACTION: Caucasian MARITAL STATUS: Divorced (12 years PTA)

OCCUPATION: Vice Pres. Small electronics firm

HEIGHT: 5 feet 11 inches

WEIGHT (lbs.): average 165; maximum 170; present 160

AGE: 52

LAST WORKING DAY: Day before admission

TEMP: 98.4F   P: 92   R: 26   BP: 110/70

CHIEF COMPLAINT: Burns over upper chest and both arms. Dozed while smoking a cigarette and shirt caught on fire.

PREVIOUS ILLNESSES: No physician visit for 6 years. No previous hospitalizations. Good health prior to last few weeks when he tired easily, lost his appetite, lost 5 pounds of weight, and noted swelling of ankles toward evening.

FAMILY DATA: Parents: Father died age 70—cancer of prostate; mother—fairly good health
Siblings: 1 sister—good health; 1 brother—adult onset diabetes
Children: none

MEDICATIONS: Anacin, DiGel, Nytol.

ALLERGIES: None known

HABITS: Alcohol—increased intake over past 12 years, now a fifth of whiskey/day; tobacco—1–2 packs cigarettes per day; drugs—none.

IMMUNIZATIONS: None since childhood

PROSTHETIC DEVICES: Prescription glasses for reading.

SOCIAL AND ENVIRONMENTAL DATA:

    Education—college graduate.

    Life style—rises at 7, no breakfast; work at 8:30, donuts and coffee at 9:30; 2 drinks before lunch; from work to bar at 5:30 pm; dinner at restaurant or pick up pizza, hamburger, etc.; read or watch television. Retire 11 pm.

    Hobbies, recreational interests: no hobbies; likes sports, but interest diminishing.

    Religious preferences or customs: baptized in Catholic church; has not attended for 12 years.

    Concerns: Expresses no concerns; has insurance for hospitalization expenses and sick leave—has "nowhere to go in dead end job anyway."

EXPECTATION OF TREATMENT: Just wants to get burns cleared up and "get the hell out of here."

SOURCE OF HISTORY—Patient. Seems reliable.

System Review	**Physical Examination**
Skin, Hair, Nails	
No changes in character or pigmentation prior to burn.	Erythema, blisters, edema, discoloration of chest, back, and arms.
Loss of hair on scalp and chest for past 5 years.	Burns extend to forearm of left, include hand on right.
	Few localized areas that have appearance of 3rd degree burn on right arm and chest.
Head	
No headache, vertigo, or loss in hearing, or smell.	No abnormality of eyes, ears, mouth, or sinuses noted.
Gums bleed easily.	Teeth in poor repair.
Wears glasses for reading.	
Neck	
Slight hoarseness.	Edema of lower neck.
Painful to swallow.	Limited motion (burn).
Lungs	
Feels like it is difficult to breathe.	Erythema and minimal edema of nasopharynx.
No cough or sputum.	No wheezing.
	Lungs clear to A and P except for inspiratory rales both bases.
Cardiovascular	
No history or present % chest pain, palpitation, orthopnea, or intermittent claudication	Heartrate 92, regular.
	PMI—5th intercostal space, anterior axillary line
Ankle swelling toward evening.	No murmurs.
Abdomen	
Heartburn for several years. Relieved by DiGel.	Moderate distension. No tenderness, rigidity, or guarding.
Emesis with "gastritis". No hematemesis.	Bowel sounds faint.
Some bloating. No jaundice.	Liver—4 cm below costal margin.
	Spleen normal.
	No hernias, masses, scars, ascites.
Rectal	
Bowels regular. No melena.	Exam—deferred

System Review *(cont.)*	**Physical Examination** *(cont.)*

Genitourinary
No urgency, frequency, incontinence, or
  hematuria.

Exam—deferred

Musculo-skeletal
No pain or limitation of motion.

No abnormalities.

Neurologic
No seizures, syncopal episodes, or paralysis.

Reflexes normal.
Coordination good.
Some decreased peripheral sensation.
? Asterixis.

Endocrine
Normal growth.
No polydipsia or polyuria.

Thyroid—midline, small.

Hematopoietic
Bruises easily.
Bleeding after cut difficult to control.
No exposure to toxic agents or radiation.

Emotional
Sleeps poorly.
Some memory loss.
Denies excessive anxiety or depression

Cognitive ability unimpaired
Answers without hesitation
May be denying some deep-rooted concerns

Impression:
Medical
  20% body surface area burns (upper chest, back, both arms—right hand involved,
  left hand unburned). Second degree burns with possible third degree of right axilla,
  forearm, and midchest.

Nursing Diagnosis
Present
1.
2.
3.
4.
Potential
1.
2.
3.
4.
5.
6.
7.

Emergency Room Care
  Received cool showering and debridement. Intravenous started—2 units albumin given,
    now infusing 5% dextrose/½ normal saline. Oxygen 35% by Venti-Mask.
  Summary of medical management after admission to floor
    Burns dressed with topical silver sulfadiazine, foley catheter inserted, and intrave-
    nous fluid infusion of colloid, blood, saline, and 5% D/W to maintain urinary output
    >65 ml/hour. Wounds were redressed every 8 hours, with whirlpool daily. Intrave-
    nous fluids were decreased on the second hospital day, and oral intake started on
    third hospital day (with further reduction in intravenous feedings).

Problem development
On the evening of his third day, the nurse noted pitting edema of his ankle, pretibial, and sacral area. Vital signs at this time were BP 130/100, P 88, R 32, T 97.8 F. His laboratory findings are as follows:

LABORATORY DATA
Blood Chemistry

	Patient	Normal
Metabolic I		
Chloride	90	95−105 mEq/L
Carbon dioxide, total	24	24−32 mEq/L
Potassium	3.4	3.5−5 mEq/L
Sodium	125	135−145 mEq/L
Urea Nitrogen	18	10−20 mg/dl
Glucose	140	58−100 mg/dl
Blood gases (arterial)		
pH	7.38	7.35−7.45
pCO_2	35	35−45 torr
pO_2	70	75−100 torr
Blood bicarbonate	20.1	22−26 mEq/L
Base excess	−3.9	0−±2 mEq/L
FiO_2 .35 (Venti-Mask)		
Hematology profile		
Leukocyte count (WBC)	8.5	5−10 thousand/cu mm
Erythrocyte count (RBC) (male)	4.1	4.5−6 million/cu mm
Hemoglobin (Hgb)	12.5	male 14−18 g/dl
Hematocrit (Hct)	38	male 40−54 ml/dl
Urinalysis		
Color	yellow	
Specific gravity	1.012	
pH	6	
Protein	Neg.	
Glucose	Neg.	
Ketones	Neg.	
Sodium	10 mEq/L	
Average hourly output	70 ml	
Metabolic II		
Protein, total	5.5	6−8.5 g/dl
Albumin	3	3.5−5 g/dl
Calcium	8.5	8.5−10.5 mg/dl
Phosphorus	4.4	2.5−4.5 mg/dl
Cholesterol, total	120	150−250 mg/dl
Uric Acid	4.1	2−8 mg/dl
Creatinine	2.2	0.7−1.4 mg/dl
Bilirubin, total	1.8	0.2−1.2 mg/dl
Phosphatase, alkaline	126	30−85 mU/ml

LABORATORY DATA   (Continued)

	Patient	Normal
Lactic dehydrogenase (LDH)	150	100−225 mU/ml
Glutamic pyruvic transaminase (GPT)	48	8−40 mU/ml
Glutamic oxalacetic transaminase (GOT)	60	7.5−40 mU/ml
Leukocyte Differential		
Neutrophils (PMN)	60	50−70%
Bands	2	0−5%
Myelocyte	0	0%
Myeloblast	0	0%
Metamyelocyte	0	0−1%
Lymphocytes	22	20−30%
Monocytes	10	2−10%
Eosinophils	8	1−4%
Basophils	0	0−0.5%
Platelets	adequate	200−500 thousand/cu mm

Skillbuilders:

1. On the patient profile list the four most likely nursing diagnoses present on admission and the seven potential diagnoses.

2. On the practicum record (6-B) list the three most likely hypotheses for the edema, listing the most likely cause first.

3. Then list the data you have that support each hypothesis and additional data needed to confirm or disconfirm.

4. Briefly outline the nursing intervention in the order of priority if the diagnosis was confirmed and the criteria by which the intervention could be evaluated. Include only intervention and criteria for the immediate period (omitting long-term plans), but list parameters by which criteria will be measured.

Feedback: We'll discuss the nursing diagnoses present on admission first. There are bound to be some variations in what different persons would list, but we considered the four most significant diagnoses to be:

1. Inadequate nutritional state.

2. Pain due to second degree burns.

3. Hypermetabolic state due to increased catecholamine secretion and elevated glucagon levels, and

4. Impairment of skin integrity resulting in evaporative water and heat loss from burned area.

To substantiate these diagnoses, nutrition is a major factor in burn healing, and the history items indicate Mr. Johnson had poor dietary habits, with a recent 5-pound weight loss.

Second degree burns are more painful than third degree burns, and it is

Possible Hypothesis/ Diagnosis	Supportive Data Available	Additional Data Needed to Confirm or Disconfirm	Nursing Intervention if Diagnosis Confirmed	Evaluation Criteria and Measurement Parameters
Edema due to:				
1.				
2.				
3.				

anticipated that Mr. Johnson will need medication and comfort measures, especially preceding dressing changes, whirlpool, and range of motion exercises.

The sympathoadrenal response to the stress of a burn continues for days or
weeks, or until the wound is closed. The metabolic rate (or heat production),
oxygen consumption, and glucogen levels are all elevated. This has implications
for nursing care, since use of an overbed heater that minimizes heat loss reduces
the metabolic rate. Glucagon levels remain elevated even in the presence of
hyperglycemia. Since the resulting high glucagon-insulin ratio stimulates gluco-
neogenesis and fosters muscle breakdown, urea production, and loss of lean
body weight, this diagnosis also has implications for importance of good dietary
intake.

The diagnosis of impaired skin integrity with the evaporative water and heat
loss from the wound cues us to reduce evaporative loss by the use of an im-
permeable membrane cover and to counteract for other functions of the skin
which have now been lost, such as barrier to infection, and reception of sensory
information about the external environment.

The following are potential nursing diagnoses we identified:

1. Fluid volume deficit due to impairment of capillary membrane.

2. Respiratory insufficiency due to airway edema and/or constrictive eschar
on chest.

3. Delirium tremens from alcohol withdrawal.

4. Infection, localized, and/or generalized sepsis.

5. Contractures of upper extremity.

6. Arterial ischemia, right arm due to edema under circumferential burn.

7. Curling's (stress) ulcer.

All except the last two diagnoses are probably familiar to you. You may have
limited understanding of the danger of arterial ischemia with a circumferential
burn. Essentially what happens is that swelling under the unyielding eschar can
act as a tourniquet to the flow of blood and lymph, with an increased swelling of
the distal extremity. The arterial supply can be compromised if the swelling
becomes extensive. Thus the color, mobility, pulses, and sensation in the extremity must be carefully monitored. Arterial ischemia can occur without loss of
distal pulses. Ischemia is prevented by escharotomy, or, in a few instances, excision of the eschar. Curling's ulcers are a frequent complication of burns. Most
physicians state the occurrence rate at 70 to 80 percent, although many ulcers do
not present clinical symptoms. Antacids are used routinely to reduce the incidence of, and hemorrhage from, ulcers.

Now we'll move on to discuss edema. The most likely hypothesis for Mr.
Johnson's edema is fluid overload due to return of third space fluid to the
intravascular space. Our knowledge that fluid which has been translocated is
returned to the circulating bloodstream on the third post burn day supports this
hypothesis. Although fluid administration was decreased in anticipation of this
occurrence, it is difficult to predict accurately the hemodynamic forces and fluid
overload can occur. The other possible hypotheses are hepatic insufficiency and
congestive heart failure due to cardiomyopathy. The decision tree for fluid
volume excess can guide our search for supportive data for the first hypothesis.

The serum sodium is low. We don't have a laboratory report for serum osmolality, but when we calculate it we find it is also low. Calculation is

$$2(Na^+) + \frac{\text{blood glucose}}{20} + \frac{\text{urea nitrogen}}{3} \text{ or } 250 + \frac{140}{20} + \frac{18}{3} = 263$$

Weight and central nervous system signs are observations that might be helpful. Since weight doesn't tell us whether fluid is in the intravascular space or third space, the information is not critical to the diagnosis in Mr. Johnson's case. We note the BUN of 18 is less than 10 times the creatinine of 2.2. Since the BUN is normally 10 times the creatinine, the disproportionate increase in creatinine is a supporting sign of fluid volume excess.

Looking at the observations in the second column of the decision tree, we know that edema and tachypnea are present so it appears there is strong support for the hypothesis of fluid volume excess. Any patient with edema also has an excess of total body sodium. SIADH is not anticipated from the history, and low urinary sodium indicates the body is conserving sodium. This is in contradiction to SIADH which is characterized by urinary concentration and urinary sodium wasting. Intervention if the diagnosis of fluid volume excess is confirmed would primarily be directed by the physician. Fluid and sodium intake (both IV and PO) would be restricted and a rapid acting diuretic like furosemide would be given by intravenous push. Keeping the patient in the upright position helps to pool fluid in the extremities and gives less interference with ventilation. Close monitoring of the patient's respiratory status that includes observation of respiration and auscultation to detect pulmonary edema would be essential.

Measures to reduce Mr. Johnson's anxiety would undoubtedly be important, since additional stress of anxiety and concern about his condition can put a heavy drain on someone whose emotional and physical resources have been depleted by the stress of his burn. Depending on the state of the patient, measures could include spending time with Mr. Johnson, giving a clear, brief explanation for the edema, and limiting requests made of him. Evaluation criteria would be:

1. Restored normovolemic state (serum osmolaity 280–300 mOsm/liter, absence of edema).

2. Absence of respiratory insufficiency (only minimal rales, normal blood gases, respiratory rate < 30, no dyspnea).

3. Control of anxiety (ability to focus attention, absence of purposeless motor activity, absence of narrowed interests and perceptual focus).

In considering the second hypothesis, hepatic insufficiency, we can be guided by the decision tree for hepatic insufficiency. The history items definitely make this a possibility that needs to be considered. Before his burn, we note he had an alcoholic intake of a fifth of whiskey per day, anorexia, and ankle swelling toward evening. Added to these factors are the trauma of the burn, fluid and electrolyte shifts, and blood transfusions. We don't have any information on his central nervous sytem functioning. Looking at the laboratory reports: his bilirubin, alkaline phosphatase, and SGOT are all slightly elevated, with total protein and albumin both low. Albumin, which is synthesized by the liver, is decreased with poor liver function to less than half of the total protein. The values on Mr. Johnson have been altered by his loss of fluid and replacement so they carry less diagnostic significance. Additional data needed are blood ammonia, prothrombin time, and gamma globulin. Abnormalities of these findings in the direction indicated would point to alcoholic liver disease, but whether the decompensation was of sufficient severity to result in hepatic insufficiency would need to be determined by further studies.

Intervention if the hypothesis were confirmed would again be primarily directed by the physician. Since the treatment for edema includes measures to get rid of the excess fluid as well as measures to treat the underlying cause, intervention measures such as fluid and sodium restriction and positioning is indicated regardless of the undelying cause. A diuretic might be given, but the dosage would be small. After the initial threat of fluid overload has been managed, long-term management of edema due to hepatic insufficiency relies on fluid and sodium restriction rather than diuretics that result in electrolyte depletion, hypovolemia, and hepatic encephalopathy. Intervention for hepatic insufficiency would include a high carbohydrate diet, administration of agents to correct any body deficiencies from poor liver function such as vitamin K and avoidance of any drugs toxic to the liver. Education about the disease and the danger of continued intake of alcohol would be indicated when condition stabilizes. Evaluation criteria would be the same as fluid volume excess, with the addition of absence of hemorrhage, improvement in altered liver function, and verbalization of knowledge of illness.

Now we'll consider our least likely hypothesis, edema due to congestive heart failure secondary to cardiomyopathy. Theory tells us that some persons who partake of alcohol develop cardiomyopathy due to the toxic effect of alcohol on the myocardium. Since the major manifestation of cardiomyopathy is congestive heart failure due to a large dilated heart that contracts poorly and empties inadequately, we can use the decision tree for low cardiac output heart failure to guide our diagnostic search. The observations to confirm (either present on admission or at time edema noted) are dyspnea, rales at the lung bases, dependent pitting edema, liver enlargement, and easy fatigability. Signs frequently associated with heart failure but not present with Mr. Johnson are tachycardia, urine output less than 30 ml/hour, a lowering of systolic Bp, and metabolic acidosis. Additional observations needed are presence of diaphoresis, state of neck veins, level of cognitive functioning, peripheral perfusion, heart size, and measurement of pulmonary artery wedge pressure and cardiac output.

Intervention for the edema would be similar to that of fluid volume excess due to return of third space fluid. Additional measures specifically aimed at the cardiomyopathy would be provision of rest, administration of digitalis and steroids as ordered, and education about the danger of continued alcohol ingestion. Evaluation criteria specifically for cardiomyopathy would be improvement of congestive heart failure and knowledge of damaging effect of alcohol on the heart. Parameters indicative of improvement in congestive heart failure are decrease in heart size, increase in cardiac output, decrease in edema (rales, pitting of extremities), and increased peripheral perfusion.

ADDITIONAL READING

Braunwald E: Edema. In Harrison T (ed). Principles of Internal Medicine, 9th ed. New York, McGraw-Hill, 1980, pp 171–175.

Metheny N, Snively W: Nurses' Handbook of Fluid Balance, 2nd ed. Philadelphia, Lippincott, 1974.

Schroeder HA: Edema. In MacBryde C. Blacknow R (eds.): Signs and symptoms, 5th ed. Philadelphia, Lippincott, 1970, pp 804–830.

Output Deviations

In health, the end products of metabolism, excess fluid, and the residue of food are excreted by the kidneys, gastrointestinal tract, skin, and respiratory tract. Complex homeostatic mechanisms maintain the balance between that which enters the body, the requirements of the body, and that which is excreted. Deficits of intake or excessive losses by one system may initiate compensatory mechanisms of conservation by another system to maintain stability. Inadequacy of the homeostatic mechanisms, dysfunction of the excretory systems themselves, or dysfunction of other body process that results in abnormalities of output results in illness. A full discussion of the many factors that alter output is not within the scope of this book, but the output of each of the major excretory systems will be briefly discussed. The assessment findings apply primarily to an acute change in the state of the patient. Persons with long-standing problems have developed compensatory mechanisms or depletion of body stores which can alter the significance of the measured parameter.

URINE

The kidneys are the primary organs for the excretion of water and solutes. By their ability to alter the volume and composition of the urine, they regulate the volume and composition of the extracellular fluid and thus the internal environment of the body. The normal kidney excretes 750–2000 ml urine in 24 hours. It contains electrolytes, end products of protein metabolism, metabolites of hormones, enzymes, bile, drugs, hydrogen ions and other trace elements. With metabolic disorders, glucose and ketones may be excreted while abnormal renal functioning can result in blood cells, casts, protein, and alterations in the excretion of electrolytes and nitrogenous end products.

ASSESSMENT

Urine volume. This is indicative of the hydration status of the body. It can also be affected by normal mechanisms, electrolyte levels, and abnormal renal states.

Oliguria. Most commonly results from decreased fluid intake, third spacing of fluid, or excessive losses from sweating, vomiting, diarrhea, or wound and fistula drainage. When the resulting fluid volume deficit is accompanied by an increase of nitrogenous products in the blood, it is referred to as prerenal failure or azotemia. Congestive heart failure and cirrhosis of the liver can also cause a prerenal type of failure, although the mechanism is due to disruption of the normal renal blood flow rather than hypovolemia. When oliguria is due to an acute or chronic problem within the kidney itself, it is termed acute vasomotor nephropathy or acute tubular necrosis. Oliguria (and sometimes anuria) can also be caused by mechanical obstruction to urinary flow, effect of certain drugs, or neurologic disorders that disrupt the innervation of the urinary bladder. When due to these causes, it is referred to as postrenal failure or postrenal oliguria. A fluid challenge may be utilized to distinguish between oliguria due to fluid volume-deficit and that due to acute vasomotor nephropathy. The challenge procedure usually consists of giving 250 ml of fluid intravenously within a 10-minute period. An increase in urine output is usually indicative of fluid volume deficit. Table 7-1 outlines the abnormal mechanisms and clinical states in which oliguria may occur.

Polyuria can result from increased fluid intake (including psychogenic polydipsia), ingestion of diuretic medications, solute diuresis (as in uncontrolled diabetes mellitus), deficiency of the antidiuretic hormone, vasopressin (as in diabetes insipidus), and some renal lesions. Renal states include nephrogenic diabetes insipidus, salt-losing nephritis, and, in a few cases, early renal insufficiency with inability to concentrate the urine but with above normal output.

Composition of the urine.   The composition provides important clues to the function of the kidney and other body systems or mechanisms. Fresh specimens should be used for analysis since some elements are unstable. Clean-catch midstream specimens should be obtained to avoid contamination from vagina or urethral meatus.

• *pH* of the urine with a normal diet is usually between 4 and 6. Alkaline urine (pH greater than 7) may result from proteus infections, metabolic alkalosis, certain medications, and renal tubular acidosis. The excretion of an acid urine with a pH below 6 by a patient in metabolic alkalosis is usually indicative of a deficit of chloride and potassium.

• *Specific gravity* is an indication of the urine's concentration. Normal specific gravity is generally considered to be 1.010 to 1.035. It may be as low as 1.001 with a water load. With a fluid volume deficit, the normal kidney will reabsorb water from the glomerular filtrate, excreting urine with a high specific gravity. With impaired renal tubular function, this concentrating ability is lost and the kidney may be unable to concentrate urine above 1.020 even with severe fluid restriction. Concentrating ability can be impaired with normal tubular function, however, in such states as diabetes insipidus, hyperthyroidism, sickle-cell anemia, and in patients on an extremely low sodium diet.

- *Osmolality* is a more sensitive indicator of urine concentration than specific gravity. Osmolality is not affected by glucose, protein, radiographic contrast media, or urine temperature in a well hydrated person as is the specific gravity. Normal urine osmolality is 100 milliosmoles per liter (mOsm/liter) greater than serum osmolality. The ratio of the urine osmolality to the plasma osmolality increases to more than 2:1 with fluid volume deficit but decreases to less than 1.1:1.0 with impaired renal tubular function. The preferred test of maximal ability to concentrate urine is the injection of ADH followed by hourly urine collections. This is generally used instead of severe water restriction, which is of itself damaging to the kidney in some patients. With normal tubular function, a well-nourished young adult after ADH injection should reach a urine osmolality of 1000 mOsm/liter. Concentrating ability decreases with age, with normal for a person in the fifth decade approximately 600 mOsm/liter.

- *Protein* is normally only present in the urine in a minute quantity. Not all proteinuria is pathologic, however. It may be increased with extreme muscular activity, maintenance of an upright position over a long period of time, and in some otherwise normal pregnancies. Organic proteinuria may accompany a number of systemic conditions such as fever, venous congestion, dehydration, hypertension, or myxedema. Excretion of more than 150 mg/day of protein is generally due to renal pathology such as with the nephrotic syndrome, glomerulonephritis, destructive parenchymal lesions and poisoning from nephrotoxins. In rare instances it is present with infectious states below the renal parenchyma.

- *Glucose* in the urine is usually due to diabetes mellitus. A few other disease states such as increase in intracranial pressure, Cushing's syndrome, and adrenocortical response to stress can result in glycosuria. The normal patient spills sugar into the urine when the blood sugar exceeds 180 mg/dl. However, individuals vary in the renal threshold for spilling sugar, and a few patients spill sugar when the blood sugar is either normal or considerably lower than 180 mg/dl (usually referred to as renal glycosuria). A high renal threshold can also occur, especially in patients with long-standing diabetes mellitus. These patients may not spill sugar in the urine until the blood sugar exceeds some 210–240 mg/dl. Thus in assessment of glycosuria, it is important initially to obtain a second voided specimen at the same time the blood sugar is drawn.

The comparison of the urine sugar with the blood sugar provides a reference for subsequent urine sugar tests. It is probably unnecessary to explain the reason for the use of a second voided specimen when testing for glycosuria. It is generally recognized that urine which has been collecting in the bladder for over a period of 3 or 4 hours is not a true indicator of the amount of sugar spilled at the present time. Thus the patient is asked to void, the specimen is discarded, and 30 minutes later he is asked to void again to obtain a current specimen. Since the methods of testing urine for sugar are found in many texts, the procedure will not be repeated here. It is important to remember that Clinitest tablets are not specific for glucose, but give a positive reaction with other sugars as well.

TABLE 7-1. Major Causes of Acute Oliguria

Abnormal Initiating Mechanism	Pathophysiology	Clinical State
I. Prenatal states Decreased renal blood flow	Inadequate renal perfusion due to decrease in volume and alteration in pressure of renal blood flow	Fluid volume deficit, low cardiac output, hypotension Increased renal vascular resistance as in hepatorenal syndrome, congestive heart failure, trauma, anesthesia, clamping of aorta Acute vasodilation, as with sepsis, antihypertensive medications
II. Renal parenchymal disease A. Acute vasomotor nephropathy (acute tubular necrosis)	Reduction in renal filtration rate with interstitial edema and impaired tubular reabsorption of water and salt due to renal ischemia or toxic agents	Major trauma, massive hemorrhage, transfusion reactions, septic shock, myoglobinuria, burns
B. Glomerulopathies	Reduction in renal filtration rate due to inflammation of the glomeruli	Glomerulonephri : acute poststreptococ , membranoproliferativ Associated with stemic disease, as syste c lupus erythematoses, iateritis nodusa, diabeti glomerulopathy, bacte l endocarditis, scl derma, amyloid glomei onthy, purpura, anap purpura (Henoch–Schönl) Serum sickness, emolyticuremic syndro.ne, toxemia of pregnancy
C. Acute cortical necrosis	Infarction of the kidney cortex with necrosis due to lack of blood supply	Abruptio placentae, infections, prolonged shock
D. Vascular lesions	Obstructive lesion to flow of blood to kidney	Renal artery thrombosis or emboli, renal artery stenosis, malignant hypertension, postpartum nephrosclerosis
E. Nephrotoxins	Damage to tubules by: Direct toxic effect	Heavy metals (mercury, arsenic, lead, uranium), carbon tetrachloride, antibiotics (cephaloridine, kanamycin, gentamicin, polymyxin, amphotericin B), pesticides
	Formation of calcium oxalate stones Sulfonamide precipitation	Ethylene glycol Sulfonamides

(continued)

TABLE 7-1. Continued

Abnormal Initiating Mechanism	Pathophysiology	Clinical State
III. Postrenal obstructive lesions		
A. Lower urinary tract	Obstruction from the bladder to the urethral meatus	Prostatic hypertrophy, bladder carcinoma, vesico-ureteral reflux, bladder infection. Neurogenic vesical dysfunction, as tabes dorsalis, diabetes mellitus, acute anterior poliomyelitis, spinal tumors, multiple sclerosis
B. Upper urinary tract	Obstruction of one or both ureters	Calculi, tumor, particulate matter (clots, crystals, pyogenic debris), injury (vascular or mechanical), congenital malformations, acute pyelonephritis, retroperitoneal fibrosis, surgical error (ureteral ligation), irradiation fibrosis

Keflin, Keflix, aspirin, and other drugs may give a false positive with Clinitest, while ascorbic acid may give a false positive with Testape or Clinistix. When determination of the renal threshold has been made, the blood sugar can be fairly accurately estimated from the urine sugar. If the urine sugar is 4+, however, it is difficult to determine if the blood sugar is at the minimum or critically elevated. A patient may spill 4+ sugar with a blood sugar of 250 mg/dl, but if the blood sugar rose to 800–900 mg/dl, the urinary sugar would still be 4+. The use of the two-drop Clinitest method is increasingly being utilized to get more definitive information on patients demonstrating 4+ by regular Clinitest or Testape measurement.

• *Ketones* in the urine are the end products of fat metabolism; acetone is the major ketone found. Ketones are not normally present but may occur with inadequate intake or disorders of carbohydrate metabolism. Ketones in the urine without glycosuria suggest starvation, while ketonuria with glycosuria indicates diabetes mellitus. Since ketones are acid, the alkaline reserve of the body can be depleted in the process of neutralizing them, resulting in metabolic acidosis, referred to as ketoacidosis. A few patients who do not develop diabetes until the sixth or seventh decade may be ketone resistant, i.e., they may develop a blood sugar of over 800 mg/dl and be comatose, but have no ketosis. This condition is referred to as hyperosmolar nonketotic coma.

• *Hematuria* can be overt or hidden and only detectable on microscopic examination of the sediment obtained from centrifuged urine. Normally no more than one or two red blood cells should be seen per high-power field. Any bleeding from the urinary tract is a serious sign that requires investigation. When bleeding is gross in alkaline urine, the urine will appear red. In acid urine, however, the color may be brown or smoky. Since red blood cells and casts may be hemolyzed or disintegrated in an acid urine, prompt analysis and testing for occult blood is essential for accurate identification. Certain drugs, food pigments, and metabolites may also give a red color to the urine. Red blood cells can result from systemic or renal states. Systemic causes include blood dyscrasias, anticoagulation therapy, collagen diseases, and scurvy. Renal causes are renal parenchymal diseases, tumors, renal calculi, infection, and trauma. The source of the bleeding is localized to the kidney by the finding of red blood cell (RBC) casts. The RBC casts generally indicate acute or subacute inflammatory lesions of the glomeruli or other structures in the renal parenchyma.

• *Pyuria* in excess of five white blood cells per high-power field denotes the presence of an inflammatory process in the urinary tract. The finding of white blood cell (WBC) casts localizes the infection to the renal parenchyma. Pyuria of renal origin is also generally accompanied by proteinuria. The number of WBC's in the urine is not a good indicator of the severity of the inflammatory process, since pyuria is intermittent or absent with some lesions.

• *Bacteriuria* can occur without pyuria. Unlike WBC's, the number of bacteria present is indicative of the severity of the infection. If the number of bacteria by quantitative urine culture is in the range of 100,000 per milliliter or more, it is indicative of significant clinical infection. Gram stain of uncentrifuged urine or examination of unstained urine sediment are quicker tests than quantitative culture, and are fairly reliable.

• *Bilirubin* in the urine is indicative of hepatic obstruction such as hepatitis, or common bile duct obstruction by stone or tumor.

• *Sodium excretion* by the kidneys is probably the most sensitive indicator of tubular function. In normal hydration, renal, and circulation states, excretion of sodium corresponds to sodium intake. With a fluid volume deficit state, a homeostatic mechanism involving increased release of ADH and aldosterone is initiated, resulting in reabsorption of sodium and water from the renal tubules in an effort to restore the volume of circulating fluid to normal. Patients with cardiac and chronic liver disease also may have an impairment of circulation to the kidney and an increased aldosterone production, with resultant diminished excretion of sodium by the kidneys. With these disorders and with a fluid volume deficit, patients have low urinary output and low output of sodium in their urine, usually less than 20 mEq/liter. The sick kidney, however, is unable to reabsorb sodium in response to a fluid volume deficit. These people have a reduced urine output, but sodium output will not be reduced, usually remaining greater than 30 mEq/liter.

• *Potassium* in a normal person is excreted or conserved to maintain the serum potassium within normal limits. Excretion or conservation is not as rapid as with sodium, however, and deficiencies or excesses may exist for several days when intake is reduced, losses are excessive, or intake is increased. In a patient with a low serum potassium, urinary excretion should be less than 20 mEq/liter. In states in which there is urinary potassium wasting, urinary concentration will probably be greater than 20 mEq/liter. Excessive amounts of potassium are lost from the urine in metabolic alkalosis, from the use of most diuretics, with osmotic diuresis from glycosuria, with aldosterone excess, and in renal tubular diseases such as renal acidosis. High serum potassium should also result in higher rates of potassium excretion unless there is inadequate excretion. Inadequate excretion occurs with renal failure, adrenal insufficiency, and large doses of diuretics that conserve potassium such as spironolactone. Plasma concentrations of potassium may rise rapidly with conditions that cause potassium to shift from within the cell to the plasma. Conditions that may cause such a shift are muscle-crushing trauma, internal hemorrhage, acidosis, and effects of certain drugs. Plasma concentration may remain dangerously elevated for a time until the kidney is able to adjust to a higher excretory level.

• *Creatinine* is normally cleared from the bloodstream by the kidneys, being excreted in the urine. Although 24-hour urine specimens were formerly used to determine the effectiveness of the kidneys in clearing creatinine, spot specimens of urine are now generally used. The normal kidneys' creatinine excretion should exceed 70 mg/dl, or be more than 10 times the plasma creatinine.

• *Amylase* in the urine may be elevated in pancreatic disease.

• *Crystals, epithelial cells, and fatty casts* may be present in urine with varying significance. The presence of porphobilinogen is diagnostic of acute porphyria, while the presence of phenylpyruvic acid is indicative of phenylketonuria.

INTERVENTION

Prerenal Oliguria. Management includes correction of fluid volume deficit, administration of drugs to improve the cardiac output, and correction of hyponatremia, hypoproteinemia, and acidosis. In selected cases vasodilators and diuretics may be indicated. Prompt and adequate treatment is essential because inadequate blood flow to the kidney when uncorrected can progress to acute vasomoter nephropathy.

Postrenal Obstruction. Frequently this is reversible when the source of the obstruction is removed. Prompt treatment is vital since if the obstruction is prolonged, the renal parenchyma may become damaged.

Renal failure. Management of renal failure depends somewhat upon the underlying cause. When glomerulopathies are associated with treatable systemic disease, the underlying disease is treated in addition to maintenance on a renal failure protocol. Renal artery occlusion can be treated surgically by bypassing the occlusion. Some renal lesions are irreversible, such as bilateral cortical necrosis, nephrosclerosis, and some types of acute glomerular nephritis. Acute vasomotor nephropathy and damage from nephrotoxins are usually reversible if the person is otherwise healthy and is carefully managed throughout the period of renal failure. Oliguria continuing for more than 3 weeks suggests irreversible disease. The primary role of the nurse is to be an astute observer of the changes in the state of the patient, provide emotional support to the patient, and work closely with the physician in the treatment of the medical condition. The goals of renal failure protocols usually include the following:

- *Maintenance of normal fluid volume state.* In most instances, all fluid is given intravenously. After adequate fluid volume has been restored, daily intake is restricted to 400–500 ml (insensible loss) plus replacement of measured external losses in urine or drainage. Accurate measurement of intake and output, daily weights, and pulmonary artery wedge pressure monitoring are utilized to evaluate fluid volume state.

- *Reduction of renal load* of metabolites and myoglobin. Prompt debridement of nonviable tissue, drainage of abscesses, and use of gastric lavage and enemas for removal of post hemorrhage blood from the gut is essential. A rise in the BUN greater than 25 mg/dl per day is referred to as hypercatabolic renal failure and signals that special efforts are needed to find necrotic tissue or infected foci.

- *Revision of medications* to eliminate those that contain potassium or magnesium and to reduce dosage of those excreted by the kidneys. Serum levels of digitalis and antibiotics are utilized to guide administration. Antibiotics toxic to the kidneys such as cephaloridine, kanamycin, gentamicin, and polymixin are only utilized when essential for treatment of infections resistant to other antibiotics.

- *Control of hyperkalemia* resulting from egress of potassium from intracellular compartment in hypercatabolic states. Prophylactic administration of a cation exchange resin such as sodium polystyrene sulfate is sometimes used. Therapeutic measures are indicated when serum potassium is greater than 5.5 or when ECG abnormalities, such as the loss of atrial activity, increase in height of T wave, or widening of the QRS complex are present. The use of larger doses of exchange resins by mouth or retention enema and administration of concentrated glucose solutions with insulin are frequently utilized methods of treatment. Calcium chloride may be given to reduce the hyperkalemic irritative effect at the myocardial membrane level. Sodium bicarbonate is occasionally used to raise the serum pH and thus drive potassium back into the cells. The high sodium load for the patient limits the usefulness of this drug.

- *Correction of severe anemia* to maintain the hematocrit above 20 percent by the use of transfusion of freshly drawn packed red cells that have been carefully crossmatched to prevent incompatibilities. Fresh blood is used to maximize red blood cell survival and minimize intake of potassium, which is always high in bank blood. Packed cells are given to prevent fluid overload. The patient needs to be closely observed during transfusion for early detection of a transfusion reaction. Moderate anemia usually appears in the second week due to a deficiency of erythropoietin, a hormone normally formed by the action of an enzyme produced by the kidney that is essential for red blood cell production in the bone marrow. Other contributors to anemia are an increase in erythrocyte destruction and defects in hemostasis that result in GI bleeding or ecchymotic bleeding into the skin. Defective hemostasis may be due to decreased platelet adhesiveness, decreased production of platelet factors, or other causes. Severe coagulopathies such as disseminated intravascular coagulation (DIC) can develop in some patients, especially with sepsis and/or shock.

- *Provision of adequate calories* for metabolic needs. With severe injury, the caloric requirement can approach 5000 calories/day. If exogenous administration does not meet the needs, the patient's muscle and fat will be used to supply them, resulting in increased azotemia from the nitrogenous end products of protein breakdown and ketones from the burning of fats. Parenteral hyperalimentation with concentrated glucose solution given into a central catheter and intravenous fat emulsions are frequently utilized to meet calorie requirements. Strict aseptic care of the hyperalimentation line is essential. Measures include reserving the lines for hyperalimentation solution only, meticulous dressing change at insertion site (with the use of an occlusive dressing), and use of solution mixed under a laminar flow hood with strict aseptic technique.

- *Maintenance of gastric pH above 5* to reduce the incidence of gastric erosions and ulceration. Aluminum hydroxide is the antacid most frequently used. Antacids containing magnesium are contraindicated due to the danger of hypermagnesemia in renal failure. Aluminum hydroxide, in addition to reducing gastric acidity, also retards the absorption of phosphate from the intestine thereby helping to control the phosphatemia that results from reduced glomerular filtration. Since serum calcium and phosphorus have a reciprocal relationship, the level of calcium drops when phosphorus (phosphate) rises, causing calcium to be deposited in soft tissues and bone. The lower serum calcium signals the parathyroids to increase calcium secretion, and a vicious cycle is initiated which can result in dangerously high levels of both calcium and phosphate in the extracellular fluid.

- *Early institution of hemodialysis* before severe toxemia develops. Early hemodialysis is generally recognized as effective in reducing the mortality rate by decreasing the incidence of sepsis and bleeding episodes and decreasing the cardiac dangers from hyperkalemia. Dialysis also helps control metabolic acidosis and makes the management of the patient easier because dietary restrictions can be liberalized. Early dialysis is used when renal failure is due to nephrotoxins to limit the damage to the kidneys.

- *Prevention of fluid and electrolyte imbalances* during the diuretic phase. Careful monitoring of serum and urinary electrolytes is required to avoid depletion of sodium, potassium, bicarbonate and extracellular fluid volume. Azotemia may continue to increase in spite of diuresis, requiring continued dialysis until the patient is able to maintain BUN under 70 mg/dl.

When renal failure fails to resolve, institution of a program for management of chronic renal failure is required. The patient will undoubtedly require assistance in making the psychologic adaptation to a chronic illness as well as education on care of his shunt, proper diet, and measures to decrease discomfort from pruritus, hiccups, and nausea.

OUTPUT OF THE GASTROINTESTINAL TRACT

The gastrointestinal (GI) tract is responsible for the digestion and absorption of food. The residue of ingested food, which is excreted as feces, varies with the type of food and fluid ingested. Normal amount is approximately 200 mg/day. Disorders of the GI tract are usually manifested by disturbances in the absorption of necessary constituents into the bloodstream or by disorders of motility. Observable signs are vomiting, a change in the number and/or character of the stools, and presence of a GI fistula. Some treatment factors such as T-tube drainage of the common bile duct also affect the output. Pathophysiology, assessment, and intervention of each of these will be discussed separately.

Vomiting

Vomiting is a cardinal symptom that accompanies many diverse illness states. It is frequently preceded or accompanied by nausea, but it can occur without nausea.

The autonomic nervous system and centers in the medulla and hypothalamus regulate and modify the functions of the GI tract. In most situations, stimulation of the sympathetic nervous system results in inhibition of intestinal smooth muscle activity. Stimulation of the parasympathetic nervous system usually results in increased tone and motility of the gastrointestinal tract. Increased parasympathetic activity with vomiting is evidenced by pallor of the skin, increased salivation, and perspiration. It may also be accompanied by bradycardia and hypotension. Vomiting can occur without participation of the higher centers, but is more often controlled by the vomiting center in the hypothalamus and the chemoreceptor center in the medulla. Activation of the chemoreceptor trigger zone results in efferent impulses to the vomiting center. The vomiting center initiates the act of vomiting in response to the stimuli from the chemoreceptor center and also in response to stimuli from the intestinal tract and the higher cortical centers that control the integrative mechanisms of the brain and the labyrinthine apparatus.

For ease in differentiating the clinical conditions that result in vomiting, the information is presented in tabular form (Table 7-2). Although vomiting may be beneficial and may be followed by greater comfort in a few situations, it is generally distressing and unpleasant. When emesis continues over a period of time, the patient can suffer serious adverse effects such as dehydration, hypokalemia, and metabolic alkalosis. With forceful vomiting some patients may suffer a rupture of the junction between the esophagus and the stomach (Mallory–Weiss syndrome). Additionally aspiration pneumonia may develop in patients with central nervous system depression who vomit. In hospitalized pa-

TABLE 7-2. Major Causes of Vomiting

Abnormal Initiating Mechanism	Pathophysiology	Clinical State
I. Gastrointestinal irritation	Gastric irritation from chemical irritants or distension, or stimulation of the chemoreceptor trigger zone	Gastritis, enteritis, poison ingestion, aerophagic syndrome Drugs, such as apomorphine, emetine, cardiac glycosides, ergot alkaloids, anesthetic agents, epinephrine, salicylates, cholinergics (neostigmine, edrophonium)
II. Obstructive lesions	Mechanical interference with normal passage of ingested food	Stricture, stenosis, atresia, volvulus, intussusception, adhesion, fibrous tissue constriction, hernia, foreign bodies, tumor
III. Inflammatory disorders	Inflammation of viscus results in sympathoadrenal reaction with decreased peristalsis and distension of the intestine by the accumulated fluid and gas	Appendicitis, hepatitis, cholecystitis, pancreatitis, pyelonephritis, peritonitis
IV. Bleeding disorders	Bleeding into esophagus or stomach causes distension, and initiates reflex mechanism	Esophageal varices, Mallory–Weiss syndrome, bleeding ulcer, gastritis, gastric tumor
V. Disordered biochemical states	Acute systemic infections accompanied by fever stimulate the vomiting center; mechanism still not understood	Acute febrile infections (especially in children)
	Hormonal changes with endocrinologic disorders, acid–base imbalance, and elevation of toxic metabolites in blood stimulates vomiting center	Diabetic ketoacidosis, Addison's disease, hyperparathyroidism, morning sickness of pregnancy, uremia, radiation sickness
VI. Disorders of central nervous system	Disruption of the psychologic integrative mechanisms of brain	Anorexia nervosa, psychogenic vomiting, pain, emotional reaction to life situations
	Hypoxemia of the vomiting center	Severe anemia, vascular occlusion, shock (cardiogenic), high altitudes, migraine headaches, hypoxia, esp. when accompanied by hypotension
	Increased intracranial pressure	Intracranial hemorrhage, concussion, cranial tumors, meningitis, lateral sinus thrombosis, internal hydrocephalus
	Excessive stimulation of the labyrinthine apparatus	Motion sickness, Meniere's disease, labyrinthitis

tients, nasogastric (NG) intubation is frequently utilized to decompress the stomach and prevent vomiting. Most of the assessment parameters outlined for a patient who is vomiting also apply to a patient with NG intubation, since both represent an abnormal loss of stomach contents.

ASSESSMENT

Volume.   The amount of the emesis or NG drainage is an indication of the amount of fluid and electrolytes lost. The electrolyte composition varies throughout the gastrointestinal tract, with higher concentrations of sodium found in the secretions of the small intestine and higher concentrations of potassium chloride present in the stomach secretions. Normal amounts of electrolytes lost with vomiting or NG drainage when the pH is normal (1.0−1.5) are sodium 60 mEq/liter, potassium 10 mEq/liter, and chloride 130 mEq/liter. When the acidity of the gastric contents is decreased, greater amounts of sodium are lost. When the pH is greater than 5, some 100−150 mEq/liter of sodium are lost.

pH.   The gastric contents provide information about the electrolyte losses previously mentioned, and also helps to differentiate between various disease states. Patients with pernicious anemia and those with a gastric malignancy generally have little or no free hydrochloric acid. Duodenal ulcers are associated with high secretion of hydrochloric acid.

Forcefulness.   The manner in which the emesis is expelled may be indicative of the underlying problem. In central nervous system disorders accompanied by increased intracranial pressure, vomiting may be projectile. Regurgitation is the term frequently used to describe emesis that is not accompanied by contraction of the abdominal and diaphragmatic muscles. Regurgitation is caused by a local condition in the esophagus or stomach such as esophageal stricture, incompetence of the gastroesophageal sphincter, or with pylorospasm.

Appearance.   The appearance of the gastric contents is important. With pyloric obstruction or diabetic gastric atony, the emesis frequently contains undigested food. When the problem is due to an obstruction low in the ileum, peritonitis, or gastrocolic fistula, the vomitus appears feculent, i.e., it is homogeneous, orangish-brown in color, and has a foul odor from the overgrowth of bacteria proximal to the obstruction. Bile, which can be identified by its characteristic yellow-green color, is normally present in the gastric contents. A large increase in the quantity of bile may be indicative of an obstructive lesion below the entry of the bile duct into the duodenum.

Time.   The relationship of vomiting to food intake can aid in the differential diagnosis. Vomiting occurring in the mornings is characteristic of pregnancy, uremia, alcoholic gastritis, and anxiety states. Vomiting that occurs during or soon after eating is suggestive of pylorospasm or gastritis. Vomiting that occurs a number of hours after eating indicates gastric retention of food and/or loss of normal motility.

Presence of nausea. Nausea may be an indicator of the cause of vomiting. Nausea is generally present when vomiting is due to abnormal conditions in the viscera or GI tract. It is frequently absent in disorders of the brain such as cerebral tumor, meningitis, and concussion.

Hematemesis. Blood may be found in a variety of disorders in the esophagus, stomach, or duodenum. It is frequently accompanied by melena which will be discussed in a later section. Vomited blood will usually be bright red if the vomiting occurs soon after the onset of the bleeding. If a period of time elapses between the bleeding and vomiting, the vomitus will be dark red or black in color, or it may have the appearance of coffee grounds due to the mixing of the blood with the hydrochloric acid in the stomach. It is important to rule out swallowed blood from a nosebleed or dental extraction as a source of the bleeding. The most frequently occurring causes for hematemesis are a duodenal ulcer, gastric ulcer, or erosive gastritis and esophageal varices from portal hypertension. Most patients can lose 500 ml of blood without untoward symptoms. The most critical indicator of hypovolemia from blood loss is postural hypotension. A decrease in systolic blood pressure greater than 10 mm Hg when a supine person sits up is an indication of volume depletion in excess of 20 percent. When blood loss approaches 40 percent, clinical signs of shock are evident: rapid and thready pulse, decreased blood pressure, and cold and clammy extremities. With massive hematemesis, a patient can lose 50 percent of his blood volume. The hematocrit will not reflect the blood loss accurately for several hours since the percentage of hemoglobin in the intravascular space does not change until hemodilution has taken place. Chronic bleeding produces a hypochromic, microcytic anemia, and occult blood positive stools, but only minimal symptoms of hypovolemia.

INTERVENTION

The goal of intervention for vomiting or losses from NG drainage is to restore homeostasis. This can involve replacement of losses, treatment of underlying causes, and provision of support, both physiologic and emotional, while the patient is in a period of reduced capacity. The specific goals for each patient would depend upon the specific problem, its etiology, degree of severity, and the patient's psychologic resources. Some of the major goals that are common to many patients will be briefly discussed.

Provision of gastrointestinal rest. Except for a few patients who have acute gastrointestinal upsets due to conditions commonly referred to as stomach flu and motion sickness, no oral intake is permitted. Carbonated beverages or sips of tea may be allowed when tolerated by the patient.

Decompression of stomach and/or intestine.   Decompression is utilized to empty the stomach of contents which may be irritating, to prevent vomiting, and to reduce distension. Since distension lessens motility and the capacity of the blood vessels to deliver blood to the involved organs, it tends to be a self-perpetuating mechanism. Nasogastric intubation is commonly utilized, with double lumen or sump tubes most frequently used. The nurse has the responsibility of maintaining the patency of the tube. This may require repositioning of the tube, insuring the suction is working properly, and irrigation. In patients with surgery of the esophagus or stomach, the nurse usually notifies the physician of malfunction rather than reposition or irrigate the tube. Air is initially used for irrigation, with small amounts of saline used when air is ineffective. Saline irrigation is used cautiously to avoid washing out of the stomach's electrolytes. Iced saline irrigations may be used to control bleeding. When bleeding esophageal varices are present, balloon tamponade by use of a tube such as the Sengstaken–Blakemore may be indicated. It is important to gavage the stomach of its contents before the balloon is inserted to avoid aspiration. A helmet is usually used to provide traction between the balloon and the gastroesophageal junction. Care must be taken not to overinflate the esophageal balloon. Scissors should be kept at the bedside to cut across the tubes for quick removal if respiratory difficulty develops.

Maintenance of normal fluid and electrolyte levels.   Accurate measurement of all fluid loss and careful administration of fluid or blood given as replacement is essential. Intravenous fluids have sodium, potassium, or chloride additives. Nasogastric drainage is frequently replaced with dextrose in half normal saline. Greater amounts of sodium are required for replacement with decreased gastric acidity. Blood and/or blood products or blood expanders are given to replace blood loss. Patients with major gastrointestinal losses generally have monitoring of the pulmonary artery wedge pressure (PAWP) for guidance in fluid volume infusion. Maintenance of the PAWP above 15 torr gives adequate fluid replacement without fluid overload.

Maintenance of normal acid-base state.   Abnormalities can include metabolic acidosis or metabolic alkalosis.

• *Metabolic acidosis* in a patient who is vomiting is usually due to diabetic ketoacidosis, severe starvation, renal disease, or ingestion of boric acid, salicylic acid, methanol, or ethylene glycol. Examination of the anion gap is helpful in determination of cause. With acidosis due to excessive bicarbonate loss, the anion gap is within the normal level of less than 15 mEq/liter. When acidosis is due to increased acid production, the anion gap exceeds 15 mEq/liter. Treatment is directed toward treatment of the underlying cause, although sodium bicarbonate may be additionally utilized if deficit is severe.

• *Gastric hyperacidity* can result in other problems such as ulceration and bleeding with a normal acid–base state. The use of antacids and/or cimetidene, a histamine H_2-receptor antagonist, is indicated in patients at risk for development of stress ulcers or with a history of previous ulcers or hepatic insufficiency.

● *Metabolic alkalosis* presents a greater threat to postoperative abdominal surgical patients than metabolic acidosis, although its danger has frequently been overlooked in the past. Increased loss of hydrochloric acid from the stomach by vomiting or NG drainage, chloride deficit with volume depletion, and severe potassium depletion from vomiting and use of diuretics are the most frequent causes. Patients with adrenal hyperfunction also have a tendency to develop metabolic alkalosis. The dangers of cardiac dysrhythmias with hypokalemia that accompanies alkalosis are well known. More recently, recognition of the deleterious effect of metabolic alkalosis on respiration, i.e., compensatory alveolar hypoventilation (in an effort to conserve CO_2) and a decrease in the dissociation of oxygen from hemoglobin at the cellular level (as demonstrated by the oxyhemoglobin dissociation curve) has prompted more intensive treatment efforts. Examination of urine electrolytes and pH is utilized to assess the extent and nature of the deficit. In early metabolic alkalosis, a urine chloride of less than 10 mEq/liter is indicative of volume and chloride deficiency. The volume deficiency causes the kidneys to conserve sodium, with excretion of higher levels of potassium. Since, in alkalosis, a large portion of the sodium is paired with bicarbonate, the kidneys reabsorb bicarbonate as well. This serves to perpetuate the alkalosis. As time passes, the supply of potassium ions to exchange for sodium are depleted, and hydrogen ions are excreted instead, giving an acid urine (termed paradoxical aciduria) and low output of sodium, potassium, and chloride in the urine. In most patients, metabolic alkalosis can be corrected by the infusion of adequate volume and replacement of electrolytes. In some severe cases, alkalosis is intractable and infusion of hydrochloric acid will be required.

Control of vomiting.   Depending on the underlying cause, a number of measures may be utilized to control vomiting. The use of nasogastric intubation has already been discussed. When vomiting is less severe, the following may be indicated:

● *Elevation of the threshold* for stimulation of the chemoreceptor trigger zone by the use of antiemetic drugs. This is of special importance after eye surgery when retching and vomiting can cause hemorrhage into the eye.

● *Decrease of cerebral cortex stimulation* of the vomiting center by control of factors that predispose to vomiting. Such factors can include pain, unpleasant sights, sounds, and odors, and also thoughts. In addition to management of general discomfort, good oral care is essential.

● *Encouragement of patient participation* in deep breathing and voluntary initiation of swallowing which can suppress the vomiting reflex.

Prevention of aspiration.   This is important in patients with altered neural regulation or muscular weakness. Turning the patient on his side and flexing the head so the chin is close to the chest decreases the possibility of aspiration of vomitus.

DIARRHEA

Diarrhea is an alteration in an individual's normal pattern of defecation characterized by an increased frequency or a loss of form of fecal output. It may or may not be accompanied by abdominal cramping (tenesmus). The increased frequency is caused by accelerated motility from the enlarged stool volume. The volume of stool increases when there is a decrease of fluid absorbed from the small intestine and/or colon or when there is a marked increase of intestinal secretion of fluid. Motility is also increased by autonomic neural and hormonal mechanisms that promote greater propulsive activity. Diarrhea is frequently categorized on the basis of the onset and duration as acute and chronic. Table 7-3 outlines the major abnormal mechanisms and clinical states in which diarrhea may occur.

Acute diarrhea occurring in an otherwise healthy person is most often related to an infectious process from viral, bacterial, or protozoal causes. The diarrhea is caused by mucosal lesions and enterotoxin-induced hypersecretion. In some cases, referred to as food poisoning, ingestion of preformed bacterial toxins is the cause rather than presence in the GI tract of the pathogens themselves. Ingestion of heavy metals, cathartic drugs, and other drugs are also causes of acute diarrhea. Less frequently involved, but possible causes requiring investigation are acute inflammatory conditions of the bowel or its appendages and psychogenic stress.

Chronic diarrhea that persists for several weeks may be a manifestation of a serious disorder, a functional symptom, or as a result of cathartic abuse. Most frequently it is due to an inflammatory state of the bowel or to the malabsorption syndrome.

Intestinal malabsorption is a complex disorder that accompanies many disease states. It may involve fats, carbohydrates, proteins, and water individually or in combination. In addition, vitamins, cholesterol, minerals, and electrolytes may be lost by a failure of absorption.

Malabsorption of fats is primarily due to a deficiency of lipase and/or bile salts. The pancreatic enzyme, lipase, is essential for the hydrolysis of the triglycerides to monoglycerides and fatty acids. Hydrolysis by lipase is more efficient when bile salts, which have been conjugated in the liver, are present, since they have detergent properties that make it easier for lipase to gain access to the water-insoluble fats. Normally the conjugated bile salts then form micelles that carry the lipids to the absorbing cells of the intestine. About 90 percent of the bile salts are reabsorbed in the ileum and are recirculated between the liver and intestine.

Malabsorption of carbohydrates is generally due to an absence of the enzyme that converts disaccharides into monosaccharides (glucose, galactose, and fructose). Most monosaccharides are readily reabsorbed across the cell membrane, but some persons congenitally have fewer carriers available for active transport of glucose and galactose.

Malabsorption of protein may result from a defect in the transport of specific amino acids from intolerance to the protein, gluten, or from passage of plasma proteins that had been previously absorbed across the gastrointestinal mucosa, referred to as protein-losing enteropathy. It occurs with many disease states. The responsible underlying pathology may be an inflammation of the intestinal mucosa, an abnormality in the structure of the mucosal cells, an increase in the lymphatic pressure, or a rupture of lymph vessels into the intestinal lumen.

Malabsorption of water is generally secondary to damage to the mucosal lining of the intestine or to osmotic gradients. It is frequently accompanied by impaired sodium transport or carbohydrate maldigestion. Diarrhea may be osmotically induced by intake of heavy metals or metabolically inert sugars.

Surgical procedures (gastrectomy, ilial resection, etc.) and the release of potent bioactive humoral agents as serotonin in tumors of the sympathetic nervous system and endocrine glands are occasionally the cause of chronic diarrhea. Functional chronic diarrhea is generally an accentuation and prolongation of the acute diarrhea from emotional tension, when tension has not been resolved. Functional diarrhea may be labeled irritable colon, functional bowel disease, spastic colon, mucous colitis, etc. Although no organic lesions are initially present, when the disordered state continues over a period of time, diverticulosis and other disorders may develop. Cathartic abuse can result in diarrhea, although intake may often be denied by the patient. Diarrhea can also be due to fecal impaction, with expulsion of loose, watery stools due to colonic distension beyond the impaction.

ASSESSMENT

The patient's description of altered fecal output combined with other history items such as age, sex, race, dietary patterns, recent travel experiences, recent stressful incidents, and drug intake (including antibiotics) may give important clues to the cause of the diarrhea. When the onset is acute and history fails to elicit psychologic or pharmaceutic causes, an infectious etiology is generally considered. Viral infections have a short duration of 1 or 2 days and have few distinguishing characteristics. In contrast, bacterial and protozoal infections are not apt to be self-limiting, and differential diagnosis needs to be made between these inflammatory states and other causes. Ongoing assessment parameters for diarrhea lasting longer than three days include:

Frequency and urgency. These parameters sometimes provide clues to the site of the lesion. Disorders of the left colon or rectum such as ulcerative colitis or amebiasis result in frequent, small bowel movements with a sense of urgency.

TABLE 7-3. Major Causes of Diarrhea

Abnormal Initiating Mechanism	Pathophysiology	Clinical State
I. Infection of GI tract	Viral changes in cellular structure of small bowel	Viral enteritis, viral gastroenteritis
	Bacterial invasion of mucosa in colon causing hyperemia and ulceration plus production of enterotoxin causing hypersecretion	Staphyloccocal food poisoning, *salmonella, shigella* enteritis (bacillary dysentery), "turista" (traveller's diarrhea), cholera, *clostridium perfringens (C. welchii)*, tropical sprue
	Protozoa and parasites produce an inflammatory colitis	Amebic dysentery (Amebiasis), giardiasis, coccidiosis, schistosomiasis, trichinosis
II. Inflammation or irritation of GI tract	Alteration of bacterial flora, overproduction of tissue-lysing enzymes, hypersensitive food reactions, autoimmune reactions, and other less well understood mechanisms initiate an inflammatory reaction, primarily involving mucosa and submucosa of small bowel, with hyperemia, ulceration, and leucocyte infiltration	Ulcerative colitis, Crohn's disease (regional enteritis), diverticulitis, drug-induced colitis (lincomycin, clindamycin, tetracycline, etc.)
III. Malabsorption		
A. Malabsorption of fats	Deficient production of the pancreatic enzyme, lipase	Pancreatitis, carcinoma of pancreas, cystic fibrosis, protein malnutrition (kwashiorkor) pancreatic resection
	Deficient production of bile salts with impaired micille formation and resultant decrease in solubilization of fatty acids	Bile duct obstruction, hepatocellular disease
	Deconjugation of bile salts by overgrowth of colonic bacteria	Jejunal diverticulosis, scleroderma, diabetic visceral neuropathy, afferent loop obstruction, blind loop syndrome
	Sequestration or precipitation of bile salts	Intake of neomycin, calcium carbonate, cholestyramine, liquid paraffin
B. Alteration of intestinal mucosa absorptive surface	Defective assimilation pathways due to deficiency of enzymes, damage to intestinal mucosa, infiltration of intestinal mucosa by other cells or matter, etc.	Celiac disease, nontropical sprue (gluten-induced enteropathy), Whipple's disease, lymphosarcoma infiltration, radiation enteritis, amyloidosis, pernicious anemia, hypogammaglobulinemia, mastocytosis
	Loss of absorptive area by surgical resection	Short bowel syndrome, gastrocolic fistula, gastroileostomy

(continued)

TABLE 7-3. Continued

Abnormal Initiating Mechanism	Pathophysiology	Clinical State
C. Metabolic abnormality	Genetic or acquired deficiency of disaccharidases, with impaired hydrolysis of disaccharides	Lactase deficiency, lactose intolerance, sucrase deficiency, glucose−galactose malabsorption
	Genetic defect in amino acid transport in intestinal mucosa and renal tubules	Cystinuria, Hartnup disease
	Release of potent bioactive humoral agents: serotonin gastrin	Carcinoid syndrome Pancreatic tumors (Zollinger−Ellison syndrome)
	Dysfunction of endocrine glands, with resultant alteration in neuromuscular function and malabsorptive disorders	Thyrotoxicosis, adrenal insufficiency, hypoparathyroidism
D. Altered vascular supply	Congestion and edema of the mucosa, abnormality of mucosal lymphatics, or ischemia from altered blood supply	Mesentery artery insufficiency/occlusion, vasculitis, constrictive pericarditis, congestive heart failure
IV. Altered neurologic function	Surgical interruption of parasympathetic nerve supply results in poor emptying of gallbladder and inadequate stimulation with malabsorptive states	Postvagotomy
	Psychogenic initiation of sympathoadrenal response	Irritable colon syndrome, anxiety states
V. Mechanical factors	Partial obstruction of the bowel causing colonic distension with frequent expulsion of liquid stool around lesion	Neoplasms, adhesions, fecal impaction, stenosis
	Osmotic effects of nonabsorbable matter with movement of fluid into bowel lumen	Laxatives (sorbitol, magnesium), heavy metals, dumping syndrome

Amount and character of stools:

• *Large bulky stools* are characteristic of malabsorption syndrome or Crohn's disease. When bulky stools are greasy and light in color with a foul odor, an insufficiency or malassimilation of fat (steatorrhea) is implicated. Steatorrhea may be due to pancreatic insufficiency, celiac disease, sprue, etc.

• *Frothy liquid stools* are indicative of carbohydrate malabsorption such as occurs with lactase or sucrase deficiency.

• *Copious watery stools* occur with a villous adenoma of the rectum.

• *Undigested food* in the stool is likely due to a gastrocolic or gastroileal fistula.

Abdominal pain. The relationship of pain to defecation and eating is significant. Functional diarrhea is associated with pain only after a formed stool or immediately after eating. Pain that is the most intense 1 to 2 hours after eating is characteristic of Crohn's disease. In ulcerative colitis, pain is often frequently intense with defecation and relieved after defecation.

Blood in stools.   This may or may not be accompanied by hematemesis. Hematemesis is most likely to occur when the bleeding site is above the duodenum, and the stool, which is frequently black and tarry, is referred to as melena. Following a single episode of upper GI bleeding, melena can persist for 1 to 3 days. The passage of red blood in the stool usually indicates a bleeding site below the duodenum, although with massive, rapid, gastric or duodenal hemorrhage, the feces can contain bright red blood. Lower GI tract bleeding is usually due to a lesion of the colon, rectum, or anus, i.e., carcinoma, polyps, inflammatory lesions (ulcerative colitis, diverticulitis), or anal fissures or hemorrhoids. Colonic ischemia can also result in bloody diarrhea. It must be remembered that dietary and drug intake can cause red or black stools and these causes must be excluded. Although all bleeding should be investigated, clinical manifestations of hypovolemia are usually not evident unless blood loss exceeds 500 ml. Occasionally, blood in the gut causes a transient temperature and blood urea nitrogen (BUN) elevation. The breakdown of proteins in the blood to urea by bacterial action in the intestine results in an elevated BUN when the glomerular filtration rate is decreased.

Mucus.   Mucus in the stool can occur with ulcerative colitis, cathartics, irritable colon, and infections such as amebiasis, salmonella, and shigella.

Weight loss.   This can accompany diarrhea with systemic disease, carcinoma, or malabsorption. Weight loss is rarely present with functional bowel disease.

Stool examination.   Collection of stool for culture, testing for occult blood, and microscopic examination for pus, ova, or parasites, and fat droplets assist in determining the problem. More accurate information about fat and protein malabsorption can be obtained by 72-hour stool collection with the patient on a controlled diet prior to and during the stool collection. Stool pH, sugar, and weight are also sometimes determined. An acid stool that is positive for sugar is indicative of a possible deficiency of an enzyme essential for the utilization of sugars and would suggest the need for further studies such as a lactose tolerance test.

Proctoscopy and sigmoidoscopy examinations.   These are indicated for bloody diarrhea or in cases that show no improvement for 4 or 5 days, when no causative agent has been identified. A rectal biopsy may be taken to aid in the diagnosis of ulcerative colitis, amyloidosis, fibrocystic disease, and such infectious states as bacillary dysentery, amebiasis, and schistosomiasis.

Roentgenologic examination.   X-ray of the abdomen followed by a barium enema and upper GI series after the acute process has subsided are frequently indicated. Abnormal findings can include bowel obstruction, gastrocolic fistula, carcinoma, inflammatory lesions, pancreatic calcification, and changes in thickness of intestinal folds and abnormal motility.

Serum carotene levels. Low levels of carotene are associated with steatorrhea.

Electrolyte losses. Diarrheal stools and surgical procedures that result in drainage from the small bowel, ileum, or colon cause electrolyte loss. Normally, the amount of potassium lost in stools is less than 10 mEq/day. With diarrhea, however, it can increase to 30 mEq/liter. Likewise, sodium losses from the GI tract which are normally negligible can increase to 90 mEq/liter. Bicarbonate and chloride loss are also increased. Serum electrolyte levels are generally utilized for determination of extent of losses rather than determinations of electrolyte content of stools themselves.

INTERVENTION

The primary goal of intervention for diarrhea is to provide supportive therapy while the underlying cause is being identified. Specific treatment is then directed at the cause. Abnormal losses of fluids, electrolytes, and other essential elements will need continued replacement until the condition is controlled. It is difficult to write specific goal statements when diarrhea can be associated with such a variety of disorders, but goals that might be included for some patients could include:

- *Decrease in peristaltic stimulation* by withholding of solid food for 24–48 hours, or until the acute period has subsided.

- *Maintenance of normal fluid and electrolyte state.* Parenteral infusion of fluid and electrolytes are utilized when oral intake is inadequate. These are used with greatest frequency for infants and the elderly. Oral glucose and electrolyte solutions have been found to be beneficial for cholera and other enterotoxin-producing bacterial disorders. Parenteral hyperalimentation may be required for severe fluid and nutritional deficits.

- *Suppression of intestinal motility* by the use of opiate-containing agents, diphenoxylate hydrochloride, or binding agents such as kaolin-pectin.

- *Adequate replacement of blood volume* and plasma protein that is lost with bleeding and from malabsorption.

- *Suppression of inflammatory process* by use of corticosteroids, and, for some patients, antibiotics.

- *Replacement of deficient enzymes,* administration of a drug to block the action of serotonin, or to bind excess bile salts.

- *Eradication of protozoan, parasitic, and bacterial organisms* by use of appropriate medication that is exactly calculated for dosage and continued for the entire prescribed course of treatment. Many medications have toxic side effects and require careful observation of the patient during the course of the therapy.

● *Dietary education.* Since many disorders that result in diarrhea show improvement with a specific dietary management, knowledge of any dietary restrictions is essential. Persons with diverticulosis improve on a high residue diet, avoidance of foods containing seeds, and intake of a bulk laxative such as psyllium extract. Those with a deficiency of lactase need to eliminate milk from their diets. It is well known that lactose is the agent in many tube feedings that is responsible for diarrhea. Although the patient when well may have been able to tolerate milk, lactase secretion seems to diminish with illness. Celiac disease in children and nontropical sprue in adults is caused by an intolerance to gluten, a protein found in wheat, oats, and barley. A gluten-free diet usually results in remission. Protein-losing enteropathies show improvement with a low fat diet. Postgastrectomy patients with dumping syndrome benefit from frequent small dry meals with no concentrated carbohydrates. Fluids are not allowed until an hour has elapsed after eating. Occasionally fat-free diets are required to eliminate steatorrhea.

● *Prevention of excoriation* of anal area by careful washing and through drying after defecation. Use of emollients or talcum powder may be beneficial for some patients. Some of the newer products on the market for protection of skin around stomas are effective for resistant excoriation that does not respond to routine care.

● *Control of psychologic stresses* may include assistance to the patient in the reevaluation of his life's goals and in meeting unresolved emotional conflicts. Frequently the knowledge of the extent his emotions are disrupting his normal physiologic functioning provides motivation for instituting changes in his responses to life.

● *Acceptance of chronic or terminal illness.* When diarrhea is due to a chronic condition or life-threatening state for which no treatment is available, the patient may need help in accepting his diagnosis and making the necessary adjustments. Specific nurse activities would depend on his assessment of his beliefs, coping mechanisms, resources, and so forth.

CONSTIPATION

Constipation can be defined as a prolonged retention and excessive dehydration of fecal matter in the colon, leading to the formation of abnormally hard and dry stools which are difficult to expel, requiring excessive use of voluntary muscles. From the frequency of complaints to health professionals and the volume of laxatives purchased, it appears there is an extreme preoccupation among persons about bowel function and a dread of contipation. Cultural beliefs, individual experiences, and misinformation have doubtless increased this preoccupation. We now know that there is a wide variation in the evacuation time in people considered to have normal elimination. It may be perfectly normal for an individual to have only one stool every 2 or 3 days while it is also normal to have two or three stools daily. In tests it has been found that one-third to one-half of the substances ingested appears in the stools 24 hours later, with the remainder usually expelled by 48 hours. The time between ingestion and expulsion depends on neural and hormonal stimuli, colonic secretion and absorption, muscular contraction, and heeding of the defecation reflex. Normally approximately 800 ml of dietary residue, cellular debris, and intestinal secretions from the small intestine pass through the ileocecal valve every day. Neural impulses and hormones released from the small intestine in response to eating (postprandial reflex) mediate the responses. The major hormones responsible for increasing colonic motility are cholecystokinin and gastrin. Emotional factors, physical activity, and fecal bulk also influence colonic motility. The urge to defecate is felt when some of the feces pass from the sigmoid colon into the rectum, stimulating the stretch receptors in the rectal wall. The sensation may be temporarily suppressed by a signal from the cerebral cortex to the defecation center in the sacral cord that results in an increase in the tone of the anal sphincters and relaxation of the sigmoid colon. As a result, the fecal matter from the rectum returns to the sigmoid colon, and the urge to defecate temporarily disappears. If the individual heeds the urge to defecate, an impulse from the cerebral cortex to the defecation center in the sacral cord causes the anal sphincters to relax and shortens the distal colon. As a result, the contents of the transverse colon are emptied into the sigmoid colon and rectum. The act of defecation is completed by a voluntary bearing-down effort which increases the intraabdominal pressure. Assumption of a position with the thighs flexed and use of the Valsalva maneuver will increase abdominal pressure.

Since constipation is such a frequently heard complaint, there may be a tendency to overlook it without investigating it adequately. A change in bowel habits, however, may be an important clue to a serious disorder and requires evaluation. Table 7-4 lists many of the clinical states that are frequently accompanied by constipation. It will be noted that a number of the disorders are not confined to the colon but are systemic.

Constipation that develops acutely without a history of drug or poison ingestion is frequently a sign of an acute abdominal problem such as an ileus, intestinal obstruction, or inflammation of the abdominal or pelvic viscera. In most of these disorders, absence of stool is accompanied by abdominal pain and distension, and may also be accompanied by vomiting. Acute porphyria is frequently accompanied by colicky abdominal pain and constipation (with or without vomiting), but it can be differentiated by the presence of porphobilinogen (PBG) in the urine. Because of the presence of several symptoms in addition to constipation in acute conditions, the remainder of the discussion will focus on chronic constipation which frequently requires more effort to determine the underlying cause.

Chronic constipation can result from the mechanical narrowing of the lumen of the intestine (as by a tumor) or from neurologic or muscular disorders,

TABLE 7-4. Major Causes of Constipation

Abnormal Initiating Mechanism	Pathophysiology	Clinical State
I. Mechanical obstruction	Intrinsic narrowing of the lumen of the GI tract by lesion, obturation, or fecal bolus	Neoplasm, intussusception, volvulus, strangulated hernia, fecal impaction
	Extrinsic lesion exerting pressure on GI tract	Pregnancy, uterine fibroids, ovarian cyst, adhesions, prostatic hypertrophy
II. Reflex inhibition	Irritation of peritoneum by chemicals (hydrochloric acid, pancreatic enzymes, colonic contents), surgical manipulation, retroperitoneal hematomas, with resultant adynamic ileus	Appendicitis, salpingitis, peptic ulcer perforation, cholecystitis, peritonitis, ureteral calculus, pyelonephritis
III. Impaired defecation	Inadequate stool volume to stimulate peristalsis	Low residue diet, extreme dehydration, chronic purgation
	Weakness of muscles with resultant inability to increase intraabdominal pressure	Rectocele, cachexia, emphysema
IV. Excessive sphincter tone tone	Painful rectal conditions with excessive sphincter tone prevent complete evacuation	Hemorrhoids, anal fissure, perirectal abscess
V. Altered neurological functioning	Voluntary delay of evacuation by cortical inhibition	Ignoring defecation reflex
	Destructive lesion of central nervous system	Tabes dorsalis, multiple sclerosis, brain and cord tumors, cerebral vascular accident, transection of spinal cord
	Deranged colonic motility due to absence of ganglion cells in a section of colon	Hirschsprung's disease
	Decreased colonic motility by suppression of ganglionic activity by drugs	Effect of opiates, ganglionic blockers, and anticholinergic drugs
VI. Altered gastrointestinal motility and tone	Atrophy of gastrointestinal musculature from inflammatory process or fibrosis	Polymyositis, scleroderma
VII. Psychogenic	Production of epinephrine with symptho-adrenal acute stress reaction inhibits cholinergic stimulation	Emotional disturbances of fear, grief, anger, anxiety, etc.
	Chronic stress activates vagal and sacral fibers to the colon resulting in hypermotility and spasm which may alternate with hypomotility	Irritable colon, spastic colon, mucous colitus
VIII. Metabolic disorders	Decreased colonic motility, sometimes termed spastic or dynamic ileus due to electrolyte imbalance and loss of muscle tone	Hypothyroidism, hypercalcemia, hypokalemia, acute intermittent porphyria, lead poisoning

but it more commonly occurs from habitual failure to heed the call to defecation. When the urge to defecate is repeatedly inhibited, the rectum in time loses its ability to initiate the defecation reflex, with resultant chronic distension of the rectum with feces and loss of elasticity of the rectal wall. Constipation in which there is no gross organic lesion or demonstrable cause has been termed functional.

ASSESSMENT

Assessment of bowel function begins with history of the onset, contributing factors, drug regime, diet, psychologic factors, etc. In Hirschsprung's disease there is always a history of constipation dating from infancy. Usually a rectal biopsy has been done to confirm the existence of an aganglionic segment in the colon. Acquired megacolon occasionally may develop in patients with longstanding rectal constipation. Identification of any abnormality that affects the function of the motor and sensory pathways responsible for defecation may suggest a causal relationship to the constipation. Systemic disease may alter the motility of the intestinal tract. Many commonly employed drugs such as codeine, morphine, some antacids, and anticholinergics have a constipating effect. The excessive use of laxatives may lead to constipation by overstimulating the bowel and conditioning of the patient to the effect. Other ingested substances that cause constipation are lead, arsenic, mercury, and phosphorus. Lack of sufficient bulky foods in the diet and/or an inadequate fluid intake may result in a deficient reflex activity. The contents are then retained longer and undergo excessive dehydration. Muscle strength must be adequate for expulsion of the feces from the colon. In addition to the muscles of the abdominal wall and intestine, the diaphragm and levator ani muscles are also utilized. Psychic factors are important in the etiology of constipation. Changes in tone, motility, and vascularity of the large intestine have all been demonstrated in response to emotional reactions. After an appropriate history has been obtained, assessment for a patient with chronic constipation could include the following:

Appearance of the stool.   The actual stool should be viewed whenever possible because what may be called a small hard stool by one person could be called a large loose stool by another. Characteristics to observe are the presence of blood or mucus in the stool, color, and the diameter of the stool. A functional disturbance most often termed irritable colon syndrome or spastic colitis is a frequently occurring gastrointestinal condition in which constipation may be alternated with diarrhea. The stool is thin, fragmented, or pelletlike, and frequently contains mucus. Clay colored stools are generally indicative of gall bladder disorders. Another observation that is important to make about the stool is the presence or absence of uniformity. The portion of feces expelled first should be firmer than that expelled last. When there is no difference in appearance, it may mean that the rectum was not evacuated completely, with retention of some feces. Although no blood may be visible, it is wise to test for the presence of occult blood.

Digital examination of the rectum.   To determine the presence of a fecal impaction, incomplete emptying of the rectum, etc., examination with a gloved finger may be indicated. The physician may examine more completely by a proctoscopic examination.

Visual inspection of the anal area.   Sometimes the call to defecation is not heeded because of accompanying pain. The elicitation of the presence of pain during the history should prompt an investigation for a possible cause such as hemorrhoids, anal fissure, or other painful anal disorders.

Stool pH.   Patients with a stool pH greater than 6 sometimes have an excessive decomposition and putrefaction of protein; these end products are constipating.

INTERVENTION

When constipation is due to an organic lesion or systemic disease, therapy is directed toward the underlying cause. When neuromuscular disorders contribute to the problem, a program of bowel retraining geared to the individual's abilities is instituted. Megacolon is generally treated by surgical resection of the aganglionic segment. It is important to remember that patients with megacolon can develop water intoxication when tap water enemas are given. The following intervention is aimed primarily at the large number of persons with functional constipation. However, with a few alterations, many portions of it would benefit a person with neuromuscular disease. Although it is desirable to decrease the dependence on laxatives, some patients have taken them regularly for so many years they are unable to defecate without them. When laxatives are required, stool softeners and hydrophilic colloids are preferred because they cause less electrolyte loss than saline and irritating cathartics. Many authorities believe the so called autointoxication that may be manifested by headache, furry tongue, foul breath, loss of appetite, and malaise is due to electrolyte depletion from harsh laxatives rather than from absorption of toxic substances from the colon. Depending on the individual, some suggested educational and demonstrable goals for a patient with functional constipation are:

Active patient participation in treatment plan.   When the patient is encouraged to identify his problems and develop the therapeutic plan, he becomes an active partner in the enterprise and is more likely to follow the plan.

Establishment of a regular time for defecation.   If the patient had a regular time before his illness, that time should be reinstituted. If there has never been a regularly established time, utilizing the gastrocolic reflex (stimulus of peristalsis from eating) by attempting to defecate following a specific meal each day is frequently successful.

Judicious use of laxatives. In some patients with long-standing dependence on laxatives, some medication will initially be required. A frequently used regimen is to take a small dose of a bulk laxative of the hydrophilic colloid type with each meal. A mild mechanical stimulating laxative such as milk of magnesia is taken once a day, with the administration timed so the effect will occur at the time of day scheduled for defecation. A hot beverage of the patient's choice is given and the patient taken to the commode or stool. It is recognized that patients who have feelings of dejection and futility commonly have an elongated slack bowel with poor tone. Therefore, if the nurse has a cheerful, optimistic, confident attitude, the patient may have better intestinal tone. Time should be allowed for the bowels to move, but the patient should not be kept on the commode any longer than he can tolerate. (It is helpful if the allotted time has been agreed upon mutually in advance.) In some instances, if defecation does not occur, a suppository or digital stimulation is used. When the patient begins to develop a bowel pattern, the medications are slowly decreased. The mechanical stimulant is decreased first and then the hydrophilic colloid. If strong laxatives and enemas are required as a preparation for radiographic examination, the patient should not be expected to have a return of normal bowel activity for 2 or 3 days, since time is required for enough residue to accumulate to stimulate peristalsis.

Maintenance of independence and privacy consistent with safety. A patient who is unable to care for himself needs to be assisted, but should be allowed to maintain as much independence as possible, in an effort to preserve his self-esteem. Emotional factors such as anger, grief, and embarrassment increase epinephrine production which inhibits peristalsis.

Use of proper position on commode or stool. The patient should be seated on the stool with both feet resting firmly on the floor and the thighs flexed in order to use accessory muscles to expel the feces. Although wheel chairs that fit over the top of a toilet are convenient and eliminate transfer of the patient, they should be used with a foot stool so the patient can push with his feet. The Valsalva maneuver, which combines closure of the glottis with diaphragmatic fixation and abdominal wall contraction does increase the muscular force. In many patients however, it can have an adverse effect on cardiovascular dynamics. The increased intrathoracic pressure that results from muscle setting with a closed glottis can reduce the venous gradient and thereby impede the venous return to the heart. Patients with compromised cardiovascular status benefit from breathing in a panting fashion with their mouths open, an activity that keeps the glottis open.

Diet that contains adequate bulk and fluids. Lack of sufficient bulky foods in the ingested diet may give a deficient reflex activity. Although the ileum and colon are capable of absorbing additional fluids, an adequate fluid intake seems to make the stool softer. Intake of hot fluids also stimulates peristalsis. Constipation on bland milk diets can be decreased by substitution of buttermilk or yogurt (or maltsuplex) for some of the milk. When gram-positive organisms or lactobacillus in the GI tract are increased, the pH is decreased to around 5 and sugar breakdown is increased, with the end products exerting a laxative effect. Sugar also spares the decomposition of protein and thus minimizes the formation of constipating end products of putrefaction.

Maintenance of a program of regular exercise.   For the ambulatory patient a brisk walk and a series of exercises to increase the tone of the abdominal muscles before the defecation time is frequently helpful. In the patient confined to bed, diaphragmatic and abdominal muscle strengthening exercises can be used.

Prevention of fecal impaction.   Persons prone to develop impaction need to have careful observation of the frequency and consistency of their stools. When impaction is suspected, digital examination is utilized for confirmation. An oil retention enema followed by a saline enema is generally effective, although manual disimpaction may sometimes be required.

EXPERIENTIAL INVOLVEMENT

CASE 7A.   Mr. Smith, 28 years old, with no history of major illnesses or surgery, received a severe injury to his left side when his motorcycle was hit by an automobile at an intersection. He arrived at the hospital in shock with internal bleeding as well as some loss of blood from skin lacerations. He was taken to surgery for exploratory laparotomy at which time a ruptured spleen was identified and removed. Although he received 8 units of whole blood and 4 units of plasma protein fraction from time of admission to the hospital until the completion of surgery, his blood pressure was never higher than 80/60 and it was as low as 60/40 for a considerable period of time. He had a dopamine (Intropin) drip running most of the surgical period and into the postsurgical period. Fluid and blood replacement continued after surgery, but although his vital signs were stabilized at 100/70 four hours after surgery, his urine output gradually decreased to 15 ml during the last hour.

   Skillbuilders:
   1. On the practicum record, 7-A, enter the two most likely hypotheses for the decrease in Mr. Smith's urine output.
   2. Then enter the data that support the hypothesis and additional data you would need to confirm or disconfirm.
   3. In the intervention column enter the activities over the next 3 or 4 days that would be indicated if the hypothesis were confirmed.
   4. In the last column list the evaluation criteria for the management of Mr. Smith during the next 3 or 4 days.

PRACTICUM RECORD 7-A

Hypothesis/Possible Diagnosis	Supportive Data to Confirm	Additional Data Needed to Confirm or Disconfirm	Nursing Intervention if Diagnosis Confirmed	Evaluation Criteria
Decrease in urine output due to: 1.				
2.				

Feedback: Probably the first thing that comes to mind with a decrease in urine output is renal failure. When we look at the table of causes of oliguria, we realize that any of the postrenal obstructive lesions would be a long shot in this previously healthy young man. Likewise there is no reason to suspect glomerulopathy or nephrotoxins. Probably no one had any trouble in identifying inadequate renal perfusion due to fluid volume deficit and acute vasomotor nephropathy as likely possibilities. Nephropathy could result from any of several states that are present, i.e., trauma with extensive tissue destruction, massive hemorrhage with a prolonged period of hypotension, and transfusion reaction with extensive hemolysis and precipitation of heme pigment in the renal tubules.

We'll discuss first the hypothesis that the decrease in urine output is due to a fluid volume deficit. The decision tree on fluid volume deficit can guide us in our search for cues. Supporting data would come from the history of blood loss from his injury and the laparatomy. With trauma and laparatomy our theoretical knowledge tells us that large amounts of extracellular fluid (in addition to blood) are lost by intraluminal and intramural collections of the extracellular fluid. This results in a deficit of the circulating fluid volume which is commonly referred to as hypovolemia. Additional physical findings which would be meaningful for Mr. Smith would be the presence of postural hypotension, signs of decreased skin turgor, low pulmonary artery wedge pressure, and flat neck veins when supine. If pulmonary artery pressure is not being monitored, greater reliance would be placed on the presence of postural hypotension. How sad it is when this is such a critical indicator that we rarely find it recorded. Laboratory data would include elevation of serum BUN and creatinine (with the BUN more than 10 times the creatinine), low hematocrit, and specific gravity of the urine greater than 1.014. The low hematocrit would be an indicator of unreplaced blood loss as the basic cause of the fluid volume deficit.

Nursing intervention would be primarily directed by the physician for this patient dependent on parenteral intake. The goal of treatment would be restoration of adequate fluid volume and prevention of dysfunctional effects. If hematocrit were low, blood would be ordered. Fluid infusion rate would be stepped up for deficits due to either blood loss or extracellular fluid. Plasma protein fraction (PPF) is generally given along with electrolyte solutions for hypovolemia to maintain the colloid osmotic pressure of the blood that is necessary to retain fluid in the intravascular space. Infusion of PPF is frequently guided by the pulmonary artery wedge pressure (PAWP). The order may be written to infuse a unit of PPF every two hours to maintain the PAWP above 15 mm Hg. Intravenous push of diuretics such as furosemide (Lasix) or infusion of mannitol would probably be ordered. It might seem strange to give diuretics that promote fluid excretion to a person with a fluid volume deficit, but the reason for their use is to prevent any dysfunctional effect on the kidneys. The danger of tubular damage from precipitation of heme and other substances is increased when the products are not washed out by a diuresis.

Evaluation again would be a continuous ongoing process for Mr. Smith. Expected criteria would be an increase in the urinary output to more than 30 ml/hour, absence of postural hypotension, normal hematocrit, and normal serum BUN and creatinine. If adequate progress was not being made, attention would need to be directed toward the possibility that the patient had an active source of blood loss. Although possible dysfunctional effects of the hypovolemia could include inadequate brain perfusion, the biggest danger is renal damage from prolonged inadequate renal perfusion. This would be indicated by loss of ability to concentrate urine, conserve sodium, or excrete nitrogenous wastes. These criteria are discussed in more detail with the next hypothesis. That brings us to the hypothesis that the decrease in urine output is due to acute vasomotor nephropathy. The only supporting datum is the decrease in urine output in a patient at risk. We can look at altered laboratory values for additional data. It is a wise nurse who takes the time to run a specific gravity on the urine and then saves the urine for sodium and creatine measurements. This may be the last urine the patient will put out and if it is discarded, valuable information will not be obtained. Many of the laboratory values are not immediately altered, so it is customary to give a fluid challenge to rule out the possibility of a fluid volume deficit. If urine output does not increase after rapid infusion of 250 ml of fluid intravenously, the probability is increased that the oliguria is due to renal insufficiency. The earliest laboratory findings to support the hypothesis are low urine specific gravity (and osmolality), low urine creatinine, and urinary sodium greater than 30 mEq/liter in a patient with decreased urine output. Since furosemide and other diuretics increase the urinary excretion of sodium, the specimen for sodium should be obtained before furosemide is given. The serum creatinine and BUN usually show only a small initial elevation, with concentration increasing as time passes. Red cells and tubular and red cell casts in the urine, when present, support the hypothesis.

Intervention for renal insufficiency is again mainly under the direction of the physician. In addition to continuous assessment and carrying out the physician's orders (with attention to insuring that the desired therapeutic effect is obtained), the nurse is responsible for keeping the patient as comfortable as possible and promoting patient compliance to the therapeutic regimen. Today hemodialysis is being initiated earlier that in the past. Thus, many patients have placement of a shunt as soon as the diagnosis is confirmed and dialysis may be started when serum creatinine and BUN are elevated only three or four times normal. Hemodialysis would be chosen over peritoneal dialysis for Mr. Smith who had a laparotomy. The dopamine drip would probably need to be continued during hemodialysis to maintain an adequate blood pressure. Even when blood pressure is within the normal range, a low dose of dopamine ($3-5$ μg/kg per minute) may be continued because of its action in increasing the blood flow to the kidney. Special attention must be given to the shunt to assure its proper functioning. Observation for blood flow includes color, warmth, fluctuation, bruit, and absence of a clot. The extremity with the shunt needs to be protected from harm with no blood pressures, intravenous infusion, or blood drawing allowed. Other aspects of management include:

  1. Fluid limitation to urine output plus insensible loss.

2. Adjustment of medications (restriction of potassium, magnesium, and antibiotics toxic to the kidneys and decrease in dosage of drugs eliminated by the kidneys).

3. Parenteral hyperalimentation with concentrated glucose solution and fat emulsion.

4. Administration of aluminum hydroxide.

5. Aseptic measures to prevent infection.

6. Control of hyperkalemia, hyperglycemia, and other potentially dangerous states.

Mr. Smith can be expected to have a rapid increase in serum potassium due to the breakdown of traumatitized cells and the high level of potassium in stored blood used for transfusion. Thus he would probably receive a cation exchange resin such as Kayexalate, in addition to hemodialysis. The resin exchanges potassium for sodium in the gastrointestinal tract with increased potassium excreted in the stools. It must be remembered that for such exchange resins to be effective in reducing potassium, they must be expelled. They are usually administered with sorbitol which is an osmotic laxative. If given orally, the patient should have 1 or 2 watery stools/day. If given as a retention enema, it should be expelled after about 1 or 2 hours or followed with a cleansing enema. Since aluminum hydroxide tends to be constipating, the addition of Kayexalate can compound the problem if attention is not paid to bowel movement.

Hyperglycemia can occur if the pancreas does not produce adequate insulin for metabolism of the intravenous glucose. Tests of urine for sugar and acetone should be done every 4 hours, with regular insulin coverage for 2+ or more sugar. Even with early hemodialysis, patients frequently have a decrease in cognitive functioning and emotional instability. Patients have been known to become extremely despondent or display irrational and noncompliant behavior such as drinking quantities of water from the tap, pulling out their shunt, etc. Thus, it is important to have an accurate assessment of the patient's psychologic and cognitive function and a nursing approach that anticipates maladaptive behavior and provides the patient with other outlets. Giving concise knowledge about the expected duration of the hemodialysis, fluid, and diet restrictions may help him mobilize his defense mechanisms more adequately. Elimination of discomfort will frequently make some of the other aspects of the regimen more tolerable. We can expect Mr. Smith to have a bad taste in his mouth and possibly stomatitis due to decreased salivary flow and the high concentration of ammonia. The urea that is secreted into the saliva breaks down into ammonia resulting in an alkaline state. The use of lemon juice and glycerine swabs helps keep the pH of the mouth down and thereby decreases the incidence of stomatitis. In acute renal insufficiency most patients do not develop the uremic frost from deposit of crystals of urea on the skin, but frequent bathing (without soap), or use of lotion to the skin may be indicated for skin discomfort.

Evaluation criteria for hemodialysis would be:

1. Decrease in elevation of creatinine and BUN.

2. Maintenance of electrolytes within safe levels.

3. Maintenance of patency of the shunt.

4. Absence of weight gain or other signs of fluid volume excess.
5. Blood glucose maintained below 200.
6. Absence of further renal damage from toxic agents.
7. Absence of infection.
8. Absence of constipation.
9. Effectiveness of patient comfort measures.
10. Maintenance of psychologic integrity.
11. Compliance with therapeutic regimen.

CASE 7B. Mrs. Schmidt, a 55-year-old woman, had a total right (R) hip replacement with a Charnley prosthesis under halothane (Fluothane) anesthesia.
She received pancuronium (Pavulon) for muscle relaxation during the surgery.
This was reversed at the end by neostygmine (Prostigmin) which was given
with atropine. She was in good general health except for hip pain and disability
since the hip had been injured in an accident 6 years previously. She had had a
previous hip operation which was unsuccessful in relieving her pain. The
surgical procedure was rather long because of scar tissue from the previous
operation. At the end of her first hour in the recovery room, her vital signs
were: BP 100/75, P 70, R 14, T (R) 36.9C (98.4F). She was noted to be shivering
considerably, but she was beginning to respond. She would not take deep
breaths when instructed and complained of being "sick at my stomach." She
vomited approximately 100 ml of greenish liquid with mucous strands.

Skillbuilders:
1. On the practicum record 7-B, list the three most likely hypotheses for Mrs.
Schmidt's vomiting in the order of their likelihood of occurrence.
2. Then list the data that support each hypothesis and additional data
needed to confirm or disconfirm.
3. In the intervention section, outline the activities that would be appropriate during the recovery room period.
4. Finally, list the criteria for evaluation of the response to Mrs. Schmidt's
vomiting.

Feedback: I think we all know that in the period of recovery from a general anesthetic, hypoxia is the most likely cause for most of the problems. Thus
our first hypothesis is vomiting due to hypoxia while the other hypotheses are
aerophagia and effect of anesthetic agents. Another possibility that you may
have listed is vomiting due to an emotional reaction. This is less likely in the early
recovery period in a person without a history of psychogenic disorder. We'll look
at hypoxia first. The supporting data are the history of a general anesthetic and
the knowledge that hypoxia, especially when accompanied by a low blood pressure can cause nausea and vomiting. The residual anesthesia can result in inadequate respiratory drive and hypoventilation. Hypoventilation can lead to
hypoxia, with other contributing factors being airway obstruction from loss of
tone of lingual and mandibular muscles, increased right to left shunting (most
frequently due to atelectasis), and increased oxygen consumption (as occurs with

PRACTICUM RECORD 7-B

Hypothesis/Possible Diagnosis	Supportive Data Available	Additional Data Needed to Confirm or Disconfirm	Nursing Intervention	Evaluation Criteria
Vomiting due to:				
1.				
2.				
3.				

shivering in emergence from anesthesia). The muscle relaxants can also contribute to hypoventilation if they have not been adequately reversed. The slow respiratory rate of 14 may be an indicator of respiratory depression. Additional datum to confirm would be the finding of a low arterial Po_2, but intervention would be initiated immediately instead of waiting for confirmation of the hypothesis.

Intervention would include administration of oxygen, encouragement of deep breathing, placing the patient in the sniffing position, and stirring-up activities to promote more rapid emergence from anesthesia. If these activities do not improve oxygenation, more vigorous therapy such as bagging with a resuscitation bag might be indicated. Additionally Mrs. Schmidt needs to be positioned on her side or semiprone and observed closely to prevent aspiration of vomitus. Evaluation criteria would be arterial Po_2 maintained above 70 torr, vital capacity greater than 12 ml/kg, no aspiration, and absence of nausea and vomiting.

Supporting data for the second hypothesis that vomiting is due to aerophagia come from the history of a general anesthetic and our knowledge that in emergence from anesthesia many patients swallow large quantities of air. Additionally, most anesthetists hyperinflate the lungs with a resuscitation bag preceding intubation. Part of the air from this bagging is forced into the stomach. Although the patient may have been NPO preoperatively, retention of gastric secretions may contribute to vomiting. Additional data to confirm the hypothesis would be palpation of the abdomen for distension. No intervention may be required if the emesis emptied the stomach. A Levine tube to suction would be indicated if distension persists. The measures to prevent aspiration would be utilized until the protective reflexes have returned. Evaluation criteria would be no vomiting or aspiration.

The third hypotheses that the vomiting is due to the effect of anesthetic agents is supported by the history of such intake and the knowledge that anesthetic agents can cause vomiting. The frequency of vomiting from anesthesia today is greatly reduced from that with previously used anesthetics. Halothane rarely causes vomiting, but the anticholinesterase agents that are used to reverse the skeletal muscle relaxants can cause increased peristalsis, especially when not given with adequate atropine. Most frequently vomiting from this cause occurs very suddenly following jolting movement. There are no additional data to confirm except that it is usually considered to be the cause when other possible factors have been ruled out. No intervention is usually indicated. Atropine may be given if excessive secretions, diaphoresis, and/or miosis indicate that neostigmine has not been adequately reversed. Antiemetic agents such as trimethobenzamide (Tigan) or prochlorperazine (Compazine) are contraindicated in the early period of recovery from anesthesia because of their tendency to cause hypotension and their prolongation of the central nervous system depression of anesthesia. They can also increase the danger of aspiration of vomitus. Since medicine to relieve every ill is a cultural expectation of our society, Mrs. Schmidt may interpret the decision to give no treatment as a lack of concern for her discomfort or welfare and/or inability of the staff to give her competent care. Thus, explanation geared to her level of understanding about why medication cannot be given at this time and assurances that the disorder is probably only transient, but that if it continues medication can be given a little later, is essential to prevent excess anxiety from lack of trust in the competence of the staff. If vomiting continues and other causes have been ruled out, antiemetic agents can be cautiously administered when the patient has recovered from the anesthesia. Evaluation criteria would be no vomiting and absence of dysfunctional effects of excess anxiety, hypotension, and aspiration.

CASE 7C. Mr. Chang is a 32-year-old admitted to the hospital 4 days ago following an accident in which the motorcycle he was riding collided with an automobile. He received a skull fracture and extensive lacerations and abrasions. His lacerations were cleaned and sutured except for a deep laceration on his right buttock that was left open with wet to dry saline packing. He has remained in a semicomatose state since admission. He has been restless and agitated. His vital signs are within normal limits and he has normal corneal and pharyngeal reflexes, with equal pupils that react to light. He is incontinent of urine and stool. He has been receiving 1500 ml daily per nasogastric tube of a low sodium milk-based formula with added amino acid, sugar, and vitamins. The formula provides 1.5 calories/ml (490 mOsm/liter). He has a history of severe allergy to penicillin, but has been receiving tetracycline 250 mg four times daily per NG tube, with medication given between formula feedings. His fluids are restricted to 2000 ml/day including the formula. He is also on dexamethasone (Decadron) 4 mg every 6 hours. Three days after admission he started having loose stools, and now on the fourth day he has had numerous loose and watery stools. His vital signs and electrolyte values (drawn on the evening of the fourth day) show some of the dysfunctional effects of the diarrhea.

BP 115/90, P 100, R 22, T (R) 38.6 C (101.5 F), Urine output 40 ml/hour

	Patient	Normal
Chloride	116	95−105 mEq/liter
Carbon dioxide	18.2	24−32 mEq/liter
Potassium	4.5	3.5−5 mEq/liter
Sodium	147	135−145 mEq/liter
Urea Nitrogen	36	10−20 mg/dl
Glucose	160	58−100 mg/dl
Blood Gases (arterial)		
pH	7.34	7.35−7.45
PCO_2	29.5	35−45 torr
PO_2	96	75−100 torr
HCO_3^-	19	22−26 mEq/liter
FiO_2	0.21	

Skillbuilders: This is another of those sneaky two-for-one problems, since we need to identify both the cause of Mr. Chang's diarrhea and the dysfunctional effects:

1. On the practicum record 7-C1, list the three most likely hypotheses for Mr. Chang's diarrhea.

2. Then list the supporting data for each hypothesis and additional data you would need to confirm or disconfirm.

3. In the nursing intervention column, list appropriate intervention if the hypothesis was confirmed.

4. Then list the evaluation criteria for the management of Mr. Chang's diarrhea.

5. On the practicum record 7-C2, list the three most likely hypotheses for present or potential dysfunctional effects of the diarrhea. Use those indicated by the blood work or history. These might not be considered to be true nursing diagnoses because the nurse might not have the primary role in their treatment, but they are disorders that have an adverse effect on Mr. Chang's state of health and for which at least part of the responsibility of assessment and intervention rests with the nurse.

6. Next enter the supporting data and additional data you would need to confirm or disconfirm each hypothesis.

7. Enter the nursing intervention activities.

8. Finally, enter the evaluation criteria for the management of the dysfunctional effects.

Feedback: We listed diarrhea due to hyperosmolar tube feeding, lactase deficiency, or tetracycline administration. Another possibility could be fecal impaction, with oozing of liquid stool around the impaction. It is unlikely, however, that an impaction could have developed so quickly. The supporting data for hyperosmolar tube feeding come from the facts that Mr. Chang is receiving a tube-feeding, with a concentration of 490 mOsm/liter and our knowledge of principles of osmosis. The tube feeding is hypertonic to the body fluids which are 290 mOsm/liter. He was only allowed 500 ml of water, and probably 400 ml of that was needed for administration of tetracycline and dexamethasone. Thus only a few ml could be given after each tube feeding and the water probably remained in the tube and did not dilute the formula. We know that fluid moves from an area of lesser concentration to an area of greater concentration. It is possible, then, that a considerable quantity of water was pulled into the bowel. In some patients this will stimulate peristaltic activity, with resultant diarrhea. There is no datum that can help confirm the hypothesis except a trial of less concentrated formula. The usual management is bowel rest for 6–12 hours, followed by a small quantity of less concentrated formula that is gradually increased as tolerated. Agents that slow intestinal motility (diphenoxylate hydrochloride with atropine (Lomotil) or deodorized tincture of opium might be ordered by the physician. Products that contained kaolin would not be used because of their absorptive properties that interfere with tetracycline therapy.

Evaluation criteria would be no more than three stools/day, with stools of

PRACTICUM RECORD 7-C1

Hypothesis/Possible Diagnosis	Supportive Data Available	Additional Data Needed to Confirm or Disconfirm	Nursing Intervention if Diagnosis Confirmed	Evaluation Criteria
Diarrhea due to:				
1.				
2.				

Hypothesis/Possible Diagnosis	Supportive Data Available	Additional Data Needed to Confirm or Disconfirm	Nursing Intervention	Evaluation Criteria
Present or Potential Dysfunctional Effects:				
1.				
2.				
3.				

formed consistency. Sometimes we include criteria for absence of dysfunctional effects, but since we are considering those individually, this time we won't list them. We have a similar type of problem with the hypothesis that the diarrhea is due to lactase deficiency. The data to confirm again come from the history that Mr. Chang is receiving a milk-base formula and our knowledge that some persons have a deficiency of the enzyme lactase that is necessary for hydrolysis of the lactose in milk. The incidence of lactase deficiency varies with races, with Orientals and American Negroes having a high incidence. The main additional data to support the hypothesis again would come from a trial of a formula without lactose and observation of the results. Ensure and Isocal are commercially available formulas that are lactose-free. They are also isotonic, but each supply only 1 calorie/ml. The administration of the formula following a period of bowel rest and possibly drugs to decrease intestinal motility is the same as that for hyperosmolar diarrhea. The evaluation criteria would also be the same. The hypothesis that diarrhea is due to intake of tetracycline is supported by the history of intake and our knowledge that both oral and parenteral intake of some antibiotics can cause diarrhea. There are no specific tests to aid the diagnosis.

Intervention is under the direction of the physician who may discontinue the antibiotic, change to another antibiotic, or continue the antibiotic and treat the diarrhea. Since overgrowth of monilial organisms may contribute to the diarrhea, lactobacillus acidophilus may be given. The administration of drugs to decrease intestinal motility and evaluation criteria would be the same as for the other hypotheses.

Now let's consider the dysfunctional effects. Because of Mr. Chang's history of incontinence and the presence of an open laceration on the buttocks, we are, of course, concerned about the potential for infection in the wound. We considered the other two dysfunctional effects to be metabolic acidosis due to bicarbonate loss in stool and fluid volume deficit due to excessive losses of fluid in stool and urine (with osmotic diuresis) in patient on controlled limited intake. The data to confirm the potential for wound infection are the history items mentioned above and the knowledge of increased susceptibility to infection with the loss of the barrier to infection of intact skin. Additional data to confirm the hypothesis would be increased redness, swelling, or drainage from the wound and positive culture. Nursing intervention would be undertaken with or without confirmation of the hypothesis because hopefully we will prevent infection. Activities would be directed toward keeping the stool from coming in contact with the lacerated area. These activities could include frequent cleansing, use of a waterproof substance over the lacerated area, and positioning on left side or semiprone. The skin in the perineal and anal area should also be protected from excoriation from the stool, which could predispose to breakdown. Additionally an external condom catheter might be used for urine incontinence. Evaluation criteria would be healing of the laceration without infection (absence of redness, swelling, drainage, or positive culture).

Were you able to identify the next dysfunctional effect as metabolic acidosis? The decision tree on metabolic acidosis will guide us here. We don't have any information on the physical signs except for tachypnea. When we look at the pH of 7.34, we know there is some type of acidosis. Since the HCO_3^- is low, we then determine the acidosis is metabolic rather than respiratory. With such a low bicarbonate, however, we would have expected the pH to be lower than 7.34. When we note the arterial P_{CO_2} is 29.5, we can see that Mr. Chang has been hyperventilating in order to blow off CO_2 and compensate for the acidosis. Bicarbonate loss from the stool can be as high as 60 mEq/liter, so this is probably the cause for the acidosis. Calculation of the anion gap will help confirm that such is the case. We can calculate the anion gap by subtracting the sum of the anions (chloride and total carbon dioxide) from the cation, sodium. Thus Mr. Chang's anion gap would be $147 - (116 + 18.2)$, or 12.8 mEq/liter. This is a normal anion gap, and is thus indicative of bicarbonate loss with compensatory hyperchloremia. Our refined diagnostic statement could thus be metabolic acidosis due to bicarbonate loss in stool, partially compensated by hyperventilation. No further data are required to confirm the diagnosis but the harmfulness to the patient of the disorder would be determined by the doctor. At the present time, the patient is almost able to compensate by hyperventilating. The reduction in P_{CO_2} results in cerebral vasoconstriction and reduced flow of blood to the brain, however, which can be deleterious for a patient with a head injury. You may have looked at this problem from the standpoint of the compensatory mechanism causing the dysfunctional effect which would not have been a wrong answer. Intervention besides control of the diarrhea would be administration of sodium bicarbonate. Evaluation criteria would be pH maintained above 7.3 and no decrease in neurologic functioning.

Everyone probably included fluid volume deficit on their list. We have discussed this with several other patient disorders which is an indication of the key role it plays in health maintenance. The decision tree on fluid volume deficit can guide our search for supporting data. The supporting data are the history of decreased water intake, diarrhea, the physical signs of tachycardia and the elevated BUN and serum sodium. Additional data to support the hypothesis would be loss of skin tugor and flat neck veins. We would not attempt to stand Mr. Chang up to determine if he had a postural drop in blood pressure, and cognitive assessment would not aid diagnosis since he had a preexisting deficit. Since there is no indication of renal failure, Mr. Chang's high BUN is indicative of the fact that he has not received sufficient water to excrete the nitrogenous waste products. He not only is receiving a high nitrogen load in the high protein tube feeding but also has nitrogen loss from the increased protein catabolism from the injury and administration of dexamethasone. A knowledge of the sympathoadrenal response to the stress of injury and treatment factors is helpful in understanding why Mr. Chang is at high risk for development of fluid volume deficit. It is somewhat complicated, but one of the essential concepts to understand. In response to the stress of injury, the body releases catecholamines and adrenocorticotropin hormone (ACTH) that stimulates release of steroid hormones by the adrenal glands. This accelerates the rate of glycogenolysis in the liver with elevation of glucose. There is a lag in the pancreas' increase in insulin production, with the elevated blood sugar initiating an osmotic diuresis. If the diuresis is sufficient to cause a decrease in fluid volume, compensatory mechanisms increase the rate of release of the antidiuretic hormone (ADH) and increase sympathoadrenal activity. Patients with head injuries frequently are temporarily low in ADH, so the sympathoadrenal response may be the major one operating with increased urinary loss of fluid. Thus it can develop into a vicious cycle if the process is not interrupted. Treatment factors also contribute to a fluid volume deficit with Mr. Chang. He is receiving dexamethasone (because it decreases cerebral edema) and sodium and fluid restriction, also to prevent cerebral edema that occurs with fluid volume excess. The dexamethasone, however, also increases glycogenolysis and the fluid restriction, when not increased to compensate for the increased losses in stool and urine, contributes to the fluid deficit. The intervention for the immediate period until the diarrhea can be controlled would be directed toward replacement of fluid volume lost in the stools. Some fluid would be allowed to replace losses, and in some instances, urinary output greater than a certain amount also would be replaced. Sodium is usually restricted to prevent cerebral edema. The tube feeding is frequently withheld for 12–18 hours until the fluid and electrolyte situation can be normalized. Evaluation criteria would be normal fluid volume state and no decrease in neurologic functioning. Normal fluid volume state would be indicated by normal skin turgor and neck veins and urinary output between 50 and 75 percent of intake with a urine specific gravity between 1.010 and 1.020. Because hyperglycemia and other electrolyte abnormalities alter the output volume and concentration, the BUN would be the most helpful parameter for ongoing evaluation of the fluid volume state in this patient who would not have a Swan–Ganz catheter for monitoring of pulmonary artery wedge pressure.

CASE 7D. Miss Anderson is a 39-year-old secretary who has had progressive systemic sclerosis (scleroderma) for 3 years. Initially the main manifestation was Raynaud's phenomena that affected the fingers and hands. Over the past year she has had some ulceration on the fingertips and increased swelling of the fingers and hands. She has developed some flexion contractures of the fingers and involvement of both knee joints. The skin of the hands, face, and upper chest has become thickened and leathery in appearance. Palpation of the knees reveals leathery crepitation. The pain has been so severe that she occasionally has to supplement aspirin with codeine to continue working. Over the past 2 weeks, she has been increasingly troubled by dysphagia, a feeling of epigastric fullness, and occasionally regurgitation of gastric contents. She has been eating only liquid and semi-liquid foods. She was admitted to the hospital for diagnostic tests to determine if esophageal stricture was present. Her orders in the hospital included full liquid diet, aspirin with Maalox (Ascriptin) 2 tabs 4×/day, codeine 65 mg every 4 hours prn, Gaviscon 15 ml after meals and hs, flurazepam HCl (Dalmane) 30 mg hs prn, and head of bed elevated 30 degrees at all times. On the day after admission she reported that she had not had a bowel movement for 4 days and that she had a feeling of abdominal bloating. She stated that she had had to take a laxative several times in the past few weeks.

Skillbuilders:

1. On the practicum record 7-D1, enter the three most likely hypotheses for Miss Anderson's lack of bowel elimination for 4 days. We have called it lack of bowel elimination because we don't know whether the exact nature of the disorder is constipation, fecal impaction, or obstipation.

2. Then enter the supporting data for each hypothesis and additional data needed to confirm or disconfirm.

3. In the nursing intervention section list the physician-directed and independent nursing activities for the relief of the disorder.

4. In the last column enter the criteria for evaluation of the effectiveness of the process.

5. On the practicum record 7-D2, enter two nursing diagnoses of physiologic problems for Miss Anderson associated with her scleroderma. These problems could have been identified on admission from the history and course of illness information. Let's not include pain and alteration in bowel elimination since they have already been discussed.

6. List the supporting data that led you to identify it as a problem area.

7. Then list the plan for nursing intervention.

8. Enter appropriate evaluation criteria.

9. On the lower portion of the practicum record, enter three nursing diagnoses of possible problems in psychosocial adjustment to her illness which should be explored with Miss Anderson for validation.

10. Then list the major signs and symptoms which would support each diagnosis. Since the nursing intervention would be cued by the patient's response in the interview, we will not ask you to include intervention and evaluation for these diagnoses.

Feedback: In a patient with progressive systemic sclerosis who is having problems from esophageal involvement, it is highly probable that there may be intestinal involvement with constipation as well. Other hypotheses would be lack of bowel elimination for 4 days from lack of bulk in the diet or from suppression of colonic motility by codeine intake. The supporting data for lack of bowel elimination from intestinal involvement of scleroderma are the history of scleroderma and the possible esophageal involvement coupled with the knowledge that the fibrosis of scleroderma can affect the intestines causing decreased intestinal motility and alteration of the intestinal mucosa with dilatation, which can result in constipation and fecal impaction. Additionally, if there has been atrophy of the muscles of the diaphragm, abdominal wall, intestine and/or rectum, the muscle strength may not be adequate for expulsion of the feces. Additional data would come from examination of the stool and anal area. The appearance of the stool would probably reflect the delayed transport by being well formed and hard. The impaired motility in the small intestine can result in abnormal stasis of the intestinal contents which allows bacterial proliferation and malabsorption. Malabsorption of fat results in steatorrhea and can be determined by examination of the stool for fat. The stool frequently appears light, bulky, and glistening. Constipation, however, is more apt to be associated with excessive

PRACTICUM RECORD 7-D1

Hypothesis/Possible Diagnosis	Supportive Data Available	Additional Data Needed to Confirm or Disconfirm	Nursing Intervention if Diagnosis Confirmed	Evaluation Criteria
Lack of bowel elimination for 4 days due to: 1.				
2.				
3.				

PRACTICUM RECORD 7-D2

Hypothesis/Possible Diagnosis	Supportive Data Available	Additional Data to Confirm or Disconfirm	Nursing Intervention if Diagnosis Confirmed	Evaluation Criteria
Scleroderma: 1.				
2.				
Difficult psychosocial adjustment to illness due to: 1.				
2.				
3.				

decomposition and putrefaction of protein, which may be manifested by a pH greater than 6. Digital examination of the rectum (to determine the presence or absence of impaction) and visual inspection of the anal area (to identify hemorrhoids or anal fissures) is important information that needs to be obtained. Barium X-ray studies and intestinal biopsy may be ordered by the physician to aid diagnosis.

Nursing intervention is primarily supportive since at the present time there is no known treatment that reverses the pathologic state. Systemically active antibiotics such as tetracycline reduce the bacterial overgrowth that results in malabsorption and excessive putrefaction. Other measures to promote improved bowel elimination include:

1. Involvement of the patient in the development of the treatment plan.
2. Establishment of a regular time for defecation.
3. High intake of water.
4. Dietary experimentation to find foods that can be ingested without dysphagia that do not contribute to constipation (a blender can frequently be utilized to liquefy high-bulk foods so they can be swallowed; concentrated sugars, fats, and milk products are the most frequent offenders in causing constipation).
5. Ingestion of hot beverages or brisk walk before defecation.
6. Use of stool softeners and laxatives, if needed.
7. Positioning on the commode that promotes use of the accessory muscles for expulsion of the feces.

Evaluation criteria would be bowel elimination at the same frequency as preillness state and absence of fecal impaction. The next hypothesis that lack of bowel elimination for 4 days is due to lack of bulk in the diet is supported by the history of dysphagia that restricted the diet to liquids and our knowledge that a certain amount of residue in the diet is needed to form a bolus to stimulate peristalsis. Additional datum would be confirmation of a small stool volume. This information is difficult to obtain, however, since stool can be retained in the gastrointestinal tract for several days. The best supporting datum comes from a trial of a high bulk diet. Miss Anderson may be unable to tolerate high residue foods with her esophageal disorder, however.

Nursing intervention would include the same measures listed for intestinal involvement from scleroderma with the exception of the use of antibiotics. The evaluation criteria would also be the same, i.e., restoration of preillness bowel elimination and absence of fecal inpaction. We have few data to support our last hypothesis of bowel elimination disorder due to suppression of colonic motility by codeine intake. We have to rely mainly on the history of codeine intake and the knowledge that codeine causes constipation in a number of persons. The datum to confirm comes from the disappearance of the constipation following discontinuance of the codeine. Intervention if this hypothesis is confirmed sometimes requires the evaluation of the relative effects of two evils. Codeine probably provides the greatest analgesia with the lowest incidence of addiction of all the available pain relieving drugs. Codeine is frequently continued if conservative measures are effective in eliminating the constipation. The measures to decrease constipation would be the same as for the other hypotheses. Evaluation criteria of absence of constipation and absence of fecal impaction are also the same as for the other hypotheses.

Perhaps we should take a break before we tackle the nursing diagnoses related to the scleroderma. There are a number of possibilities, but we listed alteration in peripheral circulation and impaired oral food intake. The data to support the alteration in peripheral circulation are the history of Raynaud's phenomena with vasospasm resulting in painful fingers, fingertip ulcers, swelling, limitation of extension, and development of flexion contractures. Nursing intervention would be direct toward educating Miss Anderson about control of vasospasm, measures to increase the digital blood flow, and prevention of infection and further deformity. Vasospasm can be reduced by avoidance of factors that precipitate it such as exposure to cold, emotional stress, smoking, and drugs such as amphetamines and ergotamine. Some patients have learned to control the temperature of their hands utilizing biofeedback to raise the threshold to vasospasm. Ulcers need to be cleaned and debrided. Topical antibiotics may be used if infection is present. Range of motion to both hands and fingers several times a day can limit flexion deformities. Sometimes hand and finger splints are worn at night to maintain extension. Evaluation during the brief period of hospitalization would primarily be by verbalization of knowledge. Criteria to evaluate the longer term effectiveness would be patient's report of decreased incidence of severe vasospasms, healing of finger ulcers without infection, and no increase in deformity.

That brings us to consideration of the nursing diagnoses of impaired oral food intake. Since we do not yet have a complete and generally accepted list of diagnostic labels, it is quite possible that you could have given a different name to this problem. The signs and symptoms that we felt supported the diagnosis are inability to swallow solid food, feeling of epigastric fullness and regurgitation of gastric contents. Nursing intervention includes education regarding lowered intake at each feeding; avoidance of eating for 2 to 3 hours before retiring, sleeping with the head of the bed elevated, and use of antacids. Some patients are helped by sublingual nitroglycerin at the start of the meal. When esophageal stricture is present, dilation may be helpful. Desirable evaluation criteria would be patient report of less difficulty in swallowing, decrease or absence of epigastric fullness, and no regurgitation of food.

We are now ready to discuss the diagnoses relating to possible psychosocial maladjustment. These are just conjectures at this point based on our knowledge of the process of adjustment to a chronic progressive illness. They would need to be refined and validated by talking with Miss Anderson and ongoing observation of her behavioral responses. Our hypotheses are alteration in body image, impaired self-determination (powerlessness), and lack of security. (It is quite likely that you might use different terminology.) Data to confirm the possibility of altered body image would include: (1) loss of normal function of the hands, fingers, and knees; (2) change in appearance of skin of hands, knees, face, and upper chest; and (3) loss of normal ability to swallow. The patient's reaction to these changes would need to be assessed to determine the extent Miss Anderson has been able to integrate the changes into her self-concept. Some signs of maladjustment would be unwillingness to talk about her body changes, denial that changes have affected her, and low self-esteem. We worded our second hypothesis impaired self-determination. It could be referred to as a feeling of powerlessness. The data which cue us to this possibility are the progression of a chronic illness in a young woman and the knowledge that almost nothing can be done to alter the course of the disease. Instead of being able to make decisions about the future based on what she would like to do and become, she is now faced with the prospect of poor health. Her deformities and finger ulceration may prevent her from continuing her work as a secretary. Discussion of the area with Miss Anderson is needed to confirm the extent of the problem. Miss Anderson's philosophy, life values, and support system will influence her response to this threat. The third hypothesis we listed is lack of security. We are strongly influenced by Abraham Maslow's hierarchy of needs and believe a problem could be present if this need is unmet. Supporting data are the enforced physical changes that are leading to social changes. The loss of the sense of security could be referred to as anticipatory grieving. The response to the lack of security could be manifested by anger and hostility or by preoccupation with self, withdrawal, and possibly regression. Anxiety and fear are also components because of uncertainty about the future. Again this needs to be explored with Miss Anderson to confirm the presence of the diagnosis and the nature and effectiveness of her coping mechanisms.

ADDITIONAL READINGS

Grant MM, Kubo WM: Assessing a patient's hydration status. AJN 75(8):1306–1311, 1975.

Lewin AJ, Maxwell M: Acute renal failure: Diagnostic and therapeutic criteria. Critical Care Med 2(6):305–310, 1974.

MacBryde CM: Dehydration, fluid and electrolyte imbalances. In MacBryde C, Blacknow R (eds.): Signs and Symptoms, 5th ed. Philadelphia, Lippincott, 1970, pp 746–800.

Peterson ML: Constipation and diarrhea. In MacBryde C, Blacknow R (eds.): Signs and Symptoms, 5th ed. Philadelphia, Lippincott, 1970, pp 381–398.

Shires GT, Canizaro PC: Fluid, electrolyte, and nutritional management of the surgical patient. In Schwartz S, et al. (eds.): Textbook of Surgery, 3rd ed. New York, McGraw-Hill, 1979, pp 65–95.

CHAPTER 8

Impaired Mobility

Impaired mobility can result from diverse causes. It can be caused by injury, be a major manifestation of a disease, be a secondary occurrence accompanying other disorders, imposed as part of a treatment regimen, or be a manifestation of a conversion syndrome. Diseases include both infectious and noninfectious disorders and may involve the skeletal, muscular, nervous, and/or endocrine systems.

Mobility is determined by the ability of muscles to contract, the transmission of the neuromuscular impulse, and the functioning of cranial and spinal motor nuclei and nerves. These functions are modified and controlled by a number of factors that include the reticulospinal system, the pyramidal and extrapyramidal systems, other proprioceptive pathways, and the cerebellum. Fractures, bone deformities, and joint dysfunction also have an effect on movement. A complete discussion of these interacting and complex mechanisms is not within the scope of this book. Assessment parameters indicative of deviations from normal movement will be outlined. The nurse interested in exploring the exact nature of the underlying pathophysiologic process of a certain affliction needs to consult a text on neurologic and musculoskeletal pathophysiology.

ASSESSMENT

History

Items of importance include incidence of trauma, other associated symptoms, presence of diseases which may have neuromuscular manifestations, and previous attacks of a similiar nature.

Physical Examination

Inspection, manipulation, and palpation are the main modalities used for assessment of mobility. Abnormalities of joints, and muscle weakness can usually all be observed by watching the patient rise from a chair, stand, and walk across the room. The examination needs to be adapted to the individual patient. If the patient denies any pain, limitation of motion, loss of sensation, or weakness and no abnormalities are present on visual observation, detailed evaluation of all aspects of the function is unnecessary. However, if any disorders of mobility are present, a more intensive examination will have to be undertaken to define the problem accurately. It is of utmost importance that the most informative assessment parameters be used and that the abnormality be described specifically and discretely so that changes in the state of the patient can be identified by others as well as yourself. It is also essential to distinguish between deformity and disability. Deformity is an anatomic abnormality while disability is the failure to function in a normal manner. Either one can be present without the other, although severe deformity is almost always accompanied by some disability. Thus, it is necessary to assess not only the extent of the deformity, but also the extent of any resulting disability.

Muscle function.   This depends primarily on strength, range of motion, and tone. *Muscle strength* is most severely affected in nutritional or wasting diseases or in advanced stages of anterior horn cell and muscle disease. For accuracy in determination of deficits in muscle strength, muscles should be tested individually. The electromyogram (EMG) gives the most definitive information about muscle strength. The strength of the muscle is usually graded from the weakest (which are those that barely support the extremity against gravity) to stronger muscles that not only withstand gravitational pull but also can exert resistance to pressures applied by the examiner. Homologous muscles should be tested simultaneously to distinguish between unilateral and bilateral weakness. The grip strength of the hand can be most accurately assessed by having the patient squeeze the bulb of a blood pressure cuff inflated to 20 mm Hg.

   Range of motion in the extremities is probably the most frequently made nursing assessment. Limited range of motion may be a reflection of muscle weakness, but more often indicates contractures or dysfunction of the involved joint. Joint disorders are most frequently caused by arthritis, rheumatism, or gout. Range of motion can be estimated, but more accurate measurements, which may be essential for evaluation of the progression of disease and response to treatment, utilize a goniometer. Motion is recorded as zero when the extremity is totally extended, with degrees recorded for the angle of greatest flexion and, when present, the angle of hyperextension. If the patient cannot extend the extremity completely, a minus sign is used before the number indicating the degrees of the angle between the patient's extension and a straight line. Tables of average ranges for each joint are available, but there is a great deal of variation among individuals and various age groups.

   Muscle tone is frequently evaluated by the extent of the muscular contraction in response to a sudden stretch produced by striking the tendon. Unilateral depression or exaggeration of reflexes or pathologic reflexes (i.e., Babinski, Chaddock's, knee jerk, etc.) are symptomatic of nervous system disorders. The major abnormalities of muscular tone are flaccidity, spasticity, and rigidity. Flaccidity is a decrease in muscle tone and weakness when the muscle is at rest. Spasticity refers to an increase in the normal muscle tone (especially of the antigravity muscles) when the muscle is stretched. Rigidity is another type of increased muscle tone that affects muscles intermittently without regard to their relation to gravity. It is manifested by stiffness and unevenness of movement.

Change in muscular volume. This needs to be assessed carefully. Atrophy of involved muscles results from impairment of movement over a period of time. Localized wasting, which frequently corresponds to a spinal segmental distribution, is seen in lower motor neuron disease. Loss of muscle mass is observable and can be measured for greater accuracy. Pseudohypertrophy is generally present with muscular dystrophy due to the paradoxical enlargement of the weakened muscles.

Postural assessment. This is primarily based on the contour of the spine. It includes a description of the cervical, dorsal, and lumbar curves, and of any lateral curvature (scoliosis). Postural deformities may be congenital or the result of trauma or disease. Decortical posturing, which results from damage to the corticospinal (pyramidal) tract above the brainstem is manifested by rigid extension of the legs and sharp flexion of the arms on the chest. Decerebrate posturing, which results from upper brainstem damage and certain metabolic disorders, such as hypoglycemia and hypoxia, is manifested by clenched jaws with all extremities rigidly extended and arms hyperpronated.

Gait. Gait is a complex activity that requires adequate muscle strength, normal skeletal system coordination, proprioception, and vestibular function. Gait should be tested by observing the person walking freely and normally, or walking a straight line with heel to toe. Skeletal system disorders interfere with the gait and require more energy to move the body. A normal gait efficiently propels the body with the least expenditure of energy, i.e., it smoothly moves the center of gravity of the body no more than 2 inches up and down and from side to side. Gaits that displace the center of gravity more (such as a limp) consume more energy and predispose to physical disability. Abnormalities of gait can be caused by pain, difference in length of lower limbs, restriction of joint motion, lower limb deformity, or paralysis of the lower extremities. Some gaits are pathognomonic of a specific disease state.

Lack of coordination of movement. Ataxia results primarily from affliction of the proprioceptor sensory nerves and/or the cerebellum. It may be aggravated by muscular weakness, spasticity, and involuntary movements.

The proprioceptive mechanism normally provides information to the motor cortex about the position of the body and its movement. Damage to the sensory nerve terminals in the muscles, tendons, labyrinth, or in the afferent pathways in the spinal cord or brainstem results in ataxia characterized by clumsiness and fumbling movements that is worsened when there is no visual guidance. The gait is wide based and uncertain, and the body sways when the eyes are closed. Fine movements are executed extremely slowly. In addition to ataxia, loss of the proprioceptive mechanism (especially when accompanied by increased time in bed), results in decreased stimulation of the extensor muscles needed to support the body, with loss of postural muscle tone. Normally muscle tone is controlled by reflex mechanisms that cause the muscle to contract upon stimulation by gravitational pull and the vestibular apparatus. Without stretch reflex contraction, the muscles atrophy and postural muscle tone is diminished. In acute unilateral impairment of vestibular function, the patient has a tendency to fall to the ipsilateral side.

Cerebellar disorders result in ataxia, tremor, and hypotonia. When only one cerebellar hemisphere is involved, motor abnormalities may appear on the ipsilateral side. Abnormalities in gait can include wavering, lurching, staggering, and jerking back and forth. There is a loss of control over the agonists, antagonists, and synergists that are concerned with a given movement. Therefore movements are characterized by an inappropriate range, rate, and combinations of each of the various components of the motor act. Observable manifestations include jerkiness of movement, intention tremor, undershooting or overshooting of intended actions, inability to perform rapid alternative movements, and slowness in acceleration and deceleration.

Sensation disturbances.   Those disturbances which affect mobility are pain and paresthesia. *Pain* is discussed in greater detail in another chapter. Assessment parameters that have the greatest relevance for mobility are determining if there was a precipitating cause, if the pain is localized or radiating, if it is migratory, aggravated, or decreased by movement, and measures (i.e., local heat, aspirin, exercise, etc.) that have proven effective in relieving the pain. In some instances, it is necessary to determine if the reduction in mobility is due to functional limitation or to limitation because of pain.

Paresthesias include both abnormal and inappropriate sensations (such as numbness, tingling, or burning) which are evoked by a normal stimulus. The range of sensations is from complete loss (anesthesia) through decreased sensory acuity (hypesthesia), to excessive sensitivity (hyperesthesia). Testing usually includes pin prick, light touch, vibration, and position sense. Alterations in sensation indicate abnormalities within the nervous system, but have little effect on mobility.

Spontaneous or Involuntary Movements.   These can interfere with voluntary movement and can also result in maladaptive psychosocial behavior. There are numerous types of movement, with several underlying causes for each type. The major types with a brief description follows:

- *Tremor* is a rhythmical succession of perceptible twitches of the head, tongue, or limbs.

- *Spasm* is a marked contraction of a muscle or a group of muscles which may be painful. If it is sustained over a period of time, it is termed a tonic spasm.

- *Fibrillation* is an irregular, flickering contraction of small muscle cells or fibers that may not be visible except when the affected muscle lies under thin skin such as on the hand. When fibrillation is coarser and involves a large collection of muscle fibers, it is termed fasciculation.

● *Athetosis,* or mobile spasm, is an involuntary condition with bizarre writhing, sinuous movements of the hands, arms, and face.

● *Choreiform movements* are characterized by irregular, jerky, and sudden involuntary movements that can occur in diverse forms. Movements are usually intensified by voluntary movement and excitement. Extreme flinging movements of the arms are termed ballism.

● *Clonic spasm,* or myoclonus, is a shocklike contraction of a muscle (or portion thereof) or a group of muscles. The focal motor seizure can occur in one area of the body or several areas at once. The spasm is usually repetitive for several seconds. Clonic jerks can sometimes build up into prolonged tonic contractions.

● *Motor tics,* or habit spasms, are a manifestation of an obsessive compulsive neurosis. They are characterized by sudden, rapid, coordinated movements of the same nature occurring in the same area. They are aggravated by emotion and lack of sleep.

Adequacy of circulation.   Adequate circulation has a high assessment priority in patients who have suffered trauma. Even when a fracture is present, the forces that produced the fracture have also injured adjacent vascular structures (with resultant neurologic impairments) that require treatment first. Arterial insufficiency of the involved extremity is usually assessed by the use of the "five P's":

1. Pain,
2. Pulses decreased or absent,
3. Paresthesia,
4. Paresis or paralysis, and
5. Pallor.

These parameters need frequent reassessment since developing edema can mechanically cause circulatory and neurologic impairment that was not initially present. Patients with chronic peripheral vascular disease have a history of leg cramps and intermittent claudication in addition to coldness and numbness in the extremities.

Other Tests

Roentgenogram examination.   X-ray will show fracture or deformities, necrosis, or other alteration of osseous structure, displacement of structures by tumors, etc.

Laboratory tests.   These are necessary for definitive diagnosis. Cultures help to identify disorders due to infection, while cell count and analysis of synovial and spinal fluid help to differentiate arthritis, gout, and some central nervous system disorders. A positive Wasserman test may be an indication of a central nervous system disorder due to syphilis. Metabolic panels may help to identify periodic paralysis related to potassium state, gout with elevated uric acid, uremic neuropathy with elevated blood urea nitrogen, Paget's disease or neoplastic diseases of the bone with elevated alkaline phosphatase and calcium, and muscle trauma with enzyme elevation. Findings of porphyrins in the urine may point to acute prophyria neuropathy, while a positive L.E. prep may indicate systemic lupus erythematosis. Special diagnostic tests such as electromyography (EMG) may be indicated for more definitive diagnosis.

Table 8-1 gives a brief overview of the major disorders that impair mobility. Many disorders have several aspects of malfunction. They have been more or less arbitrarily assigned a classification in the table which seems to represent the greatest area of malfunction.

Dysfunctional Effects of Impaired Mobility

In addition to the impairment of mobility itself, the patient frequently experiences other physiologic and psychologic alterations which can severely alter his well being. The major alterations the patient may experience as a result of immobility will be discussed.

Psychologic Effects

The patient with impaired mobility has an altered body image and ego identity and may need assistance in making the necessary psychosocial adaptations, i.e., change in role, degree of independence, occupation, economic state, and participation in activities. In addition, the patient accustomed to using physical activity for the discharge of tension and feelings of aggression may find it difficult to handle those emotions in ways acceptable to himself and those around him. Failure to adapt adequately to the limitations of the disability can result in emotional reactions such as apathy, frustration, anger, withdrawal, and regression.

Physiologic Effects

In addition to the psychologic effects of immobility, physiologic functioning is also altered. The immobility from the original disease can be intensified by musculoskeletal deterioration. The patient also can experience alterations in the normal functioning of several other body systems.

The musculoskeletal system.   This is dependent on normal motor activity for the maintenance of its structural stability. Weight bearing and muscle movement are stimuli for osteoblasts to build up the matrix of the bone. Without these activities, demineralization of the bone with osteoporosis occurs. The resulting porosity disposes to deformity and fracture, or can result in intense pain when the bones must bear the weight of the body. Closely associated with osteoporosis is the loss of muscle tone from decreased proprioceptive stimulation, which has already been briefly discussed.

The cardiovascular system. This system may be altered in three major ways by immobility: decreased ability to respond to the upright posture, decreased cardiac reserve, and predisposition to thrombus formation and embolism.

• *Decreased ability to respond to the upright posture* is manifested by postural (or orthostatic) hypotension. Decreased efficiency of the orthostatic neurovascular reflexes and loss of muscle tone are generally recognized as the cause of postural hypotension when the patient who has been confined to bed for a prolonged period tries to stand. Normally the autonomic system responds with vasoconstriction when a person changes from a supine to an erect position. This counteracts the increased hydrostatic pressure that would otherwise increase arterial and venous pressure with resultant blood pooling in the lower extremities. With a person who has been supine for a period of time, the peripheral circulation has become habituated to the lower pressure and increased diameter of the vessels and reacts sluggishly to autonomic stimuli to contract. Loss of muscle tone contributes to postural hypotension since the action of muscles massaging the veins promotes the venous return of blood to the heart. Without the contraction of muscles exerting pressure on the veins, venous blood pools in the extremities.

• *Decreased cardiac reserve* occurs because the heart has to work harder when the patient is recumbent than when he is erect or sitting. This is probably due to complex interacting forces associated with changes in the hydrostatic pressure, vascular resistance, and changes in the venous gradient resulting from the Valsalva maneuver.

• *Predisposition to thrombus formation and embolism* results from venous stasis, trauma to the intima of the blood vessels, and possibly to an increase in the tendency for the blood to clot. Venous stasis from the lack of muscular contraction which promotes venous return has already been discussed. Trauma to the intima of the blood vessels results from external pressure on the vessels. Such pressure can occur when one leg rests on another or when the bottom of the bed is gatched. The exact mechanism responsible for the increased tendency of blood to clot is unknown, but it may be related to increased viscosity or the increased levels of calcium in the bloodstream that promote conversion of prothrombin to thrombin. The serious sequel to venous thrombosis is the release of a portion or all of the clot to the pulmonary area. Other patients may have residual chronic occlusion and destruction of the venous valves. This state is referred to as the postphlebitic syndrome and is usually irreversible.

Respiratory insufficiency. This may be due to retained secretions and limited chest expansion from immobility. Removal of secretions is dependent on cough-

TABLE 8-1.   Major Disorders that Impair Mobility

Abnormal Initiating Mechanism or Clinical State	Pathophysiology	Identifying Characteristics of Disturbed Mobility
A. Cranial Lesion or Disease		
Cerebral Vascular Accident (CVA)	Intracerebral hemorrhage, thrombosis, embolism, or cerebrovascular insufficiency	Depending on site of lesion—seizures, hemiplegia, apraxia, ataxia, vertigo, hyperreflexia, areflexia, dysphagia, dysarthria
Tumor	Destruction of cranial tissue and/or secondary effects of increased intracranial pressure, cerebral edema, or compression of cranial structures (tissues, nerves, blood vessels)	Same as CVA
B. Central Nervous System Disorder		
Tabes dorsalis (Syphilitic posterior spinal sclerosis)	Degeneration of the dorsal columns of the spinal cord and of the sensory nerve trunks by syphilis spirochete	Ataxia, slapping gait, areflexia, muscular incoordination, trophic joint enlargement with impaired function, motor palsies
Poliomyelitis	Viral infection of central nervous system, with hemorrhage, edema, and nerve atrophy	Stiff neck, positive Brudzinski and/or Kernig's sign, localized or widespread muscular weakness or paralysis, muscular atrophy with subsequent contracture
Multiple sclerosis	Destruction of myelin sheath with formation of sclerotic plaques; etiology unknown but possibly autoimmune reaction; course varies with possibility of remissions	Depending on area affected, weakness of extremity, incoordination, paralysis, ataxia, intention tremor, nystagmus
Cerebral palsy	Damage to central nervous system from heredity factors or disease or trauma occurring in utero, at birth, or in early life	Mobility problems may or may not be evident at birth: hemiplegia, spastic diplegia, scissors gait, spasticity of extremities, hyperreflexia, convulsions, choreoathetosis
Parkinsonism	Nerve cell loss which may be due to infection, trauma, toxins, or unknown causes	Gait of slow, short, shuffling steps, involuntary tendency to increase the speed of walking (festinating gait), increasing muscular rigidity, hand tremor, decreased range of motion of arms
Amyotrophic lateral sclerosis	Degenerative changes in spinal cord of unknown cause; other amytrophic disorders with similar characteristics and pathophysiology are associated with underlying syphilis, diabetes, virus infections, or allergic disorders	Progressive wasting of muscles, fasciculation, hyperreflexia

(continued)

TABLE 8-1.   Continued

Abnormal Initiating Mechanism or Clinical State	Pathophysiology	Identifying Characteristics of Disturbed Mobility
Spinal cord tumor	Compression of spinal cord by lesion	Muscular weakness and spasticity corresponding to areas of lesion
Spinal cord transection	Complete or partial severance of the spinal cord	Initially, spinal shock with loss of motor, sensory, or autonomic function and areflexia, hypotonia, and flaccid paralysis from the level of the injury downward; after 3 to 6 weeks, reflex activity usually returns with an increase in tone, and reflexes that evolve into a spastic paralysis with increased deep tendon reflexes, clonus, and extensor plantar responses
C. Neuromuscular Junction Disease		
Myasthena gravis	Disturbance of acetylcholine metabolism or its concentration at the neuromuscular junction	Weakness of muscle (occular, trunk, extremities, pharyngeal) which is most pronounced after exercise; sometimes paralysis; injection of edrophonium chloride or prostigimine methyl sulfate abolishes or lessens the weakness
Periodic paralysis	Hereditary order which may be related to hypokalemia, hyperkalemia, or normokalemia	Attacks of intense weakness or flaccid paralysis lasting from a few minutes to several days, with normal mobility between attacks
D. Muscular Disease		
Muscular dystrophy	Various hereditary diseases with degeneration of muscle fibers	Progressive muscular weakness and abnormally slow relaxation after voluntary contractions are common manifestations of all types, with differences in age of onset, sex affected and area affected; the weakened muscle is paradoxically enlarged and feels rubbery to the touch
Tetanus	Exotoxin produced by anerobic bacillus that enters the CNS along the peripheral motor nerves prevents normal synaptic inhibition	Rigidity and tonic spasms of muscles of neck, back, pharynx, and extremities progressing to intermittent generalized tonic seizures

(continued)

TABLE 8-1.　Continued

Abnormal Initiating Mechanism or Clinical State	Pathophysiology	Identifying Characteristics of Disturbed Mobility
E. Connective Tissue Disorders		
Polymyositis/dermatomyositis	Inflammatory and degenerative process of muscle fibers and surrounding connective tissue, frequently followed by muscular atrophy and contractures	Muscle weakness and tenderness, most frequently involving muscles of the pelvic and shoulder girdle, thighs, and arms
Systemic lupus erythematosus	Chronic inflammatory connective tissue disorder of unknown etiology with necrosis and abnormal tissue bodies present in involved body organs	Involvement of multiple body systems, with mobility disturbances including seizures, hemiparesis, and arthritis of transient to continuous nature with resultant residual over the years or severe deformity
Scleroderma	Chronic disease of unknown cause with increase of fibrous tissue in skin, synovial membranes, and subcutaneous tissues	Increasing stiffness of face, hands, and arms with deformities of extremities from skin contractures and tinosynovial involvement
Periarteritis nodusa	Systemic disorder with lesions along the course of medium-sized muscular arteries; lesions show necrosis, fibrinoid changes, acute leukocytic infiltration, and nodule formation	Arthralgia, arthritis, muscle tenderness, and muscular weakness
Laceration	Tear caused by trauma, accompanying hemorrhage can exert pressure on surrounding tissue	Limitation of movement of affected area
F. Peripheral Neuropathies		
1. Polyneuropathies: Nutrition (vitamin B deficiency) and alcoholic neuropathy	Changes in the myelin sheath with alteration of impulse conduction	Hypoactive reflexes, sensory ataxia, weakness, and atrophy of muscles; most frequent site of manifestation is lower extremities, with loss of dorsiflexion of foot and paralysis of legs
Toxic neuropathies (heavy metals, drugs)	Myelin destruction, axis cylinder injury, and neuronal chromatolysis	Same as nutritional
Diabetic neuropathy	Intraneural vascular lesions characterized by hyalinization, stenosis, and thickening of vessel wall	Loss of proprioceptive sensation and reflexes, and cranial nerve palsies; degeneration may extend to joint with collapse of bony and articular structures

(continued)

TABLE 8-1. Continued

Abnormal Initiating Mechanism or Clinical State	Pathophysiology	Identifying Characteristics of Disturbed Mobility
Acute prophyria neuropathy	Segmental myelin degeneration of axons in the peripheral nerves	Foot and wrist drop progressing to flaccid paralysis of arms and legs, sensory ataxia, bulbar paralysis, and seizures
Uremic neuropathy	Loss of large medullated fibers in the myelin sheath and axis cylinders	Coarse twitching of muscles, and loss of motor function in feet and legs, and/or hands and forearms
Guillain–Barré	Swelling of axon cylinders with inflammatory infiltration	Ascending motor weakness with development of flaccid paralysis, loss of tendon reflexes, and distal sensory impairment
2. Mononeuropathies:		
Nerve entrapment syndromes	Persistent mechanical trauma to nerve with fibrous scarring	Muscular weakness with atrophy and loss of function of area supplied by entrapped nerve
Nerve injury	Injury to nerve itself, or injury resulting from ischemia due to edema	Ischemic changes result in Volkmann's ischemic contracture of upper extremity or anterior compartment syndrome in lower extremity
G. Joint and Bone Disorders		
1. Injuries:		
Fracture, sprain, dislocation	Break, or rupture in bone or supporting ligament or displacement of joint capsule	Pain and weakness of affected part with swelling, deformity, and loss of motion of affected area
2. Arthritic disorders:		
Polyarthritis (rheumatoid arthritis, rheumatic fever, Still's disease, ankylosing spondylitis, psoriatic arthritis, Reiter's syndrome, colitic arthropathy, etc).	Chronic systemic inflammatory conditions that involve small peripheral joints and the spine, histologic changes in the synovial membrane and subcutaneous nodules over bony prominences	Morning stiffness with joint swelling and tenderness, limitation of motion; rheumatoid arthritis affects primarily the small joints with bilateral involvement that is additive; rheumatic fever primarily affects the large joints and is migratory; arthritis associated with GI disease has an acute onset, may be migratory, and usually subsides with no residual joint damage

(continued)

TABLE 8-1.   Continued

Abnormal Initiating Mechanism or Clinical State	Pathophysiology	Identifying Characteristics of Disturbed Mobility
Degenerative joint diseases (Osteoarthritis, hypertrophic arthritis)	Increased loss of chrondroitin sulfate from cartilage matrix results in breakdown of cartilage and dysplasia of underlying bone	Joint pain and swelling, with disability when joint affected is hip or knee
Nonarticular rheumatism (Fibrositis, tendinitis, bursitis, myositis, etc.)	Inflammation of tendon sheath, bursae, or muscle, which may be accompanied by calcification	Stiffness, soreness, and tenderness of connective tissue adjacent to and supporting the joint, which may result in muscle atrophy and loss of motion in the joint
Bacterial arthritis/septic or suppurative arthritis	Microorganisms from primary infection elsewhere or from extension of infection of adjacent bone or soft tissue affect synovium with resultant edema, destruction of bone elements, formation of abscesses, and collection of necrotic debris	Abrupt onset with fever and chills. Involved joint is warm, red, swollen and painful with muscle spasms
Osteitis deformans (Paget's disease)	Initial decalcification of bone with kyphosis, flattened vertebrae, etc., followed by recalcification resulting in thickening and enlargement of deformed bones	The cumulative deformities over a period of years may lead to invalidism
Gout	Deposit of sodium urate crystals in the synovial fluid evokes an inflammatory reaction in joint with effusion	Painful swelling of joints, with limitation of motion
3. Osseous tumors, multiple myeloma, bone metastases, lymphoma of bone	Infiltration of bone by neoplastic cells results in diffuse osteoporosis, pathologic fractures, and compression of nerve roots or peripheral nerves	Painful bony lesions and fractures
H. Hysterical neurosis	Manifestation of a conversion reaction which in the early stages has no muscle wasting, although, after a period of time, it may be accompanied by muscle atrophy and osteoporosis	Motor disturbance with tremors, flaccid or spastic paresis, and contractions. May be distinguishable by normal plantar and tendom reflexes, normal electrical reaction, normal muscle function when supine with inability to stand, or standing with marked flexion of the spine

ing and changes in posture and position. Chest expansion is decreased when muscle tone is weak due to disease, disuse, or decreased innervation. Compression of the thorax from abdominal distension or supine posture also limits expansion. Inhalation of small tidal volumes over a period of time without periodical deep breaths (or sighs) combined with retained secretions result in progressive atelectasis and the development of hypostatic pneumonia.

The gastrointestinal system.   The GI system is also affected by immobility. The most common adverse effects are negative nitrogen balance and constipation. *Negative nitrogen balance* occurs because the patient who is confined to bed has decreased energy needs and thus a lower metabolic (or anabolic) rate. Catabolism is increased with immobility, however, and the accelerated protein breakdown results in protein deficiency and a negative nitrogen balance. The stress resulting from immobility can cause parasympathetic stimulation which causes anorexia, dyspepsia, and diminution of gastric and intestinal motility. Thus the patient tends to decrease his intake of food at a time when his illness is making increased metabolic demands.

   Constipation can occur due to the loss of muscle power needed to increase the intra-abdominal pressure and to expel the fecal mass. Failure to heed the urge to defecate and the necessity to use the bedpan can increase the incidence of constipation. In some instances the stool becomes hard and impacted, and liquid stool may be passed around the impaction. The underlying cause must be recognized so that the impaction will be treated instead of the diarrhea.

The urinary system.   The GU system also suffers from immobility. The loss of gravitational flow present in the erect position results in urinary stasis with resultant predisposition to infection, stone formation, and, in a few cases, bladder distension with overflow incontinence. The reason for the development of kidney stones is that the increased urinary nitrogen from protein breakdown and higher serum levels of calcium and other minerals from prolonged bed rest increases the concentration of such particles in the urine. These particles then settle in the calyces of the kidney and become the nucleus for the development of a stone. Bladder distension results if the sensation to void is ignored, or if the patient is unable to increase his intra-abdominal pressure or relax his perineal and external sphincter muscles. Overflow incontinence may result, and the higher pressure exerted on the renal system can damage the kidney nephron.

Skin.   Breakdown of the skin with decubitus ulcer formation is another adverse effect of prolonged bed rest. Causes for breakdown are prolonged pressure of body on certain areas (especially bony prominences) and the increased perspiration that increases moisture in the skin fold areas. A patient covered by bed linens is prevented from losing body heat by the normal processes of conduction and radiation and thus has increased perspiration to maintain his normal body temperature.

INTERVENTION

Intervention for mobility disturbances seeks to treat the underlying cause, when treatable, and to minimize the adverse effects of immobility on the other body systems. The major aspects will be briefly discussed.

Exercise

An exercise program for each patient needs to be planned and implemented. Exercises should include range of motion of the joints and muscle setting exercises. For maximum benefit from range of motion exercises, the patient should do them himself. Passive exercises do not give the same benefit as when the muscle actually contracts, but they can be of value for the patient unable to participate actively. Setting exercises, in which the muscles are alternately tightened and relaxed, can only be done by the patient. They are helpful to maintain the tone of the muscles of the abdomen, buttocks, and thighs when the patient is unable to stand and walk. A particularly beneficial setting maneuver is accomplished when the patient (who is lying flat on his back with his hands at his sides and his legs extended) raises his buttocks off the mattress, supporting his weight on his shoulders and heels. Exercises to decrease venous stasis in the lower extremities include alternate dorsiflexion and extension of the foot and flattening of the knee to the mattress.

Positioning

An upright position can be obtained by the use of a convalescent chair or by a bed that tilts or rotates so the patient is in an upright position with weight bearing on his feet.

   Frequent change of position of a patient while in bed is essential. Elevation of the head should be alternated with supine side lying, and, when feasible, pronation. Care should be exercised in positioning to prevent weight of one leg upon the other when the patient is lying on one side or pressure on the popliteal space by pillows or elevated bed when he is on his back. The patient should be taught (and frequently reminded) to open his mouth and exhale as he turns to prevent thoracic fixation and the Valsalva maneuver. Postural drainage positions along with clapping and vibrating techniques are indicated for patients who are unable to cough up pulmonary secretions.

Diet

Good nutrition should be encouraged. The cooperation of the dietician should be secured so the patient is given food he likes. Frequent small meals served attractively are usually better than larger feedings. Although the patient may have osteoporosis, increased dietary calcium should be discouraged because it will not be used by the bones, but will precipitate in the urine, form renal calculi, or be deposited in the muscles or joints.

Elimination

Prevention of constipation is best accomplished when the patient's preillness pattern of defecation is considered. Provision of privacy and optimal positioning to promote evacuation is essential. In some cases gentle digital stimulation or the use of stool softeners is indicated. Although laxatives and enemas should only be used when absolutely necessary, patients with lifelong laxative or enema habits will require continuation of such measures. Provision of high fluid intake and fiber in the diet are also helpful for most patients if not contraindicated.

Intake

Forcing fluids to keep the urine dilute will reduce stone formation and infection. Other measures include the maintenance of an acid urine pH by diet or intake of ascorbic acid. Position for voiding should be as nearly upright as possible, and catheterization should only be done when absolutely necessary.

Patient Involvement

Encouraging patient participation in the planning of care and the responsibility for some aspects of his treatment program will build ego strength. Helping the patient assess his progress gives him positive feedback that can reduce frustration. Adolescents and children frequently exhibit more impatience with prolonged illnesses. With immobility they are also deprived of the use of physical activity for the venting of pent-up emotions. The nurse is most therapeutic when she lets the patient know she understands how he feels and does not berate him for losing control of his feelings or from engagement in what might otherwise be considered inappropriate activities for his age such as wheelchair racing, water or pillow fights, etc. Crisis theory tells us that the period of disorganization brought about by the crisis of illness can break down previous defenses and provide opportunities for new growth. The skillful nurse can provide support to the immobilized patient that will assist him to achieve a higher level of psychologic functioning than he had before the onset of the illness.

EXPERIENTIAL INVOLVEMENT

CASE 8A. We are again using the clinical profile form to present the information on a patient who developed a mobility disturbance while hospitalized for a dislocated silastic implant.

PATIENT PROFILE

NAME: Marino, John

AGE: 60   SEX: Male   ETHNIC EXTRACTION: Italian   MARITAL STATUS: Married

OCCUPATION: Carpenter

LAST WORKING DAY: 2 years ago   HEIGHT: 5'5"

WEIGHT: Average 170; Maximum 185; Present 165

TEMP: 37.5 C   P: 96   R: 26   BP: 105/85

CHIEF COMPLAINT: Pain, deformity, and decreased motion of index finger, left hand, developed over past 3 days.

PREVIOUS ILLNESSES: History of rheumatoid arthritis for 20 years with numerous surgical procedures including left synovectomy and multiple bilateral hand silastic implants at the metacarpophalangeal joints, last surgery being 6 months ago.

FAMILY DATA: Mother died of heart attack, father died from CVA. Brothers (2) and 1 sister—all have rheumatoid arthritis. Son killed in Vietnam war.

MEDICATIONS: Prednisone: 4 mg PO Tues and Thur; 5 mg PO Mon, Wed, Fri, Sat, Sun
Ibuprofen (Motrin): 800 mg TID
Mylanta: 30 cc TID with above drugs, and prn heartburn

ALLERGIES: none known

HABITS: alcohol—none; tobacco—none

IMMUNIZATIONS: None past 40 years

PROSTHETIC DEVICES: Bifocal glasses, nonremovable partial plate.

SOCIAL AND ENVIRONMENTAL DATA:
Education: grade 10
Customary day: Rises at 7:30 AM. Eats 3 meals/day. Does small repair jobs, but spends most of time watching TV and preparing meals. Wife on chemotherapy since radical mastectomy 1 year ago. Retires 10:00 PM.
Hobbies—Recreational interest: Likes building model cars, but has not been able to past 3 years.
Religious preferences: Catholic
Concerns: Worried about wife's health. On disability insurance with hospital coverage.

EXPECTATION OF TREATMENT: Wants relief for knuckle pain and return of function.

SOURCE OF HISTORY: Patient and reliable informant

System Review	Physical Examination
Skin, Hair, Nails	
Has had sweating of face and both hands	Rheumatoid nodules both elbows and back of right hand
Nails are brittle and break easily	Palmar erythema
	Skin over fingers shiny and atrophic
Bruises easily	Numerous ecchymoses
Head	
No headaches, vertigo or syncope	Small cataract, right eye
Gums bleed easily	"Moon" facies
Neck	
No hoarseness or trouble in swallowing	Limited and painful motion
	No masses
Nodes	
Has noticed no swelling	Enlarged node left axilla
	Moderate bilat. inguinal lymphadenopathy
Lungs	
Short of breath with exertion	Labored respiration
Morning cough with clear sputum	Mild inspiratory stridor and crepitant rales
	Diffuse rhonchi
	Expiratory wheeze
	Dullness to percussion posterior lung bases

System Review	**Physical Examination**

Cardiovascular
  Sleeps on 3 pillows
  No chest pain or palpitation
  Ankle swelling toward evening

Regular heart rhythm
Grade II/VI systolic ejection murmur
Distant S_1, S_2
Physiologic splitting S_1
Distended neck veins
Lt. pitting edema lower extremity
Pulses intact $1-2+/2+$ in all extremities

Abdomen
  Occasional heartburn

  Appetite fair

Liver 2 cm below R costal margin, edge
    rounded and tender
No splenomegaly
Abdomen soft—no masses
Bowel sounds normal

Rectal
  Diarrhea with heavy Mylanta intake
  Stools sometimes dark

Good sphincter tone
No hemorrhoids
Prostate not enlarged

Genitourinary
  Nocturia $\times$ 1

  No hesitancy, dysuria, or dribbling

Normal adult male genitalia
Circumcised
No discharge or hernia

Musculoskeletal
  Morning stiffness for 1–2 hours on
    arising
  Pain in both arms from elbows down.
  Pain in left knee and toes of both feet
  Unable to grasp with left hand

Severe deformity of index finger left hand
    with dislocation of implant on meta-
    carpophalangeal joint, swelling, tender-
    ness, and increased warmth
Swan neck deformities both hands
Volar subluxation of the left wrist
Cannot increase pressure on BP cuff with
    left hand
Right grasp: 4 mm Hg on BP cuff

ROM (in degrees)	R	L
Elbow flexion	60	50
Elbow extension	-10	-20
Hip flexion	90	65
Hip extension	15	10
Knee flexion	90	80
Knee extension	-5	-10

Atrophy of left quadriceps muscle
Enlargement both knees. Scar on left
Right knee: bogginess above and beside
    patella
Moderate cock-up toes
Kyphosis

Neurologic
  Numbness of both toes and fingers
  Burning in calf left leg

Gait: walks slowly, with right hip higher
    than left and limp. Valgus position of
    left knee
Normal deep tendon reflexes
Decreased sensation in toes and fingers
Coordination OK

System Review	Physical Examination
Endocrine	
No polydipsia or polyuria	Thyroid not enlarged
Cold sweats	
Socialpsychologic	
Memory OK	Answers questions logically and consistently but response is delayed
No trouble with sleeping	No restless or involuntary movements
Decreased interest in sex	
No activities outside home	
Denies depression about physical disability	Speaks without emotion; seems detached. Is anxious about index finger, but seems unaware of other disabilities and deformities
States his only concern is his wife's health	
Cannot name activity enjoyed the most in the past 3 months	Rather careless grooming

LABORATORY DATA
Blood Chemistry

	Patient	Normal
Metabolic I		
Chloride	98	95−105 mEq/liter
Carbon Dioxide, total	30	24−32 mEq/liter
Potassium	3	3.5−5 mEq/liter
Sodium	125	135−145 mEq/liter
Urea Nitrogen	16	10−20 mEq/liter
Glucose	110	58−100 mg/dl
Hematology Profile		
Leukocyte count WBC	12	5−10 thousand/cu mm
Erythrocyte count (RBC)	3.85	4.5−6 million/cu mm
Hemoglobin (Hgb)	11	14−18 g/dl
Hematocrit (Hct)	34.2	40−54 ml/dl
Mean corpuscular volume (MCV)	77	84−94 cu microns
Metabolic II		
Protein, total	5.6	6−8.5 g/dl
Albumin	2.8	3.5−5 g/dl
Calcium	9	8.5−10.5 mg/dl
Phosphorus	2.2	2.5−4.5 mg/dl
Cholesterol, total	220	150−250 mg/dl
Uric acid	6.5	2−8 mg/dl
Creatinine	1.8	0.7−1.4 mg/dl
Bilirubin, total	0.8	0.2−1.2 mg/dl
Phosphatase, alkaline	40	30−85 mU/ml
Lactic dehydrogenase (LDH)	200	100−225 mU/ml
Glutamic pyruvic transaminase (GPT)	36	8−40 mU/ml
Glutamic oxalacetic transaminase (GOT)	30	7.5−40 mU/ml
Creatine phosphokinase (CPK)	170	50−180 IU/L

LABORATORY DATA (Continued)

	Patient	Normal
Leukocyte Differential		
Neutrophils (PMN)	60%	50–70%
Bands	2%	0–5%

Impression

Medical Diagnosis:
1. Dislocation of silastic implant netacarpophalangeal joint, L index finger. Possible infectious process.
2. Congestive heart failure
3. Microcytic anemia

Possible Nursing Diagnoses:
1.

2.

3.

4.

5.

6.

7.

8.

Summary of medical management and patient response:
Fluid aspirated from L index finger, with culture positive for *Staphylococcus aureus*. Started on Nafcillin 2 gm every 4 hours. Other medications in addition to prednisone, ibuprofen, and Mylanta were a stat intravenous dose of furosemide (Lasix) 40 mg followed by hydrochlorothiazide (Hydrodiuril) 50 mg BID and Klorvess–QID. He was taken to surgery for removal of the silastic implant with postoperative irrigation of the wound with Betadine. Wound appeared to be healing. On the eighth day after admission, patient suddenly developed an acute painful swelling of the right knee with inability to move the knee. He had chills and shivering followed by elevation of the temperature to 38.2 C (100.8 F).

Skillbuilders:
1. List the eight most likely nursing diagnoses, present on admission or potential, which you would want to explore with the patient or consider when planning his care.

2. Then on practicum record 8A, enter the two most likely hypotheses for the inability to move the knee and associated signs and symptoms.

3. Next enter the data that support each hypothesis and additional data you would need to confirm or disconfirm.

4. In the intervention column enter the physician directed and independent nursing activities that would be indicated if the diagnosis were confirmed.

5. In the last column list the criteria for evaluation of the response to Mr. Marino's acute episode.

PRACTICUM RECORD 8-A

Hypothesis/Possible Diagnosis	Supportive Data Available	Additional Data Needed to Confirm or Disconfirm	Nursing Intervention if Diagnosis Confirmed	Evaluation Criteria
Inability to move right knee due to: 1.				
2.				

Feedback: The nursing diagnoses at this point are only tentative—some of them will need further exploration and validation with the patient while others will need more data for confirmation. Our list includes:
1. Impaired functional performance.
2. Impaired immune response.
3. Fluid volume excess.
4. Inadequate affect (cortisone vs limited psychologic capacity).
5. Decreased socialization.
6. Decreased sexual functioning.
7. Potential gastrointestinal blood loss.
8. Potential hypokalemia.

We are sure that many of you agreed with a number of these. You may have additional ones that are valid that we did not include. We will briefly substantiate those that may have been more obscure. Mr. Marino has been on long-term cortisone therapy which decreases the resistance to infections and the ability to localize infections as well as masks some of the normal responses to infection. The absence of fever, white count elevation, or increase in polymorphonuclear leukocytes on admission with an infected finger joint are indicative of impairment of the normal immune response. This means that extra care needs to be exercised to protect him from infection (scrupulous skin care, good aseptic technique in wound care, protection from personnel or other patients with infection, etc.). Also important is careful observation for any sign of a developing infection.

We included potential gastrointestinal blood loss on our list. Mr. Marino's low hemoglobin, hematocrit, and mean corpuscular volume (MCV) on admission are indicative of anemia due to chronic blood loss or iron deficiency. Although patients with rheumatoid arthritis may have anemia, the type of anemia is usually normocytic (as evidenced by normal MCV) rather than microcytic with low MCV. Cortisone predisposes to gastrointestinal hemorrhage. Mr. Marino has reported some dark stools. It is important for the nurse to be alert to such blood loss. The patient should either use a commode or be asked to not flush the toilet until the nurse has checked his stool. Stools can also be tested for blood. The medication schedule should be arranged so Mylanta is given with the medications and the patient encouraged to report the need for prn Mylanta to relieve any gastric distress.

Perhaps we should also discuss the diagnosis of potential hypokalemia. On admission Mr. Marino had a low serum potassium of 3 mEq/liter. It does seem as though we're blaming cortisone therapy for everything, but cortisone promotes sodium retention and potassium loss. Additionally Mr. Marino will now be receiving a thiazide diuretic which increases the renal exchange of sodium for potassium and kaliuresis. He is on an oral potassium supplement which will supply 80 mEq of potassium daily.

It is probably not necessary for the nurse to be able to calculate the potassium deficit, but we will do it for those interested. There are graphs in many texts that show the potassium depletion or excess represented by the concentration of serum potassium at different blood pH levels. The serum concentration of potassium is affected by pH since acidosis causes potassium to leave the cell while potassium moves into the cell with alkalosis. With a normal acid-base state, there is a 5 percent depletion of potassium when the serum concentration is 3.5 mEq/liter, a 10 percent depletion at 3 mEq/liter, and a 20 percent depletion at 2.5 mEq/liter. Normal body potassium for an average sized adult is 3200 mEq. A 10 percent depletion would mean 320 mEq. The 80 mEq/day replacement may not be adequate so we will need to watch Mr. Marino for signs of hypokalemia. Critical indicators are muscle weakness, increased lethargy and fatigue, and cardiac rhythm changes such as premature contractions and tachycardia. The ECG may show characteristic alterations of the waveforms and time intervals.

Now let's move ahead in time to Mr. Marino's eighth day of hospitalization and his inability to move his right knee. Our two most likely hypotheses are loss of motion due to septic arthritis or gout. The supporting data for septic arthritis are the history of a staph infection, previous knee damage from rheumatoid arthritis, and his increased susceptibility to infection from cortisone intake. Other supporting data are the abrupt onset accompanied by chills and fever and the intense local reaction of swelling, tenderness, and limitation of motion of the joint. Although this acute state could possibly be an extension of the rheumatoid arthritis to another joint, the rapid onset and severity of the symptoms is indicative of an infectious process. Additional data needed are joint aspiration with examination of the synovial fluid for cell count, glucose, gram stain, and culture.

Intervention, if the hypothesis was confirmed, would include following the physician's orders for administration of antibiotics and pain medication. Prednisone dosage would probably be increased during the stressful period. Close observation of the joint for extensive swelling would be important for recognition of pus accumulation that required aspiration. Joint destruction is increased when pus is allowed to exert pressure on the structures and generate proteolytic enzymes. If tube drainage is instituted, attention would be directed toward maintaining patency of the tube.

Temporary splinting of the knee will make Mr. Marino more comfortable and will reduce the flexion deformity. As the inflammation subsides, range of motion exercises will increase the return of joint function. Mr. Marino will need supportive nursing activities which could include:

1. Demonstration of concern and caring.

2. Use of a cradle to keep the weight of the covers off the painful knee.

3. Assistance with turning and position change.

4. Exercise of noninvolved extremities to provide kinesthetic stimulation and prevent loss of function.

5. Diversional activities geared to his interests to prevent boredom.

6. Provision of assistance to his wife.

Evaluation criteria would be:

1. Clearing of infection.

2. Return of preillness joint function.

3. Maintenance of psychologic integrative ability.

4. Development of trust in staff.

5. Effective coping by wife.

That brings us to discussion of the hypothesis that the inability to move the right knee is due to gout. Supporting data are the history of intake of a thiazide diuretic which interferes with urate excretion and the clinical picture of acute onset with chills and low grade fever and the intense inflammatory reaction of swelling, tenderness, and loss of mobility. Additional data to confirm would be elevation of uric acid on the metabolic panel and the finding of urate crystals in the synovial fluid.

Intervention would include following the physician's orders for drug to combat gout and analgesic. Colchicine is the usual drug of choice for gout. An initial dose of colchicine is given followed by successive doses every 1 to 2 hours until pain is relieved or gastrointestinal symptoms of nausea, vomiting, cramping, or diarrhea develop. Since most patients develop the gastrointestinal side effects simultaneously with the relief of pain, education of the patient regarding the expected occurrence will increase the patient's reporting and also his tolerance for the discomfort. Another diuretic would probably replace hydrochlorthizide or a drug such as allopurinol (Zyloprim) would be added to control the serum urate level. Supportive intervention could be similar to that outlined for septic arthritis except that with the shorter duration and lesser severity of the illness, less assistance would be required. Evaluation criteria would include relief of the pain within 24–48 hours, restoration of preillness knee function, and serum uric acid within normal levels.

CASE 8B.   Mr. Mason is a 34-year-old single owner of a small plastic fabrication business. He leads an active physical life, jogging daily and participating in racquet ball and kung fu. While on a skiing trip, he fell and suffered a comminuted fracture of the proximal femoral shaft of his right leg. His leg was splinted and he was transported to the nearest hospital where the fracture was reduced. A threaded Steinman pin was inserted in the tibial tubercle with balanced suspension using a half-ring Thomas splint and flexion of the knee. He withstood the trauma well with only minimal fluctuation of the vital signs, and no other signs of distress. He did have considerable swelling of the right leg. Ice was kept continuously on the leg but the swelling continued to increase after he was placed in traction. Four hours after initiation of traction, the circumference of the right mid-thigh was 2 inches greater than the left. His treatment plan is to maintain skeletal traction for 6 weeks, and then progress to ambulation with crutch assist.

Skillbuilders: This is a slightly different type of problem. The reason for Mr. Mason's impaired mobility is known to us. This is frequently the case when immobilization is used as a treatment modality. For these patients, the nurse's overall goals are to maximize the potential for early restoration of function and to minimize the development of psychosocial or physiologic dysfunctional effects. Therefore, for Mr. Mason we are asking you to:

1. Enter on practicum record 8-B1, the five most likely hypotheses for potential physiologic nursing diagnoses for Mr. Mason that could result from his injury, the immobilization or other treatment factors. Select the untoward states for which nurses have the major responsibility for assessment and *prevention,*

PRACTICUM RECORD 8-B1

Hypothesis/Possible Diagnosis	Theoretical Data to Support the Hypothesis	Assessment Data for Early Detection	Preventive or Ameliorative Nursing Intervention	Evaluation Criteria
Immobilization and other treatment factors makes patient at risk for potential:				
1.				
2.				
3.				
4.				
5.				

rather than those that are the major responsibility of the physician. We are stressing prevention rather than maintenal problems.

2. List the theoretical data that support the hypothesis and the assessment parameters that would be the most helpful in the early detection of the untoward state.

3. In the nursing intervention column, list the nursing activities over the next 3-week period for prevention of the development of the untoward state or ameliorative activities to minimize the dysfunctional effects of the disordered state (both independent and physician directed).

4. Enter the criteria for evaluation of the effectiveness of the nursing intervention for the 3-week period.

5. On the practicum record 8-B2, list the three most likely hypotheses for nursing diagnoses for Mr. Mason in the area of psychosocial adjustment to his illness.

6. Then briefly enter the rationale for each hypothesis.

7. Describe in a few sentences the general aspects of the nursing approach for each hypothesis. We are not asking you to name specific nursing activities since they rely so heavily on the information obtained during the process of hypothesis validation (either with the patient or by other appropriate methods).

8. In the evaluation column, list criteria which would probably be appropriate to evaluate the effectiveness of the nursing response if the hypothesis was confirmed.

Feedback: It is anticipated that there will be differences of opinion on the most likely hypotheses. We listed potential impairment in circulation, potential neurologic impairment, potential impairment of musculoskeletal function, potential infection, and potential impairment of skin integrity. The theoretical data to support the hypothesis of potential impairment in circulation are the knowledge that arterial embarrassment can result from thrombosis secondary to contusion, or damage to the artery intima with increased incidence in persons who have a high impact fracture. Circulatory impairment can also result from arterial vasospasm from compression by a hematoma, from fat embolism, and from thromboembolic problems. Assessment data for early detection of arterial occlusion include the five P's: pain (which becomes more intense with toe motion), pulses decreased or absent, paresthesia, paresis or paralysis, and pallor with coolness. When these clinical signs of diminished blood supply in the distal limb are present, further testing and examination will be required to determine the responsible pathologic state. Suspected arterial injury, or occlusive state, is generally confirmed by arteriography.

Fat embolism usually occurs within the first few days after an injury. Additional assessment parameters for fat embolism are the presence of petechiae on the upper torso, conjunctiva, of buccal membranes, tachycardia, and fever. Fat emboli lodged in the lung cause tachypnea and dyspnea, while lodgement in the brain results in altered states of cognition and consciousness. The signs and symptoms of venous thrombosis (thrombophlebitis, phlebothrombosis) differ from those found with arterial occlusive states, but the physical signs are much

PRACTICUM RECORD 8-B2

Hypothesis/Possible Diagnosis	Rationale for Hypothesis	Nursing Intervention if Hypothesis Confirmed	Evaluation Criteria
Difficult psychosocial adjustment due to: 1.			
2.			
3.			

less reliable. Superficial phlebitis is usually manifested by swelling, redness, and increased warmth and tenderness. Deep phlebitis can occur with no physical signs, or it may be accompanied by pain, edema, warmth, tenseness and firmness of muscles of extremity, and a positive Homan's sign. In a few instances it is accompanied by arterial vasospasm which makes it harder to differentiate from arterial occlusive phenomena. Venography as discussed in a previous chapter is utilized for definitive diagnosis.

Preventive nursing activities are directed toward prevention of any external pressure on the leg that would interfere with blood supply and promotion of venous return. Muscle exercises to increase venous return include dorsiflexion, foot exercises, and, after 2 or 3 days, gentle but progressive quadriceps drill. Nursing attention would also be directed toward decreasing the anxiety the patient would undoubtedly be experiencing with the threat of impaired circulation. Appropriate activities will be discussed in more detail with the psychosocial hypotheses.

Activities directed by the physician can include:

1. Embolectomy or thrombectomy for arterial occlusion.

2. Administration of vasodilator drugs or sympathetic blockade in some instances of arterial spasm.

3. Heparinization for arterial or venous thrombosis, fat embolism, and pulmonary embolism (from leg thrombus which breaks off and becomes lodged in the lung).

4. Local application of heat for venous thrombosis (heat is contraindicated for arterial thrombosis).

5. Fasciotomy if hematoma has caused acute swelling of the anterior tibial compartment.

6. Provision of adequate oxygenation to the brain and other vital organs if embolism develops.

Anticoagulation with heparin to prevent further propagation of the clot is the mainstay of treatment which all the foregoing circulatory disorders have in common. The usual dosage is 30,000–45,000 units/24 hours given either as a continuous intravenous infusion or as an intravenous bolus every 4–6 hours. It may occasionally be given subcutaneously instead of intravenously. Administration is continued for 8 to 12 days, with gradual conversion to coumarin therapy. While on heparin, the alteration in blood clotting is usually monitored daily by the partial thromboplastin time (PTT). The therapeutic range is considered to be $1^1/_2$ to $2^1/_2$ times the control. When heparin is given intermittently, blood for the PTT should be drawn immediately prior to the bolus injection. Oral administration of coumarin preparations is monitored by the prothrombin time (PT). The therapeutic range is 10–20 percent, or $1^1/_2$ to $2^1/_2$ times the control. Laboratory determination of PTT or PT does not replace careful nursing observation for signs of bleeding. Frequent sites that can show an increased tendency to bleed are the gums, skin, gastrointestinal tract (with dark stools positive for occult blood), urinary tract (with hematuria), site of insertion of Steinman pin, and sites of IV or IM injections. Heparin does not have a long-term effect on blood clotting. Four hours after therapy is terminated, it is no longer active. Thus, minor bleeding may be treated by suspension of heparin.

If hemorrhage is more severe, protamine sulfate will be given to neutralize the heparin. Protamine must be diluted with saline and be given slowly. It is one of those situations in which the antidote can cause as much harm as the toxic drug it was neutralizing. The effect of the coumarin drug is cumulative and prolonged, so hemorrhage is usually treated by administration of vitamin K. Phytonadione (Aquamephyton) is the vitamin K product most frequently used. If it is given intravenously, it must also be given slowly to avoid precipitating a hypotensive episode. Careful monitoring of other drugs given with a coumarin preparation is also essential since many drugs interact with the coumarin in vivo and their effects can be harmful. Perhaps we should mention prophylactic administration of heparin for prevention of thromboembolic phenomena. Although it may be used for patients at high risk for development of emboli, it would probably not be indicated for Mr. Mason because it is felt that heparin administration retards fracture healing. Many orthopedic surgeons place their patients on around the clock aspirin which they believe reduces the incidence of thrombophlebitis.

Evaluation criteria would include absence of impaired circulation from arterial thrombosis, arterial vasospasm, fat embolism, or thrombophlebitis, and absence of undue anxiety. Although careful nursing observation and preventive measures can reduce the incidence or the severity of these disordered states, they cannot eliminate their occurrence. Thus if circulatory impairment developed, other criteria would be required. Depending on the nature of the underlying disorder and treatment factors, criteria could include one or more of the following:

1. Preservation of function in extremity.
2. Restoration of preillness cognitive level.
3. Restoration of normal pulmonary function.
4. Absence of bleeding.
5. Absence of untoward effects from administration of protamine or vitamin K.

Now let's discuss the second hypothesis that Mr. Mason has potential neurologic impairment. The theoretical data to support the hypothesis come from the knowledge that nerve damage can occur at the time of the initial injury or be associated with treatment factors during the healing process. Because of the cushion of muscle between the bone and the nerve, damage to the nerve does not occur frequently with the injury. It does occur however, with poorly managed traction. The common peroneal nerve is especially vulnerable to injury since its lateral position as it courses around the fibular neck make it especially susceptible to external pressure. Arterial occlusion and the anterior tibial compartment syndrome mentioned under impaired circulation can result in ischemic degeneration of the nerves if intervention is not successful in relieving the obstruction or pressure within 6–8 hours.

Assessment data that would be obtained at frequent intervals for early detection of nerve damage are the presence of numbness, tingling, or paresthesia over the lateral aspect of the lower leg and dorsum of the foot, eversion of the foot, and loss of ability to dorsiflex the foot. Careful attention to the traction apparatus is important in preventing nerve injury. Management includes prevention of external rotation of the leg, avoidance of padding at the head of the fibula that can put direct pressure on the nerve, keeping the Achilles tendon area of the heel free from pressure, and encouragement of patient movement to avoid continuous pressure on any one nerve area. Correction of impaired arterial circulation would also be important. Evaluation criterium would be preservation of normal nerve function of extremity.

The third hypothesis was that Mr. Mason has potential impairment of musculoskeletal function. The theoretical data to support the hypothesis are the knowledge that a fracture of the femur will require immobilization with resultant muscular atrophy and demineralization of the bones. Additionally, comminuted fractures generally are accompanied by considerable soft tissue injury and hematoma formation. Secondary fibrosis in a muscle belly can cause shortening of the muscle and limitation of joint motion. Nonunion or malunion of the fracture of course lengthens the treatment period and increases the potential disability. Assessment data are muscle strength, range of motion, and changes in muscular volume. During the first 3 weeks after fracture, the knee is usually kept immobile, so muscle testing is limited to the foot and the quadriceps. Since muscles are commonly observed during exercise, the movement will be more completely discussed under intervention. Frequent roentgenogram examination is ordered by the physician to check alignment of the bone and position of the fragments. The nurse also needs to examine the traction set-up to ascertain that weights hang free, ropes are unobstructed, ropes and pulleys are freely movable, that the heel of the right leg is free of the bed and that hip flexion is maintained at 20 degrees.

Nursing intervention includes muscle and joint exercises of right leg, encouragement of bodily activity and development of muscles of upper extremity, maintenance of proper body alignment, relief of pain, and minor adjustment of the traction. Perhaps it should be mentioned that the bed must be fitted with an overhead trapeze. Muscle exercises for the injured leg start with dorsiflexion, eversion, inversion, and circumduction of the foot for a period of at least 5 minutes every waking hour. The patient should be encouraged to exercise his feet simultaneously. After 3 or 4 days, quadricep setting exercises are begun. Mr. Mason will require instruction and assistance to learn the technique of contracting the quadriceps muscle (or the top part of the thigh) while raising his heel slightly and dorsiflexing his toes. Since he has to maintain knee flexion, the usual quadriceps setting has to be modified. Encouraging Mr. Mason to place a hand on his anterior thigh and feel the muscles tighten will probably increase the effectiveness of the exercise. Active movement of the knee joint is usually not encouraged for 6 to 8 weeks. In addition to exercise of the injured leg, the patient will need to develop his arm muscles for crutch walking. Although an athletic person probably has good muscle strength, the muscular movement is also beneficial because it stimulates osteoblasts to build up the matrix of the bone. The body needs to be maintained in proper alignment to prevent contractures. The foot must be maintained with the toes pointing upward to prevent development of permanent foot drop. We have already discussed the danger of peroneal nerve damage from external rotation of the leg. A trochanter roll or use of a pillow under the thigh and a second under the calf can help maintain proper alignment. Relief of pain is important not only for the comfort of the patient, but also because joint motion is greater without the inhibiting effect of pain. Because large amounts of tissue are being reorganized and the femur is incompletely healed, pain is to be expected. If moderate pain increases in intensity, however, thorough investigation is indicated. Adjustments of the traction apparatus may be done by the nurse in some practice settings. Whether the nurse actually makes the adjustment or notifies the responsible person of a problem, the nurse must fully understand the principles of the balanced suspension traction and the desired position of the patient in order to recognize the need for either adjusting or reporting.

Evaluation of effectiveness of nursing activities to prevent impairment of musculoskeletal function at the end of the 3-week period could include:

1. Absence of muscle atrophy in right thigh or calf (could be determined by comparison of circumference of midthigh and midcalf with that of left leg if edema has resolved).

2. Full range of motion of right foot.

3. Absence of claw foot or foot drop.

4. Ability to raise upper torso off bed, maintain for 5 seconds, and lower gradually.

5. Good alignment of the femur fracture and fragments.

6. Patient statement that pain was controlled.

Now we can move on to discuss the hypothesis that patient is at risk for development of potential infection. The theoretical data to support the hypothesis come from the knowledge that although infection is less likely to develop when the fracture is reduced by the closed method, it can occur from the septic breakdown of dead and devitalized tissue (including hematomas) or from migration of bacteria through the pin site insertion. Additionally, urinary tract infection can develop from urinary stasis with the loss of gravitational flow, and pulmonary infection may develop from decreased chest expansion or nonclearance of secretions from the pulmonary tree.

Nursing activities to prevent the development of infection include: (1) scrupulous cleaning of the pin site with a disinfectant such as Betadine; (2) early recognition of redness, swelling, drainage, or odors; (3) turning, coughing, and encouragement to maintain deep breathing; (4) forcing fluids; (5) providing privacy during use of the urinal; and (6) instructions in the use of external pressure above the pubis and muscular bearing down to empty the bladder more completely.

Evaluation criteria would be absence of infection at site of pin insertion, absence of pneumonia, and absence of urinary infection. It is hoped that early recognition of deeper wound infection will result in its eradication without loss of function, but this cannot be adequately evaluated within the 3-week period.

We're now ready to discuss the last hypothesis that Mr. Mason is at risk for development of potential impairment of skin integrity. You may not have listed this as one of your hypotheses because it is less likely to occur in a young man in good physical condition. We did include it, however, because its development delays recovery and is an area in which the nurse needs to maintain continual vigilance with all immobilized patients. The theoretical datum that supports the hypothesis is the knowledge that continuous pressure on the skin results in ischemia with impaired nutrition that can result in a break in the skin and destruction of the tissues. Preventive nursing activities include frequent position change, massage of bony prominences, use of padding to protect the skin from contact with the ring of the Thomas splint, use of a heel protector on left foot (which is used to assist in the turning process), and prevention of lying on any reddened area that has a potential for breakdown. There are a number of products available on the market to reduce the incidence of decubiti. Such products include the antigravity pad, alternating pressure mattress, egg crate mattress, sheep skin, and covering reddened areas with Op-Site dressings. Many are useful adjuncts but none can take the place of the outlined nursing activities. Evaluation criteria for this hypothesis would simply be absence of impairment of skin integrity.

Now that we have identified the physiologic problems and their management, let's look at the possible psychosocial problems. These could be worded in many different ways. We listed difficult psychosocial adjustment due to: (1) conflict over forced dependency for previously independent person; (2) loss from alteration in physical activity status; and (3) anxiety about possible loss of business and social status. The rationale for the hypothesis that Mr. Mason would find the enforced dependency difficult to accept is based primarily on the fact that his illness requires such a radical change in lifestyle. Since he has been very active, competitive, and his own boss, it is highly likely that he will react to the enforced dependency, passivity, nonproductivity, and loss of control over many aspects of his life associated with his hospitalization and treatment. The nurse can be most therapeutic for Mr. Mason by conveying her understanding that she knows it must be difficult for him to be tied down to the bed with others telling him what to do, but that it is just a temporary thing. Letting him make as many decisions about his care as possible and pointing out the ways he can help himself recover can decrease his feeling of dependency.

Evaluation criteria would be:

1. Absence of noncomplaint behavior.

2. Absence of change in affect or behavior (no withdrawal, development of sustained hostility, refusal to participate in care, etc.).

3. Verbalization of feelings regarding enforced dependency with delineation of factors which increased tolerance.

The rationale for the second hypothesis that Mr. Mason would experience a feeling of loss from the alteration in physical activity status is based on the fact that he was extremely active physically. Additionally, when physical activity has been used as an outlet for release of emotional tension, excess tension can build up when it is curtailed. In addition to alteration of participation in sports activities, he will also experience an alteration in sexual functioning. There are also a number of other physical activities that will be altered such as eating, grooming, voiding, and defecating. The nursing approach would be somewhat similar to that for the first hypothesis. It is important to convey a feeling of empathetic understanding as well as the knowledge that the situation is temporary. Other outlets for physical activity in addition to the exercises already mentioned should be found. These could include a punching bag from the overbed frame, or encouragement of competition with a roommate in some activity. In the past, available activities were confined to cards, checkers, or chess. With the advent of electronic games that utilize the television screen found in many hospital rooms, the variety of activities is more extensive. At the present time, sexual needs of a hospitalized patient who is unable to go out on pass have been pretty much overlooked. The increased awareness on the part of the nurse of these needs and willingness to discuss them, however, has probably been of some therapeutic value. Evaluation criteria could be patient verbalization that his needs for physical activity were satisfied, and absence of signs of frustration and acting-out behavior.

Now let's look at the last hypothesis that states Mr. Mason could have difficulty in psychosocial adjustment to his illness because of his anxiety about possible loss of business and social status. We have combined business and social status because, in our society, a man's status in the community generally is derived from the man's occupation or financial condition. Other rationale for identifying this as a possible diagnosis is that small businesses frequently suffer when the owner is unable to be actively involved in the conduct of affairs. Anxiety about the business may be difficult for Mr. Mason to work through without the customary release of physical activity. This can result in a vicious cycle of increasing anxiety that interferes with the ability to see the problems clearly or which may even distort reality. The nursing approach during a period of severe anxiety includes remaining with the patient and conveying the impression that you believe he is competent to handle the situation. When severe anxiety has subsided, the patient should be encouraged to talk about his concerns. He may need guidance in the problem solving process, if anxiety makes it difficult for him to focus on the problem. He may also find discussion with a social worker helpful. With the use of a telephone at his bedside, Mr. Mason can continue to take care of some of his business affairs. Evaluation criterion would be control of anxiety (absence of muscle tension, perspiration, narrow perceptual field, decreased cognitive function, trembling, and feeling of dread). It is also desirable that Mr. Mason's business does not suffer, but this is not within the control of the nurse.

ADDITIONAL READING

Blake FG: Immobilized youth, A rationale for supportive nursing intervention. AJN 69:2364−2369, 1969.

Kelly MM: Exercises for bedfast patients. AJN 66:2209−2213, 1966.

Kinnaird LS: Preserving skeletal muscle tone in inactive patients. AJN 69:2662−2663, 1969.

Landau W, O'Leary J: Disturbances of Movement. In MacBryde CM, Blacklow R (eds.): Signs and Symptoms, Philadelphia, Lippincott, 1970, pp 692−710.

McCormick GP: Stroke: The double crisis. AJN 79:1410–1411, 1979.

Olson EV: The hazards of immobility. AJN 67:780–797, 1967.

Prior J: Physical Diagnosis: The History and Examination of the Patient, 5th ed. St Louis, Mosby, 1977, pp 375–445.

Walleck C: Neurological assessment for nurses: A part of the nursing process. J Neurosurg Nursing, 10(1):13–16, 1978.

Webb K: Early assessment of orthopedic injuries. AJN 74:1048–1052, 1974.

CHAPTER 9

Pain

Pain is probably the most frequently reported symptom. Most persons associate pain with illness and may disregard other signs and symptoms when they are not accompanied by pain. The significance the lay person attaches to pain, however, is not without scientific foundation. There are very few illnesses that do not have a painful component, and, in numerous illnesses, pain is the principal identifying characteristic of diagnosis. The major causes of pain are listed on Table 9-1. In spite of its familiarity and frequency of occurrence, there is no definition that is universally acceptable by all disciplines or any theoretical concept that adequately explains the complex biopsychosociocultural nature of pain.

Pain is a disagreeable sensation that is subjectively experienced by a conscious, attentive person in response to a stimulus. It is frequently a warning to the individual that one or more protective barriers have been breached. Pain receptors can be stimulated by electrical, thermal, mechanical, chemical, or psychic stimuli. The individual is not consciously aware of the pain stimulus until it has been transmitted to the thalamocortical level of the nervous system. Individuals differ in the manner in which they perceive pain and also in their reactions to pain. Reactions can include autonomic, musculoskeletal, and emotional behavior. Each of these major aspects of the pain experience will be briefly discussed.

GENERAL DISCUSSION

Noxious Stimulation

The stimulus that gives rise to a sensation of pain varies with the type of tissue involved and with the number and type of nerve receptors in the area. Different receptors are responsive to various forms of stimuli. Some examples of the different types of stimuli that result in pain in various body structures follow. The receptors in the skin are most frequently stimulated by tissue injury such as cutting, crushing, burning, or freezing. In the gastrointestinal tract this type of stimulation causes little pain. The stomach and intestine are stimulated by local

TABLE 9-1. Some of the Major Causes of Pain

Abnormal Initiating Mechanism	Pathophysiology	Clinical State	Character of Pain
I. Ischemia	Blood supply to involved area is reduced due to arteriosclerosis, external pressure on artery, vasospasm, or occlusion; when muscles do not receive an adequate supply of blood and oxygen for aerobic metabolism, have anaerobic metabolism with accumulation of lactic acid and cellular breakdown with release of bradykinin and histamine which stimulate the nerve endings	Myocardial ischemia, myocardial infarction, angina pectoris, mesenteric infarct/ischemia, pulmonary infarction, chronic arterial occlusion, Reynaud's disease, compartment syndrome, sickle-cell crisis, cerebral thrombosis	Constricting, squeezing, burning, or heaviness which may be provoked by exercise or stress
II. Increased arterial pulsation	The rhythmic stretch and relaxation of sensitive arterial walls with each systolic impulse stimulates pain receptors in response to the mechanical stretching	Malignant hypertension headache, migraine headache, arteritis, vascular headache	Throbbing and aching localized to involved area and sometimes accompanied by tenderness to pressure on area; pain increased by activity that increases systolic pressure such as exercise, bending over, fever, etc.
III. Pressure of mass on adjacent structure	Presence of a space-occupying mass exerts pressure on the nerves and displacement and traction on surrounding organs	Intracranial mass, hemorrhage, neoplasm, hiatus hernia, urinary retention, torsion of ovarian cyst	Constant aching, most often severe, intensified by movement of involved area
IV. Spasm of a hollow viscus	Distension of an organ with air or fluid causes pain from overstretch of the tissues and the forcible peristaltic moving of the contents against resistance	Ileus, intestinal colic, intestinal obstruction, impacted stone in bile duct, gastroenteritis, labor, ureteral colic or spasm	Rhythmic cramping that increases to very severe and then subsides; with repetition every few minutes; in late obstructive disease pain becomes continuous as ischemia develops

V. Chemical irritation	Irritating chemical substances like hydrochloric acid, pancreatic enzymes, and bile come in contact with the naked nerve terminals in the peritoneum or pancreatic bed	Peptic ulcer disease, pancreatitis, heartburn, esophageal reflux, esophagitis	Steady burning or gnawing
VI. Inflammatory process	The elaboration of kinins, toxins, and other chemical substances in response to injury, invasion and multiplication of microorganisms, or other pathology lowers the threshold for pain; additionally the accompanying swelling from collection of exudate or edema puts pressure on nerves of adjacent organs	Chest: pericarditis, pleuritis, pneumonia, myositis, acute tracheitis	Steady aching that frequently radiates and is accentuated with movement or increased abdominal pressure; when more severe, sharp and penetrating (knife-like)
		Abdomen: appendicitis, cholecystitis, peritonitis, diverticulitis, hepatitis, subphrenic abscess, pyelonephritis	
		Other: sinusitis, phlebitis, reaction to foreign body, prostatitis, acute pelvic inflammatory disease	Same as above
VII. Tissue injury A. External penetration	When tissue is damaged, the pain receptors in the free nerve endings in the skin and deeper structures are stimulated; the tissue reaction of swelling also stimulates the pain receptors responding to mechanical pressure	Surgical incision	Pricking, burning, aching in area affected
		Wounds: Laceration, bruise, burn	
B. Internal disruption	Rupture or tear of a structure	Dissecting aortic aneurysm, pneumothorax, mediastinal emphysema, rupture of esophagus, perforated duodenal ulcer, perforated viscus	Abrupt onset with quick progression to agonizing severity
		Ectopic pregnancy: tubal abortion, tubal rupture	
		Rupture of uterus	
		Rupture of corpus luteum cyst, rupture of graafian follicle	Abrupt onset but pain of lesser severity than when larger organs are involved, and pain gradually subsides instead of becoming more severe

(continued)

TABLE 9-1. Continued

Abnormal Initiating Mechanism	Pathophysiology	Clinical State	Character of Pain
VIII. Metabolic or toxic disorder	Metabolic abnormalities resulting in hypercalcemia, porphobilinogen, sodium and fluid depletion, and/or metabolic acidosis	Hyperparathyroidism, acute intermittent porphyria, adrenal insufficiency, uremia, diabetic ketoacidosis	Abdominal pain of varying degrees of severity which may be continuous, colicky, or intermittent cramping
	Pain from toxin ingestion or bite of black widow spider	Heavy metal poisoning, arachnidism, food poisoning	Severe cramping pain in abdomen
IX. Osseous injury or lesion			
A. Skeletal bones	Disruption of continuity, tension on the periosteum, or alteration in the function of joints and overlying tissue (nerves, ligaments, tendons, or bursae) stimulate the pain receptors; if edema develops, pain is intensified from stimulation of pressure receptors	Fractures, sprains, ruptured tendons, scurvy, rickets, arthritis, bursitis, osteomyelitis, Paget's disease	Ache or deep pain in general area of lesion that is increased with movement and pressure on area
B. Vertebral column	Irritation of the fascia ligaments or tendons of the back, demineralization of the bones, or degenerative or traumatic changes in the disks with softening, loosening, and displacement of the nucleus pulposus, exerting pressure on (or stretching) adjacent ligaments and/or nerve roots	Sciatica, intervertebral disk disease, osteoarthritis of the spine, ankylosing spondylitis	Backache, which may be accompanied by abnormal posture, limitation of motion of the spine, and, if nerve root involved, radiation of pain, sensory alterations, and altered tendon reflexes; nerve root pain is exacerbated by sudden increases in intraspinal pressure as from coughing, sneezing, or straining

	Tumors extending from vertebral bodies or from extraspinal spaces through intervertebral foramens and other osseous lesions cause resorption of normal osseous tissue by production of substances that lyse bone, resulting in bone deformity, pathologic fractures, and destruction and narrowing of the intervertebral disks	Primary extramedullary spinal cord tumors Secondary to: neoplastic diseases, lymphoma, tuberculosis	Same as above
X. Muscular spasm or contraction	The contracting muscle compresses the intramuscular blood vessels with a reduction in flow of blood to the area but an increase in the metabolic rate of the muscle, resulting in relative muscle ischemia	Tension headache, muscle cramp, muscle strain	Spasmodic muscular contraction, with knot in muscle sometimes palpable
XI. Nerve root, sensory ganglions, peripheral nerve disorders	Compression, stimulation, traction, or inflammation of nerve roots, sensory ganglions, or peripheral nerves results in pain	Trigeminal neuralgia, glossopharyngeal neuralgia, herpes zoster, tabes dorsalis, entrapment neuropathies, neuritis (intercostal, peripheral, etc.)	Sharp, lancinating, or throbbing occurring in quick succession, and frequently triggered by end organ stimulation
XII. Psychogenic, psychologic needs, secondary gain	Various psychologic factors are responsible for pain by precipitation of physiologic changes (vascular changes, muscle tenseness, hypo and hypersecretion of glands), by conversion of an emotional conflict into a physical complaint, or by development of delusions	Hysterical pain, hypochondriacal pain, phantom pain (in some cases), spastic colon, delusional pain, conversion symptoms, psychosomatic pain, psychologic augmentation of pain	Pain may be of any nature. Most frequently described as a sharp aching in the region of organ to which it is attributed

tissue reactions such as inflammation, distension, or spasm of the smooth muscle, and the elaboration of irritating or chemical substances such as acetylcholine, histamine, bradykinin, gastric juice, pancreatic enzymes, and bile. There are fewer visceral pain receptors compared to those on the body surfaces so the pain is more diffuse, duller, and of longer duration than superficial pain. The metabolic products of muscle ischemia coming in contact with nerve receptors are the stimuli for pain in intermittent claudication, angina pectoris, and myocardial infarction. Pain in the skeletal muscles can also result from tissue injury such as tears, necrosis, hemorrhage, or the injection of irrigating solutions. The most intense stimulator of pain in the arteries is increased pulsation. The stimulus for pain in some instances is thought to come from the person's mental or psychologic state. Such psychic stimuli, which seem to be based on long-standing inabilities to resolve emotional needs or conflicts, are responsible for hysterical pain, hypochondriacal pain, and, in some instances, phantom pain.

Perception of Pain

There is general agreement among the theorists who have studied pain that when pain receptors are stimulated, the impulse is carried by nerve fibers in the peripheral sensory nerves. The peripheral nerve fibers enter the spinal cord through the dorsal roots, with impulses transmitted by various tracts through the spinal cord. It has already been said that the pain receptors in the various structures of the body differed in their responsiveness to various forms of stimulation. The nerve fibers serving the receptors also differ. The major differences are in the speed of conduction and the threshold for pain recognition. The threshold for pain is the lowest intensity of noxious stimulation of the nerve which is perceived as painful. The two major types of peripheral nerve fibers involved in the transmission of pain are the myelinated type A and the unmyelinated type C. The myelinated fibers are subtyped according to their size, with A beta the largest fiber, A gamma medium in size, and A delta the smallest. The unmyelinated fibers in type C are even smaller than A delta fibers. The fiber size correlates with the velocity of conduction of the impulse and with the threshold for pain. The large A beta fibers have the most rapid conduction and the lowest threshold for pain. They transmit mechanical impulses that arise in the corpuscular receptors with few synaptic delays to the thalamus, with projections to the sensory cortex. The smaller fibers conduct impulses that arise in the free nerve endings, with impulses being conducted more slowly and the pain threshold higher. They transmit impulses through the T-cells of the dorsal horn with multiple relays terminating in the reticular formation of the brain stem or in the intralaminar nuclei of the thalamus or diffusely conducted to various brain centers.

In addition to this difference in the speed of conduction and the pain threshold, the nature of the stimulus received is also influenced by the distribution of the variously sized fibers since the pain receptors sensitive to certain stimuli are generally served by specific fiber sizes. Tht body surface as a whole is supplied with nerve fibers of all sizes from the large A beta to the smallest C. There are specialized body surface areas, however, that are served primarily by the large A beta fibers, whose receptors are sensitive to mechanical pressure such as stroking or vibration. These areas lie below the epidermis of the palms and soles, in mucocutaneous regions, and in the deeper layers of the skin and in the subcutaneous tissue. Impulses transmitted through the A gamma and A delta fibers give the sensation of pricking pain. Impulses transmitted through C fibers give the sensation of burning and aching. Most of the visceral and deeper somatic structures are supplied with the small nerve fibers of the A delta and C range. Stimulation of the receptors in the viscera and deeper somatic structures (such as the skeletal structures) gives the sensation of aching or burning, with more intense pain felt as sharp, or penetrating.

Transmission of Pain

Although there is general agreement on the concept that peripheral and central nervous system pathways have specialized functions related to reception and conduction of pain stimuli, the pain theorists have conflicting theories to explain the mechanism whereby these pathways transmit the stimulus that results in the sensation of pain. Since we do not have precise knowledge about the transmission of pain, the theorists have proposed models to explain the clinical phenomena of pain. Although complete understanding of these models is not expected of the beginning student, they are briefly presented for the benefit of those especially interested in the field. The basis of nursing intervention aimed at decreasing the perception of pain comes from these models. Early theories were based on the specificity doctrine that proclaimed that there were specific pain receptors in the skin that, when stimulated, always resulted in the sensation of pain, with a direct and unvariable relationship between stimulus intensity and perceived pain. Such a stimulus-response relationship failed to explain individual differences in perception of pain, why a person with a chordotomy could still have pain, or psychic pain. Several pattern theories were proposed to explain the inconsistencies of the specificity theory. They were based on the concept that the duration and location of a pain stimulus formed a pattern that was transmitted to the brain, with the perception of pain depending on the central summation of the various stimuli.

The most adequate explanation for pain at the present time is generally believed to be the gate control theory which was proposed by Melzack and Wall. This theory embodies the early ideas of physiologic specialization of the nervous system pathways and the concept of central summation, but describes a different mechanism for alteration of the impulses from small fibers before they enter the T-cells of the dorsal horn. According to the theory, the pain impulses from the nerve receptors can be modified or blocked before they reach the T-cells of the dorsal horn by a gating mechanism located over the entire length of the spinal cord in the cells of the substantia gelatinosa which surrounds the T-cells. It is postulated that when stimulation of the large nerve fibers occurs, the rapid conduction of the impulse to the brain can inhibit the transmission of impulses from the small fibers in which conduction is slower. The process by which this is said to occur is a negative inhibiting feedback resulting from the large fiber impulses that reach the brain giving a "downflowing" impulse to the substantia gelatinosa cells which closes the gate to further transmission of small fiber impulses. With stimulation of the small nerve fibers, however, the small fiber impulses that reach the substantia gelatinosa provide a positive excitatory feedback that opens the gate and facilitates the transmission of later-arriving small fiber impulses. The nature of the stimuli that are transmitted through the spinal cord thus depends on the relative balance of activity in the small and large fibers. When small fibers are predominately stimulated, the gate is opened wider and the transmission of the impulse through the T-cells is facilitated. When large fibers are predominately stimulated, the gate is closed and central transmission of small fiber impulses occurring at the same time is inhibited, although this reaction weakens over time. Since the large fiber receptors have a lower threshold, they can be stimulated by gentle stroking. Stronger mechanical stimulation of the surface area results in stimulation of the smaller nerve fibers, which have a higher threshold.

The gate control theory further postulates that there are other modulating influences on the open or closed status of the gate which involve sensory discriminative, affective, and cognitive factors. The sensory discriminative system is believed to localize incoming stimuli. Not arising solely from the gate control theory, but important to discuss is the difficulty in determining the location of visceral pain. Visceral pain is poorly localized; this is partially due to the small number of pain receptors and also to the mechanism of referred pain. Referred pain occurs because visceral pain fibers synapse in the spinal cord with pain fibers from the body surfaces. With intense stimulation of visceral pain fibers, the stimuli spread to the body surface fibers, and the person feels the pain on the body surface. The actual body surface involved is the area from which the organ developed embryologically. Returning to the specifics of the gate control theory, the motivational affective system is activated when small fiber activity reaches a certain intensity, interprets the impulses as unpleasant, and provides the impetus for action aimed at stopping or reducing the noxious stimulation. The cognitive central control system determines how the sensory discriminative input is perceived and/or how the motivational affective system is controlled. It evaluates and analyzes the input of the other systems in terms of past experience, possible outcomes, symbolic meaning of pain, and preset response strategies. After this central summation of pain, the organism responds by facilitating or inhibiting influences on the discriminative or motivational systems, as well as directly signaling for opening or closure of the gate. After the initial perception of pain, subsequent perception of pain is integrated and modified in terms of the continuous monitoring of the central control system in the thalamus and cerebral cortex. Psychologic factors such as anxiety, fear, and apprehension heighten the perception of pain since their activation of the thalamocortical circuit results in cortical excitability that augments pain perception.

Endogenous Mechanisms

The role of endogenous mechanisms in the perception of pain is currently being studied. It has been found that when noxious stimuli activate the ascending system and are relayed in the gray matter of the brain to activate the descending systems, endogenous peptides, which produce a morphine-like analgesia, are released. Theories regarding the nature and release of these endogenous analgesics do not contradict the gate control theory, but perhaps explain a mechanism of inhibition that reduces the perception of pain. The two major groups of compounds involved are enkephalins and endorphins. The term endorphin means endogenous morphine-like substance. Since the administration of a narcotic antagonist such as naloxone has reversed the analgesic effect of the endogenous peptides, the compounds are called morphine-like. Enkephalins are manufactured, stored, and released by periaqueductal gray matter of the brain and the interneurons in the spinal cord. Endorphins come from sites in the brain. Betaendorphin is believed to be manufactured in the hypothalamus, stored in the same pituitary granule as ACTH, and released with ACTH in response to stress. The most recent peptide to be isolated is dynorphin. It is secreted by the pituitary gland and is 200 times more potent than morphine.

Although there are many still unexplained elements about endogenous mechanisms that will require future research, present knowledge of their actions has provided explanations of several previously mystifying occurrences. Some of the major findings and their generally accepted explanations will now be briefly summarized.

Electrical stimulation of the periaqueductal and periventricular gray matter and the limbic system provides analgesia. It is believed that there are stereospecific receptors in these areas that bind the morphine-like peptides. Electrical stimulation is one means of increasing release of the morphine-like transmitter. Stainless steel electrodes, which have been implanted into some patients experiencing pain, allow them to stimulate the opiate receptor sites voluntarily.

Placebo reactors, who obtain relief of organic pain after administration of a substance that ordinarily has no effect on pain, are believed to have activation of the descending system by the stereoreceptor sites in the limbic system. The limbic system is generally considered to be concerned with the way sensory sensations are experienced. There is a possibility that pain control by hypnosis, autogenic training, and some behavior modification techniques also occurs as a result of activation of the receptor sites in the limbic system.

The elevation of the pain threshold by acupuncture and transcutaneous electrical stimulation and the reversal by a narcotic antagonist have been clinically measured. This blocking of the stereospecific receptors by an antagonist is believed to support the concept that the beneficial effect of these pain relief measures is due to the increase in the release of enkephalins.

Adequate levels of dopamine, norepinephrine, and serotonin are required for normal functioning of the descending pathway that goes down the dorsal horn of the spinal cord to effect pain inhibition. This is believed to explain the lower threshold for the perception of pain in depressed persons and the analgesic effect of antidepressant drugs that increase the concentration of one or more of the catecholamines or other biogenic amines (as serotonin) at the central adrenergic receptor sites in the limbic cortex and hypothalamus. Antidepressant drugs are frequently given in combination with opiates to potentiate the action of the opiates.

Enkephalins are degraded by carboxypeptidase in the central nervous system. It appears that agents that inhibit the production of enzymes for the degradation of peptides (such as D-phenylalanine) exert an analgesic effect. Closely associated is the antagonistic action of prostaglandins on enkephalins. The pain relief from acetylsalicyclic acid is believed to be due to its inhibition of prostaglandin synthesis.

Reaction to pain

After noxious stimuli transmitted to the brain are interpreted as painful, the organism may respond with altered activity of the skeletal muscles and the autonomic nervous system, and by changes in the affective state. The nature of these responses will be discussed further under assessment of associated manifestations.

ASSESSMENT

Assessment of pain relies heavily on the patient's statements since pain is a subjective symptom. For patients unable to report, or for those whose actions are contrary to their statements, observation of changes in physiologic or psychologic behavior assumes greater importance. The physical examination is directed toward finding an abnormal physical state responsible for the pain and/or the reproduction of the pain. In addition to the pain itself, variables that might influence the perception of, and/or response to pain need to be assessed. The terminology used to describe the characteristics of pain and the sequential steps in its assessment may differ in various texts, but the following factors are generally included.

Location or Site of Origin

When the site of the pain is a superficial somatic structure, such as the skin, it is easily localized. In deep somatic structures and the viscera, the pain is diffuse, poorly localized and may not be felt in its actual location but may be referred according to the spinal segmental distribution of its roots. Examples of referred pain are: myocardial ischemia in which the pain may be in the left shoulder, down the inside of the left arm, and in the back; gall baldder pain which is felt in the back between the shoulder blades; and male kidney disorders, with pain referred to the testicles. In some instances, the location of the pain may spread to the segmental division of neighboring nerve roots, with pain from myocardial ischemia being referred to the neck, throat, lower jaw, and ear as well. Referred pain is said to radiate when it can be described as extending in some direction from its site of origin. Since patterns of radiation with different disorders are highly consistent, they have diagnostic significance. Pain of myocardial ischemia and gall bladder may be described as starting in the involved organs and radiating to the structures mentioned above. Another example of radiation is the pain from a herniated intervertebral disc that compresses the lumbar root extending down the lateral thigh and leg. Occasionally a patient will report that pain radiates from a distant area toward the disordered area. Psychogenic pain follows no location pattern, but is frequently located in the region of the organ to which it is attributed.

Duration and Other Temporal Relationships

Some pain, such as angina pectoris and intestinal colic, lasts only a few minutes. Ulcer pain however, may continue for several hours unless terminated by food or drug ingestion. Some pain, such as the skeletal pain of metastatic carcinoma, is worse at night while the pain of arthritis is most severe upon arising. In addition to the duration and time of day, it should be determined if the pain is steady or intermittent. Angina pectoris, peptic ulcer, gall bladder colic, and renal colic are all characterized by steady pain. Intermittent abdominal or epigastric pain is suggestive of an obstructive lesion in a hollow viscus.

Quality

Terms frequently used to describe the quality of pain are sharp, dull, pricking, aching, throbbing, crushing, squeezing, cramping, burning, gnawing, and stabbing. Some patients describe pain in terms of a familiar painful experience such as a cramp, bee sting, or an electric shock. Others use a simile such as "it felt like a knife was sticking in there," or "like a hot poker was being run down my leg." Oftentimes the similes accurately describe the sensations resulting from an altered state, but when they are dramatically presented with much elaboration and are inconsistent with an organic process, the possibility of psychogenic pain should be investigated. Neurogenic pain, in which a number of different stimuli can be so altered by damage to the nerves that they are experienced as pain, frequently cannot be described accurately because it does not correspond to any previous experience.

Quantity or Intensity

Reports of intensity of the pain frequently contain the terms mild, severe, excruciating, bearable, or unbearable. Although there is a high correlation between the intensity of the noxious stimulation and the severity of the pain, many variables influence the patient's report of pain intensity. A report of pain reaching great intensity almost immediately after its appearance suggests a rupture of tissue such as a dissecting aortic aneurysm or perforation of a peptic ulcer.

Associated Manifestations

The reaction to pain, as discussed in the introductory section, has three components.

Altered skeletal muscle activity.   Initial skeletal muscle activity when there is an external source of pain consists of the reflex action of voluntary withdrawing from the pain source. When the pain source is internal, there is usually a reflex tightening and rigidity of muscles of the affected area. Regardless of the pain source, there is frequently a reflex clenching of the fists and teeth, and facial tensing evidenced as grimaces, tight lips, frowns, and wrinkles in the forehead. The initial reflex action may be followed by diffuse physical activity which is frequently an effort to relieve the pain. This can consist of restless, purposeless movement of the extremities, clutching of the painful area, or pacing of the floor. When movement increases the pain, there may be decreased skeletal muscle activity with avoidance of any movement of the painful area, assumption of unnatural postures such as drawing the knees up to the chin, and a change in gait.

Autonomic nervous system reactions. When most patients experience pain, the sympathoadrenal response is initiated as with other types of stress. As has been previously mentioned, this includes the stimulation of the sympathetic division of the autonomic nervous system (with the liberation of norepinephrine) and adrenal stimulation (with increased release of adrenocorticosteroid hormone). This response is a protective mechanism to help the person mobilize his defenses to fight the pain or escape from the pain by flight. The major effects of sympathoadrenal stimulation are elevation of the blood pressure, heart rate, and respiratory depth and rate, dilation of pupils, localized perspiration, pallor (from skin arteriolar constriction), gastrointestinal distress (from decreased motility and tone of stomach and intestines), and hyperglycemia (from glycogenolysis). With severe deep pain, or in patients who are unable to mobilize the sympathoadrenal response (such as adrenal crisis, severe catecholamine depletion, etc.), the response of the nervous system may be different, and parasympathetic activity to conserve energy will predominate. The major observable effects of parasympathetic stimulation are a decrease in blood pressure, heart rate, and depth of respiration, increased tearing, salivation, and sweating (from increased secretion of lacrimal, salivary, and sweat glands), and diarrhea (from increased intestinal peristalsis). When pain is not relieved in a patient with severe hypotension and bradycardia, the patient can faint (vasopressor syncope) and the condition can progress to vascular collapse and shock.

Changes in the affective state. Changes in the affective state, which are sometimes referred to as the psychic reactions to pain, may be manifested by verbalization of pain, moaning or groaning, negativism, focusing attention on self with decreasing response to the environment, irritability or other mood shifts, and a decrease in cognitive functioning. There is extreme variability among persons in their affective response to pain which seems to be due primarily to the meaning that each person attaches to the pain, cultural conditioning, and psychologic factors such as level of anxiety, adequacy of adaptive mechanisms, and degree of support received from health care providers and/or family or significant others. It has already been mentioned that psychologic factors such as anxiety, fear, and apprehension heighten the perception of pain. Since patients frequently react to the experience of pain by increased anxiety, anxiety and other related emotions can trigger a pain cycle that results in intensification of the pain. Initial anxiety preceding or accompanying the painful experience increases the perception of pain. When the patient reacts with new or greater anxiety, the pain is perceived as more intense—which triggers an even greater affective response of anxiety, and so on.

Aggravating and Alleviating Factors

The patient should be questioned regarding any medications, diet, or activities that affect the amount of pain experienced. Patient reports of bodily activities, physiologic states, and environmental factors that help to alleviate or aggravate pain are helpful in identifying the disorder responsible for the pain and also point to intervention for relief of the pain. Bodily activities that may increase the stimuli and/or the perception of pain are movement, muscular exertion, posture, position of dependency, maneuvers that increase intraspinal pressure (such as coughing, sneezing, straining), and skin contact in painful areas. Body activities that may alleviate pain are rest, postures that decrease the pressure on painful areas, elevation of painful extremities, and gentle stimulation of adjacent uninvolved areas. Physiologic states that may aggravate pain are increased systolic blood pressure, masses that put pressure on adjacent structures, increased peristaltic activity, and high acid secretion by the stomach. Environment factors which may intensify pain are pressure from clothing, bright lights or glare, high noise levels, disagreeable odors, exposure to rays from the sun, extremes of temperature and humidity, high altitudes, air pollution, and limitation of sensory input. The application of heat or cold may alleviate some types of pain. Cooling is usually most effective for pain of inflammatory origin, while warmth is more effective for pain from damaged nerves.

Influencing Variables

The patient's perception of, and reaction to, pain is influenced by physiologic, cultural, and psychologic variables.

Physiologic variables.   Physiologic variables have been partially outlined in the foregoing assessment parameters. Higher feelings of pain can usually be correlated with intense pain that involves an extensive area, with observable skeletal-muscular and autonomic reactions, and in which there are bodily activities, physiologic states, or environmental factors present to aggravate the pain. Pain appears to have a cumulative effect; when pain appears simultaneously in two or more areas of the body, the perception of pain is heightened. Pain is also affected by the level of consciousness. Drugs, cranial lesions (trauma, tumor, infection, hematoma, etc.), and other states that affect consciousness may decrease the perception of pain. In addition, physical fatigue may affect a patient's pain experience. Fantasies and hallucinations have a tendency to occur with fatigue, and the resultant anxiety and apprehension can activate the thalamocortical circuit and augment pain perception. Perhaps an additional comment should be made about chronic pain. When pain is present over a prolonged period of time, the capacity of the body to tolerate the pain is reduced, and the entire nervous system can be adversely affected. Reactions to chronic pain can include loss of emotional stability, increased irritability, insomnia, and poor appetite.

Cultural conditioning.   Cultural conditioning influences the interpretation of noxious stimuli as painful and the reaction. Members of some cultural groups have a tendency to refrain from overt emotional expressions, while others are more publicly demonstrative. Women frequently react more freely to pain than men. This is probably due to the equation of stoicism and maintenance of control with manliness. Religious beliefs can alter the reaction to pain. Some patients feel that the pain is punishment for wrongdoing and that it should be borne bravely for the spiritual gains that are derived. Others may use prayer or religious ritual to help them tolerate pain. Cultural conditioning that certain parts of the body should not be talked about may result in no mention of pain in the genital area or in the organs for excretion of urine and feces. Although acceptable attitudes and responses are usually learned in childhood, exposure to other cultures may alter a person's affective reactions to pain. There is also a great deal of variation in the reaction to pain within a cultural group, so stereotyping is to be avoided.

Psychologic variables.   These are primarily associated with the cognitive control system that evaluates sensory input and controls the action response system. Previous pain experiences affect the central summation of pain by the cognitive system since the patient tends to transfer the knowledge gained from past experience with pain to new experiences. Individual differences in the characteristic manner of perceiving and interpreting pain (reduction, augmentation, or realistic toleration), affect pain perception. The symbolic meaning associated with the pain, such as threat to life or manner of living, not only influences the central summation of pain but can also lead to anxiety which increases the perception of pain. Factors which influence the meaning of pain for the patient are his knowledge and understanding of the cause of the pain and the degree of control he feels he has over it. Some adaptive mechanisms such as intellectualization, withdrawal, denial, and purposeful diversion to distract attention from pain may decrease the perception of pain. The presence, attitudes, and suggestions of family and professional staff can also influence the patient's pain experience. A few patients use pain to meet other psychologic needs such as attention from loved ones, control of the action of others, and avoidance of certain responsibilities. These outcomes are termed secondary gains because the pain is used by the patient to fulfill his otherwise unmet psychologic needs. When the need for secondary gains is strong enough, readiness to feel pain is increased and there may be more concern with the response of others than with the relief of pain.

INTERVENTION

After the characteristics of pain and the influencing variables have been identified, a plan for intervention to interrupt or modify the pain in the circuit from source to reaction can be initiated and implemented. With the wide variability in the stimuli that cause pain and the influence of the underlying physiologic and psychosocial processes on the perception and reaction to pain, the possibilities for intervention are almost endless. Some of the broad goals which are common to many patients will be briefly discussed. Specific activities which might be employed for goal attainment will be suggested for each goal, although many activities overlap and may further more than one goal. Some activities are primarily in the realm of the physician, some are shared, while the nurse may assume the primary responsibility for others.

Elimination (or Alteration) of the Stimulus at the Source of Pain

• *Avoidance of unnecessary movement* and/or use of supportive measures to decrease pain from movement. Activities may include instruction in the use of muscles in other areas to accomplish the movement, splinting a painful part to prevent muscle strain, and use of slow and steady movement with pauses whenever resistance is felt. When the weight of a supportive structure is such that more than one person is needed for movement, synchronization of efforts is essential. When the patient is moving the painful area himself, he should be allowed to take as much time as he needs. Movements that increase pain by elevation of intraspinal pressure such as coughing, sneezing, and straining should be modified.

• *Modification of muscular exertion* is needed to decrease pain of angina pectoris and intermittent claudication in which the irritating metabolic products of muscle ischemia come in contact with the nerve receptors.

• *Positioning* is necessary to prevent tension or pressure on body structures. Activities may include elevation of an inflamed, edematous extremity, manipulation of posture to decrease the pressure on painful organs, and encouraging patient with a spinal headache to lie flat in bed.

• *Drugs* are required to reduce the noxious stimuli such as antacids (for gastric hyperacidity), antibiotics (for infectious processes), anti-inflammatory agents (for inflammatory processes), and vasodilators (for inadequate tissue perfusion).

• *Prevention and/or relief from distension* of gastrointestinal tract and urinary bladder by use of nasogastric intubation and action as appropriate to empty urinary bladder.

• *Removal of any existing identifiable source* when advisable. Activities could include skin cleansing to remove caustic or irritant, removal of foreign body (splinter, surgical equipment, etc.), and removal of diseased organ.

• *Use of external applications* of hot, cold, or counterirritants to decrease the number of noxious stimuli coming from the pain source.

• *Control of environmental factors* that may intensify the existing noxious stimulation or provide new stimuli. Activities may include the avoidance of cutaneous stimulation from the pressure of clothing, bedclothes, adhesive tape, etc.; control of bright lights, glare, or high noise levels; provision of meaningful sensory input; regulation of room temperature and humidity; and education regarding the potential dangers of exposure to the sun, high altitudes and air pollution.

Modification of the Impulses

The impulses can be modified from the small nerve fibers before they enter the spinal cord by stimulation of the large (A beta) fibers. Gentle stroking, vibration, and back rubs may close the gate and thus inhibit the transmission of pain impulses by the small nerve fibers.

Alteration of the Pain-Conducting Pathway

Alteration in the spinal cord can be achieved by nerve blocks, cordotomy, rhizotomy, etc.

Elevation of the Threshold for Perception of Pain at the Thalamocortical Level

- *Modification of anxiety*, fear, and apprehension that heighten the perception of pain. During the period of anticipation of pain, intervention is focused on reducing the fear of the unknown by providing accurate information about the expected pain. One technique termed autogenic training involves rehearsal of the anticipated procedure with descriptions of the sensations that will be felt. For a patient experiencing pain, intervention is directed toward reducing anxiety which increases cortical excitability. Measures may include the administration of tranquilizer drugs and providing information. Other activities to lessen anxiety will be discussed under intervention for the reaction to pain.

- *Relaxation techniques* which reduce the muscular tension which contributes to the intensity of pain.

- *Acceleration of the release of endogenous analgesics* by the use of acupuncture, electrical stimulation (by transcutaneous or implanted stimulator), antidepressant drugs, or placebos with autosuggestion. Although a placebo is an inactive substitute that can have no direct effect on pain, when both the administrator and the receiver have the attitude that it will be effective, it may stimulate the release of endorphins. Other agents, such as those to inhibit the degradation of endorphins (D-phenylalanine) are still in the experimental stage. Some of the activities that alter the central summation of pain may owe part of their effectiveness to release of endogenous analgesics.

- *Alteration of the central summation of pain.* Cognitive control is increased by clarifying misconceptions and giving knowledge and understanding that assists in the placement of a more realistic meaning on the pain experience. The motivational affective component is altered by hypnosis and some group therapy in which positive suggestions are accepted that alter the interpretation of pain as unpleasant and increases the ability to tolerate discomfort. The intensity ascribed to the pain by the sensory discriminative system can be decreased by the administration of analgesic drugs, provision of adequate rest and sleep to prevent physical fatigue, and the use of distraction. Analgesic drugs are more effective when they are given before a painful experience or in the early stages of pain, since intense pain intensifies cerebral cortex activity. Biofeedback training in alpha wave control, rhythmic breathing patterns, and waking-imagined analgesia (WIA) are three techniques that use the principle of distraction. WIA is the imaginary reliving of all the sensations of a previous pleasant experience when pain is present or anticipated.

• *Therapeutic adaptive mechanisms* must be maintained and encouragement to replace potentially harmful adaptive mechanisms with other more helpful responses. Advance information about painful procedures allows time for mobilization of adaptive defenses.

• *Support* must be provided for ego strength and self-esteem by health care providers and/or family or significant others. Acceptance of the patient's behavioral responses to pain, remaining with the patient during difficult periods, allowing the patient to have more control over deciding what to do for pain, and the use of touching activities such as stroking the forehead, pressing the hand, patting the shoulder, etc., are especially helpful for the patient whose pain has been present over a period of time. They also can reduce anxiety which increases the pain. The family may need suggestions of ways they can provide assistance. Explanations of the reason for the pain may reduce their feelings of anxiety and anger related to the patient, which otherwise might be communicated to the patient.

• *Use of behavior modification techniques* with a system of rewards that are given for substitution of other responses (i.e., relaxation, distraction) for the customary response to pain.

• *Provision of assistance* in finding other ways to meet psychologic needs (i.e., attention of loved ones, control of the actions of others, avoidance of responsibilities) instead of the use of pain for its secondary gains. Psychotherapy may be indicated for hysterical or hypochondriacal pain when there is a long-standing inability to resolve conflicts or establish meaningful interpersonal relationships.

• *Assistance in realistic integration of the pain experience* after the pain has been controlled to avoid conditioning that would result in greater sensitivity to future painful stimuli.

EXPERIENTIAL INVOLVEMENT

Case 9A. Mrs. Cannon, a 22-year-old black woman with known sickle-cell anemia was brought to the emergency department by her husband. He related that when he came home from work she was complaining of severe abdominal pain and a feeling of weakness. She had been feeling well before the attack of pain. She described the pain as steady and sharp with the greatest intensity in

Hypothesis/Possible Diagnosis	Supportive Data Available	Additional Data Needed to Confirm or Disconfirm	Nursing Intervention if Diagnosis Confirmed	Evaluation Criteria
Lower right abdominal pain due to: 1.				
2.				
3.				

the right lower abdomen. The pain had been present for 4 to 5 hours, but had become more severe in the last hour. She had eaten nothing since breakfast. Her vital signs were: BP 105/85, T 37.8 C (100.1 F), P 90, R 22.

Skillbuilders:

1. On the practicum record 9-A, enter the three most likely hypotheses for Mrs. Cannon's abdominal pain. We don't expect you to name the specific clinical state, but list the body systems that are most likely involved.

2. Then enter the data that support the hypothesis and additional data you would need to confirm or disconfirm. Focus primarily on the interview and physical examination data that you could gather.

3. In the intervention column list the immediate activities, both physician directed and independent, that would be appropriate for the next 24 hours.

4. In the last column enter the evaluation criteria for the management of Mrs. Cannon for this 24-hour period.

Feedback: When a previously well young woman with sickle-cell anemia develops severe abdominal pain the first possibility that comes to mind is a vascular disorder from microthrombi that occur with a sickle-cell crisis. Other hypotheses would be a disorder in the gastrointestinal system or reproductive system. Let's discuss the sickle-cell crisis first. Supporting data would come from the theory that persons with sickle-cell anemia can suffer vasoocclusive phenomena in various parts of the body, especially the abdomen, chest, and joints. History items, in addition to a history of the anemia, would include the sudden onset, the sharp steady character of the pain, the low grade fever, narrow pulse pressure, and the accompanying anorexia. Additional data to support the hypothesis would be presence of abdominal distension, absence of rebound tenderness, normal or increased bowel sounds and absence of rigidity. Other definitive diagnosis depends on negative findings for other acute disorders.

Nursing intervention if the hypothesis was confirmed would primarily be geared to minimizing the dysfunctional effects from the crisis. Goals and activities would include:

1. Maintenance of adequate tissue oxygenation by oxygen administration. Hypoxemia with arterial Po_2 less than 60 torr increases intravenous sickling and mechanical obstruction of the microcirculation.

2. Control of pain by administration of analgesics. Medications are given with close observation of effect to prevent respiratory depression that would result in increased hypoxia.

3. Restoration of normal fluid state since fluid volume deficit results in greater viscosity of the blood and circulatory stasis in vulnerable organs, with both factors increasing sickling. Intravenous fluids will be required until oral fluid intake can be resumed.

4. Maintenance of adequate hemoglobin levels by transfusion of packed cells. Transfusion is not usually given if the hematocrit is over 25 ml/dl, because the higher viscosity with greater red cell concentration increases sickling. For severe crises or surgery, hypertransfusion with replacement of 50 percent or more of the patient's blood with donor blood may be used. Daily administration of folic acid is generally used to meet the increased requirements generated by the need for red blood cell replacement.

5. Correction of severe acidosis by the administration of sodium bicarbonate might be beneficial since acidosis lowers the oxygen affinity of the red blood cell, increasing the deoxygenation of the blood and thus increasing sickling.

6. Prevention of infection is important not only because of the greater susceptibilty to infection but also because infections increase sickling.

Evaluation criteria would be

1. Disappearance of abdominal pain

2. Arterial Po_2 maintained between $65-100$ torr

3. Adequate hydration (could be determined by adequate urine output, good skin turgor, absence of postural hypotension, etc.)

4. Hematocrit between $18-25$ ml/dl (or preillness state)

5. pH of the blood maintained between 7.2 and 7.45

6. Absence of infection

Although educational activities are not appropriate during the initial acute period, communication with the patient should enable the nurse to make an evaluative statement concerning Mrs. Cannon's knowledge about sickle-cell disease and her desire for further services such as genetic counseling. Now let's consider the hypothesis that the lower right abdominal pain is due to a disorder in the gastrointestinal (GI) system. We did not think it was the nurse's responsibility to attempt to make the fine determination between ischemic, obstructive, chemical, inflammatory, tissue injury, or metabolic disorder. Many of these possible clinical states, however, are unlikely because the pain was of a steady rather than a crampy or colicky nature and the pain was located in the lower abdomen rather than the epigastric area. Because of her age and report of feeling well prior to the episode, the most likely underlying GI source would probably be acute appendicitis. Data to support a GI disorder would include the history of a sudden onset of pain, presence of anorexia, and low grade fever.

Other data to confirm would be the presence of tenderness and altered bowel sounds. Many of the physical findings vary with the location, type of disorder, and time after onset. Data which should be collected to help substantiate the presence of a GI disorder and differentiate the exact nature of the disorder include more precise information about the character of pain, the coincidence with physiologic functions as respiration or urination, the aggravating and alleviating factors (effect of food, vomiting, belching, defecation, expulsion of flatus, body movement, posture, etc.), and identification of any past episodes of similar pain. Many aspects of the physical examination of the abdomen may be the nurse's responsibility, while other portions of the examination are almost always done by the physician. The modalities of inspection, palpation, percussion, and auscultation are all used. The most helpful information for Mrs. Cannon would be identification of rebound tenderness, rigidity or guarding, cutaneous hyperesthesia, distension, vascular bruits, and pitch and frequency of bowel peristalsis sounds. Rectovaginal examination provides essential information about both GI and reproductive system disorders.

Laboratory tests may help to rule in or rule out clinical states. The urinalysis, serum and urine amylase, and blood count provide the most information. High amylase levels are suggestive of acute pancreatitis. Elevated white count is indicative of an inflammatory process, but since persons with sickle-cell anemia normally run a white count of $12-15,000$ cu mm, leukocytosis requires careful interpretation. Abdominal X-ray films, studies with contrast material in the GI tract, injection of dye into the arterial tree, diagnostic paracentesis, and colonoscopy are examinations which may be used by the physician. Intervention if the hypothesis is confirmed depends to a great extent on the exact nature of the clinical disorder. Acute appendicitis is almost always treated by early operation to avoid perforation and generalized peritonitis. The special care of a patient with sickle-cell anemia following surgery is discussed under the next hypothesis.

During the preoperative period, Mrs. Cannon and her husband will undoubtedly need assistance in making the psychologic adjustment to surgery. Since any surgery carries a much greater risk in a patient with sickle-cell anemia, it can provoke severe anxiety. Additionally, patients who enter the hospital through the emergency service and are then transferred to a hospital bed for a short period before surgery are deprived of an adequate period of time to develop a relationship with the personnel. Frequently the securing of specimens for testing, X-ray examination, and preparation of the skin for surgery takes precedence over emotional needs. Thus, the nurse must be skillful in utilizing the small amount of time available to help both Mr. and Mrs. Cannon mobilize their emotional resources. Supportive treatment to maintain homeostasis and prevent dysfunctional effects that would increase sickling include adequate hydration, supplemental oxygen, blood transfusion, and control of pain. Analgesics are used sparingly to avoid masking the symptoms but positioning the patient on her left side with her right knee drawn up frequently promotes comfort. These supportive measures were discussed more completely with the first hypothesis.

Evaluation criteria would include those listed for sickle-cell crisis plus some more specifics for the hypothesis of GI disorder. It is difficult to list specific evaluation criteria for a system disorder when intervention differs with the clinical state. We listed absence of signs of generalized peritonitis (increased nausea and vomiting, distension, rigidity, inability to pass feces or flatus, hypotension, tachycardia, thirst, oliguria, and decreased or absent bowel sounds). Another criterion is absence of severe anxiety (supported by behavior and patient and husband validation).

That takes us to our third hypothesis—that the cause of the lower right abdominal pain was due to a disorder of the reproductive system. The supporting data are the knowledge that tubal abortion, tubal rupture, torsion of an ovarian cyst, rupture of a corpus luteum cyst, and rupture of a graafian follicle all cause sharp unilateral lower abdominal pain. The clinical picture is most characteristic of a tubal abortion or torsion of an ovarian cyst. Tubal rupture usually results in hemorrhage into the peritoneal cavity with rapid development of hypotension and shock. The pain from a ruptured cyst or follicle usually decreases rather than increases in severity. Other data to support the hypothesis would be the referral of pain to the shoulder, diffuse pelvic tenderness, and menstrual history. Pain with menses is indicative of a luteum cyst, pain midway between menses is indicative of a graafian follicle, while skipped menses may mean an ectopic pregnancy.

Intervention if the hypothesis is confirmed is supportive (as outlined above) except for tubal abortion or tubal rupture. Immediate surgery is required for these states, and intervention would include the supportive and preoperative preparation as previously outlined.

Special nursing attention will be required during the period of emergence from anesthesia. Hypoventilation from continued central respiratory depression by anesthesia can result in hypoxemia with occurrence of sickling. Thus Mrs. Cannon needs special attention to stirring up activities, supplemental oxygen, and encouragement to breathe deeply. If unable to cooperate with deep breathing, periodic hyperinflation of the lungs with oxygen-enriched air from a resuscitation bag is indicated. Clearance of secretions by coughing should be encouraged, but Mrs. Cannon needs to be restrained from efforts that require moderate or severe physical exertion since they increase the oxygen requirement. Reduction of both psychologic and physiologic stress is important to decrease the metabolic oxygen requirement. Measures to reduce stress have been previously discussed.

Evaluation criteria include all of the previously mentioned criteria. There are no additional criteria, but the major desired outcome is adequate tissue oxygenation. This is vital since it is the deoxygenation of hemoglobin that predisposes to sickling, sickle-cell crisis, and functional damage to vital body organs such as the lung, liver, and kidneys.

CASE 9B. Miss Kaplan is a 28-year-old high school teacher of English literature and drama who writes poetry and is also very active in community theater productions. She noticed an enlarged gland in her neck four months ago. She has no history of previous serious illnesses. Around the time she became aware of the neck swelling, she also noted that she would waken at night bathed in perspiration and had a general feeling of malaise. She attributed these symptoms (and an 8 pound weight loss) to a rather stormy break-up with her boyfriend of 3 years. Cervical node biopsy revealed lymphoma of the Hodgkin's type. Upon further examination, mediastinal lymphadenopathy was found but a staging laparotomy was negative for involvement below the diaphragm. Her diagnosis was Hodgkin's disease, Stage II B.

She received 4000 rads of radiation to the "Mantle" supradiaphragmatic field and is now to be started on the MOPP program of chemotherapy. This protocol combines the use of nitrogen mustard, vincristine, procarbazine, and prednisone. She is to receive 6 cycles of therapy with 2 weeks of treatment followed by 2 weeks of rest. She is to be hospitalized for the first 2 weeks of therapy, but will probably receive the rest on a day treatment basis. She is scheduled to receive prophylactic radiation in the "inverted-Y" field below the diaphragm after chemotherapy is completed.

Upon admission to the hospital for the chemotherapy, her outlook was optimistic. She roamed around the unit "cheering-up" the other patients. She became extremely friendly with Mrs. Agnew who was just completing a course of chemotherapy. Mrs. Agnew claimed she had always loved the theater and wished she could have had drama training. Miss Kaplan made several telephone calls and arranged for Mrs. Agnew to audition for the next community theater production.

Miss Kaplan seemed to tolerate the chemotherapy fairly well. She was given an injection of prochlorperazine (Compazine) a half hour before nitrogen mustard was injected into the intravenous tubing, which effectively controlled nausea and vomiting most of the time. Her appetite was poor, however, and she ate less than half of the food on her tray. As she began her last week of treatment, she spent much less time interacting with the other patients. She was noted to be writing rather lengthy letters and spending many hours on the phone. She had few visitors and hardly any cards.

Now on her eighth day of chemotherapy treatment, Miss Kaplan is complaining of chest pain which she describes as a feeling of constriction and burning, most severe just below the sternum with radiation upward. She states she has had similar pain before, but it has never been this severe. Her pulse was a little rapid (90) and her respirations were hyperpneic. Her skin was moist but warm.

Skillbuilders:

1. On practicum record 9B, list the three most likely hypotheses for the chest pain that you would want to differentially consider if you were caring for Miss Kaplan. Refer to the Table 9-1 and try to select causes that have some bases in the history, personality, or treatment factors to account for the pain.

2. Then list the data that support each of the hypotheses and additional data needed to help confirm or disconfirm.

3. In the nursing intervention column, outline your plan to reduce the pain.

4. In the last column, list the criteria for evaluation of the process in response to the report of pain.

Feedback:

As we look at Table 9-1, our task is made easier if we can eliminate some of the less likely causes. Although any person can develop pain in the chest from myocardial ischemia or the ischemia resulting from a pulmonary infarction, there is no reason to suspect these disorders in Miss Kaplan. Additionally, the account of previous similar pain is not characteristic of pulmonary embolism with infarction. (We primarily consider pulmonary infarction because a pulmonary embolus may be present with no pain.) We can also put in the less likely category those disordered states which are rarely responsible for chest pain such as increased arterial pulsation, spasm of a hollow viscus, and metabolic or toxic disorders. We can rule out some of the other abnormalities after brief deliberation:

1. There is a possibility that a lymphoma in the nodes in the chest could cause the pain, but our knowledge of Hodgkin's disease tells us that there is no pain in the early stages.

PRACTICUM RECORD 9-B

Hypothesis/Possible Diagnosis	Supportive Data Available	Additional Data Needed to Confirm or Disconfirm	Nursing Intervention if Diagnosis Confirmed	Evaluation Criteria
Chest pain due to: 1.				
2.				
3.				

2. There is a possibility of tissue injury from pneumothorax, mediastinal emphysema, or rupture of the esophagus, but the pain for these disordered states would have been much more severe initially, and accompanied by greater systemic deterioration.

3. Although there is no indication of an osseous injury, there is a possibility of osseous involvement of the vertebrae or sternum. It would be highly unlikely, however, that this would occur to such an extent as to cause pain so soon after the staging procedure that showed involvement limited to cervical and mediastinal nodes.

4. Nerve root involvement would be considered very unlikely for the same rationale as the osseous lesions.

You may have noted that we skipped over a few abnormal mechanisms. These are the ones that would take a little more investigation to rule out, and thus form our hypotheses. We've worded them:

1. Chest pain due to chemical irritation from esophagitis caused by irradiation and/or *Candida* infection from immunosuppressive drugs.

2. Chest pain due to pericarditis with possible pericardial tamponade from irradiation.

3. Chest pain due to psychosomatic pain or psychologic augmentation of pain from pectoral muscle tension.

We'll try to explain the rationale that led to the selection of these hypotheses. We'll start with the hypothesis of esophagitis first. The supporting data are:

1. The history of radiation therapy and treatment with immunosuppressive agents.

2. The knowledge that radiation can cause irritation, edema, and occasionally erosion of the esophageal mucosa.

3. The knowledge that opportunistic infections tend to develop in patients whose immune mechanisms are impaired, especially in irritated tissue, with Candida being the most frequent type of infection in the esophagus.

4. The nature of the retrosternal pain that radiates upward is consistent with that present with esophagitis.

Additional data to support the diagnosis would come from more precise information about the pain. The pain of esophagitis appears after meals, especially large meals or with intake of alcoholic beverages or spicy foods. It is aggravated by bending over, lying down, or straining. It is often relieved by intake of antacids. It may also cause difficulty in swallowing, with a complaint of solid food "sticking" in the lower esophagus. Since both irradiation and *Candida* infection can also affect the oropharynx, you would expect to see some edema and irritation of this area (with radiation) and white patches (with *Candida* infection). When chest pain presents with the characteristic picture outlined above, it is usually considered sufficient for acceptance of the diagnosis of esophagitis without further testing or studies.

Nursing intervention directed by the physician would include a bland diet with four or five small feedings, antacid therapy every 1−2 hours, and, if *Candida* infection seemed likely, the use of nystatin (Mycostatin) mouthwash and nystatin oral tablets. Independent nursing activities would be directed toward coordination of treatment activities and patient education. Frequently, scheduling of treatment activities so the patient can receive the greatest benefit is a difficult task. Nutrition is vitally important for Miss Kaplan in order to maintain a positive nitrogen balance in the face of the catabolic forces of tissue destruction from irradiation and chemotherapy. Yet we need to keep her meals small and continue her chemotherapy. The nitrogen mustard is probably the most difficult drug to schedule because it results in intense nausea and vomiting and thus should not be given too close to a meal. It may be that bedtime would be the best time for administration of this drug. When preceded by the injection of prochlorperazine and perhaps a sedative, Miss Kaplan may be able to sleep through the period that might otherwise be accompanied by nausea. Patient education is important since the patient will be going home and can be anticipated to have a continuing problem throughout her period of chemotherapy.

Education would include knowledge of diet, oral hygiene, use of medications, sleeping position, and avoidance of emotional stress. Diet education includes knowledge of the basic food groups necessary for maintenance of adequate nutritional state and the need to avoid intake of alcoholic beverages and spicy foods. If Miss Kaplan feels she cannot forego all alcoholic beverages, intake of beer is preferred to beverages with a higher alcoholic content. Oral hygiene is directed toward maintenance of the integrity of the skin and oral mucosa, since breaks in the skin predispose to opportunistic infections. There is always a danger that a localized infection can spread to the bloodstream with development of generalized septicemia.

Miss Kaplan needs to realize that her antacid and nystatin medications are not to be taken just when she has pain, but they have a preventative and curative effect and must be taken on a continuing basis. If she dislikes the taste or texture of the antacid liquid in the hospital, she will have a tendency to skip it at home. Thus some experimenting may need to be done to find an agent that she likes. Antacid tablets are not as effective, because they do not provide the desired coating action of the esophageal mucosa. She may likewise object to the nystatin medication. Although nystatin is available in tablets, patients with oral or esophageal lesions are generally given vaginal suppositories to suck. In the hospital the nurse usually removes the packaging before giving them to the patient. If Miss Kaplan does not know what to expect and the reason for their use, she may not continue the nystatin at home when she sees they are labelled vaginal suppositories.

The importance of sleeping with the head elevated to reduce reflux of gastric juice into the lower esophagus with resultant increased irritation has been discussed with other case studies. The last aspect of education we listed was avoidance of emotional stress. Stress does contribute to increased pain because the sympathoadrenal response results in constriction of the sphincter in the lower esophagus which, combined with the decreased motility from sympathetic stimulation, results in painful esophageal spasm. However, we all know that telling someone to avoid emotional stress probably does nothing for the problem. What is needed is an exploration of the factors which contribute to feelings of tension or evoke strong emotions. Then problem solving with the patient should help outline a program to reduce the tensions or avoid them at meal times. Sometimes such simple alterations as relaxing before meals by a method effective for the patient (yoga, meditation, exercises, waking-imagined activity, listening to music, etc.) or avoidance of situations that create stress (not listening to the news at mealtimes, taking the telephone off the hook, etc.) can make a decided difference in the patient's physiologic response.

Evaluation criteria would be absence or decrease in chest pain, absence of generalized infection, ability to swallow food without difficulty, verbalization of knowledge and rationale of therapeutic regimen to be continued at home, and verbalization of understanding of effect of emotional stress on physiologic state.

This leads us to consideration of the second hypothesis that chest pain is due to pericarditis (and possible pericardial tamponade) from irradiation. Although the final responsibility for the definitive diagnosis for all these disorders does rest with the physician, the nurse has the responsibility of making the critical assessments to report to the physician. If present, pericardial tamponade is an emergency state requiring prompt intervention to prevent cardiac arrest. The nurse who recognizes it as a possible hypothesis to explain the chest pain and is thus cued to look at critical assessment parameters may be influential in saving the patient's life. The supporting data are the knowledge that chest radiation can cause acute pericarditis, chronic constrictive pericarditis, or chronic myocarditis, with acute pericarditis accompanied by subacute effusion into the pericardial space the most common manifestations. Another supporting datum is the character of the pain. The pain can vary from a steady constrictive pain that radiates upward and into either arm to a severe, sharp, stabbing pain that is aggravated by respiratory maneuvers. If the pericarditis develops slowly following radiation, there may not be any pain. Datum to support the hypothesis would be the presence of a pericardial friction rub.

A pericardial friction rub is not present continuously, so frequent auscultation may be necessary to detect its presence. It is best heard during inspiration or forced expiration with the patient upright and leaning slightly forward while exerting pressure on the bell of stethoscope. The friction rub disappears when a pleural effusion develops, but may be supplanted by the development of a paradoxical pulse if the effusion develops rapidly. We have discussed paradoxical pulse before. Briefly, it is best detected by sphygmomanometric measurement of systolic blood pressure with the patient breathing slowing. A difference greater than 10–15 mm Hg between systolic pressure audible at the end of expiration and the pressure when sounds are audible throughout the entire respiratory cycle is indicative of paradoxical pulse. Paradoxical pulse is due to the compression of the heart by the pericardial effusion and the resultant alteration of pressures throughout the respiratory cycle with a decrease in left ventricular output. Since the presence of a paradoxical pulse is an indication of a rapidly developing pleural effusion that can result in pericardial tamponade, its presence cues us to look for other signs of tamponade. These signs may include faintness of heart sounds, dyspnea, orthopnea, narrow pulse pressure, tachycardia, increase in size of the heart, and ECG changes. The ECG shows elevation of the ST segment in standard limb lead II and III, and chest leads V2 through V6 (with reciprocal depression of ST segment in aVR and V1.) The QRS remains unchanged. After several days, the ST segments return to normal and the T waves become inverted.

Other tests that can support the hypothesis are primarily the responsibility of the physician. They include pericardiocentesis (with examination of the fluid), echocardiography, and cardiac catheterization with angiocardiography. Intervention if the hypothesis of pericarditis were confirmed would depend on the presence or absence of pericardial tamponade. For tamponade, pericardiocentesis is an emergency procedure. When pericarditis is not accompanied by extensive effusion, it may not require treatment. In many cases, the disorder may progress to a chronic state with constriction of the heart. This usually requires surgical intervention with wide excision of both visceral and parietal pericardium.

Intervention should also include emotional support measures for Miss Kaplan. Culturally the heart is accorded great significance and dysfunction of the heart can be extremely anxiety-provoking and difficult to face. In discussions with the patient it is important that she realize that there is nothing wrong with the heart itself, but that the problem is an irritation of the sack around the heart. The fact that it does occur with some frequency and can be successfully treated are psychologic bolsters which can strengthen the patient's defenses to withstand the disorder. Evaluation criteria would be:

1. Freedom from chest pain.

2. Absence of dysfunctional effects from low cardiac output due to pericardial tamponade.

3. Return to normal of altered states, i.e., ECG, paradoxical pulse, pulse rate, pulse pressure, and respiratory effort.

4. Control of anxiety with prevention of high levels of psychologic stress from the disorder.

This brings us to the last hypothesis that chest pain is due to psychosomatic pain or psychologic augmentation of pain from pectoral muscle tension. Supporting data are the knowledge that emotional conflict can create a physiologic tension state that is painful and may be amplified by the patient. It has been found that chest pain in some persons results from an unconscious and prolonged increase in the pectoral muscle tone from emotional tension. It is often enhanced by an accompanying hyperventilation that increases muscle contraction, vasoconstriction, and accumulation of lactic acid in the muscle. Additional support comes from knowledge of the traits and behavior patterns which are frequently manifested by artistic and imaginative persons. Although we want to avoid type-casting persons without confirmation, we know a number of people in this group have what has been classified as an "hysterical personality" and exhibit overreactive behaviors. Thus they may have a large swing in mood from enthusiasm and joy to depression and despair. This tendency to overreact may be manifested by an intense reaction to organic pain that is out of proportion to the noxious stimulus.

The following are history items that tend to support the hypothesis (but which would require validation): (1) her somewhat inappropriate affect on admission, which could be indicative of denial of the true seriousness of her condition; (2) her behavior change during hospitalization from outgoing optimism to withdrawal with more covert activities; (3) the indication that possibly she had a very limited number of true friends she could count on for support; (4) the possibility that she may have just begun to realize that she will probably lose her hair from the chemotherapy and may become sterile from the radiation; and/or (5) the necessity to make some decisions about the future as time for hospital discharge approaches. Additional data would come from exploration of these various possibilities with Miss Kaplan and observance of her behavioral reactions. Intervention if the hypothesis is confirmed is difficult to outline, since it would depend upon the nature of the problem identified by the additional assessment. Some activities which might be appropriate include discussion of plans for the future, correction of any misconceptions about her illness, assistance in arrangements for relaxation activities or biofeedback distraction techniques of Miss Kaplan's choice, administration of pain medication, and, for some patients, administration of muscle relaxants and antidepressant medications. It is important to remember that although the pain may have no organic basis, it is nonetheless a true pain to Miss Kaplan. All medications and activities for pain relief need to be undertaken with a positive approach that they will help the patient. The nurse needs to be aware of her own feelings so unconscious attitudes do not prevent her from being therapeutic. Evaluation criteria would be freedom from chest pain, patient assumption of some of the responsibility for prevention and/or management of pain, and future planning that reflects both hope and realism.

ADDITIONAL READING

Pain, Part I: Basic concepts and assessments; programmed instruction. AJN 66(5):1085–1108, 1966.

Beland IL, Passos JY: Care of persons in pain. In Clinical Nursing-Pathophysiological and Psychosocial Approaches, 3rd ed. New York, Macmillan, 1975, pp 271–282.

Engel GL: Pain. In MacBryde E, Blacklow R (eds.): Signs and Symptoms, 5th ed. Philadelphia, Lippincott, 1970, pp 44–61.

Halpern L: Neurophysiological theories of pain. In Postoperative Pain, Plainfield, NJ, Chirurgecom, 1979.

Mastrovito RC: Psychogenic pain. AJN 74(3):514–519, 1974.

McCaffrey M: Nursing management of the patient with pain. Philadelphia, Lippincott, 1972.

Siegele DS: The gate control theory. AJN 74(3):498–502, 1974.

Smith D, Germain C: The patient in pain. In Care of the Adult Patient. Philadelphia, Lippincott, 1975, pp 134–145.

CHAPTER 10

Cognitive Impairment

There is no generally accepted terminology to describe the continuum of brain functioning that ranges from the maximum integrative ability to frank coma. Consciousness has different meanings to the psychologist, the physician, and the nurse. All recognize that consciousness embodies both the state of arousal or awareness and mental functioning, expecially the cognitive processes of thinking, learning, and remembering. Each discipline, however, has focused on the aspect it found most relevant.

Physicians primarily assess consciousness by observation of general behavior and reaction to overt stimuli, measures of the state of awareness to the environment. Consciousness is thus equated with awareness of environment and unconsciousness is a state of unawareness of the environment.

Psychologists primarily use the patient's verbal account of his introspections substantiated by observable action to determine the content of the mental functioning, which they equate with consciousness. A number of persons in the field of philosophy and clinical psychiatry, as well as some in the field of psychology have substituted the term, cognition, to describe the content of thought and the processes involved in thinking. These disciplines have also given a different meaning to the term, unconsciousness. To them it represents thoughts, feelings, and emotions of which a person is unaware, but which influence his behavior.

In nursing literature, several terms have been used to describe various aspects of the function, with much overlapping of characteristics. Terminology used include the aforementioned cognitive functioning and levels of consciousness, and also impaired thought processes, confusion, disorientation, and lack of understanding. In spite of the different terms used, there appears to be a consensus that the nursing profession is concerned about the continuum of mental functioning. Mind and body are not viewed separately, but rather physical health is recognized as affecting mental functioning, while mental disturbances can result in physical disorders. Additionally, the emphasis has shifted to early recognition of developing physiologic disorders when brain dysfunction is still reversible and/or the underlying disorder can be successfully treated. Likewise, in mental health, attention is on the early recognition of psychologic patterns that adversely influence attitude and behavior responses. More and more, immature cognitive processes are being identified as responsible for maladaptive behavior. This preventive focus makes it essential to identify slight alterations in cognitive functioning rather than wait for the more well-known signs of impaired function such as increased intracranial pressure, stupor, and coma. These manifestations are more easily understood when they can be related to underlying pathophysiology.

Arousal and cognition require continuous and effective interaction between two functionally intact parts of the brain; the cerebral hemispheres and the ascending reticular activating systems of the brainstem. Although normal function depends upon interaction between the two, arousal is believed to be primarily the function of the brainstem structures, with cognition the function of the cerebral hemispheres. Impaired cognition is a warning signal, but it is not a specific indicator of any one disorder. It may be due to a structural disorder within the brain or nervous system; it may be due to a disorder within the brain or elsewhere in the body that interferes with cerebral metabolism; or it may be an indication of psychologic maladjustment. Table 10-1 outlines the major causes of cognitive impairment. Each of the categories will be briefly discussed.

CAUSES

Structural Disorders

Structural disorders within the brain or nervous system can be caused by a lesion (mass, hemorrhage, abscess, etc.) in a cerebral hemisphere that squeezes and compresses the brainstem, or a lesion within the brainstem that compresses and destroys the reticular formation. The signs and symptoms that occur with lesions in the two areas, and those that occur with metabolic disorders and psychiatric diseases help to differentiate the cause of the dysfunction.

Cerebral hemisphere lesions (frequently referred to as supratentorial lesions) usually produce focal motor and/or sensory signs before cognitive impairment. Early signs and symptoms are frontal headache, focal seizures, and focal hemispheral signs that reflect the site of the pathologic process, e.g., sensorimotor defect, aphasia, and visual field defects. The extent of cognitive impairment varies with the site of the lesion. If the pathologic process is not corrected early, signs of increased intracranial pressure may develop indicating the lesion is exerting remote effects on the opposite hemisphere and the deep diencephalon and caudally on downward. If the disorder is not alleviated, herniation into the tentorial notch with permanent brain damage and/or death can occur. Signs of impending herniation are deeper stupor, respiratory alterations (sighs, yawns, periodic respirations), bilateral rigidity or spasticity of extremities with extensor plantar responses, and pupil changes. Pupils may both constrict to 1−2 mm in diameter, with maintenance of ability to react to light, or they may become unequal in size, with one pupil dilated and unreactive to light. Oculoves-

TABLE 10-1.   Major Causes of Cognition Impairment

Abnormal Initiating Mechanism	Pathophysiology	Clinical State
I. Structural disorders		
A. Brain tumors	Proliferation of cells, edema development, and sometimes bleeding into the tumor produces pressure on the reticular activating system in the brainstem and can cause herniation	Brain tumors, brain-stem tumors, metastatic brain lesion
B. Cerebral vascular lesions		
Hemorrhage	Bleeding causes pressure on surrounding structures and development of edema and inflammatory reaction in surrounding area	Intracerebral hemorrhage, subarachnoid hemorrhage, ruptured aneurysm, ruptured arteriovenous malformation, cerebellar hemorrhage
Thrombosis	Obstruction of artery by coagulation of the blood deprives the brain in the area of blood and oxygen, resulting in ischemic necrosis (infarction); neurologic deficit is localized initially, but as vascular congestion, inflammation, and edema increase the size of the lesion, it begins to exert pressure on surrounding structures	Cerebral artery infarction, brainstem infarction, venous thrombosis of superior longitudinal sinus
Embolism	Blockage of cerebral artery by embolic material causes loss of blood supply to affected area with acute inhibition of neural functioning; later edema formation and vascular congestion can cause increased pressure by same mechanism as thrombosis	Air embolus, clot embolus, fat embolus, calcium embolus (arteriosclerotic plaque)
Hematoma formation	Trauma to arteries or vessels results in bleeding with formation of a hematoma that exerts pressure on the surrounding brain structures, with increased ICP and possible progression to herniation	Acute subdural hematoma, chronic subdural hematoma, epidural hematoma, intracerebral hematoma
Abscess	Infectious process causes necrosis of the brain tissue, pressure on other structures, and increased ICP; elaboration of toxins also impairs brain metabolism	Brain abscess, subdural empyema
Occult hydrocephalus	Interference with reabsorption of spinal fluid by a block near the tentorium with enlargement of the ventricles and compression of the plexuses	Noncommunicating hydrocephalus
II. Cerebral metabolism interference		
A. Intrinsic failure of neuronal metabolism	Diffuse cerebral degenerative states with interference with normal neuronal and glial function; in some disorders, cause can be a chromosomal defect, but the mechanism is poorly understood	Alzheimer's disease, Pick's disease, Creutzfeldt–Jakob disease, Huntington's chorea, Parkinson's disease, senile dementia, progressive myoclonic epilepsy

(continued)

TABLE 10-1.   Continued

Abnormal Initiating Mechanism	Pathophysiology	Clinical State
B. Trauma	Chemical alterations interfere with electrical conduction	Concussion
	Deformation or acceleration of the skull and associated edema causes increased ICP with lowered cerebral perfusion pressure	Contusion Skull fracture
C. Seizures	Intense neuronal activity depletes cerebral oxygen supply, resulting in anoxia	Epilepsy
	With continued seizures, have cumulative and severe cerebral anoxia	Status epilepticus
	Following seizure have metabolic cerebral depression due to systemic hypoxia during attack	Postictal state
D. Systemic disorders Deprivation of oxygen	Decreased Po_2 and oxygen content of blood from pulmonary disease, alveolar hypoventilation, or high altitudes	Hypoxemia (respiratory insufficiency)
	Decreased oxygen content due to loss of ability of hemoglobin to bind and transport O_2	Anemic anoxia, carbon monoxide poisoning, methemoglobinemia
	Decreased cardiac output causes decrease in cerebral blood flow (CBF)	Cardiac arrest, Stokes–Adams syndrome, acute myocardial infarction, congestive heart failure
	Decreased peripheral resistance in systemic circulation results in pooling of blood in periphery and decreased flow to brain	Orthostatic syncope, vasovagal syncope, carotid sinus hypersensitivity
	Decreased CBF due to increased vascular resistance	Hypertensive crisis, hyperventilation syndrome (respiratory alkalosis)
	Decreased CBF due to numerous small vessel occlusions	Disseminated intravascular coagulopathy, systemic lupus erythematosus, cerebral malaria
Deprivation of substrate	Deficiency of glucose, the brain's only substrate, resulting in impaired cerebral metabolism and synthesis of high energy phosphate compounds such as adenosine triphosphate (ATP)	Hypoglycemia, insulin reaction
Deficiency of cofactor	Deficiency of essential components for the enzymatic functions in the degradation of glucose	Wernicke's/Korsakoff's encephalopathy, pellagra, pyridoxine deficiency, vitamin B_{12} deficiency
Endogenous intoxicants Ammonia	Toxic nitrogenous products from the bowel such as ammonia gain access to systemic circulation, causing aerobic glycosis in brain	Hepatic insufficiency, hepatic cirrhosis
Urea	Retention of urea and other nitrogenous waste products gives cerebral depression	Renal insufficiency, uremia

(continued)

TABLE 10-1.　Continued

Abnormal Initiating Mechanism	Pathophysiology	Clinical State
CO_2	Hypoventilation from damage to the lungs or from effect of drugs results in CO_2 retention, which depresses cerebral metabolism	Respiratory acidosis, hypercapnea, CO_2 narcosis
Porphyrins	Disordered porphyrin metabolism with excessive accumulation of porphyrin, a heme biosynthesis precursor	Porphyria, acute intermittent
Exogenous intoxicants		
Sedative drugs: barbiturates, opiates, tranquilizers, ethanol	Cortical and brainstem depression due to interruption of synaptic transmission and interference with enzymatic processes of cerebral metabolism	Drug overdose, drug withdrawal, ethanol intoxication, dilirium tremens
Acid poisons: paraldehyde, methyl alcohol, ammonium chloride	Acidity of substance or acid breakdown products depresses cerebral metabolism	Metabolic acidosis
Enzyme inhibitors: heavy metals, cyanide, salicylates	Poisons inhibit enzymatic activities essential for metabolic process	Lead poisoning, cyanide poisoning, salicylate poisoning
Endocrine abnormalities		
Adrenal deficiency	Deficiency of cortisone results in lowering of free amino acid content in brain and impaired cerebral metabolism	Addisonian crisis
Thyroid deficiency	Thyroid hormone is necessary for normal oxidative metabolism, so there is decreased cerebral oxygen uptake	Myxedema crisis
Thyroid excess	Excess thyroid increases metabolic rate, increasing cardiac work and may precipitate cardiac failure and anoxia	Thyrotoxic crisis or thyroid storm
Pancreas deficiency	Lack of insulin results in accumulation of ketones in blood and inhibition of enzymatic activities which causes cerebral dysfunction	Diabetic ketoacidosis
	Hyperosmolar state from high blood glucose results in severe fluid volume deficit, with cerebral dehydration as water moves from cells to intravascular compartment	Hyperosmolar hyperglycemic nonketonic state
Pituitary deficiency	Mechanism for altered cerebral function is unknown, but possibly related to accompanying adrenocortical deficiency and hypoglycemia	Hypopituitary coma
Fluid and electrolyte abnormalities		
Water and sodium	Volume of extracellular water relative to salt is increased, and lowered sodium concentration results in increased neuronal excitability	Water intoxication, hyponatremia, fluid volume excess

(continued)

TABLE 10-1.   Continued

Abnormal Initiating Mechanism	Pathophysiology	Clinical State
	Inadequate fluid intake or excessive losses result in a decrease in the volume of extracellular water relative to salt, resulting in brain cell dehydration	Hypernatremia Fluid volume deficit
Calcium deficiency	Inadequate levels of calcium result in neuromuscular excitability and decreased cardiac muscle activity, with lowered cardiac output	Hypocalcemia, hypoparathyroidism
Calcium excess	High levels of calcium interfere with cerebral metabolic processes	Hypercalcemia, hyperparathyroidism
Magnesium deficiency	Without magnesium, have loss of an important mediator of neural transmission in the CNS	Hypomagnesemia
Magnesium excess	Excess magnesium reduces neuromuscular irritability and causes CNS depression	Hypermagnesemia
Bicarbonate excess	With excess bicarbonate, the amount of ionized calcium is reduced, with neuromuscular irritability and decreased cardiac output	Metabolic alkalosis
Temperature regulation impairment	Body temperatures less than 32 C are associated with slowing of all body functions, inadequate cardiac output, hypoglycemia, hypoxemia, etc., with deficient cerebral metabolism	Hypothermia
	Increase in metabolic rate with elevated temperatures and loss of heat dissipating mechanisms causes relative hypoxia, protein denaturation, and altered cell membrane and capillary permeability	Heat stroke
Infectious disorders	CNS is damaged by production of toxins and/or inhibition of enzymatic processes	Meningitis, encephalitis, sepsis
III. Psychologic maladjustment		
A. Personality disorders	Disordered process of thinking and distortion of perceptions in a manner not consistent with reality or logic	Anxiety reaction, reactive depression
B. Conversion symptom	Physiologic manifestation of frustrations and psychologic conflicts rather than a mental disturbance	Hysterical trance, amnesia, syncope, narcolepsy, somnambulism
C. Functional psychoses	Severe inability to control thoughts and misinterpretation of experiences	Manic state, endogenous depression, catatonic schizophrenia
IV. Abnormal sensory states	Reduction in the amount, intensity, or variety of the sensory input, with resultant decrease in ability to accurately interpret the environment	Sensory deprivation
	Misinterpretation of stimuli of normal intensity due to fatigue	Sleep deprivation

(continued)

tibular response is preserved until the very later stages. Electroencephalogram (EEG) shows focal or unilateral slowing of activity.

Early manifestations of brainstem lesions (frequently referred to as subtentorial lesions) are cranial nerve dysfunction, slight alterations in alertness, and localized asymmetrical signs of focal brainstem dysfunction as occipital headache, nystagmus, diplopia, nausea, vomiting, and ataxia. In contrast to supratentorial lesions, abnormalities of the pupillary light reflex and dysconjugate eye movements toward the irrigated ear with oculovestibular testing (caloric stimulation) are usually present early. Stupor and coma are later developments.

Interference with Cerebral Metabolism

Cerebral metabolism can be interfered with by a disorder within the brain or elsewhere in the body. The cognitive defect is indicative of diffuse cerebral cortex depression. The brain stem is also frequently involved, with signs of alteration in alertness. The distribution is usually symmetrical, showing selective involvement of certain functions in both hemispheres, and there is rarely any sensory impairment. Thus, both the pupillary light reflexes and the oculovestibular response are preserved, and the EEG is symmetrical but slow. In a few instances it may be difficult to differentiate primary metabolic disorders that are due to a disorder within the brain with disorders that are secondary to systemic (or exogenous) disorders. Differentiating signs include the nature of the onset and the type of impairment. Systemic or exogenous metabolic disorders have an acute or subacute onset while intrinsic metabolic brain disorders have a gradual onset. Both have cognitive impairment, but intrinsic brain disorders are less apt to be accompanied by alteration in alertness and rarely progress to stupor and coma. Disorientation to place is frequently a characteristic of intrinsic brain disorders while systemic disorders are characterized more by disorientation to time. Thus, the main sign of intrinsic disorders of the cerebral hemispheres is gradual impairment of cognitive function, referred to as dementia. The dementia is usually progressive and irreversible. Chronic brain syndrome is an overall term frequently used to describe a number of disorders producing dementia. In contrast, systemic disorders are often reversible and, in addition to cognitive impairment, have signs of altered alertness and affect, and may be accompanied by delirium.

Psychologic Maladjustment

Psychological maladjustment may be responsible for an impairment in cognitive functioning. The disorder can be in the nature of a personality disorder, conversion symptoms, or a functional psychosis.

A personality disorder is a noticeable deviation from the normal range for a specific trait with increased potential for neurotic responses such as anxiety, depression, or suspiciousness. Intense emotions have a disorganizing effect on cognition. Persons with personality disorders frequently have a disorder of thinking that results in their misinterpretation of certain types of experiences in an idiosyncratic way that is not consistent with reality and logic. They may edit their perceptions, make arbitrary inferences, exaggerate external problems, and selectively accommodate their perceptions to concepts of themselves. There is often a reciprocal interaction between the distorted thoughts and aroused feelings, with one reinforcing the other. Thus, the disordered process of thinking and distortion of perception may result in reactive depression in the patient who perceives a stimulus as a loss. Likewise an euphoric manic state may be exhibited in response to a stimulus perceived as gain; an anxiety neurosis (or anxiety reaction) may be the response of a stimulus perceived as danger; and a paranoid state may be a response to a stimulus perceived as an affront or unjust treatment.

Conversion symptoms are the result of an intrapsychic process whereby frustration and psychologic conflicts (such as arise when a person has an idea, wish, or fantasy that is unacceptable) are manifested by a physical rather than a mental disturbance. The syndrome is also referred to as a conversion reaction or hysteria. A hysterical personality is frequently described in the literature as possessing the characteristics of attention-seeking, egocentricity, and emotional instability, although hysteria can occur in other types of people. A period of discouragement and depression frequently precedes the appearance of conversion symptoms, and the physical illness seems to be a socially acceptable escape from reality. Manifestations of conversion reactions in the cognitive and awareness field can include the memory disorders of amnesia and fugue, a momentary disorder of consciousness termed syncope (which may last long enough to be classified as stupor or coma), convulsions, and sleeping disorders such as narcolepsy and somnambulism.

Features that assist in the differentiation of conversion symptoms from physical illness in addition to the personality of the patient and the circumstances surrounding their development are their incompatibility with known disorders. The disorientation with psychogenic amnesia includes person in addition to time and place, whereas, with medical illness, disorientation to person is a very late development. Coma in a conversion reaction can usually be differentiated by flaccidity of the extremities, resistance to passive eye opening, and normal response to oculovestibular testing (i.e., nystagmus with the slow component toward the irrigated ear and the fast component toward the opposite ear). A conversion convulsion rarely follows the grand mal seizure stereotype. Tongue biting and incontinence are infrequent, there is no loss of corneal, pupillary, and deep reflexes, and motor activity does not follow the usual tonic and then clonic pattern. Motor activity may include flailing of the arms, rolling from side to side, bizarre posturing, and tearing at the clothes. Consciousness is not usually completely lost, and the patient can report some details of the seizure. Seizures rarely occur when the person is alone, and postictal confusion is unusual. The EEG is normal with both conversion coma and convulsion.

Functional psychoses are the last type of psychologic maladjustment to be discussed. Both schizophrenia and manic depressive psychosis may result in impaired cognition. Inability to control thoughts in schizophrenia and assignment of erroneous value on self and misinterpretation of experiences in manic or depressed states is similar to the impaired cognition with personality disorders. They can usually be differentiated from physical illness by the preservation of recent memory orientation and mental ability. When hallucinations occur, they are usually auditory rather than visual as with metabolic brain disorders. Physical states that are extremely difficult to differentiate from schizophrenia are amphetamine intoxication, alcoholic withdrawal, and psychomotor epilepsy. Catatonic stupor accompanying schizophrenia is difficult to differentiate from physical disorders since EEG, autonomic, and endocrine function may all be abnormal.

ASSESSMENT

History

The usual practice of history taking, physical examination, and diagnostic testing may not be appropriate for the patient with impaired cognition or arousal. Immediate measures to insure adequate respiration and circulation and prevent permanent brain damage are sometimes indicated. After life-threatening problems have been alleviated, information should be sought about the past medical history, speed of onset of disorder, and symptoms or events that preceded it. If the patient is unable to give reliable information, the family or significant others will need to be consulted. Of special significance are head trauma, convulsive seizure, recent changes in mood or behavior, access to drugs, alcoholic intake, presence of poisons or toxins in environment, and complaints of headache. After this information has been obtained, assessment is directed toward determination of the extent of the dysfunction and the nature of the underlying cause. The following ordering of assessment parameters is frequently used. History items or patient appearance, however, may indicate a different order, with physical examination of the scalp or certain laboratory tests given first priority. Although the emphasis in this chapter is on cognitive impairment, it does not seem feasible or appropriate to attempt to confine assessment parameters to a certain level on a continuum, since with any patient whose state is deteriorating, assessment continues even though there is no longer any cognitive functioning. The focus of assessment then shifts to identification of any response to environmental stimuli.

Level of Functioning

There is general agreement on the use of terms such as lethargy, stupor, etc., to describe the various levels of arousal or awareness. Terminology for levels of cognitive functioning, however, is still in the developmental phase. In some of the literature, cognition includes awareness as well as the more commonly acknowledged components of perception, learning, thinking, understanding, and remembering. It is always preferable to describe a behavior completely instead of labeling it with a term that may be interpreted differently by someone else. Since patients rarely display all the characteristics of a disorder and the extent of any deficit can vary, actual description provides greater accuracy in detection of improvement or deterioration in the state. The following levels of functioning have been useful to the authors because they provide a more precise differentiation of early changes than the frequently used levels of consciousness. They are arranged in order of decreasing levels of function. In any individual patient, however, the observable signs and symptoms may not follow this sequence. The progression of the deficit depends on the underlying pathophysiology and the patient's individual response to his altered state.

Slight impairment of cognitive function. This is recognized by dulling of mental ability and changes in pattern of attentiveness. The level of functioning can differ so little from the patient's usual functioning that it can be overlooked. Sometimes the observable behavior is increased irritability or negativism, which may be the patient's response to his inability to organize his thoughts or think clearly.

The earliest signs of deterioration in mental ability are usually manifested by reduced grasp of the situation and decreased capacity for problem solving. Orientation, ability to follow simple commands, and participation in casual conversation is unchanged. There are a number of tests of cognitive function, both verbal and written. Tests of recent memory, attention, construction capacity, and abstract reasoning are most helpful since they are usually affected early and are not dependent on education. Recent memory is frequently tested by setting three objects to be remembered for 5, 10, and 30 minutes. Mathematical tasks that require carrying over such as serial subtraction of 7 from 100 or counting by three provide information about attention span. Construction capacity can be tested by asking the patient to draw a simple object like a clock or to solve a task such as the recognition of errors in pictures or assembly of parts of puzzles. Impaired abstract reasoning may be demonstrated by an inability to determine whether two words are alike or different. Words used for testing are common words like auto and car, stop and go, apple and orange, boast and brag. Interpretation of test performance must take into account preillness ability.

Changes in patterns of attentiveness are sometimes referred to as disorders of receptivity or alterations in vigilance. This is generally considered to be a type of cognitive functioning, with the emphasis placed on the awareness and response to stimuli rather than the ability to perform mental functions. The terms distractability, hypovigilance, and hypervigilance have been used for the different behavior patterns of attentiveness. Distractability is described as difficulty in directing the train of thought, with thought wandering aimlessly under the influence of chance stimuli. Hypovigilance is a decrease in attention to the environment with delayed and/or incomplete verbal response to questions and delayed and/or incomplete motor response to commands. Increased stimulation may be required to evoke a response. This is sometimes described as lethargy, indifference, somnolence, or withdrawal. Hypervigilance is an increase in the susceptibility to all environmental stimuli with frequent overreaction to stimuli and increased purposeless psychomotor activity.

Moderate to severe impairment of cognitive function.   This is characterized by more obvious deficits in mental functioning and marked reduction in awareness. There is frequently disorientation to time, place, and person, difficulty in following all but the most simple commands, loss of remote as well as recent memory, and misinterpretation of stimuli. Sometimes disorientation and misinterpretation of stimuli can result in delirium and hallucinations. Delirium may be accompanied by hyperactivity and agitation, and can alternate with lucid periods in which drowsiness is present. Obtundation is sometimes used to describe the loss of mental functioning accompanied by extreme drowsiness; the patient can be awakened, but response is slow.

Stupor.   Stupor is a state of extremely difficult arousal in which it is impossible to determine the mental state. The patient can be aroused only by vigorous and repeated stimulation. The patient may open his eyes and seem to look at persons or objects and will frequently respond to a bright light by closing his eyes. Simple questions may receive a one or two word response or result in increased motor activity and behavior to avoid further stimulation. Tendon and plantar reflexes are usually normal.

Semicoma.   Semicoma is responsiveness only to noxious stimuli such as pricking or pinching the skin, distension of the bladder, etc. The response may be semiappropriate movement or moaning. Plantar reflexes may be either flexor (normal) or extensor (referred to as a positive Babinski's sign).

Coma.   Coma is the absence of any meaningful response to external stimulus or inner need. The unresponsiveness remains for a period of time in contrast to syncope, which is a brief loss of consciousness. In its deepest stages, corneal, pupillary, pharyngeal (gag), tendon, and plantar reflexes are all absent. Noxious stimulation may result in decorticate or decerebrate posturing. Deep coma is a self-limiting state. Patients who survive usually begin to waken in 2 to 4 weeks, but they may not recover mental ability.

Persistent vegetative state.   This is a term used to describe the patient who has awakened from a coma but who demonstrates no signs of conscious intelligence.

Associated Neurologic Signs

Although all cranial nerve function and body systems under neural control may be assessed, the most valuable information is gained from the size and reactivity of the pupils, the eye movements and responses, changes in the vital signs, and the skeletal muscle motor responses. These are frequently referred to as neurologic checks or checks for increased intracranial pressure (ICP). Although these are important, their limitations need to be recognized. It has already been mentioned that these signs do not reflect early increases in ICP. Additionally, primary damage to the brainstem can occur with very little increase in ICP, while some patients with high ICP appear to have no abnormality in neurologic functioning. Cerebral edema following anoxia, ischemia, or trauma is primarily intracellular and may not increase ICP. The greatest value of the neurologic signs are in ongoing assessment to detect deterioration in the state of the patient.

Pupillary signs include size, equality, and reaction to light. The pupils should be examined first for size and equality. Lighting should be the same for subsequent examinations to avoid variations. Size may be expressed in millimeters or as normal, dilated, or constricted. Both morphine and structural brain damage can cause constriction. Reactivity is best examined in a dimly lighted room. Pupils are observed separately to see how they constrict to light from the side. In some instances the consensual reflex (reaction occurring in the opposite eye) is also tested. Response is usually described as brisk, moderate, sluggish, or fixed. The consensual reflex is usually slightly less than the direct reflex. As previously mentioned, the absence of pupillary light reflexes is usually indicative of structural brain disorder. Obviously, the presence of an eye prothesis or blindness must be differentiated from organic nonreaction.

Eye movement alteration is usually described as medial or lateral deviation of one or both eyes, convergence, divergence, dysconjugate gaze (independent eye movement), or nystagmus (rhythmical, involuntary movement, with both eyes moving conjugately or simultaneously). Oculocephalic and oculovestibular reflexes may be assessed. The oculocephalic reflex, commonly called the doll's eye maneuver, is tested by rotating the head horizontally and then vertically while holding the eyes open. In an unconscious patient with no damage to the neural pathways the eyes move in the opposite direction from that to which the head is turned like the eyes of a doll. In psychogenic unresponsiveness, the eyes either do not move or move inconsistently. In brain-stem lesions and severe brain pathology, the pupils are fixed in the midline and do not rotate with movement of the head. Oculovestibular testing, commonly called calorie stimulation, is usually performed by the physician. Irrigation of each ear with cold water will normally cause nystagmus away from the stimulated side. With lesions or severe depression of brainstem activity, the response is continuous lateral or vertical deviation without nystagmus. When nystagmus and oculomotor paralysis (opthalmoplegia) occur in a patient with cognitive impairment, the possibility of thiamine deficiency encephalopathy (Wernicke's disease) should be immediately considered; if thiamine is not received, cardiovascular collapse and death can follow.

Vital sign changes in the past have been termed compensatory mechanisms to increase perfusion pressure to the brain when ICP was elevated. Changes usually include changes in the respiratory pattern, slowing of pulse, and increase in systolic pressure (with unchanging diastolic pressure) resulting in an increase in pulse pressure. Slow pulse, however, occurs with heart block and use of some drugs. Hypertension also occurs in a number of patients, but the diastolic pressure is frequently also elevated, so pulse pressure is not increased. When a low pulse rate, periodic breathing, and systolic blood pressure elevation are all present, increased ICP is highly probable, but changes do not usually occur until ICP exceeds 50 mm Hg. Thus, they are probably more a result of the increased ICP than a compensatory mechanism for it.

Respiratory patterns are useful in localizing the area of the brain involved. This also is subject to limitations, since metabolic and neurogenic influences on respiration can overlap. Changes that can be observed in respiratory patterns beginning with metabolic or neurogenic influences on the forebrain and progressing down to the medulla are posthyperventilation apnea, Cheyne–Stokes breathing, central neurogenic hyperventilation, apneusis, cluster breathing, ataxic breathing, and apnea. Central neurogenic hyperventilation must be differentiated from the Kussmaul's respiration of diabetic ketoacidosis or uremic acidosis. Slow breathing may also be due to morphine administration, barbiturate intoxication, or myxedema crisis. Yawning is another respiratory abnormality, but its meaning is difficult to interpret. Persons with severe central nervous system dysfunction usually die from respiratory arrest, so recognition of need for ventilatory assistance may be crucial. When respirations are normal and the patient is cooperative, assessment of extent of hyperventilation apnea may allow differentiation of psychologic maladjustment from metabolic or neurologic dysfunction. The patient is instructed to take five deep breaths. Normally, the period of apnea following the deep breaths is less than 10 seconds. Those with brain damage may have a period of apnea lasting 12 to 30 seconds or more.

An excessively high fever (41–44 C) associated with dry skin suggests heat stroke. Moderate to high elevation of temperature can indicate pressure on the thermoregulation center in the hypothalamus, but it can also be due to infection, ingestion of anticholinergic, salicylate, or phenothiazine drugs, or other causes. It must be remembered that hyperthermia increases the metabolic demands for oxygen. Thus elevations need to be assessed to guide treatment.

Skeletal muscle motor response provides information about the geographic distribution of the neurologic dysfunction. The ability to move all four extremities as well as the strength of each extremity is tested. In the responsive patient, movement and strength is checked by simple commands such as "squeeze my fingers," "push your foot against my hand," etc. Both sides should be tested and compared to determine weakness or paralysis of one side of the body. With paralysis of one side (hemiplegia), the paralyzed limb when lifted from the bed falls faster than the normal limb and the cheek puffs out in expiration on the paralyzed side.

Involuntary movements such as tremor, asterixis, and multifocal myoclonus are manifestations of metabolic brain disorders but are rarely present bilaterally with structural brain lesions. Tremor, however, can be present with psychologic maladaption states. Tremor is coarse, irregular, has a frequency of 8 to 10 per second, and usually disappears at rest. Asterixis is a sudden palmar flapping movement of the hands at the wrists that persists with lethargy but usually disappears with stupor or coma. It can be best elicited by asking the patient to extend his hands, spread the fingers, and dorsiflex the wrist.

Multifocal myoclonus is characterized by a sudden, nonrhythmic, gross twitching that involves parts of muscles or groups of muscles. It frequently affects the facial muscles but can affect other muscles as well. It rarely appears in a patient who is not stuporous or comatose. Other movements such as restlessness, grasping, picking movements of one or all extremities, or complex avoidance movements can occur with either structural or metabolic disorders. The presence of exaggerated prehensile sucking, reflex tonic grasping of the hand or foot, and skeletal muscle paratonia are observations that have been more recently recognized as useful evaluation parameters. Skeletal muscle paratonia, or motor negativism, is tested by passive movement of the extremities, head, or trunk. There is little resistance with very slow movement, but with more rapid movement resistance increases up to "stickiness" or intense rigidity.

In patients unresponsive to verbal stimulation, motor function can be estimated by observing the response to noxious stimuli applied to various body areas. Appropriate responses include ipsilateral grimace with supraorbital pressure, closure of the eyelid wth corneal stroking, gagging with glossopharyngeal stimulation, and plantar flexion with stroking of the outer edge of the sole of the foot. Absence of normal response or inappropriate responses are signs that need to be observed and recorded, although their interpretation is sometimes extremely complex. With brain injury, the major inappropriate motor responses with noxious stimulation are decorticate rigidity and decerebrate rigidity. Decorticate rigidity is characterized by flexion of the arm, wrist, and fingers, with adduction in the upper extremity and extension, internal rotation, and plantar flexion in the lower extremity. Decerebrate rigidity is manifested by opisthotonus, clenched teeth, arms stiffly extended, adducted, and hyperpronated, and the legs stiffly extended with the feet plantar flexed. In some patients, only fragments of the responses are elicited or the differences are blurred, with a combination of responses resulting. For example, decerebrate changes in the arms can be combined with either flaccidity or weak flexor responses in the lower extremity.

Physical Examination

The order of the examination is frequently determined by the history, other symptoms reported, manifestation of cognitive impairment, etc.

• *Scalp and skull examination* may reveal contusions, lacerations, gunshot wounds, or skull fracture. Edema frequently overlies a fracture line; there may be loss of bloody spinal fluid from the nose or ear; and blood pigment stains may be visible behind the ear (Battle's sign) or around the orbit of the eye.

• *Skin inspection* may yield evidence of trauma or needle puncture marks indicative of use of drugs or insulin. Cyanosis of the lips and nail beds points to inadequate oxygenation. Other color changes of notable value are the cherry-red coloration of carbon monoxide poisoning, the icterus of hepatic insufficiency, the hyperemic face and conjunctiva that accompanies intake of alcohol. The presence of a rash may indicate a meningeal infection or endocarditis. Hemorrhagic blisters will have formed over pressure points if the patient has been motionless for a period of time. Crops of petechial hemorrhages over the chest and flanks following skeletal injury may indicate fat embolism.

● *Breath odor* can indicate ketoacidosis if acetone present (odor resembles spoiled fruit), uremia if odor resembles urine, hepatic insufficiency if odor is musty, and acute alcoholism if alcohol, or aldehydes, are present.

● *Neck flexion resistance* when unaccompanied by resistance to extension or turning can indicate meningeal irritation or impending herniation into the tentorial notch.

● *Fundoscopic examination* of the retinal vessels and disks of the eyes may reveal venous congestion, edema, and elevation of the disk margins characteristic of papilledema that occurs with increased ICP and with long-standing arterial hypertension as well. Other abnormalities and visual field losses are frequently indicative of specific disorders such as arteriosclerosis, malignant hypertension, diabetes, subarachnoid hemorrhage, space-occupying brain lesion, and so forth.

● *Oral cavity examination* may reveal tongue lacerations from biting during a convulsive seizure or ulceration and/or discoloration from ingestion of poison.

● *Auscultation of the bifurcation of the carotid arteries* may reveal a systolic bruit indicating carotid insufficiency which can cause transient ischemic attacks (TIAs).

● *Chest examination* may reveal the consolidation of pneumonia, the wheezes and obstructive sounds suggesting CO_2 retention with narcosis, or the presence of other states resulting in respiratory acidosis and/or hypoxemia.

● *Abdominal examination* may reveal an enlarged liver and ascites characteristic of hepatic insufficiency, masses that can be a source of brain metastasis, or distension due to a ruptured viscus with impending shock. The occurrence of vomiting with no physical abnormality of the abdomen may indicate poison intake. Projectile vomiting without preceding nausea may indicate a central neurological lesion. Hiccoughs may also be an indication of neurologic lesion.

Monitoring

The physiologic parameters of electroencephalogram (EEG), intracranial pressure (ICP), and cardiac output are monitored. The EEG in metabolic brain disorders is generally slow but symmetrical. In structural brain disorders, signs are unilateral with the early EEG showing signs of disorganization with random slow waves of varying voltages. As the patient's condition deteriorates, the EEG usually changes to slow low voltage waves or even suppression of all organized electrical activity. In psychologic maladaptive states, the EEG is normal or may show an increase in frequency of the alpha waves with a decrease in voltage. In disordered states, slow EEG activity usually correlates with reduction in cerebral blood flow.

Intracranial pressure can be continually measured by a pressure transducer connected to a catheter inserted into a cerebral ventricle. Normal pressures are 0–15 mm Hg; pressures between 15–40 mm Hg are considered elevated; while those in excess of 40 mm Hg are in the danger zone for most patients, especially when they develop rapidly. Any nurse involved with this monitoring needs to be well versed in the factors that control ICP and in the recognition of the different patterns of ventricular fluid pressure. Intracranial pressure is controlled by the volume and pressure in the cerebral arteries, the venous outflow, the rate of formation and reabsorption of cerebrospinal fluid, and the osmotic gradients between cerebrospinal fluid, the brain, and the plasma. With a small brain mass or lesion, cerebrospinal fluid is expressed from the intracranial space to accommodate the expansion with no change in ICP. This mechanism, however, is limited, so with an increase in the size of the mass, the ICP rises. In monitoring ICP, importance is accorded not only to the top pressure reading, but also to the patterns of the pressure waves. The recognition of plateau waves, which are believed to be related to transient cerebral hypoxia with resultant permanent damage to the brain, is of special importance.

Cardiac output can be monitored by thermal dilution techniques or estimated from the pulmonary artery wedge pressure. Adequate cardiac output is required for adequate cerebral perfusion. Central mean arterial pressure monitoring is useful in conjunction with the intracranial pressure, since the pressure for cerebral perfusion is roughly equivalent to the mean arterial pressure minus the intracranial pressure.

Laboratory Procedures

Almost all tests can be included since the causes of cognitive impairment are so numerous. Certain tests, however, are of special importance because of their delineation of life-threatening metabolic defects that require prompt treatment. The significance of some of the tests will be briefly discussed.

- *Serum glucose* for detection of hypoglycemia, diabetic ketoacidosis, and hyperglycemic, hyperosmolar, nonketonic state. Hypoglycemia when not promptly corrected can cause prolonged and irreversible coma and/or death. It can develop with patients receiving insulin, in alcoholics with chronic liver disease, with functional psychoses of the manic type, in Addisonian crisis, and in other states with no identifiable cause. Some physicians, after drawing the blood for blood sugar determination, give intravenous glucose to patients suspected of having hypoglycemia to prevent further cerebral damage. Hyperglycemia can occur with a cerebral lesion as well as with a defect in carbohydrate metabolism.

• *Blood gases* and arterial pH determination for determination of acid-base abnormalities and hypoxemia. Acidosis or alkalosis due to both metabolic or respiratory causes can cause cognitive impairment. Severe acid-base abnormalities are incompatible with life. Hypoxemia can exist without respiratory acidosis. Cerebral hypoxia may also occur with normal blood oxygenation when cerebral blood flow is reduced. Additionally, significant deviations in oxygen consumption occur with brain dysfunction.

• *Electrolyte level* abnormality can cause impaired cognition. The ionic concentration of sodium probably causes the greatest deficit, but abnormally low levels of calcium and magnesium can also result in impairment. Known systemic disorders may provide clues to the cause of the abnormality. Examples are the low serum sodium of Addison's disease and myxedema, the low serum calcium of hypoparathyroidism, high calcium with hyperparathyroid states and multiple myeloma, and the low serum magnesium in chronic alcoholism and toxemia of pregnancy.

• *Blood urea nitrogen* (BUN) provides information about renal function, and, to a lesser extent, the fluid volume state.

• *Blood count and differential* may be helpful in identification of hypoxemia due to anemia and presence of sepsis.

• *Drug levels* may assist in identification of an overdose or precipitation of a neurologic disturbance by the administration of a neurotropic drug or a drug that blocks the normal myoneural action and thus potentiates the effect of muscle relaxants.

• *Analysis of contents* obtained by gastric lavage will sometimes identify the drug or poison ingested.

• *Urinary findings* of low specific gravity and high sugar in the urine (glycosuria) can occur with diabetes mellitus or a massive cerebral lesion. Acetone in the urine is indicative of diabetic ketoacidosis or ketoacidosis from severe malnutrition. The presence of porphyrins is indicative of porphyria.

Special Diagnostic Studies

These may include lumbar puncture, cerebral angiography, echoencephalography, computerized axial tomography (CAT) scan, brain isotope scan, and roentgenograms of the skull and cervical spine. These studies are the responsibility of the physician and will not be discussed except for lumbar puncture. The use of lumbar puncture in assessment is not without its drawbacks. Removal of cerebrospinal fluid (CSF) may result in acute decompensation due to structural shifts in the intracranial compartment. Its use is generally reserved for identification of a suspected meningitis, and when the initial pressure is high, fluid is slowly withdrawn over a period of 15 to 20 minutes. CSF is usually tested for Wasserman reaction, white cell count, protein, and sugar. Bacterial culture and microscopic examination of gram stain of centrifuged fluid helps to identify the presence of meningitis, especially when accompanied by a high white cell count and low sugar. In some centers, CSF is tested for pH, Pco_2, HCO_3^-, lactate, and pyruvate. The lactate-pyruvate ratio is considered to be an extremely sensitive indicator of hypoxic brain damage.

Psychologic Adaptive Structure Assessment

This assessment may determine the relationship between psychologic maladaptation and impaired cognition. Complete assessment is, of course, an extremely lengthy and difficult process. A psychiatric consultation for specific diagnosis and direction of intervention is usually requested when history, physical examination, and diagnostic tests indicate the need for consultation. The major components of the assessment process include precise determination of the nature of the disorder, identification of predisposing factors, and delineation of the precipitating factor or factors.

• *The nature of the disorder* is determined after data on the presenting signs and symptoms have been organized into a clinical profile. This profile is compared with that of various psychologic disorders to find a match. Data that exclude other conditions which may produce similar symptoms are also obtained to strengthen the accuracy of the diagnosis. From this point, assessment of the functional psychoses may proceed in a different manner from the personality disorders and conversion symptoms, since the functional psychoses are generally believed to be due to deranged neural metabolism in a genetically predisposed person. Environmental disturbances are believed to influence the onset of symptoms in functional psychoses but the extent of their role is not believed to be as direct or as essential as it is with personality disorders and conversion symptoms.

• *Predisposing factors* are those attributes within an individual's psychologic and physiologic state that make him vulnerable to emotional disturbances. The psychologic factors are frequently found within the personality of the individual. Personality refers to the temperament, attitudes, and predictable responses that characterize the way the individual meets the various life situations. It embodies the influences of genetic constitution, intelligence, and experience. Personality factors frequently found include low self-esteem, tendency to amplify, limited coping capacity (including mental retardation), attention seeking, and tendency to misinterpret perceptual stimuli. The major physiologic factor is the individual's general health status, since physical illness affects the central nervous system, reducing the person's capacity to cope with untoward circumstances. Chronic illness seems to have an especially devastating effect on the individual's defenses. There are also certain physiologic states that are more commonly associated with psychologic disorders, particularly those of the depressive type. Disorders that have a high correlation with depression include hepatitis, influenza, Cushing's or Addison's disease, and stroke.

- *Precipitating factors* are untoward circumstances, events, or experiences that can disrupt the emotional equilibrium. Some examples are conflicts that require a decision (particularly when the outcome can affect social or economic success), distressing life experiences or severe fright, and troubled life circumstances such as a death or loss of a loved one or discouragement. Frightening experiences can cause a phobic anxiety syndrome that is self-perpetuating even after the original cause for fright has been dissipated. Troubled life circumstances usually cause a disturbance in stability, security, effectiveness, or worth that alters the self-concept and leaves the individual vulnerable to psychologic distress. There are several scales that have been developed to measure the amount of stress to which an individual has been subjected, or the social readjustment an individual has been required to make. They have been found useful in quantifying the precipitating factors, although signs of psychologic maladjustment do not consistently appear with scores above a certain level.

Sensory Stimuli Assessment

This may help to identify cognitive impairment due to altered sensory environmental input or sensory limitation of the individual (i.e., loss of vision, hearing, or kinesthetic sensation) that prevents him from receiving the stimuli. Examples of forms of sensory alteration are sensory deprivation (reduction in the amount and intensity of the sensory input), perceptual disturbances (distortion of sensory input), perceptual monotony (lack of variety of stimuli), sensory overload (increase in amount and intensity of the stimuli), social isolation (decreased social interaction), and immobilization (decrease in kinesthetic stimulation). The presence and extent of most of these altered states can usually be determined by assessment of the patient's environment, any sensory deficits, and observation of his reaction. Validation with the patient will usually help to strengthen the assessment process. Patients with perceptual distortion may attempt to conceal and/or be hesitant to discuss their experiences. If the patient's behavior indicates he may be perceiving something inappropriate or actively hallucinating, the use of such terms as dream or nightmare is more likely to elicit a response than the term, "hallucination."

INTERVENTION

The overall goal of intervention is to maintain adequate brain perfusion while identifying and treating the responsible underlying cause. Because hypoxia, hypoglycemia, and thiamin deficiency can cause death, if any of these are suspected, the deficit is frequently replaced immediately without waiting for the completion of the entire assessment process. In addition to these three acute states, there are numerous other disorders with an almost infinite list of possible interventions. This book will only attempt to cover the major goals and activities. Again, the order of activities would depend on the state of the patient, but attention is generally directed to maintenance of basic physiologic mechanisms and safety needs first.

Maintenance of Adequate Oxygenation

Oxygen, which is vital for normal cerebral function, is not stored by the brain, so a constant source must be provided. Po_2 is usually maintained above 75 torr. Measures to improve oxygenation include: establishment of a patent airway, administration of oxygen, careful removal of secretions, and transfusions for significant anemia.

• *A patent airway* can frequently be achieved by turning the patient on his side, with an oral airway used when required to keep the tongue from obstructing the airway due to the relaxation of the pharyngeal and glottic musculature in less responsive states. Extension of the neck will also help to prevent airway obstruction.

• *Oxygen* may be given by mask, but intubation with the use of a respirator is frequently indicated. Positive pressure maintained by respirators can decrease the cerebral venous return. Negative pressure modes on pressure-cycled respirators have frequently resulted in inadequate ventilation, so the treatment of choice is the use of intermittent mandatory ventilation (IMV) with a volume respirator. Because only a few respirations per minute are assisted, cerebral venous return is rarely compromised.

• *Removal of secretions* can increase airway patency, but the main objective is prevention of atelectasis and pneumonia. Use of the lateral or semiprone position and gentle suctioning are the usual methods employed. Adequate hyperinflation of the lungs should precede suctioning to prevent hypoxia during the suctioning procedure. Postural drainage is generally contraindicated because of the danger of increased ICP when the head is positioned lower than the rest of the body.

• *Transfusion* when hemoglobin concentrations are less than 8 g/100 ml is advisable to prevent hypoxia from lowered oxyhemoglobin carrying ability.

Maintenance of Adequate Cerebral Blood Flow

This goal overlaps to some extent with oxygenation, since oxygen transport depends on an adequate blood flow. In addition to anoxia, the accumulation of potentially toxic waste products and lactic acid is to be avoided. Of prime importance, however, is an adequate systemic arterial pressure to pump the blood through the arterial system and maintain adequate cerebral perfusion pressure. The perfusion pressure is the difference between intracranial pressure and mean systemic arterial pressure. Thus there is no one arterial pressure that will provide adequate cerebral blood flow, but a range of pressures depending on the intracranial pressure. Normally autoregulation (changes in the diameter of the resistance vessels) maintains cerebral blood flow at a constant level despite changes in perfusion pressure. When ICP increases above 33 mm Hg, however, this autoregulation is impaired, and cerebral blood flow varies more directly with arterial pressure. The potential danger of this situation can be readily seen, for example, in the patient with intracranial pressure of 70 mm Hg and mean arterial pressure of 80 mm Hg. The extremely low perfusion pressure (10 mm Hg) would result in brain cell hypoxia. The importance of adequate blood volume and cardiac output for maintenance of blood pressure has been mentioned in previous chapters. With the usual complexity present in bodily disorders, however, effective intervention is not clear cut. In patients with cerebral edema and increased ICP, increasing blood volume can cause increased cerebral edema. Vasopressors and vasodilators may be indicated to increase blood flow through ischemic areas or for disorders associated with vasospasm, but they can increase intracranial bleeding and also increase ICP in patients with deficient autoregulatory mechanisms. Thus, intervention depends on many complex factors and must be constantly evaluated for its effectiveness.

Prevention of Sustained, Increased Intracranial Pressure

Major activities are the elimination of the cause, when possible, and reduction or control of increased ICP.

Elimination of the cause can include restoration of normal brain volume by removal of a tumor or hematoma, reduction in extent of edema, reduction in cerebral blood volume by restoration of vascular tone, and decrease in volume of CSF by removal of intraventricular obstruction or increased absorption of spinal fluid from the intracranial space.

Control of ICP relies primarily on measures that remove CSF or reduce cerebral edema. Mannitol, an osmotic diuretic, is frequently given in doses of 1 g/kg initially, followed by a continuous intravenous drip that does not exceed 5 g/kg every 24 hours. Other agents to reduce edema include dexamethasone, urea, 10 percent glycerol, and low molecular weight dextran. Of these agents, dexamethesone is the only one in frequent use. Dosage is generally 10 mg intravenous push followed by 4 mg every 6 hours. Antacids are generally given concomitantly with steroid therapy to reduce the risk of associated gastrointestinal hemorrhage.

Hyperventilation on a volume respirator may be utilized to lower the Pco_2 to between 25 and 30 torr. The resultant cerebral vasoconstriction decreases the cerebral edema. Care must be taken to maintain Pco_2 above 25 torr to prevent cerebral ischemia from intense cerebral vasoconstriction.

Proper positioning is extremely important. Flexion of the neck can obstruct venous outflow and increase ICP. The head must also be kept in alignment with the body when the patient is turned to prevent compression that compromises carotid arterial flow and venous return. If the patient can cooperate, he should be encouraged to exhale while turning, since holding the breath increases intrathoracic pressure and further impedes venous return. For most patients, the head is kept elevated 30 degrees.

Constipation should be prevented by institution of a regular bowel program. Straining at stool and the Valsalva maneuver increase intracranial pressure as well as adversely affecting other pressure levels.

If the ICP rises to a dangerous level in spite of the preceding efforts at control, more aggressive therapy such as drainage of ventricular fluid is indicated. If a cannula is already in place for pressure monitoring, fluid may be withdrawn through it. Otherwise a twist drill or burr hole will need to be made and a catheter inserted. The catheter is usually left in place so that ventriculostomy fluid will drain into an external collection device. Any patient with continuous ventriculostomy drainage must have precautions taken to prevent changes in the height of the head or the level of the fluid in the collection system. All personnel and visitors must be aware of the potential dangers involved.

Control of Body Temperature

Extremes of temperature interfere with cerebral metabolism. Hyperthermia, with a temperature over 42 C is accompanied by coma. Efforts to lower the temperature have high priority because of the potential brain damage resulting from the elevated temperature as well as the anoxia from the increased oxygen required for cellular metabolism. (Remember that oxygen requirements increase 7 percent for each degree increase in temperature.) Many patients have moderately elevated temperatures because of damage to the thermal regulation center in the hypothalamus. Other disorders can cause hypothermia. Cognitive ability is reduced when the temperature is less than 32 C, with onset of coma below 26. Warming methods are usually used to maintain the temperature above 32 C, but moderate hypothermia (32–36 C) is sometimes desired. Moderate hypothermia may reduce ICP and cerebral need for oxygen. When hypothermia is being maintained, excessive shivering is controlled with chlorpromazine or diazepam, since shivering increases oxygen consumption. In some patients, bradycardia may develop with hypothermia. Atropine should not be given to increase the heart rate since the temperature may not return to normal after atropine injection.

Maintenance of Normal Blood Sugar

The danger of hypoglycemia has already been mentioned. Frequently, if insulin reaction or other cause for hypoglycemia is suspected, 25 g of glucose are given IV push after blood is withdrawn for electrolyte and chemical analysis. Evaluation of the patient's response and serum glucose is used as a guide to further treatment. Diabetic ketoacidosis and hyperglycemic hyperosmolar state can also cause cognitive impairment. The treatment of these disorders has been discussed in preceding chapters. Briefly, treatment requires insulin and fluid replacement. Fluid is almost as essential as insulin because of the severe dehydration resulting from the osmotic diuresis with glycosuria.

Replacement of any Deficient Cofactor

Although thiamine is the B vitamin most often responsible for decreased cognition, other B deficiencies (such as niacin, pyridoxine (B_6), and cyanocobalamin (B_{12}) can also require replacement.

Maintenance of Normal Fluid and Electrolyte Levels

Sodium, calcium, and magnesium are the electrolytes most likely to be associated with impaired cognition. Electrolyte deficiencies are usually remedied by addition of the electrolyte to the intravenous fluid. High concentrations of electrolytes are usually managed by withholding the electrolyte, but occasionally more aggressive methods are required. Diuretics may be used to decrease the levels of sodium, while administration of phosphate or mithramycin may be ordered to lower serum calcium.

Hypotonicity due to the syndrome of inappropriate secretion of antidiuretic hormone (SIADH) is a more difficult state than electrolyte abnormality to recognize and treat. SIADH is fairly frequently associated with intracranial lesions, and results in ADH being secreted in abundance without the normal stimulus of hypovolemia or hyperosmolality. As a result of the ADH secretion, abnormal quantities of water are retained in the intravascular compartment, diluting the electrolytes and resulting in a hypotonic state. This is especially dangerous for a patient with increased intracranial pressure, since fluid moves by osmosis from the compartment of the lesser concentration to the compartment of greater concentration, in this case into the brain cells, increasing cerebral edema. In addition to the addictive effect on the cerebral edema already present, the cause of the problem may not be recognized and the increased ICP may be blamed on the underlying pathology rather than to a fluid volume excess with hypotonicity. Treatment generally includes severe restriction of water intake and the use of sodium-retaining steroids. Hypertonic saline (3–5 percent) may be given in acute situations.

Frequently, hypertonicity can also occur with hypernatremia. Some of the reasons are excessive restriction of fluid intake, osmotic diuresis from administration of mannitol, and deficient vasopressin (ADH) release with pituitary lesions (diabetes insipidus). Treatment is administration of fluid, restriction of electrolytes, and (for patients with diabetes insipidus) medication with vasopressin or antidiuretic substance.

Treatment of Infection

Full doses of an antibiotic, to which the infecting organism is sensitive, are given intravenously. Treatment is usually continued for 10 days. Any focus of infection such as mastoiditis, paranasal sinusitis, infected shunt, or cranial osteomyelitis needs to be identified and drained. Prolongation of fever may be due to development of a subdural empyema or brain abscess.

Provision of Safety

Activities to safeguard the patient from undue harm include protection from falls or other bodily injury, prevention of aspiration, prevention of overdistension of the bladder, and prevention of, or competent care during, seizures. Aspiration must be guarded against when there is impaired ability to swallow or a disturbance in the gag reflex. Suctioning of the mouth and pharynx and maintenance of the patient on his side are basic. Use of nasogastric intubation with suction to prevent reflux of gastric contents may be necessary. If the patient is receiving nasogastric tube feedings, the volume of the feedings should be small (300 ml or less), the head of the bed should be elevated during and after administration, and the residual volume in the stomach should be ascertained before the next feeding is administered. If the residual is greater than 50 ml, the physician usually directs the feeding to be withheld. Patients at high risk of aspiration who are going to require long-term tube feeding are sometimes managed with jejunostomy feedings. These feedings rarely cause problems with aspiration, but diarrhea can be increased. Some patients require use of an elemental diet that is rapidly absorbed without residue to control diarrhea.

The other major safety aspect to be discussed is seizure. Seizures can sometimes be prevented by administration of anticonvulsant medication or reduction of physiologic or psychologic stimuli. Repetitive generalized seizures may sometimes be aborted (when they have premonitory signs such as muscular twitching) by the administration of 5−10 mg of diazepam. The drug should be administered over a 3- to 5-minute period, since too rapid administration can cause hypotension and/or cardiac or respiratory arrest. Patients with continuous EEG monitoring frequently exhibit a series of spikes or sharp waves interrupting the alpha and beta waves that warn of an impending seizure. A bite stick or padded tongue blade should be kept at the bedside for insertion between the teeth to prevent biting of the tongue. After the jaws are set in a tonic spasm, however, there should be no attempt to force a wedge between the teeth. Bruising of the gums and breaking of the teeth can result, with no actual benefit—since if the tongue was between the teeth when the jaws become clenched, it has already been damaged. During the early phase of the seizure it is helpful to loosen tight clothing and turn the head to the side. A small pillow or other padding placed under the head will help to lessen the trauma of the head banging against a hard surface during the clonic phase.

In some instances, the patient does not follow the usual pattern of regaining consciousness after a seizure, but will have a series of convulsions. This state, referred to as status epilepticus, must be stopped as quickly as possible to prevent brain damage from anoxia in the presence of increased cerebral metabolism. Diazepam or other rapid acting anticonvulsant drugs are given intravenously, and longer-lasting drugs are used to maintain control. If the seizure activity cannot be controlled, general anesthesia may be used for a period of 1 or 2 days. Anesthetized patients are placed on a mechanical volume respirator, of course, and are continually monitored for EEG, ECG, and arterial blood pressure.

Prevention of Complications from Immobility

The major complications are development of decubitus ulcers, thrombophlebitis, and occurrence of deformities and contractures. These and other complications of immobility have been discussed in the chapter on mobility disturbances. Because prevention is so crucial, the major complications will be briefly
discussed from the standpoint of the semicomatose or comatose patient.

- *Decubitus ulcers,* or bedsores, can develop when the patient is unaware of
pressure on vulnerable tissue and/or unable to change his body position to
relieve the pressure. Sheepskin, alternating pressure air mattress, egg crate
mattress, flotation pad or bed (utilizing silicone gel, water, or air to distribute
pressure), and the Stryker frame or Circ-O-Lectric bed are all used. Probably any
of these can help prevent the development of decubiti, but they cannot be used
as a substitute for essential nursing activities. Rotation of position, with
avoidance of body weight or other pressure on the susceptible or affected areas,
is the keystone of both prevention and treatment of decubiti. Other essential
preventive measures are keeping the skin clean and dry (air exposure may be
necessary), massaging bony prominences, and ensuring adequate nutrition.
There are numerous agents that have been applied to a decubitus with varying
rates of success. Regardless of the agent used, wound cleansing and debridement
are important. The effectiveness of the treatment must be continuously
evaluated, so the agent used can be changed if it is not beneficial.

- *Thrombophlebitis* prevention primarily depends on reduction of venous stasis
and adequate management of a phlebitis from intravenous infusion or other
venous injury. Measures to decrease venous stasis of the lower extremities include range of motion, dorsiflexion of the ankles with flattening of the calf to the
mattress, and antiembolic stockings. Care in positioning to avoid pressure from
one leg on the calf of the other leg or popliteal pressure from bed gatching at the
knees helps to reduce venous injury. Intravenous sites need to be carefully
observed for signs of infiltration or phlebitis. The site of the infusion should be
changed at the first signs of phlebitis and the arm should be elevated on pillows
and heat applied. Deep venous thrombosis is generally treated by anticoagulation with heparin therapy to prevent extension of the thrombosis and/or
pulmonary embolism. When anticoagulation is contraindicated or pulmonary
embolism occurs in spite of anticoagulation, the vena cava may be ligated or
partially occluded with an "umbrella" or other device.

- *Deformities and contractures* cannot always be prevented, but correct body
alignment, use of supportive devices, and range of motion exercises to the joints
are helpful. Plantar flexion of the foot (footdrop) and hip flexion contractures
can develop insidiously. Preventive measures for footdrop include keeping the
weight of the covers off the feet and the use of a footboard or sandbags to maintain dorsiflexion of the feet. The upper legs need to be slightly internally rotated
to prevent hip flexion. To maintain the position, trochanter rolls or sandbags

are usually needed. Sometimes joints are splinted or prosthetic appliances are utilized to maintain proper alignment.

Provision of Reality Orientation

Conversation needs to be geared to a level understandable to the patient. The use of simple sentences is usually preferred. Declarative statements coupled with hopeful predictions are frequently helpful, e.g., "It must be frustrating to not be able to think clearly but it is just a temporary thing." Encouraging meaningful physical activity, calling attention to the patient's progress, and frequent reorientation are other therapeutic activities. Other measures to improve orientation are discussed under sensory input.

Regulation of Sensory Input

When cognitive impairment is intensified by altered sensory environmental input, misinterpretation of stimuli, or limitation in ability to receive stimuli, nursing measures to control the sensory input are needed. The specific measures utilized would, of course, depend on the assessment of the environment and the patient's reaction. Intervention for some of the stimuli that have been found to contribute to sensory disturbances in a number of patients will be briefly outlined.

Visual, auditory, and tactile stimuli are the environmental factors that have been most frequently implicated. Intervention directed toward control of visual stimuli include reduction of glare, replacement of bright lights with softer lights, use of low illumination at night, positioning of furniture and use of even illumination in room to avoid shadows that can be misinterpreted, and bed placement so patient can see both the outside and the doorway. The presence of a calendar and a clock in the room are only useful if they are placed in the patient's line of vision and are large enough for the patient to see. Use of glasses by a patient who ordinarily wears them should not need to be mentioned.

Measures to regulate auditory stimuli are aimed primarily at the amount of noise and the meaningfulness of the auditory stimuli. In most hospitals, there is too much, rather than too little, noise. An elevated noise level over a period of time can be as distressing as occasional, unexpected loud noises. Measures to control noise include closing the door of the room, turning off the audible "beep" on the ECG monitor, keeping respirators as far from the patient as possible (with the outflow valve pointing away), keeping conversation near the bed at a minimum, and use of audible paging systems only when essential. Meaningless noise can be controlled by talking to the patient instead of about him, using familiar terminology that he can understand. Voices need to be loud enough to be heard by a person who has a hearing problem. The use of a radio or television needs to be guided by the patient's desires and observed reaction. If the patient is unable to indicate his wishes, the choice of programming should be determined by the usual desires of persons of his age group and culture. Programs with a great deal of conversation or a complicated plot should be avoided.

Measures to increase tactile stimuli are frequently indicated, especially for the patient who has impaired mobility. In addition to providing needed stimulation of the ascending reticular activating system, touch supplies an emotional component of acceptance. The use of tubes, wires, and restraints that interfere with patient movement should be kept to a minimum. With hyperesthesia which accompanies meningitis and other states, unnecessary kinesthetic stimulation is avoided because of the overreaction which may be harmful.

Measures to reduce misinterpretation of sensory input include promotion of rest to reduce fatigue, meaningful diversion to reduce monotony, adequate control of pain, increase in frequency and/or duration of contacts with isolated patients, provision of knowledge about environment, and encouragement to talk about experiences. Reassurance that other patients also have problems and that they are usually transitory is helpful to most patients.

Modification of Cognitive Structures

This is the major intervention for patients whose cognitive impairment is due to psychologic maladjustment. The relatively recent development of the school of cognitive psychology with its technique of cognitive therapy claims success in treating some forms of maladjustment, especially depression. It utilizes both verbal and behavior modification techniques. The major focus of the therapy is to get the patient to believe that he can successfully execute behavior required to produce outcomes. Initially behavioral techniques such as list-keeping and planning productive activities are utilized to focus the patient's attention away from himself and provide a sense of accomplishment. Then the therapist and the patient work together to identify the content and the process characteristics of the patient's distorted cognition and reality-test their appropriateness. The patient's dysfunctional beliefs and inaccurate assumptions are identified, and the patient is helped to use a more realistic way of processing information. It can be seen that the cognitive theorists believe in the adverse effect of lack of self-determination that has been identified by the concept of powerlessness. The patient is said to feel powerless when he believes that he is incapable of influencing the outcome he seeks. Although major cognitive restructuring is not within the realm of the nurse, measures to increase a patient's control in a situation and reengage him in life experiences in which he can be successful, help him to develop a more realistic outlook. Likewise, encouraging the patient with a personality disorder to express his feelings and discuss his circumstances may result in the patient spontaneously recognizing causal factors for his difficulties. Identification of the cause usually results in an improvement in the patient's mood which may be followed by ideas for problem resolution.

Pharmacologic agents such as antidepressants, tranquilizers, and sedatives are used to modify some psychologic maladaption disorders. They are most effective for short-term acute personality disorders or they are used in combination with psychotherapy for the functional psychoses. Noncompliance with prescribed drug program, untoward side effects, and danger of suicide are some of the problems that arise with drug administration. Conversion symptoms are usually managed by persuasive techniques. A dramatic show of some kind is often helpful, since symptoms present for a period of time cannot be easily abandoned without embarrassing the patient. Embarrassment is minimized if the patient can report that the doctor eliminated the cause of the trouble by a special treatment modality, administration of a new drug, or hypnotic trance. Effective treatment, in addition to removing the manifested symptoms, includes assistance in resolution of the intrapsychic conflict and in dealing with the threatening life situation that initiated the disorder.

Provision of Assistance to the Family

Cognitive impairment that does not resolve places a strain on the family. They may feel helpless, anxious, depressed, or angry. Oftentimes fears regarding the possibility of other family members being affected or the social stigma they may experience make them withdraw from the patient. The nurse can help the family or significant others understand the nature of the disorder and make realistic plans with and for the patient that will maintain his sense of self-worth and social integrity.

EXPERIENTIAL INVOLVEMENT

CASE 10A. Mrs. Wollenski is a 42-year-old widow who has been in moderately good health except for two severe cases of pneumonia. Since her last bout of pneumonia 1½ years ago, she has had some dyspnea on exertion which was felt to be due to a mild form of emphysema. She works as a bookkeeper for a construction firm. Most of her time when not working is devoted to her two children, ages 10 and 14. She has not smoked for the last 1½ years. She has an occasional social drink. She takes no drugs except vitamins. For the past 2 months she has had constipation with pain radiating to the back which became progressively worse. She entered the hospital with acute intestinal obstruction where sigmoidoscopy revealed the presence of a tumor at the sigmoid flexure. After antibiotic preparation, an abdominal resection with colostomy was performed. Two units of blood were used during surgery and a third unit was given in the surgical intensive care unit on the evening of surgery. Weight after surgery was 60 kg (132 pounds). The first postoperative day she was alert and responsive and seemed relieved that the surgeons had been able to resect the entire tumor mass and that there was no evidence of spread to the lymph nodes. Her rectal temperature in the afternoon was 38 C (100.4 F). She cooperated well with turning but cough was nonproductive. She was able to raise 1½ balls on the Triflow incentive deepbreathing exerciser (inspiratory capacity approximately 750 ml). Her Foley catheter was removed on the morning of her second postoperative day but she was still on IV's and NPO. On the afternoon of her second postoperative day she still had no bowel sounds. Her nasogastric tube drained 1200 ml/24 hours for which she received replacement with electrolyte solution. Her last injection of meperidine was 5 hours ago. Her physical findings and laboratory reports at this time are: T(R) 38.5 C (101.5 F), P 98, R 24, BP 120/80 (supine), 118/80 (sitting upright) Wt 59.5 kg, neck veins normal.

	Patient	Normal
Metabolic I		
Chloride	92	95−105 mEq/L
Carbon dioxide	34	24−32 mEq/L
Potassium	4.5	3.5−5 mEq/L
Sodium	132	135−145 mEq/L
Urea Nitrogen	12	10−20 mg/dl
Glucose	155	58−100 mg/dl
Hematology profile		
(WBC)		
Leukocyte count	15,500/cu mm	5−10 thousand/cu mm
(RBC)		
Erythrocyte count	4.5 million/cu mm	4.2−5.4 million/cu mm
Hemoglobin (Hgb)	13 g/dl	12−16 g/dl
Hematocrit (Hct)	42 ml/dl	36−47 ml/dl
Blood Gases (arterial)		
pH	7.33	7.35−7.45
P_{CO_2}	50	35−45 torr
P_{O_2}	65	75−100 torr
Blood bicarbonate	28	22−26 mEq/L
$F_{I_{O_2}}$	0.21	room air 0.21
Leukocyte Differential		
Neutrophils (PMN)	80%	50−70%
Bands	8%	0−5%
Output past 4 hours	150 ml	
Urine	pH 6	
Urine Sp. G	1.014	

It is noted that she responds less to her environment. She is slow to answer when spoken to, and does not know the time of day. She does not cooperate with Triflow treatments or help turn herself. When asked to repeat a series of 5 numbers, she only repeated the first 4 numbers. When given pairs of words and asked to say if they mean the same thing or if they were different, she only answered correctly for 3 out of 5 of the pairs. Several times the question had to be repeated to get any response at all. She has no signs of neuromuscular irritability.

Skillbuilders:

1. On the practicum record 10-A enter the three most likely hypotheses for Mrs. Wollenski's cognitive impairment.

2. Then enter the data that support the hypothesis and additional data you would need to confirm or disconfirm.

3. In the intervention column enter the plan for nursing care for the next 2−4 days if the diagnosis were confirmed.

4. In the last column list the evaluation criteria for Mrs. Wollenski.

Hypothesis/Possible Diagnosis	Supportive Data Available	Additional Data Needed to Confirm or Disconfirm	Nursing Intervention if Diagnosis Confirmed	Evaluation Criteria
Cognitive impairment due to:				
1.				
2.				
3.				

Feedback: With such a large number of possible causes, we think it helps to eliminate those that are unlikely to be responsible. Referring to the table of causes of cognitive impairment will aid our search. With the history information and the development of the disordered state acutely following surgery, it is unlikely that structural disorders, failure of neuronal metabolism, trauma, seizures, deficiency of cofactors, hepatic insufficiency, porphyria, exogenous intoxicants, endocrine disorders, or impairment of temperature regulation are responsible for the cognitive impairment. A few other states that cannot be ruled out by history information alone can be by the physical and laboratory findings. Thus a blood glucose of 155 rules out hypoglycemia; a normal BUN rules out uremia; the almost normal levels of sodium, stable weight, and normal neck veins rule out fluid volume excess and sodium deficit or excess; the lack of postural hypotension, lack of hemoconcentration of sodium, BUN, Hct, and Hgb, weight loss less than 5 percent, normal neck veins, and urine output greater than 30 ml/hour rule out fluid volume deficit; the absence of signs of neuromuscular irritability (combined with absence of history of parathyroid disorder or necessary time frame for magnesium) rule out calcium or magnesium excess or deficit; the normal blood pressure and hematocrit rule out decreased cerebral blood flow from anemia, low cardiac output, or hypertensive crisis; and the lack of isolation or sensory deficit rules out abnormal sensory states. Our hypotheses then are cognitive impairment due to respiratory insufficiency, sepsis, or reactive depression.

We will discuss respiratory insufficiency first using the decision tree for respiratory insufficiency. It is, of course, acceptable if you used the terms hypoxemia and respiratory acidosis, but they are parts of the one disordered state so they cannot be used as two separate hypotheses. The supporting data come from the history of mild emphysema, the reduced vital capacity (normal vital capacity is more than 15 ml/kg or more than 900 ml), the impaired cognitive functioning, and arterial blood gas analysis. To analyze the blood gases, the pH less than 7.35 is indicative of acidemia. When we look at the P_{CO_2}, the elevation to 50 torr indicates the cause of the acidemia is respiratory. The slightly elevated bicarbonate indicates that there is no metabolic component, and that the problem has been present for several days, although not necessarily to the same extent. The low P_{O_2} is indicative of hypoxemia which, combined with respiratory acidosis, meets our criteria for respiratory insufficiency. Additional data which would help to confirm the hypothesis are signs of labored respirations and abnormal breath sounds plus knowledge of preoperative arterial blood analysis. Since Mrs. Wollenski is known to have mild emphysema, the present blood gases may only be minimally changed from her preoperative state. If this were the case, respirations were not increasingly labored, and the chest clear to auscultation and percussion, the hypothesis would probably be rejected. If the data support the hypothesis, further testing such as chest X-ray, sputum culture, and calculation of physiologic shunting would probably be indicated to confirm the hypothesis and provide baseline data to guide intervention and evaluation. The nursing intervention if the hypothesis of respiratory insufficiency were confirmed would depend to some extent on the underlying cause of the problem.

Certainly the most likely cause is atelectasis due to retained secretions and alveolar hypoventilation in a patient with an inadequate volume of inspired air due to an abdominal surgical incision and chronic obstructive pulmonary disease. Pneumonia could contribute to the problem, although it is a little early for its development. Pneumonia would probably be treated by appropriate antibiotic agents in addition to the following measures indicated for atelectasis and emphysema:

1. Clearance of secretions from the pulmonary tree by coughing, postural drainage with chest physiotherapy, and suctioning (if needed).

2. Maintenance of an adequate volume of inspired gas by periodic deep breathing with or without an inspiratory incentive spirometer, appropriate use of multiple small doses of pain medication, encouragement to expel all air by pursing of lips and audible sighing with expiration, and preventing abdominal viscera from exerting pressure on the diaphragm by elevation of the head and maintenance of proper functioning of the nasogastric tube.

3. Maintenance of normal distribution of air throughout the lung fields by turning every 2 or 3 hours around the clock.

4. Maintenance of adequate oxygenation by administration of oxygen at a flow rate of $2-3$ liters/minute (oxygen flow rate is, of course, ordered by the physician).

If Mrs. Wollenski ran an arterial Po_2 of 65 torr preoperatively, oxygen might not be ordered for her. With the increased shunting from atelectasis (or pneumonia), however, she will probably require oxygen adjunct to maintain an adequate Po_2. More aggressive treatment, such as intubation and mechanical ventilation, would not be indicated at the present time with the present severity of symptoms. If you did not include all the above intervention on your record, review the intervention section in the chapter on respiratory alterations. The criteria for evaluation would be:

1. Restoration of blood gases to preoperative levels
2. Chest clear to auscultation and percussion
3. Vital capacity greater than 900 ml
4. Normal cognitive functioning
5. Normal chest X-ray
6. Negative sputum culture

That brings us to the second hypothesis which states the cause of the impaired cognitive functioning is sepsis. Supporting data are the history of possible sources of infection (chronic lung disorder, Foley catheter, intravenous administration, and colon surgery), and the physical and laboratory findings of fever, tachypnea, decrease in cognitive function, and increase in white count with neutrophils 80 percent and bands 5 percent. Additional data to confirm the hypothesis would come primarily from observation of the suspected foci and culture and gram stain of the blood, wound drainage, urine, sputum, and tip of the intravenous catheter. In a few cases of sepsis, no positive cultures can be obtained. The other signs on the decision tree are helpful in the early stages of an infection when white count and differential are not available. Although Mrs. Wollenski has many of the criteria for the diagnosis of sepsis, her deviation from normal is only slight and there could be other explanations for most of her abnormal findings. For example, the body's response to both intestinal obstruction and surgery includes inflammation, fever, and leukocytosis. After major surgery the white count can be elevated 50 percent and remain elevated for 3 to 5 days. Thus a positive culture or gram stain and/or findings of a focus are needed for accuracy in diagnosis. Intervention if sepsis were confirmed would include appropriate antibiotic therapy as directed by the culture and sensitivity findings and ordered by the physician, specific treatment measures geared to the focus of infection, and measures to combat the dysfunctional effects of sepsis.

Intervention for the specific focus could include:

1. Urinary infections managed by avoidance of trauma to the urinary tract from instrumentation, dilution of urine by forcing fluids to maximum allowed, and measures to ensure complete emptying of bladder with no residual urine

2. Infections from intracaths treated by removal of intracath, warm moist compresses to involved site, and when septic phlebitis is present, removal of involved vein.

3. Wound infections with collections of pus treated by incision and drainage with packing to prevent the wound from closing at the surface before the deeper focus has been eradicated.

Measures to combat the dysfunctional effects of sepsis would include:

1. Reduction of anxiety from unexpected complication.

2. Provision of adequate parenteral intake of protein and carbohydrate to prevent negative nitrogen balance and hypoalbuminemia from the accelerated metabolic state.

3. Maintenance of adequate intravascular fluid volume by infusion of colloid and fluid to counteract for the vasodilation and third-spacing of fluid that occurs with sepsis.

4. Administration of oxygen to counteract hypoxemia that results from impaired oxygen utilization.

5. Administration of sodium bicarbonate for severe lactic acidemia.

6. Administration of sympathomimetic drugs such as isoproteranol (Isuprel) and dopamine (Intropin) to counteract myocardial depression and venous constriction.

Concerning the last point, in a few instances vasoconstrictive drugs such as levarterenol (Levophed) and metaraminol (Aramine) might be given to counteract arterial dilation. Most physicians prefer to treat the hypovolemia physiologically by massive fluid administration and only use vasoconstrictive drugs when such infusion cannot maintain an adequate blood pressure to perfuse the vital organs.

Evaluation criteria would be:

1. Patient's validation that she felt competent to handle the anxiety-provoking situation with the support given by the staff

2. Negative culture or other evidence of elimination of source of infection.

3. Normothermia.

4. Normal respiratory rate.

5. Absence of cognitive impairment.

6. Normal white blood count.

7. Healing of wound (or other focus of infection).

8. Limitation of severity of dysfunctional effects and absence of damage from same.

Measures under point 8 would include: (a) Po_2 maintained above 55 torr and absence of brain damage from hypoxemia; (b) absence of signs of a fluid volume deficit or kidney damage from inadequate renal perfusion; (c) pH maintained above 7.25; and (d) blood pressure maintained above 85 systolic.

This should bring us to our last hypothesis, that the cognitive impairment was due to a reactive depression. The supporting data come primarily from the theoretical knowledge that a person can suffer a depression following surgery that gives the individual a sense of loss, with the extent of the depression depending on the value accorded the loss and the person's past responses to other losses. Colostomy surgery to a middle-aged widow who already had to adjust to a chronic obstructive lung disease could be viewed as a disaster because of its body disfigurement, the possible loss of a job and the earnings needed to support her children, and possible restrictions in her social life. Patient behaviors consistent with reactive depression are withdrawal, loss of interest, apathy, slowness of speech, and cognitive impairment. Since psychological data do not lend themselves to numerical criteria or laboratory testing, additional data to confirm the hypothesis would come from interviewing Mrs. Wollenski and receiving her validation of the relationship between the loss she felt and her emotional state. Nonverbal communication should be noted, since it can reinforce or contradict what is said. The facial expressions or voice may translate unhappiness and/ or dejection. Nervous repetitive movements such as foot or finger tapping or shrugging of the shoulders may be a cue to unexpressed emotions or conflicts. Psychologic testing may be needed to confirm the hypothesis. Nursing intervention if the hypothesis is confirmed would be directed toward assimilation of the changes in body image and increasing Mrs. Wollenski's self-esteem. Preliminary to this is development of a good interpersonal relationship, as discussed in greater detail in a previous chapter. Activities would include:

1. Encouraging Mrs. Wollenski to express her feelings with acknowledgment that the feelings are understood and accepted

2. Assisting Mrs. Wollenski to help herself

3. Use of kindness and firmness

4. Provision of knowledge about her colostomy with a realistic interpretation of what it will alter in her life and what it will not

5. Encouragement and assistance in grooming

6. Provision of information about resources available to the patient (financial, child care, ostomy clubs, etc.)

The physician may order a tricyclic antidepressant such as amitriptyline (Elavil). The supportive relationship needs to continue as Mrs. Wollenski's depression is lifting, because the conflict the depression masked is revealed and painful feelings accompanying it are exposed.

Evaluation criteria would include:

1. Resolution of depression

2. Patient making realistic plans for discharge

3. Interest in grooming and dressing

4. Absence of untoward effects from medication

There is an additional step that can increase the accuracy of diagnosis for complicated cases such as Mrs. Wollenski's. The step entails looking at all the abnormal findings to see if they can be explained by the proposed hypotheses, or if, perhaps, there are other possibilities that have not been considered. The one major abnormality that has not been considered is the elevated blood glucose of 155 mg/dl. Since the sympathoadrenal response to stress is increased, with a release of adrenocortical steroid that accelerates the conversion of liver glycogen to glucose, the high glucose could be a manifestation of stress. The stress could come from the surgery itself and/or the reaction to the surgery as manifested by the depression. An additional explanation is that when sepsis is present, insulin (both endogenous and exogenous) is less effective in transporting glucose into the cells. Thus, the glucose elevation can be explained and does not need to be considered as pathogenic.

CASE 10B. Mr. Alexander, a 50-year-old white divorced resident of Las Vegas, was on a business trip to Los Angeles when he suffered pain in the right lower abdominal quadrant. He took Alka-Seltzer with little relief. The pain kept recurring for the next 2 days. However, he was very busy with appointments during the days and evenings and he was able to ignore the pain. He ate very little and took two sleeping pills at night. On the afternoon of the third day, the pain became much more intense and when it continued for several hours and he began to vomit repeatedly, he went to the emergency room of the nearest hospital. Examination and tests at this time showed generalized abdominal tenderness, rigidity of the abdominal wall, presence of a palpable mass in the right inguinal area, absent peristaltic sounds, and leucocytosis of 20,000 per cubic millimeter. The diagnosis of perforated appendix with inflammatory process in the right inguinal area was made. He was admitted to the hospital for initial medical management, with later surgery anticipated.

His past history showed him to have been a heavy drinker for 15 years with a hospital admission for cirrhosis 2 years ago. He denied any drinking for the past 2 years. Other history was essentially negative.

His initial treatment after hospital admission included gastric suction, antibiotics, and parenteral fluid therapy with electrolytes and vitamins added. After 3 days, his symptoms became more intense and his white count increased to 24,000; there was an increase in pain, abdominal rigidity, and fever. He was taken to surgery where he was explored and an abscess in the right peritoneal gutter was located. The perforated appendix was removed and the abscess drained. He was returned to an isolation room after surgery where he did well for 2 days, being maintained on nasogastric suction, antibiotic therapy, and parenteral fluid.

On the second postoperative day, his nasogastric tube was clamped off without discomfort. However, on the evening of the second postoperative day he became nauseated, distended, and diaphoretic. His Levine tube was reconnected to suction with copious bright red drainage returning. His blood pressure dropped to 90/60 and his pulse was increased to 120. He was transferred to an isolation room in the surgical intensive care unit. Blood and iced saline irrigations were started which controlled the bleeding within 3 hours. He received a neomycin enema which was expelled with dark red stool. He received four units of blood as well as albumin and electrolyte solution during the 8-hour period after the bleeding started. At the end of the 8 hours, he appeared alert and well oriented, but exhibited signs of fatigue and seemed concerned about his condition. He was started on intravenous cimetidine (Tagamet), 300 mg every 6 hours and antacids by NG tube every hour, with clamping of the NG tube for 30 minutes after administration. His intravenous rate was slowed and he was watched closely for rebleeding. Parameters continuously monitored included ECG, central arterial blood pressure, and pulmonary artery pressure (PAP). His pulmonary artery wedge pressure (PAWP) and urine output were measured hourly, with testing of the urine for specific gravity and pH. Blood from the arterial line was drawn every 8 hours for blood gas determination.

Eighteen hours after the bleeding episode, the patient was noted to be less responsive. He was slow to follow commands such as squeezing the nurse's hand, but he finally did squeeze with both hands. He seemed unaware of the activity occurring around him, did not know the time of day, and was slow to answer when spoken to. When asked to count by 3, he got to 12 but then seemed to be unable to think of the next number and gave up the effort. He denied having pain but said his abdomen hurt when he coughed. He had received no medications other than antibiotics, cimetidine, and antacids for the past 18 hours. The physical findings and laboratory data for Mr. Alexander at this time: T (R) 38.4 C (101.1 F), B = 110/80, BP = 110, R = 24, PAWP = 11 mmHg, Urine output last hour 30 ml, pH = 6, Sp G. = 1.018

	Patient	Normal
Metabolic I		
Chloride	90	95−105 mEq/L
Carbon dioxide, total	18	24−32 mEq/L
Potassium	4.5	3.5−5.0 mEq/L
Sodium	128	135−145 mEq/L
Urea nitrogen	30	10−20 mg/dl
Glucose	85	58−100 mg/dl
Blood Gases (arterial)		
pH	7.48	7.35−7.45
P_{CO_2}	26	35−45 torr
P_{O_2}	92	75−100 torr
HCO_3^-	17.8	22−26 mEq/L
Base excess	−3.4	0−±2 mEq/L
$F_{I_{O_2}}$	.21	.21 (room air)
Hematology Profile		
Leukocyte count (WBC)	20,000	5−10 thousand/mm³
Erythrocyte count (RBC)	4 million	4.5−6.0 million/mm³

	Patient	Normal
Hemoglobin (Hgb)	12.5	14–18 g/dl
Hematocrit (Hct)	36	40–54 ml/dl
Metabolic II		
Protein, total	5	6–8.5 g/dl
Albumin	2.3	3.5–5.0 g/dl
Calcium	9	8.5–10.5 mg/dl
Phosphorus	4	2.5–4.5 mg/dl
Cholesterol total	250	150–250 mg/dl
Uric acid	7	2–8 mg/dl
Creatinine	1.8	0.7–1.4 mg/dl
Bilirubin, total	7	0.2–1.2 mg/dl
Phosphatase, alkaline	100	30–85 mU/ml
Lactic dehydrogenase (LDH)	240	100–225 mU/ml
Glutamic pyruvic transaminase (GPT)	210	8–40 mU/ml
Glutamic oxalacetic transaminase (GOT)	190	7.5–40 mU/ml
Leukocyte Differential (Percent)		
Neutrophils (PMN)	75	50–70
Bands	18	0–5
Lymphocytes	6	20–30
Monocytes	1	2–10

Skillbuilders:

1. On practicum record 10-B, list the three most likely hypotheses for the primary disorder responsible for Mr. Alexander's cognitive impairment. Use the table of major causes of cognitive impairment to guide you. Try to distinguish between primary disorders and secondary disorders that occur as a result of a compensatory mechanism for a primary disorder. This differentiation is not easy since in one situation a disorder may be a primary cause while in another it is a compensatory mechanism. Those whose list contains only primary disorders get an automatic "A."

2. Next list the supporting data and additional data needed for each hypothesis.

3. Outline the nursing activities, both those which would be directed by the physician and those independently undertaken by the nurse.

4. List the criteria for evaluation of the response to Mr. Alexander's cognitive impairment.

Feedback: Since Mr. Alexander's case history was somewhat complicated, a little explanation of the rationale for the management prior to the development of cognitive impairment may be helpful. Most patients with acute appendicitis and those with perforation are treated by emergency surgery. When 3 to 5 days have elapsed since the onset of symptoms, however, and there is a palpable

Hypothesis/Possible Diagnosis	Supportive Data Available	Additional Data Needed to Confirm or Disconfirm	Nursing Intervention if Diagnosis Confirmed	Evaluation Criteria
Cognitive impairment due to primary disordered states of: 1.				
2.				
3.				

mass present, operation is delayed. The reason for the delay is that a phlegmon rather than a definitive abscess will be found, and operation can cause the infection to spread, resulting in a generalized peritonitis involving the entire abdominal cavity. A second aspect of the clinical course that might profit by explanation is the episode of gastrointestinal bleeding. The peritonitis and surgical procedure are both highly stressful events and it is not unusual for the patient to develop a stress ulcer with hemorrhage. The presence of blood in the gut and the need to give multiple blood transfusions is a source of concern for a patient with impaired liver function, since the liver has to metabolize the nitrogenous substances absorbed from the intestines and red cell breakdown. The neomycin enema was given to promote expulsion of the blood in the gut and because neomycin decreases the bacterial flora in the intestine and thus decreases the production of ammonia. Remember that normally the ammonia produced by bacterial action in the intestine is changed to urea by the liver and excreted by the kidneys. With liver cell disease, the Krebs cycle does not function properly, and ammonia instead of urea is present in the serum in abnormally high amounts. Although high ammonia is not the only cause of hepatic encephalopathy, it is probably the major cause. We will refer to the abnormal mental state associated with chronic liver disease as hepatic encephalopathy. In some of the literature it is now being called portal-systemic encephalopathy, or PSE. Cimetidine is a histamine hydrogen ion antagonist that inhibits gastric acid secretion. It is given with antacids to decrease the incidence of rebleeding. Now let's look at the problem of cognitive impairment.

Our hypotheses are:

1. Cognitive impairment due to primary hepatic insufficiency with secondary respiratory alkalosis

2. Cognitive impairment due to sepsis with compensatory respiratory alkalosis

3. Cognitive impairment due to altered sensory state (sensory deprivation or sensory overload)

We'll follow our usual practice of starting at the top. The decision tree for hepatic insufficiency can guide our search. Data to support the hypothesis that cognitive impairment is due to hepatic insufficiency would include the history of stressful states, previous cirrhosis, changes in blood volume state, and blood transfusions. Since active cirrhosis is associated with diffuse bleeding tendencies, the gastrointestinal bleeding could be an indication of reactivation of a latent cirrhotic process with a deficiency of clotting factors or portal hypertension. We have already mentioned that persons with impaired liver function have increased levels of ammonia in the blood following GI bleeding and/or multiple transfusions. This elevation of ammonia interferes with cerebral metabolism and leads to hepatic encephalopathy. An additional physical finding to support the hypothesis would be the presence of asterixis, which is a peculiar "flapping tremor" that is marked by an intermittent lapse of the assumed posture of the extremities, head, and trunk. The flapping can be observed every few seconds when the patient who has extended his hand with the wrist dorsiflexed sustains the posture for a period of time. Laboratory data to support the hypothesis are the elevation of bilirubin, alkaline phosphatase, and SGOT, and the low total protein and albumin. Additional laboratory data to support the hypothesis would be an elevated ammonia and gamma globulin and a prolonged prothrombin time. Although the high number of abnormal laboratory values are indicative of hepatic insufficiency, the levels would need to be compared with preillness values. Many patients with cirrhosis due to alcoholic intake who have stopped drinking may have regained somewhat normal liver function but still have an elevated bilirubin and alkaline phosphatase and low serum albumin. Thus cognitive impairment would not be ascribed to hepatic causes unless these parameters showed more extensive alteration. The physician frequently orders a needle biopsy of the liver to confirm the extent of the disease process.

Let's discuss the possibility of respiratory alkalosis before we talk about intervention. Using the decision tree for respiratory alkalosis, we find that Mr. Alexander satisfies the criteria of a pH greater than 7.45, with a Pco_2 less than 35 torr, and a HCO_3^- less than 22. With an arterial Po_2 of 92, we can say that his hyperventilation must be in response to an underlying cause other than hypoxia. Hepatic insufficiency is one of the disordered states frequently accompanied by hyperpnea with resulting respiratory alkalosis. The exact mechanism responsible for the hyperventilation is not known. Intervention if the hypothesis of hepatic insufficiency was confirmed would be directed toward reducing the blood levels of ammonia and other toxic nitrogenous substances, correction of factors that potentiate the encephalopathy, promotion of liver healing, and education. Measures to reduce ammonia and other nitrogenous levels include:

1. Exclusion of any protein intake for 3 or more days

2. Administration of neomycin to decrease the bacterial production of ammonia in the gut

3. Avoidance of narcotics, sedatives, tranquilizers, and diuretics containing ammonium or amino compounds

4. The administration of lactulose to lower the fecal pH and suppress the ammonia-forming bacteria

5. The prophylactic measures to prevent gastrointestinal rebleeding already discussed

An additional measure to prevent bleeding could be administration of vitamin K if prothrombin time is prolonged. Correction of factors that potentiate the encephalopathy includes control of infections which increase catabolism, administration of folic acid for macrocytic anemia, inhalation of a 5 percent carbon dioxide mixture for respiratory alkalosis, and management of fluid and electrolyte imbalances. It is noted that Mr. Alexander has hyponatremia. Sodium replacement, however, would not be indicated until it was determined if the hyponatremia was due to dilution. Dilution occurs when there is an excess of total body fluid, which is frequently the case with cirrhosis. Therefore, you should search for evidence of edema, ascites, and other signs of fluid volume excess. Fluid volume excess would be treated by free water restriction and sodium restriction. Salt-poor albumin would be given to increase the colloid osmotic pressure within the intravascular space. When we calculate the serum osmolality by the formula previously discussed (on the decision tree for fluid volume excess), we obtain the value of 274 mOsm/liter. Since the normal serum osmolality is 290, we can recognize the need for colloid administration to decrease movement of fluid from the intravascular to interstitial space. If edema were severe, small doses of an aldosterone antagonist diuretic like spironolactone (Aldactone) might be given. Potent diuretics would be avoided because of the danger of increasing the hepatic encephalopathy.

Activities to promote liver healing are the administration of a high carbohydrate diet, supplemental vitamins, and avoidance of intake of alcohol and drugs metabolized by the liver or toxic to the liver. As the acute phase subsided, Mr. Alexander's knowledge about his liver disorder would need to be assessed. He may have a number of unanswered questions about the illness from the time of onset 2 years ago. The exacerbation now gives us an opportunity to meet some of these previously unmet needs. For example, decreased libido and impotence may accompany the disorder. This, or other problems he was experiencing, may have troubled him but reticence could have kept him from inquiring about them. He states that he has not had a drink for 2 years. There is a great tendency among health professionals to give little credence to the patient's report of alcoholic intake. Experience has probably demonstrated that many patients do not report accurately. Some of you may have listed delirium tremens as a hypothesis. This certainly should always be considered in a patient with a history of alcoholic intake who has cognitive changes. The usual period for it to occur, however, is some 3 or 4 days after a period of drinking. It thus does not fit the time frame for Mr. Alexander. It is important for the patient to understand that the liver does heal to a certain extent, but that intake of alcohol or onset of certain disordered states can result in hepatic insufficiency. Preillness function can usually be regained with recovery from the disorder, but continued alcoholic intake can result in the pathologic alterations of portal hypertension which are not reversible. Additionally he needs to be aware that sedatives are tolerated poorly by patients with impaired liver function, and that their intake can precipitate encephalopathy. Regardless of the cause of the cognitive impairment, we know the experience is likely to be stressful for Mr. Alexander and it is important for us to minimize the dysfunctional effects of the experience. We will discuss appropriate activities briefly at this time, although they would be equally important with the other hypotheses. Activities would include:

1. Reality orientation to time and place
2. Use of simple sentences geared to Mr. Alexander's level of understanding
3. Assurances that the state was only temporary
4. Regulation of sensory input to avoid overload of visual and auditory stimuli, reduction or elimination of meaningless stimuli, provision of tactile stimuli, and promotion of rest and comfort

Evaluation criteria would include:

1. Improvement in cognitive state
2. Return of altered laboratory values toward normal
3. Absence of further gastrointestinal bleeding
4. Patient verbalization of knowledge about his illness (including the effect of alcohol) and his feedback that he was satisfied both with the response to his concerns and the support he received during the period of cognitive impairment

One criterion listed here is improvement in cognitive state. Evaluation is most helpful when we have a numerical component to rate the cognitive level. Therefore, administration of one of the simple cognitive tests that are available from a number of sources at the onset of the disorder with follow-up evaluations every 3 to 5 days is far superior to the subjective evaluation methods that are sometimes employed. These tests include the ability to construct figures, to write, to calculate, to connect various numbers by a series of lines over a measured period of time, etc. Perhaps the best known test is the Reitan trailmaking test. Dr. Conn has devised a simplified version of the trailmaking test, called the Number Connection Test, which can be administered serially and provides a good method of evaluation.

We're now ready to look at the second hypothesis that cognitive impairment is due to sepsis with compensatory respiratory alkalosis. The data to support the hypothesis are the history of a perforated appendix with peritonitis and abscess formation and the knowledge that other abscesses or foci of infection may develop, with incidence of infection higher in patients with liver damage. The decision tree for sepsis can guide our search for cues. Data do require evaluation, however, since Mr. Alexander would be expected to have many positive findings because of his known abscess of 3 days ago. The clinical picture suggestive of new abscess formation or new focus of infection is an initial return of parameters toward normal followed by an intensification of symptoms, physical findings, and laboratory abnormalities. In many instances patients on antibiotic therapy have suppression of physical signs and alteration of other manifestations.

Evaluation of the supporting data could follow the following reasoning:

1. Temperature elevation is indicative of sepsis, but it would carry greater weight if Mr. Alexander had had a shaking chill, and if elevation was higher that the same time on the previous day. Abscess formation is accompanied by a fever that rises in a stepwise fashion, and septicemia is accompanied by a chill at the time bacteria enter the bloodstream. The increased metabolic rate with the stress of surgery and tissue catabolism can result in elevation of fever without infection.

2. The presence of tachycardia, while supportive of sepsis, could also be due to alterations mentioned for fever.

3. The hyperpnea and impaired cognitive function are supporting data. We only have a recording of an increased respiratory rate, but since we have laboratory findings of respiratory alkalosis, we know that respirations are deep as well as rapid. As you gain more experience in caring for patients, you will be more alert in looking for sepsis in any patient who does not have hypoxemia or other known cause for respiratory alkalosis.

4. The white count elevation with the left shift of PMN's (or polys as they are commonly called) to 75 percent and increase in immature forms such as bands supports the hypothesis of sepsis. Greater weight would be added if the PMN's had decreased after the abscess had been drained and now show a second increase. The presence of immature forms of neutrophils, while indicative of sepsis, can also indicate that the body has exhausted its supply of polys in fighting the original infection and is thus mobilizing immature forms.

Additional data we should obtain to rule in or rule out the hypothesis are the presence or absence of lymphadenopathy, splenomegaly, worsening ileus (postoperative ileus usually clears after 2 or 3 days), and if systolic blood pressure is decreased from previous levels. Blood pressure may be difficult to evaluate since the bleeding episode caused a drop in the blood pressure and there has been inadequate time to determine Mr. Alexander's expected pressure. Not included on the decision tree, but essential information for patients suspected of having an abdominal infection or abscess is inspection of the wound for signs of a wound infection such as redness, swelling, drainage, and tenderness. Data which are usually the responsibility of the physician are the determination of other intraperitoneal abscess by the methods of abdominal palpation for the presence of a mass and scanning techniques (gallium, ultrasound, computerized tomography, etc.).

Intervention if the diagnosis was confirmed would include following the physician's orders for treatment of the infectious process and independent nursing activities to prevent dysfunctional effects from the infection. Abscesses are generally drained by surgical means, although drainage may not be done until localization has occurred. At the time of surgery, a multiple lumen catheter such as a Shirley or Abramson may be placed for irrigation of the infected focus. The nurse is responsible for managing the irrigation. Special attention is frequently needed to prevent dislodgement of the catheter, to maintain patency of the tubing, to promote removal of irrigating fluid by suction, and to maintain dryness around the irrigating catheter. Since patients with sepsis have large losses of fluid from the intravascular space, intravenous therapy orders need to be followed with accuracy and on time. A patient whose IV infiltrates or otherwise becomes nonfunctional, needs to have a new intravenous started promptly. A delay of 1 or 2 hours can result in development of hypovolemia and shock which may be irreversible. Accurate measurement and prompt replacement of losses from NG drainage are also essential. In the chapter on output deviations we talked about the nurse's responsibility for patients with nasogastric intubation. Since the distension accompanying ileus lessens motility and the capacity of the blood vessels to deliver blood to the involved organs, the nurse must maintain patency of the NG tube to prevent this dysfunctional self-perpetuating mechanism of continued ileus that results when the gastrointestinal tract is not decompressed. Activities could include repositioning of the tube, insuring the suction is working properly, and irrigation. Aspiration should be done at 3- or 4-hour intervals before instillation of antacid to be certain that stomach contents are not being retained. Also important for patients with NG intubation of good oral hygiene to maintain comfort and prevent dysfunctional effects of oral lesions. Emotional support and explanation need to be provided to prevent the dysfunctional effects of excess anxiety. Evaluation criteria could include improvement in cognitive state, healing of wound, control of infection, blood pressure maintained above 90 systolic, return of altered laboratory values toward normal, resolution of ileus, and control of anxiety.

This takes us to the last hypothesis that cognitive impairment is due to an altered sensory state. Supporting datum comes from the knowledge that disturbances in sensory input can upset the balance of function of the reticular activating system (RAS), with a decrease in the ability to process stimuli accurately.

Sensory deprivation theory tells us that altered sensory environments can produce changes in perception, affect, and cognition. Other supporting data from the history are:

1. Mr. Alexander's social isolation (he was away from home, placed in an isolation room, and moved from one floor to the intensive care unit with different personnel)

2. His exposure to meaningless, unpatterned sensory input from the ECG monitor, suction machine, arterial blood pressure line, Swan–Ganz catheter, and intravenous infusion

3. His concern about his condition

4. His inability to get adequate sleep because of the frequency of treatment and evaluation activities

5. The report of administration of no pain medication for the past 18 hours; in confused states or with stoic patients, pain assessment should not be limited to the patient's report.

Respiratory alkalosis is not commonly present with cognitive impairment from abnormal sensory state. If the patient, however, also has changes in his affective state (anxiety, fear, depression, etc.,) they can be manifested by hyperventilation and respiratory alkalosis. Thus assessment should include identification of changes in affective and perceptual states which could be due to the altered sensory environment as well as the change in cognitive state. Additional data to support the hypothesis could include exploration with Mr. Alexander of the various sensory stimuli to determine their effects. Most patients, however, have cognitive impairment to such an extent that they are unable to determine the effect of stimuli rationally. Nursing intervention would probably be undertaken without definite confirmation of the hypothesis since such confirmation may only be obtained by a positive response to activities to control the sensory input. Activities would include:

1. Control of pain

2. Scheduling of activities to provide for periods of uninterrupted rest in a darkened environment

3. Increase in mobility, with use of a cardiac chair for position change and encouragement of range of motion exercises

4. Giving of accurate information geared to the patient's level of understanding about his condition

5. Pointing out progress the patient is making

6. Reducing environmental noise and conversation about the patient at his bedside

7. Provision of diversional activities of the patient's choice.

8. Protection from harm during the period of cognitive impairment

Evaluation criteria would include improvement in cognitive state, absence of injury, return of pulse, respirations, and arterial blood gases to normal, and patient's report that he felt secure rather than distressed during the period of cognitive impairment.

CASE 10C. The last case study has been taken from the files of a nurse practitioner. It involves an elderly man with a gradual change in cognitive behavior. We thought you might like to try your skill with this type of problem.

PATIENT PROFILE

Case 10 C

NAME: Carl Wagner

AGE: 78　　　SEX: Male　　　ETHNIC EXTRACTION: German

MARITAL STATUS: Married

OCCUPATION: Retired butcher

HT: 5'3"　　WT: Average 170; Maximum 180; Present 170

PULSE 88　RESP. 20　BP 170/100

TEMP. 36.9C (98.4F)

CHIEF COMPLAINT: Tiredness, inability to concentrate, loss of memory, and headaches.

INFORMANT: Patient accompanied by his wife, age 62 (second wife—married 10 years) who
　provides most of the information.

HISTORY OF THE PRESENT ILLNESS: Has felt tired, with decreased interest in activities used to en-
　joy for past 6 months. Some dizziness with standing. Fell approx. 5 weeks ago when
　getting up to go to the bathroom. No loss of consciousness. Had small abrasion on head
　which hit bedside stand. Wife has noticed his speech is slower and briefer. Does not
　watch television shows formerly enjoyed because he can't follow plots. Wife has taken
　over payment of bills because he gets confused with computations. Recently has be-
　come extremely irritable and upset over trivial matters.

PREVIOUS ILLNESSES: TURP 7 years ago. Hypertension for 15 years.

FAMILY DATA: Mother died of stroke (83). Father died of pneumonia (78). No siblings or
　children.

MEDICATIONS:
　Hydrochlorthiazide (Hydrodiuril): 50 mg daily (15 years)
　Methyldopa (Aldomet): 250 mg 4×/day for past 6 months
　Vitamin E: 4 capsules/day.

ALLERGIES: none

HABITS:
　Alcohol—2 cans beer/day
　Tobacco—Formerly 1 pack/day—none past 15 years

PROSTHETIC DEVICES:
　Wears bifocals
　Has hearing aid
　Partial (upper) dentures

SOCIAL AND ENVIRONMENTAL DATA:
　Education: 8th grade
　Life Style: Gets up at 8:00 AM. Has good breakfast, Main meal of day at 2:00 PM. Soup,
　　cheese, and bread at night. Dozes throughout day. Looks at newspaper some and
　　watches television. In bed by 10:00 PM.
　Diet: Regular with no added salt. Wife prepares food
　Religious Preferences: Lutheran. Has not been going to services past year. Doesn't like
　　new minister.
　Hobbies: Used to enjoy gardening. Since moved to apartment, have no yard.
　Concerns: Patient—seems unaware of most everything. Wife—afraid he's losing his
　　mind.

System Review	Physical Examination

Skin, Hair, Nails
  Itching at times—?due to commercial
    laundromat.
	Numerous bruises
	Skin color rather sallow
	Skin turgor decreased

Head
  Always troubled by headaches,
    have been worse lately
  Wears glasses for vision
  Occasional blurring of vision
  Hearing (wears hearing aid)
	Healed abrasion right temple area.
	  No bone deformity
	Partial upper plate
	Gingivitis, calculus
	Fundoscopic—diffuse narrowing of
	  retinal arterioles (arteriolar/venous
	  diameter 1/3 to 1/2), few "cotton wool"
	  exudates.

Neck
  No hoarseness or trouble in
    swallowing
	No masses
	Some nuchal rigidity
	Nodes not enlarged
	No carotid bruit

Lungs
  No cough or sputum
  Short of breath when climbs more
    than 6-8 stairs.
	Lungs clear
	Fat padding in upper abdomen
	  limits chest excursion

Cardiovascular
  No chest pain
  Ankle swelling in evening
	Heart rate regular, no murmurs
	Neck veins flat
	Peripheral pulses good

Abdomen
  Decreased appetite
  No pain or bloating
	Soft, bowel sounds normal
	No tenderness
	Liver 2 cm below costal margin
	No hernia
	Inguinal nodes not palpable

Rectal
  No change in bowel habits
  No bleeding
	Fair spincter tone
	Prostate—diffuse 1+ enlargement
	Brown stool negative for occult blood

Genitourinary
  Nocturia ×2
  Occas, dribbling
  No urgency, burning, or dysuria
  Difficulty maintaining erection
    past 6 months
  No ejaculation
	Normal circumcised male
	No discharge
	No scrotal masses

Musculoskeletal
  Rheumatism in knees and hands—
    takes an hour to limber up in
    mornings
	No spinal curvature
	Gait is slow, steps are short, but no
	  shuffling
	Drags left side slightly
	Enlargement of joints both hands,

System Review	**Physical Examination**
	deformity of fingers, Heberden's nodes
	Right knee crepitus

Neurologic

Vertigo with change to upright posture	Pupils equal, react to light
No seizures or syncope	No limitation of visual field (blinks with stimulus from both sides)
	Slight facial weakness with grimace on left
	Motor strength good in all extremities, slightly weaker on left
	Deep tendon reflexes (DTSs)
	Scale: 2 = normal; 1 = diminished; 3 = exaggerated

	Bicep	Tricep	Pat.	Achilles	Plantar
R—	2+	2+	2+	2+	↓
L—	3+	2+	3+	3+	↑↓

Sensory—responds to pinprick in all extremities

Decreased sensation along medial aspect left calf

Emotional/Mental

Recent deterioration in memory	Dull affect
Becomes irritable when has to make decisions, postpones decisions	Immediate recall of 3 numbers out of a series of 5
Has withdrawn from church activities, meetings with friends	Unable to subtract 7 from 100 serially
	Answers questions slowly—does not elaborate on explanations
Sleeps frequently during day, fitfully during night	When questioned further, explanation may be unrelated to question
Decreased interest in sex	Does not seem to understand complex directions
	General appearance neat
	Verbal responses consistent with observable behavior
	Appears dejected

LABORATORY DATA
Blood Chemistry

	Patient	**Normal**
Metabolic I		
Chloride	99	95−105 mEq/liter
Carbon dioxide, total	26	24−32 mEq/liter
Potassium	4.7	3.5−5 mEq/liter
Sodium	135	135−145 mEq/liter
Urea nitrogen	37	10−20 mg/dl
Glucose	120	58−100 mg/dl

	Patient	Normal
Metabolic II		
Protein, total	5.8	6−8.5 g/dl
Albumin	3.2	3.5−5 g/dl
Calcium	7.8	8.5−10.5 mg/dl
Phosphorus	6	2.5−4.5 mg/dl
Cholesterol, total	225	150−250 mg/dl
Uric Acid	10	2−8 mg/dl
Creatinine	2.4	0.7−1.4 mg/dl
Bilirubin, total	0.8	0.2−1.2 mg/dl
Phosphatase, alkaline	106	30−85 mU/ml
Lactic dehydrogenase (LDH)	252	100−225 mU/ml
Glutamic pyruvic transaminase (GPT)	50	8−40 mU/ml
Glutamic oxalacetic transaminase (GOT)	42	7.5−40 mU/ml
Hematology Profile		
Leukocyte count (WBC)	12	5−10 thousand/mm³
Erythrocyte count (RBC)	4.3	4.5−6.0 million/mm³
Hemoglobin (Hgb)	14	14−18 g/dl
Hematocrit (Hct)	38	40−54 ml/dl
Urinalysis		
Color	yellow	
Appearance	clear	
Specific gravity	1.016	
pH	5	
Glucose	negative	
Protein	negative	
Occult blood	small	
Ketone bodies	negative	
Bilirubin	negative	
WBC	0−2	
RBC	9−11	
Squamous	few	

Skillbuilders:

1. On practicum record 10-C, list the four most likely hypotheses for Mr. Wagner's decrease in cognitive function. Include both medical and nursing diagnoses that are pertinent. List them in the order of their priority for consideration, listing those first that may require prompt intervention to reduce or limit the dysfunctional effects.

2. List the data that support each hypothesis and additional data needed to confirm or disconfirm.

3. In the intervention section, list appropriate intervention, both physician directed and independent nursing activities. If the disorder is an acute state, list the intervention which would be appropriate for the acute period. If it is a more chronic type of disorder, describe the intervention planned for a longer period of time.

PRACTICUM RECORD 10-C

Hypothesis/Possible Diagnosis	Supporting Data	Additional Data to Confirm or Disconfirm	Nursing Intervention if Hypothesis Confirmed	Evaluation Criteria
Decrease in cognitive function due to:				
1.				
2.				
3.				
4.				

4. List the criteria for evaluation of the effectiveness of the nursing process for Mr. Wagner.

Feedback: Our diagnoses, in order of priority are decrease in cognitive function due to a cranial lesion, cerebral arteriosclerotic changes in small arteries, depressive psychosis, or intake of methyldopa. The rationale for suspecting a cranial lesion and listing it first is because the clinical picture is compatible with that, and if the nature of the lesion were that of a chronic subdural hematoma, it is essential to treat it before the patient becomes comatose and the damage cannot be reversed. The decision tree on cranial lesion can guide our search for cues. We need to bear in mind, however, that the trees are designed primarily for acute changes in the state of the patient and slowly developing disorders generally show fewer alterations with less deviation from the normal state. The characteristics on the tree that are present to support the hypothesis are the presence of headaches, decrease in cognitive functioning, personality change, decreased motor function and exaggeration of DTR's on left side, and history of trauma 5 weeks ago.

Although these altered signs and symptoms could occur with an intracranial neoplasm and other cranial lesions, the potential harm to the patient of a chronic subdural hematoma cues us to consider this probability first. The length of time from injury and the lack of focal neurologic signs essentially rules out other hematomas. It may be helpful to review the signs and symptoms, course, and underlying pathophysiology of a chronic subdural hematoma. It can follow a head injury which may be trivial and, in some cases, not remembered. The physical signs and symptoms, which can vary, include intermittent headaches, giddiness, drowsiness, slowness in thinking, exaggeration of certain personality traits, seizures, hemiparesis, and aphasic disturbance. The presence of signs may fluctuate over the period of intervening time, with the greater severity or the development of symptoms not previously present providing the impetus for seeking medical care. The pathophysiology explains the reason for the increasing symptoms. The hematoma that forms between the dura and subarachnoid space may initially be quite small and asymptomatic. Fibrous membranes grow from the dura to encapsulate the hematoma. As the red corpuscles hemolyze and the blood proteins disintegrate, the osmotic pressure within the encapsulated area rises and fluid enters. The fluid enlarges the lesion and increases its compressive effect. Compression of the cerebral cortex may result in herniation through the tentorium with compression of the cranial nerves and possible brainstem hemorrhage. Additional data to support the hypothesis comes from arteriography and computerized axial tomography (CAT) scan. Roentgenograms are frequently negative and spinal tap does not usually assist diagnosis.

Intervention is the prompt surgical procedure of burr holes with evacuation of the clot and neomembrane. The nurse can help Mr. Wagner and his wife adjust to the rapid scheduling of diagnostic procedures and surgery. Because the disorder can develop without any of the symptoms the public customarily associates with a brain lesion, the possibility is startling and may be met with a variety of behaviors such as denial, severe anxiety, extreme disorganization of behavior, etc. Education for the wife (and the patient based on level of under-standing) that reduces the emotional impact includes (1) the use of a drawing that shows the location of the hematoma; (2) the explanation that the surgical process does not invade the gray matter of the brain; (3) the reassurance that noticeable deformity of the skull does not result from the procedure; and (4) the reassurance that, with removal of the clot compressing the brain, normal functioning is usually restored.

Nursing measures during the postoperative period are directed toward maintenance of patency of the drainage catheter, prevention of cerebral edema (careful control of fluid intake, administration of dexamethasone, etc.), provision of safety (prevention of falls, injury from seizure, etc.), prevention of wound infection, and provision of psychologic support to patient and family. Evaluation criteria would include improvement in cognitive function, absence of neurologic deficit, wound healing without infection, absence of physical injury, and absence of undue anxiety of both patient and spouse. Treatment for other cranial lesions and evaluation criteria would of course be somewhat different. We will not attempt to give feedback on all the various lesions. The other hypotheses have no particular priority for treatment, so we listed decrease in cognitive function due to cerebral arteriosclerotic changes in the small arteries second, since it probably has the greatest frequency of occurrence. Supporting data come from our knowledge that hypertension accelerates the atherosclerotic process, both throughout the body and in the cerebral circulation. Areas commonly affected in the brain are sites where the flow is altered by acute angulation or bifurcation of vessels. Occlusion of one of these major vessels can result in the clinical picture of stroke. Atherosclerosis can also affect the smaller penetrating arterial branches that supply the internal capsule, basal ganglia, thalamus, pons, and cerebellum. Arteriosclerosis present over a period of time with small artery involvement results in a decreased cerebral blood flow, perivascular hemorrhages, focal cerebral ischemia (with multiple small areas of necrosis or infarction), decrease in ability to establish effective collateral circulation, cerebral edema, and progressive degeneration of the brain. There are indications that the kidney has also been affected by the hypertension and, possibly, the atherosclerotic process. With increasing age, the rate of glomerular filtration is slowed, and the BUN may be slightly elevated. The elevation to 37 mg/dl is abnormal, however, and indicates impaired renal function. The elevated creatinine and uric acid and red blood cells in the urine also reflect this impairment.

Some of you may have listed uremia as a cause of the decrease in cognitive function. Uremia can result in the cognitive change described, but in persons with slowly developing uremia, the cognitive changes do not usually occur until the BUN exceeds 100 to 120 mg/dl. Thus the data to support the hypothesis of small cerebral artery arteriosclerotic changes would then include:

1. History of hypertension
2. Fundoscopic findings of narrowing retinal arterioles; "cotton wool" exudates
3. Occasional blurring of vision
4. Headaches

5. Dizziness
6. Left-sided weakness and exaggerated DTRs
7. Memory loss and inability to concentrate
8. Personality changes
9. Hypercholesterolemia

There are no reliable additional data to support the hypothesis. Small artery occlusions and/or stenosis are not visible with four vessel angiography. Confirmation of the hypothesis frequently relies on negative findings for other causes of impaired cognition. Nursing intervention is primarily directed toward helping the patient adjust to the chronic disorder and education about factors that may slow the degenerative process and reduce the incidence of other complications. Education about dietary factors seems indicated with a serum cholesterol of 255 mg/dl, overweight, and only minimal sodium restriction in previous regimen. Protein should be reduced in addition to sodium, cholesterol, and calories to reduce danger of increasing azotemia. He may also require adjustment of his hypertensive medications and more frequent followup. Moderate physical activity should be encouraged. The physician is responsible for directing the care. The blood pressure cannot be lowered rapidly or to levels considered normal without decreasing the blood supply to the brain and, perhaps, causing a stroke. The nurse plays an instrumental role in providing information, motivation, and encouragement to the patient. It is important to include the wife in the sessions whenever possible since she prepares the food and her attitude will influence Mr. Wagner. It is important for both the nurse and the wife not to expect more of the patient than he is able to understand or carry out. Working with brain-damaged persons requires patience. It can also be stressful for the nurse because it triggers his/her own fears concerning old age. Evaluation criteria would be serum cholesterol less than 240 mg/dl, weight loss 4 pounds or more a month, blood pressure at prescribed level, good relationship with spouse, and same or improved cognitive level.

Now we are ready to discuss the hypothesis that the decrease in cognitive function is due to a depressive psychosis. The supporting data come from the knowledge that a depressive psychosis can cause fatigue, inability to focus attention, psychomotor retardation (slowness to respond to stimuli, sparse speech, etc.), difficulty in making decisions, sleep disturbances, loss of appetite, and decreased libido. Theory also tells us that depression is a common reaction to loss. The older person suffers many losses. Those identified for Mr. Wagner are:

1. Loss of gainful activity (with probable loss of respect that is accorded by society to a working person)
2. Loss of contact with the church, and other friends
3. Loss of gardening outlet since move to an apartment
4. Loss of muscular strength and physical dexterity
5. Decrease in sexual functioning (perhaps particularly distressing with a younger wife)
6. Loss of ability to function independently
7. Loss of meaning in life

Another factor that has been found to contribute to depression has been fear of approaching death. Mr. Wagner's father died when he was 78, the patient's present age. Some persons consider that an omen that they will also die at that age. Additionally, in our society an older person is a target of prejudice. They are sometimes relegated to the "gray ghetto" because of society's hostility, indifference, stereotyping, and prejudice. The effect of these variables on Mr. Wagner's mood would need to be explored. Additional data to confirm the hypothesis may be obtained by more discrete testing of cognitive ability. Although the depressed patient may state he can't think or concentrate; when he is calmed and reassured and given more time and encouragement during testing, his performance will frequently improve. Intervention is directed toward alteration of the disordered mood. Psychotherapy is the mainstay of treatment, with chemotherapy utilized for some patients. Therapeutic nursing approaches are those that:

1. Demonstrate respect and concern for Mr. Wagner
2. Give him an opportunity to succeed
3. Encourage him to express his feelings (including anger, resentments, etc.)
4. Reduce environmental influences that contribute to cognitive impairment
5. Encourage reminiscence of past achievements (includes asking advice in his area of expertise, i.e., "Where does a Spencer steak come from?")
6. If he indicates a readiness for this step, help to make plans to "mend his fences"

It could be that his estrangement with the church has deprived him of needed support. Sometimes if an uninvolved person offers to contact the minister, consent will be given. Such activities that help the patient to "save face" may restore much needed support. Medical therapy might also be directed toward restoring some of the physical losses that contribute to the depression. This could include medication to reduce the stiffness from rheumatism and investigation of the decrease in sexual functioning.

Although there may not be a treatable cause, the coincidence of the onset of the problem of sexual functioning with the addition of methyldopa to his hypertensive regimen makes us suspicious that the problem could be drug related. Methyldopa is known to cause impotence and decreased libido. Since methyldopa increases renal blood flow in addition to lowering blood pressure, it is especially valuable in patients with impaired glomerular filtration. Hydralazine (Apresoline) also increases renal blood flow and might be a suitable substitute. Since sexual functioning can also be decreased with depressive states, it may improve with resolution of the depression. Evaluation criteria could include increase in cognitive level, absence of signs of depression, increased participation in physical activities, more involvement in community activities, and improvement in sexual functioning (or acceptance of impairment). This takes us to discussion of the last hypothesis that decrease in cognitive function is due to intake of methyldopa. Support data come from the history of methyldopa intake and to the knowledge that, in addition to impotence, intake of methyldopa can cause headaches, weakness, impaired cognition, and paresthesias. Additional data to support the hypothesis would probably come from the disappearance of these parameters after cessation of methyldopa therapy. Intervention, which would be directed by the physician, could include substitution of another drug, such as hydralazine. Evaluation criteria would be increase in cognitive levels and improvement in other altered parameters.

ADDITIONAL READING

Back A: Cognitive Therapy and the Emotional Disorders. New York, International Univ. Press, 1976.

Bolin R: Sensory Deprivation: an Overview. Nursing Forum 13(3):241–258, 1974.

Engel G: Conversion symptoms. In MacBryde C, Blacklow R (eds.): Signs and Symptoms, 5th ed. Philadelphia, Lippincott, 1970, pp. 650–668.

Holmes T, Rahe R: The social readjustment score. J Psychosom Res 11:213, 1967.

Kovacs M, Beck A: Maladaptive cognitive structures in depression. Am J Psychiat 135(5):525–533, 1978.

O'Leary J, Landau W: Coma and convulsion. In MacBryde C, Blacklow R (eds.): Signs and Symptoms, 5th ed. Philadelphia, Lippincott, 1970, pp 669–690.

Mauss N, Mitchell: Increased intracranial pressure. Heart Lung 5(6):918–926, 1976.

Meinhart N, Aspinall M: Nursing intervention in hypovigilance. AJN 69(5): 994–998, 1969.

Meyd C: Acute brain trauma. AJN 78(1):40–44, 1978.

Plum F, Posner J: Diagnosis of stupor and coma, 2nd ed. Philadelphia, Davis, 1972.

Decision Trees

A NOTE ABOUT DECISION TREES

Dennis G. Fryback

Decision trees are perhaps the most visible tool of the discipline of decision analysis. Certainly they have come to symbolize decision analysis. Because this book makes use of decision trees but is not intended to be a primer on either decision analysis nor the construction of decision trees, the purpose of this note is to provide a brief guide to the history and literature for readers who wish to delve more deeply.

Decision analysis is a young discipline. It involves the application of mathematical and analytical tools to assist decision makers in making the "best" choice. It is a hybrid technology with roots in economics, engineering, mathematics, statistics, and psychology.[1,2] Major areas of application now include business and government. Perhaps the fastest growing area of application is health care.[3]

The basic tenets of decision analysis are few. First, it is assumed that decision makers wish to maximize some measure of overall "happiness" or preference for outcomes of decisions. Second, it recognizes that people are generally limited in the amount of information they can handle about complex decision situations at any one time. So, third, its goal is to "divide and conquer," i.e., to break complex decisions into smaller, more easily assimilated pieces that human decision makers *can* handle well, then to use mathematical techniques to put all the pieces together to solve the larger, more complex decision problem faced by the decision maker.

The decision tree is extremely useful in this pursuit because it provides a diagram showing the interrelationships of the many pieces of the problem.

349

A decision tree is simply a flow chart showing all possible sequential "paths" representing combinations of decisions and decision outcomes from the initial decision to the decision outcomes of interest. In medical diagnosis, the initial point might be the decision to do a workup for a problem or not. If it is elected to proceed with a workup, then a decision must be made concerning which observation to make or which test to do first. Each test or observation has several potential outcomes. Depending upon the particular test selected and the particular outcomes, we then must decide what to do next, continue the workup or stop. And so forth. The myriad combinations that are possible rapidly become mind boggling without some assistance in keeping track of everything. Providing this assistance is the function of the decision tree.

Several texts exist which teach decision tree construction, although these are mostly oriented toward business students.[4-6] Clinicians will find numerous short tutorials listed by Albert[3] in his excellent review of decision analysis in health care; but none thus far deals with the "nuts and bolts" of decision tree construction at the same level that is found in business-oriented texts.

Decision trees are called "trees" because they are branching diagrams; each line, or "branch," represents a decision alternative, or an event that might occur or influence the outcome of choosing a particular decision alternative. These branches are set end to end to represent combinations of decision/observation contingencies as shown in the illustration.

The left-most point is the starting point of the tree (the "root" of the tree). It represents the present decision. In the illustration, this is a decision to proceed first with one of three tests. For illustration here, Test B is assumed to result always in exactly one of two possible observa-

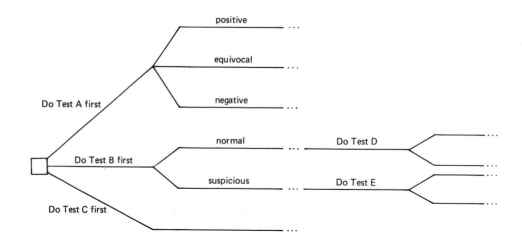

tions, "normal" or "suspicious." If Test B is selected and it is normal, then the next step is to do Test D; if B were to result in a "suspicious" value, then the next step is Test E. And so forth.

The rules for decision tree construction are simple. At every node in the decision tree from which branches emanate, the branches must represent mutually exclusive possibilities, only one may occur, and they should exhaust the set of possibilities, i.e., one of them *must* occur. Finally, the left-to-right ordering of events in the decision tree must faithfully represent the order in which information becomes available to the decision maker and the order in which decisions must be made.

These rules guarantee that each left-to-right path through the tree represents a unique scenario for the problem and, further, the scenario that will in fact occur is included in the tree.

Of course, in reality these guarantees are but ideals we approximate. If *all* eventualities were represented, instead of a sleek and useful decision tree, we would have a "bushy mess."[4] Hence the construction of decision trees is as yet an art in which the decision analyst strives to achieve a sufficiently complete picture of the problem so that the major concerns of the decision maker are represented, yet a simplified enough picture so that it is useful without being overwhelming. Some quick experimentation by the reader will show that even simple-sounding problems can result in complex trees rapidly expanding beyond the bounds of a page. But perusal of the literature also reveals that useful representations of complex problems can be achieved in trees that appear simple but can capture in one gestalt diagram interactions that are very difficult to think about sensibly without the assistance of the decision tree.[7-9]

Use of decision trees as flow charts for decision making requires no special expertise. One merely "begins at the beginning," as Alice would say, and follows the appropriate branches. Of course, one must be careful to follow the instructions.

The references cited form an excellent starting point for the serious professional wishing to learn more about application of decision trees and the other machinery of decision analysis to problems of patient management. Though not a panacea by any means, the emerging field of medical decision analysis should prove thought provoking and, I hope, useful to clinicians and their patients.

REFERENCES

1. Edwards W: The theory of decision making. Psych Bull 51:380−417, 1954.
2. Matheson JE, Howard RA: An introduction to decision analysis. In Howard RA, Matheson JE, Miller KL (eds): Readings in Decision Analysis. Menlo Park, Ca, Stanford Res. Inst, 1976.

3. Albert DA: Decision theory in medicine: A review and critique. Milbank Memorial Fund Quarterly/Health and Society 56:362–401, Summer, 1978.
4. Raiffa H: Decision Analysis: Introductory Lectures on Choices under Uncertainty. Reading, Ma, Addison, 1968.
5. Schlaifer R: Analysis of Decisions under Uncertainty. New York, McGraw-Hill, 1969.
6. Brown RV, Kahr AS, Peterson C: Decision Analysis for the Manager. New York, Holt, 1974.
7. Schwartz WB, Gorry GA, Kassirer JP et al. Decision analysis and clinical judgment. Am J Med 55:459–472, 1973.
8. Pauker SG: Coronary artery surgery: The use of decision analysis. Ann Int Med 85, 1:8–18, July, 1976.
9. Pauker SP, Pauker SG: Prenatal diagnosis: A directive approach to genetic counseling using decision analysis. Yale J Bio Med 50:275–289, 1977.

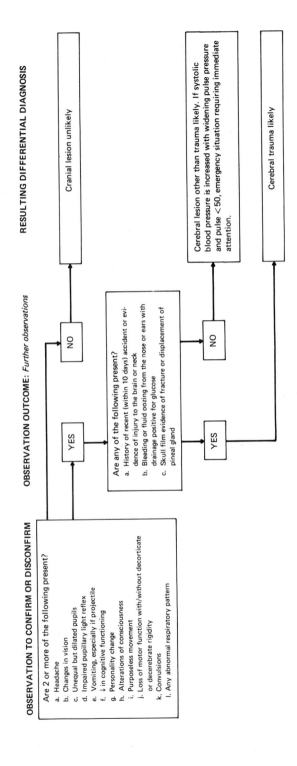

FIGURE A-1. Possible diagnosis: Cranial lesion (trauma, tumor, CVA, hematoma, aneurysm, infection).

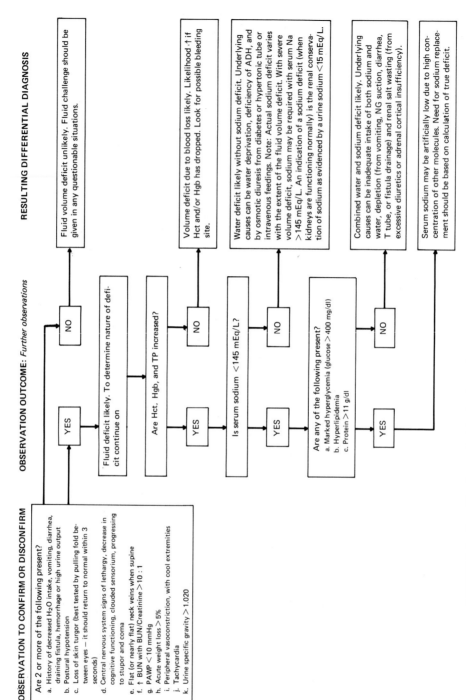

FIGURE A-2. Possible diagnosis: Fluid volume deficit (hypovolemia, dehydration, hemorrhage).

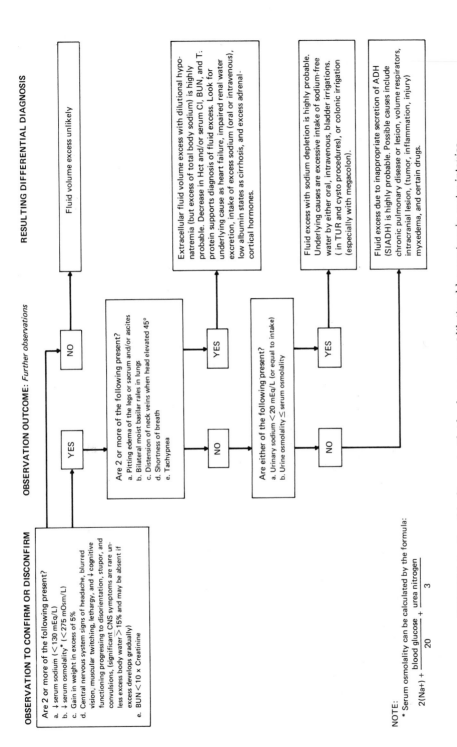

FIGURE A-3. Possible diagnosis: Fluid volume excess [dilutional hyponatremia, water intoxication, syndrome inappropriate secretion of antidiuretic hormone (SIADH)].

NOTE:
* Serum osmolality can be calculated by the formula:

$$2(Na+) + \frac{blood\ glucose}{20} + \frac{urea\ nitrogen}{3}$$

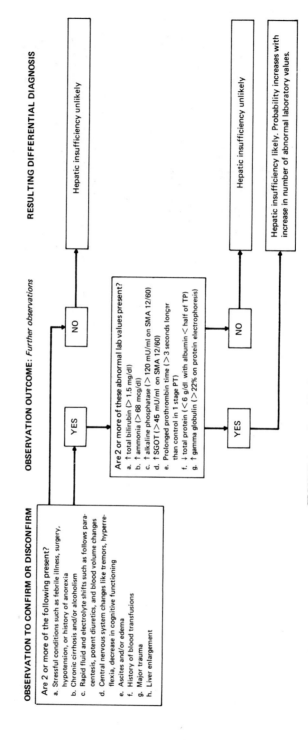

OBSERVATION TO CONFIRM OR DISCONFIRM

Are 2 or more of the following present?

a. Stressful conditions such as febrile illness, surgery, hypotension, or history of anorexia
b. Chronic cirrhosis and/or alcoholism
c. Rapid fluid and electrolyte shifts such as follows paracentesis, potent diuretics, and blood volume changes
d. Central nervous system changes like tremors, hyperreflexia, decrease in cognitive functioning
e. Ascites and/or edema
f. History of blood transfusions
g. Major trauma
h. Liver enlargement

OBSERVATION OUTCOME: *Further observations*

YES

NO

Are 2 or more of these abnormal lab values present?
a. ↑ total bilirubin (> 1.5 mg/dl)
b. ↑ ammonia (> 68 mcg/dl)
c. ↑ alkaline phosphatase (> 120 mU/ml on SMA 12/60)
d. ↑ SGOT (> 45 mU/ml on SMA 12/60)
e. Prolonged prothrombin time (> 3 seconds longer than control in 1 stage PT)
f. ↓ total protein (< 6 g/dl with albumin < half of TP)
g. ↑ gamma globulin (> 22% on protein electrophoresis)

YES

NO

RESULTING DIFFERENTIAL DIAGNOSIS

Hepatic insufficiency unlikely

Hepatic insufficiency unlikely

Hepatic insufficiency likely. Probability increases with increase in number of abnormal laboratory values.

FIGURE A-4. Possible diagnosis: Hepatic insufficiency.

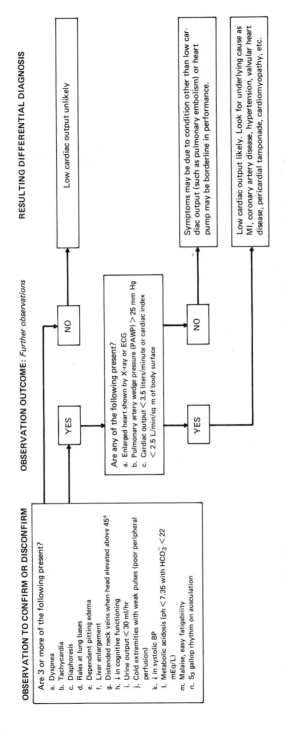

FIGURE A-5. Possible diagnosis: Low cardiac output heart failure (congestive heart failure, cardiogenic shock).

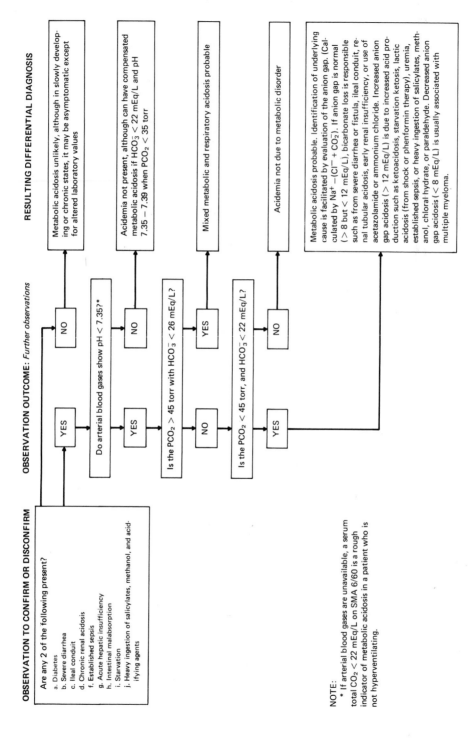

FIGURE A-6. Possible diagnosis: Metabolic acidosis (diabetic ketoacidosis, lactic acidosis).

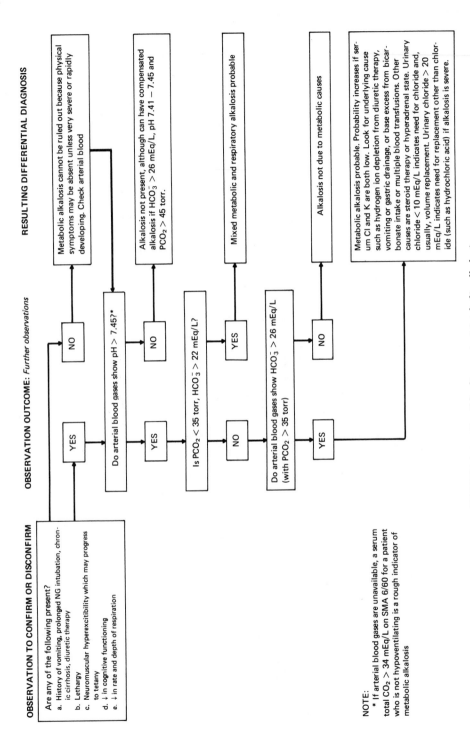

FIGURE A-7. Possible diagnosis: Metabolic alkalosis.

359

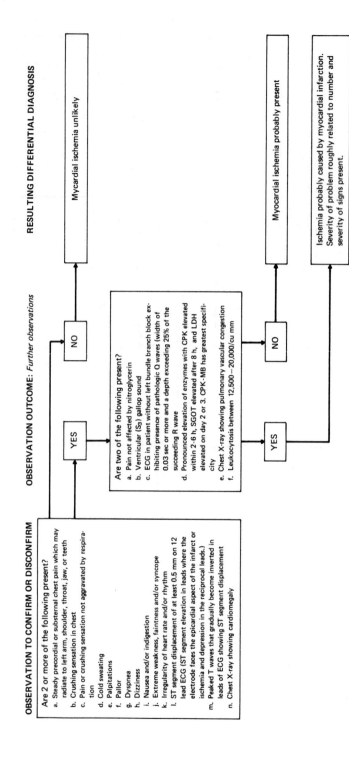

OBSERVATION TO CONFIRM OR DISCONFIRM

Are 2 or more of the following present?

a. Steady precordial or substernal chest pain which may radiate to left arm, shoulder, throat, jaw, or teeth
b. Crushing sensation in chest
c. Pain or crushing sensation not aggravated by respiration
d. Cold sweating
e. Palpitations
f. Pallor
g. Dyspnea
h. Dizziness
i. Nausea and/or indigestion
j. Extreme weakness, faintness and/or syncope
k. Irregularity of heart rate and/or rhythm
l. ST segment displacement of at least 0.5 mm on 12 lead ECG (ST segment elevation in leads where the electrode faces the epicardial aspect of the infarct or ischemia and depression in the reciprocal leads.)
m. Peaked T waves that gradually become inverted in leads of ECG showing ST segment displacement
n. Chest X-ray showing cardiomegaly

OBSERVATION OUTCOME: *Further observations*

YES → NO → Mycardial ischemia unlikely

Are two of the following present?

a. Pain not affected by nitroglycerin
b. Ventricular (S3) gallop sound
c. ECG in patient without left bundle branch block exhibiting presence of pathologic Q waves (width of 0.03 sec or more and a depth exceeding 25% of the succeeding R wave
d. Pronounced elevation of enzymes with CPK elevated within 2-6 h, SGOT elevated after 8 h, and LDH elevated on day 2 or 3. CPK-MB has greatest specificity
e. Chest X-ray showing pulmonary vascular congestion
f. Leukocytosis between 12,500 – 20,000/cu mm

RESULTING DIFFERENTIAL DIAGNOSIS

NO → Myocardial ischemia probably present

YES → Ischemia probably caused by myocardial infarction. Severity of problem roughly related to number and severity of signs present.

FIGURE A-8. Possible diagnosis: Myocardial ischemia.

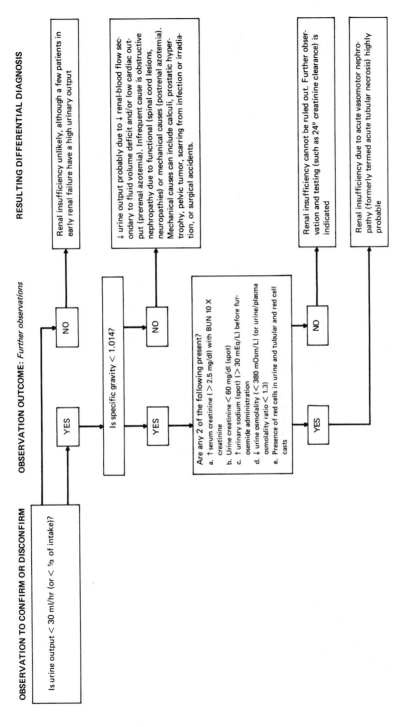

FIGURE A-9. Possible diagnosis: Renal insufficiency (acute vasomotor nephropathy, acute tubular necrosis).

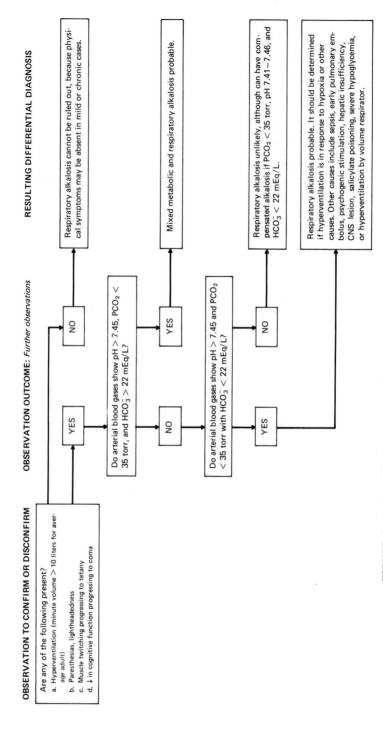

FIGURE A-10. Possible diagnosis: Respiratory alkalosis (hyperventilation, hypocarbia).

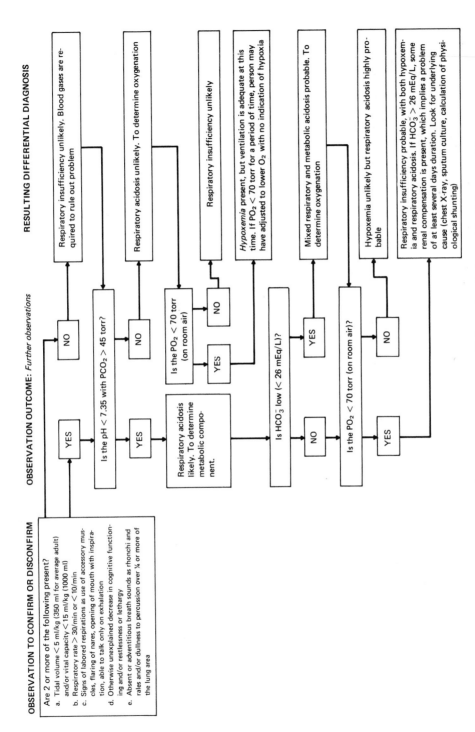

FIGURE A-11. Possible diagnosis: Respiratory insufficiency (respiratory acidosis, hypoxemia).

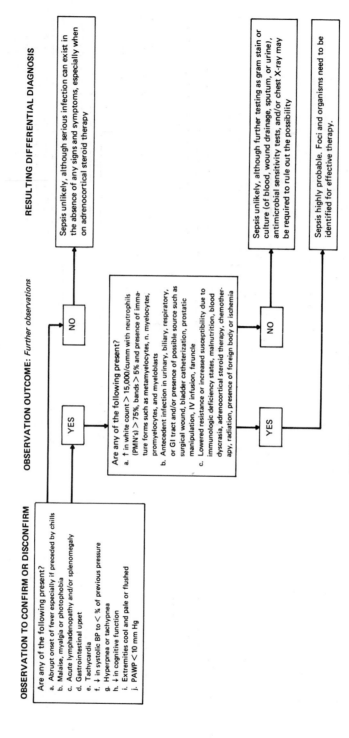

FIGURE A-12. Possible diagnosis: Sepsis.

OBSERVATION TO CONFIRM OR DISCONFIRM

Are any of the following present?

a. Abrupt onset of fever especially if preceded by chills
b. Malaise, myalgia or photophobia
c. Acute lymphadenopathy and/or splenomegaly
d. Gastrointestinal upset
e. Tachycardia
f. ↓ in systolic BP to < ⅔ of previous pressure
g. Hyperpnea or tachypnea
h. ↓ in cognitive function
i. Extremities cool and pale or flushed
j. PAWP < 10 mm Hg

OBSERVATION OUTCOME: *Further observations*

RESULTING DIFFERENTIAL DIAGNOSIS

YES

NO

Sepsis unlikely, although serious infection can exist in the absence of any signs and symptoms, especially when on adrenocortical steroid therapy

Are any of the following present?

a. ↑ in white count > 15,000/cumm with neutrophils (PMN's) > 75%, bands > 5% and presence of immature forms such as metamyelocytes, n. myelocytes, promyelocytes, and myeloblasts
b. Antecedent infection in urinary, biliary, respiratory, or GI tract and/or presence of possible source such as surgical wound, bladder catheterization, prostatic manipulation, IV infusion, furuncle
c. Lowered resistance or increased susceptibility due to immunologic deficiency states, malnutrition, blood dyscrasia, adrenocortical steroid therapy, chemotherapy, radiation, presence of foreign body or ischemia

YES

NO

Sepsis unlikely, although further testing as gram stain or culture (of blood, wound drainage, sputum, or urine), antimicrobial sensitivity tests, and/or chest X-ray may be required to rule out the possibility

Sepsis highly probable. Foci and organisms need to be identified for effective therapy.

Index

f indicates figure; *t* denotes table